A

PHILOSOPHICAL AND POLITICAL

HISTORY

OF THE

SETTLEMENTS AND TRADE

OF THE

E U R O P E A N S

IN THE

EAST AND WEST INDIES.

———◆———

REVISED, AUGMENTED, AND PUBLISHED,

IN TEN VOLUMES,

BY THE ABBÉ RAYNAL.

———◆———

NEWLY TRANSLATED FROM THE FRENCH,

BY J. O. JUSTAMOND, F. R. S.

WITH A

New Set of Maps adapted to the Work, and a copious Index.

IN SIX VOLUMES.

VOL. III.

SECOND EDITION.

NEGRO UNIVERSITIES PRESS
NEW YORK

Originally published in 1798
by J. Mundell & Co., London

Reprinted 1969 by
Negro Universities Press
A DIVISION OF GREENWOOD PUBLISHING CORP.
NEW YORK

Library of Congress Catalogue Card Number 69-18996

SBN 8371-1553-1

CONTENTS.

VOL. III.

BOOK VII.

BOOK VIII.

BOOK X.

A

PHILOSOPHICAL AND POLITICAL

HISTORY

OF THE

SETTLEMENTS AND TRADE

OF THE

EUROPEANS

IN THE

EAST AND WEST INDIES.

BOOK VII.

Conqueſt of Peru by the Spaniards. Changes that have happened in this Empire ſince that Revolution.

IT has not been my intention to be the panegyriſt of the conquerors of the other hemiſphere. I have not ſuffered my judgment to be ſo far miſled by the brilliancy of their ſucceſſes, as to be blind to their crimes and acts of injuſtice. My view is to write hiſtory, and I almoſt always write it with my eyes bathed in tears. Aſtoniſhment hath ſometimes ſucceeded grief. I have been ſurpriſed that none of theſe ſavage warriors ſhould have preferred the more certain mode of mildneſs and humanity, and that they ſhould have rather choſen to ſhow themſelves as tyrants than as benefactors. What ſtrange infatuation hath prevented them from perceiving, that, while they deſtroyed the countries which they ſeized upon, they were injuring themſelves, and that their cruelties obliged them to give up a more quiet and more lucrative poſſeſſion of them?

BOOK VII.

Can the conqueſts of the Spaniards in the New World be approved of?

BOOK
VII.

It hath been afferted, that, in countries where man had not yet appeared, the moft timid animals came near him without fear. I can never be perfuaded, that, at the firft afpect of an European, the favage man can have been more wild than the animals. It was undoubtedly a fatal experience which informed him of the danger of fuch familiarity.

What then! fhall nations be more cruel among themfelves, than the moft oppreffive fovereigns are towards their fubjects? One fociety muft then devour another! Man will be more fierce than the tyger! Shall reafon have been given to him merely as a fubftitute in him to every maleficent inftinct; and fhall his annals be nothing more than the annals of his perverfenefs? O God! why didft thou create man? Thou certainly didft know, that, for one inftant in which thou fhouldft be able to look upon thy work with complacency, thou fhouldft turn thine eyes away from it a hundred times! Thy prefcience certainly forefaw the atrocious acts which the Spaniards were to commit in the New World!

We are here going to difplay fcenes ftill more terrible than thofe which have fo often made us fhudder. They will be uninterruptedly repeated in thofe immenfe regions which remain for us to go over. The fword will never be blunted; and we fhall not fee it ftop till it meets with no more victims to ftrike.

Extravagances and cruelties that mark the firft fteps of the Spaniards in South America.

We fhall again begin our accounts with Columbus. This great man had difcovered the continent of America without ever landing upon it. It was not till after the ifland of San Domingo was firmly eftablifhed, that he thought proper to extend his enterprifes. He imagined, that beyond this continent there was another ocean, which muft terminate at the Eaft Indies; and that thefe two feas might have a communication with each other. In order to difcover it, he failed, in 1502, as clofe along the coaft as poffible. He touched at all places that were acceffible; and, contrary to the cuftom of other navigators who behaved in the countries which they vifited in fuch a manner as if

they were never to return to them, he treated the in- B O O K
habitants with a degree of kindnefs that gained their ⁀ VII.
affection. The gulf of Darien particularly engaged
his obfervation. He thought that the rivers which
poured into it were the great canal he had been in
fearch of through fo many imminent dangers and exceffive fatigues. Difappointed in thefe expectations,
he wifhed to leave a fmall colony upon the river Belem, in the country of Veragua. The avidity, the
pride, and the barbarifm of his countrymen prevented
him from having the fatisfaction of forming the firft
European eftablifhment upon the continent of the
new hemifphere.

Some years elapfed after this, and ftill the Spaniards
had not fixed themfelves upon any fpot. As thefe adventurers only received from government the permiffion of making difcoveries, it never once entered their
minds to employ themfelves in agriculture or commerce. The profpect of diftant fortunes that might
have been made by thefe prudent means, was far above
the prejudices of thefe barbarous times. There was
nothing but the allurement of immediate gain that
could ftimulate men to enterprifes fo bold as thofe for
which this century was diftinguifhed. Gold alone attracted them to the continent of America, and made
them brave dangers, difeafes, and death, which they
were expofed to in the courfe of their voyage, at their
arrival, or on their return; and, by a terrible but juft
vengeance, the cruelty of the Europeans, and their
luft of gold, exhaufted at once the two hemifpheres of
their inhabitants, and deftruction raged equally among
thofe who were the plunderers and affaffins, as among
the plundered people.

It was not till the year 1509, that Ojeda and Ni-
queffa formed, though feparately, the defign of making folid and lafting conquefts. To encourage them
in their refolution, Ferdinand gave to the firft the government of the countries that begin at Cape de la
Vela, and terminate at the gulf of Darien; and to
the fecond, that of all the fpace extending from this

famous gulf to Cape Gracias à Dios. They were both of them to announce to the people, at their landing, the tenets of the Chriſtian religion, and to inform them of the gift which the Roman pontiff had made of their country to the king of Spain. If the ſavages refuſed to ſubmit quietly to this double yoke, the Spaniards were authoriſed to purſue them with fire and ſword, and to reduce whole nations to ſlavery.

Is it then the head of the moſt holy of all religions who gives to another what does not belong to him? And is it a Chriſtian ſovereign who accepts of the gift? And are the conditions agreed upon between them, ſubmiſſion to the European monarch, or ſlavery; baptiſm, or death? Upon the bare recital of a contract ſo unheard of, we ſhudder with horror, and we pronounce, that the man who does not partake of the ſame ſenſation, is a ſtranger to every idea of morality, to every ſentiment, and to every notion of juſtice; a man who is unworthy of being argued with. Abominable pontiff! And if theſe countries of which thou doſt diſpoſe have a lawful proprietor, is it thy advice that he ſhould be ſpoiled of them? If they have a legitimate ſovereign, is it thy advice that his ſubjects ſhould break their allegiance? If they have Gods, is it thy advice that they ſhould be impious? And thou, ſtupid prince, doſt thou not perceive, that the perſon who confers theſe rights upon thee, arrogates them to himſelf; and that, by accepting of them, thou doſt abandon thy country, thy ſceptre, and thy religion, to the mercy of an ambitious ſophiſt, and of the moſt dangerous ſyſtem of Machiaveliſm?

But it was a more eaſy matter to grant theſe abſurd and atrocious privileges, than to put the barbarous and ſuperſtitious adventurers, who ſolicited ſuch rights, in poſſeſſion of them. The Indians rejected every kind of intercourſe with a ſet of rapacious ſtrangers, who threatened equally their life and their liberty. Arms were not more favourable to the Spaniards, than their perfidious careſſes. The people of the continent, accuſtomed to carry on war with each other, received

them with a boldnefs unexperienced in the iflands that
had been fo eafily fubdued. Poifoned arrows were
fhowered upon them from all quarters; and not one
of thofe that were wounded efcaped a death more or
lefs dreadful. To the arrows of the enemy, other
caufes of deftruction were foon joined: fhipwrecks
unavoidable in thefe unknown latitudes; an almoft
continual want of fubfiftence upon a country totally
uncultivated; and difeafes peculiar to this climate,
which is the moft unwholefome one in America. The
few Spaniards who had efcaped fo many calamities,
and who could not return to San Domingo, collected
themfelves at St. Mary's, in the province of Darien.

They lived there in a ftate of anarchy, when Vafco
Nugnès de Balboa appeared among them. This man,
who was honoured by the companions of his crimes
with the furname of Hercules, had a robuft conftitution, an intrepid courage, and a popular eloquence.
Thefe qualities made them choofe him for their chief;
and all his actions proved that he was worthy to command the villains whofe fuffrage he had obtained.
Judging that more gold would be found in the inland
parts than upon the coafts, from whence it had been
fo repeatedly taken, he plunged himfelf among the
mountains. He found at firft in the country, it is faid,
fome of that fame fpecies of little white men, as are to
be met with in Africa, and in certain of the Afiatic
iflands. They are covered with a down of a gliftening
white colour. They have no hair; their eyes are red;
and they only fee well in the night-time. They are
feeble; and their faculties appear to be more circum-
fcribed than thofe of other men. Thefe favages, if it
be true that they exifted, were few in number; but
others were found of a different fpecies, brave and
hardy enough to defend their rights. They had a very extraordinary cuftom among them, which was, that
the hufbands on the death of their wives, and the
wives on the death of their hufbands, ufed to cut off
the end of a finger; fo that by looking merely on

BOOK their hands, one might fee whether they were widow-
VII. ers or widows, and how often they had been fo.

Nothing has hitherto been, or will probably ever
be faid, that can fatisfactorily explain the various per-
verfions of reafon. If the women alone had been
obliged to practife this whimfical ceremony, it would
be natural to fufpect that it had been intended to prevent the impofture of a widow, who might wifh to
pafs for a virgin to her fecond hufband. But this conjecture would lofe its force, when applied to the hufbands, whofe condition could never be a matter of
fuch confequence, as that it fhould be carefully indi-
cated by indelible figns. This cuftom hath obtained
in other countries; but the following is peculiar to
Darien.

When a widow died, fuch of her children whofe
tender age rendered it impoffible for them to provide
for their own fubfiftence, were buried in the fame
grave with her. As no one would take the charge of
thefe orphans, the nation deftroyed them, to prevent
their being ftarved to death. The charity of thefe
barbarians extended no further. This is the moft atrocious act to which the deplorable ftate of favage life
was ever able to impel mankind.

Notwithftanding thefe ferocious manners, Balboa,
fupported by the obftinacy of his difpofition, fpurred
on by the infatiable cupidity of his foldiers, and with
the affiftance of fome packs of thofe blood-thirfty dogs
which had been of fo much fervice to the Spaniards in
all their conquefts, at length fucceeded in deftroying
the inhabitants of Darien, and in difperfing or fubduing them.

The Spani-   One day, as the conquerors were difputing with
ards acquire each other about gold, with a degree of warmth that
the firft no-
tion of Pe- feemed to threaten fome act of violence, a young Ca-
ru.   cique overturned the fcales in which they were weighing it. *Why*, faid he to them, with an air of difdain,
*why do you quarrel for fuch a trifle? If it be for this ufe-
lefs metal that you have quitted your country, and that you
maffacre fo many people, I will conduct you into a region*

where it is ſo common, that it is employed for the meaneſt purpoſes. Being urged to explain himſelf more clearly, he aſſured them, that, at a little diſtance from the ocean which waſhed the country of Darien, there was another ocean which led to this rich country. The opinion immediately and univerſally prevailed, that this was the ſea which Columbus had ſo earneſtly ſought after; and on the firſt of September 1513, one hundred and ninety Spaniards, attended by a thouſand Indians, who were to ſerve them as guides, and to carry their proviſions and baggage, ſet out to reconnoitre it.

From the place whence this troop began their march, to the one they were going to, there was no more than ſixty miles; but it was neceſſary to climb ſo many ſteep mountains, to paſs ſuch large rivers, to traverſe ſuch deep moraſſes, to penetrate into ſuch thick foreſts, and to diſperſe, perſuade, or deſtroy ſo many fierce nations; that it was not till after a march of five-and-twenty days, that men accuſtomed to dangers, fatigues, and wants, arrived at the place of their expectations. Without a moment's delay, Balboa, armed at all points, in the manner of the ancient chivalry, advanced ſome way into the South Sea. *Spectators of both hemiſpheres,* exclaimed this barbarian, *I call you to witneſs that I take poſſeſſion of this part of the univerſe for the crown of Caſtile. My ſword ſhall defend what my arm hath given to it.* Already was the croſs planted upon the continent, and the name of Ferdinand inſcribed upon the bark of ſome of the trees.

Theſe ceremonies gave to the Europeans in thoſe days the dominion of all the countries in the New World, where they could introduce their ſanguinary ſteps. Accordingly, the Spaniards thought they had a right to exact from the neighbouring people a tribute in pearls, metals, and proviſions. Every teſtimony was united in confirming what had been at firſt ſaid of the riches of the empire that was called Peru, and the robbers who meditated the conqueſt of it, re-

B O O K turned to Darien, where they were to collect the forces
VII. neceffary for fo difficult an enterprife.

Balboa expected that he fhould be employed to conduct this great defign. His companions had placed
their confidence in him. He had thrown into the
public coffers more treafure than any one of thefe adventurers. In the opinion of the public, the difcovery
he had juft made, had put him on a level with Columbus. But by an inftance of that injuftice and ingratitude fo common in courts, where merit cannot
prevail againft favour ; where a great commander is
fuperfeded in the midft of his triumphs by an unfit
perfon; where a diffipating and rapacious favourite
difplaces an economical minifter of finance ; where the
general good, and fervices done, are equally forgotten;
and where revolutions in the great offices of ftate often
become objects of mirth and pleafantry ; Pedrarias was
chofen in his ftead. The new commander, as jealous
as he was cruel, had his predeceffor confined ; he ordered him to take his trial, and afterwards caufed
him to be beheaded. His fubalterns, by his orders,
or with his confent, pillaged, burnt, and maffacred
on all fides, without any diftinction of allies or enemies ; and it was not till after they had deftroyed to
the extent of three hundred leagues of the country,
that in 1518 he transferred the colony of St. Mary,
on the borders of the Pacific ocean, to a place that
received the name of Panama.

Three Spa-   Some years paffed away without this eftablifhment
niards un-   having been able to fulfil the great and important
dertake the
conqueft of purpofes for which it was deftined. At length, three
Peru with-   men of obfcure birth undertook, at their own expence,
out any af-
fiftance   to fubvert an empire that had fubfifted with glory for
from go-   feveral ages.
vernment.
Francis Pizarro, who is the moft known among
them, was the natural fon of a gentleman of Eftra-
madura. His education had been fo neglected, that
he could not read. The tending of flocks, which was
his firft employment, not being fuitable to his charac-

ter, he embarked for the New World. His avarice B O O K
and ambition infpired him with inconceivable activity. VII.
He joined in every expedition, and fignalized himfelf
in moſt of them; and he acquired, in the feveral fituations in which he was employed, that knowledge of
men and things, which is indifpenfably neceffary to
advancement, but efpecially to thofe who by their
birth have every difficulty to contend with. The ufe
he had hitherto made of his natural and acquired abilities, perfuaded him that nothing was above his talents; and he formed the plan of exerting them againſt
Peru.

To thefe defigns he affociated Diego de Almagro,
whofe birth was equivocal, but whofe courage was proved. He had ever been found temperate, patient, and
indefatigable, in thofe camps in which he had grown
old. In this fchool he had acquired a franknefs which
is more frequently learnt here than in other fituations;
as well as that obduracy and cruelty which are but too
common.

The fortune of two foldiers, though confiderable,
being found infufficient for the conqueſt they meditated, they joined themfelves to Fernanda de Luques.
He was a mercenary prieſt, who had amaffed prodigious wealth by all the methods which fuperftition renders eafy to his profeffion, and by fome means peculiar to the manners of the age he livid in.

As the bafis of their affociation, the confederates
mutually agreed, that each fhould engage the whole
of his property in this enterprife; that the wealth ac-
cruing from it fhould be equally fhared, and that they
fhould reciprocally obferve an inviolable fidelity. The
parts that each of them were to take in this great ſcene
were diſtributed as the good of the common caufe required. Pizarro was to command the troops, Almagro
conduct the fuccours, and Luques prepare the means.
This plan of ambition, avarice, and ferocioufnefs, was
completed by fanaticifm. Luques publicly confecrated a hoft; part of which he ate, and divided the reſt
between his two affociates; all three fwearing, by the

B O O K blood of God, that, to enrich themfelves, they would
   VII.   not fpare the blood of man.

The expedition, commenced under thefe horrible
aufpices, towards the middle of November 1524, with
one veffel, one hundred and twelve men, and four
horfe, was not fortunate. It was feldom that Pizarro
was able to land ; and in the few places where it was
poffible for him to come on fhore, he met with nothing
but plains deluged with water, impenetrable forefts,
and fome favages, little difpofed to treat with him.
Almagro, who brought him a reinforcement of feventy men, did not meet with more encouraging adven-
tures ; and he even loft an eye in a very fharp engagement he was obliged to fuftain againft the Indians.
More than one half of thefe intrepid Spaniards had
perifhed by hunger, by the fword, or by the clmate ;
when Los Rios, who had fucceeded to Pedrarias, fent
orders to thofe who had efcaped fo many calamities,
to return to the colony without delay. They all obeyed ; all of them, except thirteen, who, faithful to their
chief, refolved to follow his fortune to the end. They
found it at firft more adverfe than it had hitherto been ;
for they were obliged to pafs fix whole months in the
ifland of Gorgon, the moft unwholefome, moft barren,
and moft dreadful fpot there was perhaps upon the
globe. But at length their deftiny grew milder : with a
very fmall veffel, which had been fent them merely from
motives of compaffion, to remove them from this place
of defolation, they continued their voyage, and landed
at Tumbez, no inconfiderable village of the empire
which they propofed one day to invade. From this
road, where every thing bore the marks of civilization, Pizarro returned to Panama, where he arrived
at the latter end of the year 1527 with fome gold duft,
fome vafes of that precious metal, fome vicunas, and
three Peruvians, deftined, fooner or later, to ferve as
interpreters.

Far from being difcouraged by the misfortunes that
had been experienced, the three affociates were inflamed with a more ardent paffion for treafures which were

now better known to them. But they were in want B O O K
of foldiers and of fubfiftence ; and the colony denied VII.
them both thefe fuccours. The miniftry, whofe fupport Pizarro himfelf had come into Europe to folicit,
were more favourably inclined. They authorifed, without referve, the levying of men, and the purchafe of
provifions; and added to this indefinite liberty every
favour which drew nothing from the treafury.

Neverthelefs, the affociates, by combining all their
means, could not equip more than three fmall veffels;
nor collect any more than one hundred and forty-four
infantry, and thirty-fix horfe. This was very little
for the great views that were to be fulfilled ; but in
the New World the Spaniards expected every thing
from their arms and their courage ; and Pizarro did
not hefitate to embark in the month of February 1531.
The knowledge he had acquired of thefe feas, made
him avoid the calamities that had thwarted his firft
expedition; and he met with no other misfortune than
that of being obliged, by contrary winds, to land at
the diftance of one hundred leagues from the harbour
where he had intended to difembark. The Spaniards
were therefore obliged to go to the place by land.
They followed the coaft with great difficulty, compel-
ling the inhabitants on their march to furnifh them
with provifions, plundering them of the gold they poffeffed, and giving themfelves up to that fpirit of rapine and cruelty which diftinguifhed the manners of
thofe barbarous times. The ifland of Puna, which
defended the road, was taken by ftorm, and the troops
entered victorious into Tumbez, where diforders of
every kind detained them for three whole months.
The arrival of two reinforcements, that came from
Nicaragua, afforded them fome confolation for the
anxiety they felt on account of this delay. Thefe
reinforcements, indeed, confifted only of thirty men
each ; but they were commanded by Sebaftian Benalcazar and by Ferdinand Soto, who had both of them
acquired a brilliant reputation. The Spaniards were

B O O K not difturbed in their firft conqueft, and we muft men-
   VII.   tion the reafon of it.

Manner in   The empire of Peru, which, like moft other domi-
which Pi- nions, had in its origin but little extent, had been fuc-
zarro, the
chief of the ceffively enlarged. It had in particular received a
expedition, confiderable aggrandizement from the eleventh empe-
makes him-
felf mafter ror, Huyana Capac, who had poffeffed himfelf by force
of the em- of the vaft territory of Quito, and who, to legitimate
pire.
as much as poffible his ufurpation, had married the
fole heirefs of the dethroned monarch. From this
union, reprobated equally by the laws and by prejudice, Atabalipa was born, who after the death of his
father claimed the inheritance of his mother. This
fucceffion was contefted by his elder brother Huafcar,
who was born of another bed, and whofe birth had
no ftain upon it. Two fuch powerful interefts induced the competitors to take up arms. One of them
had the people in his favour, and the cuftom imme-
morial of the indivifibility of the empire; but the
other had previoufly fecured the beft troops. The
one who had the troops on his fide was conqueror,
put his rival in chains, and becoming more powerful
than he had expected, was mafter of all the provinces.

   Thefe troubles, which for the firft time had agitated
Peru, were not entirely appeafed when the Spaniards
appeared there. In the confufion in which the whole
kingdom was ftill involved, no one thought of molefting them on their march, and they arrived without
the leaft obftruction at Caxamalca. Atabalipa, whom
particular circumftances had conducted into the neighbourhood of this imperial palace, immediately fent
them fome fruits, corn, emeralds, and feveral vafes of
gold or filver. He did not however conceal from their
interpreter his defire that they fhould quit his territories; and he declared that he would go the next
morning to concert with their chief the proper meafures for this retreat.

   To put himfelf in readinefs for an engagement, without fuffering the leaft preparation of war to be perceived, was the only difpofition that Pizarro made

for the reception of the prince. He planted his ca- valry in the gardens of the palace, where they could not be feen: the infantry was in the court; and his artillery was pointed towards the gate where the emperor was to enter.

Atabalipa came without fufpicion to the place appointed. He was attended by about fifteen thoufand men. He was carried on a throne of gold, and gold glittered in the arms of his troops. He turned to the principal officers, and faid to them : *Thefe ftrangers are the meffengers of the gods; be careful of offending them.*

The proceffion was now drawing near the palace, which was occupied by Pizarro, when a dominican, named Vincent de Valverdo, with a crucifix in one hand, and his breviary in the other, came up to the emperor. He ftopped the prince in his march, and made him a long fpeech, in which he expounded to him the Chriftian religion, preffed him to embrace that form of worfhip, and propofed to him to fubmit to the king of Spain, to whom the Pope had given Peru.

The emperor, who heard him with a great deal of patience, replied, *I am very willing to be the friend of the king of Spain, but not his vaffal; the Pope muft furely be a very extraordinary man, to give fo liberally what does not belong to him. I fhall not change my religion for another; and if the Chriftians adore a God who died upon a crofs, I worfhip the fun, who never dies.* He then afked Vincent where he had learned all that he had faid of God and the creation? *In this book,* replied the monk, prefenting at the fame time his breviary to the emperor. Atabalipa took the book, examined it on all fides, fell a-laughing, and, throwing away the breviary, added, *This book tells me nothing of all this.* Vincent then turned towards the Spaniards, crying out with all his might, *Vengeance, my friends, vengeance! Chriftians, do you not fee how he defpifes the gofpel? Kill thefe dogs, who trample under foot the law of God.*

The Spaniards, who probably had with difficulty re-

B O O K ſtrained that fury, and that thirſt of blood, which the
VII. ſight of the gold and of the infidels had inſpired them
with, inſtantly obeyed the dominican. Let the reader
judge of the impreſſion that muſt have been made on
the Peruvians by the ſight of the horſes who trampled
upon them, and by the noiſe and effect of the cannon
and muſketry which beat them down. They fled with
ſuch precipitation, that they fell one upon another.
A dreadful maſſacre was made of them. Pizarro himſelf advanced towards the emperor, made his infantry
put to the ſword all that ſurrounded his throne, took
the monarch priſoner, and purſued all the reſt of the
day thoſe who had eſcaped the ſword of his ſoldiers.
A multitude of princes of the race of the Incas, the
miniſters, the flower of the nobility, all that compoſed
the court of Atabalipa, were maſſacred. Even the
crowd of women, old men, and children, who were
come from all parts to ſee their emperor, were not
ſpared. While this carnage continued, Vincent ceaſed not to animate the aſſaſſins who were tired with
ſlaughter, exhorting them to uſe not the edge but the
point of their ſwords, to inflict deeper wounds. When
the Spaniards returned from this infamous maſſacre,
they paſſed the night in drunkenneſs, dancing, and all
the exceſſes of debauchery.

The emperor, though cloſely guarded, ſoon diſcovered the extreme paſſion of his enemies for gold.
This circumſtance determined him to offer them for
his ranſom as much of this metal as his priſon, which
was two-and-twenty feet in length, and ſixteen in
breadth, could contain, and to as great a height as
the arm of a man could reach. His propoſal was accepted. But while thoſe of his miniſters, in whom he
had moſt confidence, were employed in collecting what
was neceſſary to enable him to fulfil his engagements,
he was informed that Huaſcar had promiſed three
times as much to ſome Spaniards who had found an
opportunity of converſing with him, if they would
conſent to reinſtate him upon the throne of his an-

ceftors. He was alarmed at this incipient negotiation; B O O K and his apprehenfions made him refolve to ftrangle a VII. rival who appeared fo dangerous.

In order to diffipate the fufpicions which fuch an action muft neceffarily excite in his keepers, Atabalipa urged with frefh zeal the collecting of the metals ftipulated for the recovery of his liberty. They were brought in from all fides as faft as the diftance of the places, and the confufion that prevailed, would allow. The whole would have been completed in a little time; but thefe heaps of gold, inceffantly expofed to the greedy eyes of the conquerors, fo inflamed their cupidity, that it was impoffible to delay any longer the diftribution of them. The fifth part of the whole, which the government had referved to itfelf, was delivered to the agents of the treafury. A hundred thoufand piaftres, or 540,000 livres [22,500l.], were fet apart for the body of troops Almagro had juft brought up, and which were ftill upon the coafts. Each of Pizarro's cavalry received 43,200 livres [1800l.], and each of his infantry 21,600 [883l. 6s. 8d.]. The general, and the officers, had fums proportioned to their rank in the army.

Thefe fortunes, the moft extraordinary that have ever been recorded in hiftory, did not mitigate the barbarity of the Spaniards. Atabalipa had given his gold, and his name had ferved to keep the people in fubjection: it was now time, therefore, to put an end to him. Vincent faid that he was a hardened prince, who ought to be treated like Pharaoh. The interpreter Philippillo, who had a criminal intercourfe with one of his women, might be difturbed in his pleafures. Almagro was apprehenfive, that, while he was fuffered to live, the army of his colleague might be defirous of appropriating all the booty to itfelf as part of the emperor's ranfom. Pizarro had been defpifed by him, becaufe, being lefs informed than the meaneft of the foldiers, he knew not how to read. Thefe circumftances, even more perhaps than political reafons, occafioned the emperor's death to be determined upon.

B O O K   The Spaniards had the effrontery to bring him to a
   VII.   formal trial; and this atrocious farce was followed
with those horrid consequences that must necessarily
have been expected from it.

After this judicial assassination, the murderers over-
ran Peru with that thirst of blood and plunder which
directed all their actions. Had they shown some degree of moderation and humanity, they would probably have made themselves masters of this vast empire
without drawing the sword. A people naturally mild,
accustomed for a long time past to the most blind sub-
mission, ever faithful to the masters it had pleased Heaven to give them, and astonished at the terrible spec-
tacle they had just been beholding; such a nation
would have submitted to the yoke without much reluctance. The plundering of their houses and of their
temples, the outrages done to their wives and daughters; cruelties of all kinds succeeding each other without interruption: such a variety of calamities stirred
up the people to revenge, and they found commanders to guide their resentment.

Numerous armies at first obtained some advantages
over a small number of tyrants lost in these immense
regions; but even these trifling successes were not durable. Several of the adventurers, who had enriched
themselves by the ransom of Atabalipa, had quitted
their standards, that they might go elsewhere to enjoy,
in a more peaceable manner, a property so rapidly acquired. Their fortune inflamed the minds of men in
the Old and in the New World, and they hastened
from all quarters to this country of gold. The consequence of this was, that the Spaniards multiplied in a
less time at Peru than in the other colonies. They
soon amounted to the number of five or six thousand;
and then all resistance was at an end. Those of the
Indians who were the most attached to their liberty,
to their government, and to their religion, took refuge
at a distance among inaccessible mountains. Most of
them submitted to the conqueror.

A revolution so remarkable hath been a subject of

aſtoniſhment to all nations. Peru is a country very в о о к VII. difficult of acceſs, where one muſt continually climb mountains, and perpetually march in narrow paſſes and defiles. Troops are there obliged to be inceſſantly paſſing and repaſſing torrents or rivers, the banks of which are always ſteep. Four or five thouſand men, with a moderate ſhare of courage and ſkill, might deſtroy the beſt diſciplined armies. How then could it poſſibly happen that a great nation did not even venture to diſpute a territory, the nature of which was ſo well known to them, againſt a few plunderers, whom the ocean had juſt brought to theſe ſhores?

This event took place for the ſame reaſon that an intrepid robber, with the piſtol in his hand, ſpoils with impunity a body of men, who are either quietly reſting by their fire-ſides, or who, ſhut up in a public carriage, are going along the road without miſtruſt. Though the robber be alone, and though he may have only one or two piſtols to fire, yet he ſtrikes the whole company with awe, becauſe no one chooſes to ſacrifice himſelf for the reſt. Defence implies a mutual agreement, which is the more ſlowly formed, as the danger is leaſt expected, as the ſecurity is more complete, and as it has laſted a longer time. This was exactly the caſe with the Peruvians. They lived without uneaſineſs and without moleſtation for ſeveral centuries. Let us add to theſe conſiderations, that fear is the offſpring of ignorance and aſtoniſhment; that a diſorderly multitude cannot ſtand againſt a ſmall number of diſciplined forces; and that courage unarmed cannot reſiſt cannon-ſhot. Accordingly, Peru muſt neceſſarily have been ſubdued, if even the domeſtic diſſenſions which then ſubverted it had not paved the way for its ſubjection.

This empire, which, according to the Spaniſh hiſtorians, had flouriſhed for four centuries paſt, had been founded by Manco Capac, and by his wife Mama Ocello, who were called Incas, or Lords of Peru. It has been conjectured that theſe two perſons might be the deſcendants of certain navigators of Europe, or the Origin, religion, government, manners, and arts of Peru, at the arrival of the Spaniards.

Canaries, who had been shipwrecked on the coasts of
Brazil.

To support this conjecture, it has been said, that the
Peruvians divided the year, as we do, into three hundred and sixty-five days, and that they had some notion of astronomy; that they were acquainted with
the points of the horizon, where the sun sets in the
summer and winter solstice, and in the equinoxes;
marks which the Spaniards destroyed, as being monuments of Indian superstition. It has been asserted, that
the race of the Incas was whiter than that of the natives of the country, and that several of the royal family had beards; and it is a known fact, that there
are certain features, either ill formed, or regular, that
are preserved in some families, though they do not
constantly pass from one generation to another. And
lastly, it has been said, that it was a tradition generally
diffused throughout Peru, and transmitted from age to
age, that there would one day arrive by sea men with
beards, and of such superiority in arms, that nothing
could resist them.

If there should be any of our readers disposed to
adopt so improbable an opinion, they must necessarily
allow, that there must have elapsed a considerable
space of time between the shipwreck and the foundation of the Peruvian empire. If this be not admitted,
we cannot explain why the legislator should not have
given the savages, whom he collected together, some
notions of writing, though he should not himself have
been able to read? Or why he should not have taught
them several of our arts and methods of doing things,
and instructed them in certain tenets of his religion?
Either it was not an European who founded the
throne of the Incas, or we must necessarily believe,
that the vessel of his ancestors was wrecked on the
coast of America, at an era so remote, that the succeeding generations must have forgotten all the customs of the place from whence they sprang.

The legislators announced themselves to be children, sent by their father to make men good and hap-

py. They certainly thought that this prejudice would B o o k
inflame the minds of the people whom they meant to VII.
civilize, would elevate their courage, and infpire them
with greater love for their country, and with more
complete fubmiffion to the laws.

It was to a fet of naked and wandering men, without agriculture, without induftry, without any of thofe
moral ideas that are the firft ties of fociety, that their
difcourfes were addreffed. Some of thefe barbarians,
who were imitated by others, affembled round the legiflators in the mountainous country of Cufco.

Manco taught his new fubjects to fertilize the earth,
to fow corn and pulfe, to wear clothes, and to provide
dwelling-places for themfelves. Ocello fhowed the
Indian women how to fpin, to weave cotton and wool;
and inftructed them in all the occupations fuitable to
their fex, and in all the arts of domeftic economy.

The ftar of fire, which difpels the darknefs that covers the earth, which draws the curtain of the night,
and fuddenly difplays to the eyes of aftonifhed man
the moft extenfive, the moft auguft, and the moft
pleafing of all fcenes; which is faluted at its rifing
by the cheerfulnefs of animals, by the melody of birds,
and by the hymn of the being that is endowed with
the faculty of thinking; which advances majeftically
above all their heads; which, in its progrefs through
the regions of the fky, traverfes an immenfity of fpace;
which, when it fets, plunges the univerfe again into
filence and melancholy; which diftinguifhes the feafons and the climates; which collects and diffipates
the ftorms; which lights up the thunder, and extin-
guifhes it; which pours upon the fields the rains that
fertilize them, and upon the forefts thofe that nourifh
them; which animates every thing by its warmth,
embellifhes every thing by its prefence, and the privation of which produces in all parts a ftate of languor
and annihilation: the fun, in a word, was the god of
the Peruvians; and, indeed, what being is there in nature more worthy of the homage of the ignorant man,
who is dazzled with its fplendour, or of the grateful

B O O K man, on whom its benefits are lavifhed? The worfhip
  VII. of the fun was accordingly inftituted. Temples were
built to this deity, and human facrifices were abolifhed. The defcendants of the legiflators were the only
priefts of the nation.

The laws pronounced the pain of death againft
murder, theft, and adultery. Few other crimes were
treated with the fame feverity. Polygamy was prohibited. No one was allowed to have concubines except the emperor, and that becaufe the race of the fun
could not be too much multiplied. Thefe concubines
were felected from among the virgins confecrated to
the temple of Cufco, who were all of his own race.

A moft wife inftitution enjoined that a young man,
who fhould commit a fault, fhould be flightly punifhed ; but that his father fhould be refponfible for him.
Thus it was that found morals were always inculcated
by a good education.

There was no indulgence for idlenefs, which was
confidered, with reafon, as the fource of all crimes.
Thofe who, from age and infirmities, were rendered
unfit for labour, were maintained at the public charge,
but on condition that they fhould preferve the cultivated lands from the birds. All the citizens were obliged to make their own clothes, to raife their own
dwellings, and to fabricate their own inftruments of
agriculture. Every feparate family knew how to fupply its own wants.

The Peruvians were enjoined to love one another,
and every circumftance induced them to it. Thofe
common labours, which were always enlivened by
agreeable fongs ; the object itfelf of thefe labours,
which was to affift every one who had occafion for
fuccour ; that apparel that was made by young women devoted to the worfhip of the fun, and diftributed by the emperor's officers to the poor, to the aged,
and to orphans ; that union which muft neceffarily
reign in the decuries, where every one was mutually
infpired with refpect for the laws, and with the love of
virtue, becaufe the punifhments that were inflicted for

the faults of one individual fell on the whole body; BOOK
that cuftom of regarding each other as members of VII.
one fingle family, which was the empire : all thefe
circumftances united, maintained among the Peruvians concord, benevolence, patriotifm, and a certain
public fpirit ; and contributed, as much as poffible, to
˚ıbftitute the moft fublime and amiable virtues in lieu
    perfonal intereft, of the fpirit of property, and of
ˈɹ ue ufual incentives employed by other legiflators.

The fe virtues were rewarded with marks of diftinction, as much as if they had been fervices rendered to
the country. Thofe who had fignalized themfelves by
an exemplary conduct, or by any diftinguifhed actions
of advantage to the public good, wore, as a mark of
ornament, clothes wrought by the family of the Incas.
It is very probable that thofe ftatues, which the Spaniards pretended that they found in the temples of the
fun, and which they took for idols, were the ftatues of
men, who, by the greatnefs of their talents, or by a
life replete with illuftrious actions, had merited the
homage or love of their fellow-citizens.

The fe great men were alfo ufually the fubjects of
poems compofed by the family of the Incas for the
inftruction of the people.

There was another fpecies of poetry conducive to
morality. At Cufco, and in all the other towns of
Peru, tragedies and comedies were performed. The
firft were leffons of duty to the priefts, warriors, judges,
and perfons of diftinction, and reprefented to them
models of public virtue. Comedies ferved for inftruction to perfons of inferior rank, and taught them the
exercife of private virtues, and even of domeftic economy.

The whole ftate was diftributed into decuries, with
an officer that was appointed to fuperintend ten families that were intrufted to him. A fuperior officer had
the fame infpection over fifty families ; others over a
hundred, five hundred, and a thoufand.

The decurions, and the other fuperintending officers, up to the fuperintendant of a thoufand, were

obliged to give an account to the latter of all actions
whether good or bad, to folicit punifhments and rewards for each, and to give information if there were
any want of provifions, clothes, or corn, for the year.
The fuperintendant of a thoufand made his report to
the minifter of the Inca.

He had feldom any caufe of complaint againft the
part of the nation intrufted to his care. In a country
where all the laws were thought to be prefcribed by
the fun, and where the leaft infringement of them was
confidered as a facrilege, thefe tranfgreffions muft have
been very uncommon. When fuch a misfortune happened, the guilty perfons went of their own accord to
reveal their moft fecret faults, and to folicit permiffion
to expiate them. Thefe people told the Spaniards that
there never had been one man of the family of the Incas who deferved punifhment.

The lands of the kingdom, that were fufceptible of
cultivation, were divided into three parts ; one appropriated to the fun, another to the Inca, and a third to
the people. The firft were cultivated in common, as
were likewife the lands of orphans, of widows, of old
men, of the infirm, and of the foldiers who were with
the army. Thefe were cultivated immediately after
the lands appropriated to the fun, and before thofe of
the emperor. The feafon of this labour was announced by feftivals : it was begun and continued with the
found of mufical inftruments, and the chanting of
hymns.

The emperor levied no tribute ; and exacted nothing from his fubjects, but that they fhould cultivate
his lands ; the whole produce of which, being depofited in public magazines, was fufficient to defray all the
expences of the empire.

The lands dedicated to the fun provided for the
maintenance of the priefts, the fupport of the temples,
and of every thing that concerned public worfhip.
They were partly cultivated by princes of the royal
family, clad in their richeft habits.

With regard to the lands that were in the poffeffion

of individuals, they were neither hereditary, nor even eftates for life : the divifion of them was continually varying, and was regulated with ftrict equity according to the number of perfons which compofed every family. There was no other wealth but what arofe from the produce of the fields, the temporary enjoyment of which was all that was granted by the ftate.

This cuftom of moveable poffeffions has been univerfally cenfured by men of underftanding. It has been their general opinion, that a nation would never rife to any degree of power or greatnefs, but by fixed, and even hereditary property. If it were not for the firft of thefe, we fhould fee on the globe only wandering and naked favages, miferably fubfifting on fuch fruits and vegetables as are the fole and fcanty production of rude nature. If it were not for the fecond, every individual would live only for himfelf ; mankind would be deprived of every permanent advantage, which paternal affection, the love of a family name, and the inexpreffible delight we feel in acting for the good of pofterity, urge us to purfue. The fyftem of fome bold fpeculators, who have regarded property, and particularly that fpecies of it which is hereditary, as an ufurpation of fome members of fociety over others, is refuted by the fate of all thofe inftitutions in which their principles have been reduced to practice. Thefe ftates have all fallen to ruin, after having languifhed for fome time in a ftate of depopulation and anarchy.

If Peru hath not fhared the fame fate, it is probably becaufe the Incas, not knowing the ufe of impofts, and having only commodities in kind to fupply the neceffities of government, muft have been obliged to ftudy how to multiply them. They were affifted in the execution of this project by their minifters, by inferior officers, and by the foldiers themfelves, who received nothing but the fruits of the earth for their fubfiftence and the fupport of their rank. Hence arofe a continual folicitude to increafe thefe productions. This attention might have for its principal object the intro-

B O O K duction of plenty into the lands of the fovereign ; but
VII. his patrimony was fo mixed and confounded with that
of his fubjects, that it was not poffible to fertilize the
one without fertilizing the other. The people, encouraged by thefe advantages, which left little fcope to
their induftry, applied themfelves to labours, which
the nature of their foil, of their climate, and of their
confumptions, rendered very eafy. But notwithftanding all thefe advantages ; notwithftanding the ever
active vigilance of the magiftrate ; notwithftanding
the certainty that their harvefts would never be ravaged by a turbulent neighbour ; the Peruvians never
enjoyed any thing more than the mere neceffaries of
life. We may venture to affert, that they would have
acquired the means of diverfifying and extending their
enjoyments, if their talents had been excited by the
introduction of rented, transferable, and hereditary
property.

The Peruvians, though at the very fource of gold
and filver, knew not the ufe of coin. They had not,
properly fpeaking, any kind of commerce ; and the
more minute arts, which owe their exiftence to the
immediate wants of focial life, were in a very imperfect ftate among them. All their fcience confifted in
memory, all their induftry in example. They learned
their religion and their hiftory by hymns, and their
duties and profeffions by labour and imitation.

Their legiflation was undoubtedly very imperfect
and limited, fince it fuppofed the prince always juft
and infallible, and the magiftrates poffeffed of as much
integrity as the prince ; fince not only the monarch,
but his deputies, a fuperintendant of ten, of a hundred, or of a thoufand, might change at pleafure the
deftination of punifhments and rewards. Among fuch
a people, deprived of the ineftimable advantage of
writing, the wifeft laws, being deftitute of every principle of ftability, muft infenfibly be corrupted, without there being any method of reftoring them to their
primitive character.

The counterpoife of thefe dangers was found in

their abfolute ignorance of gold and filver coin; an B O O K ignorance which, in a Peruvian defpot, rendered the VII. fatal paffion of amaffing riches impoffible. It was found in the conftitution of the empire, which had fixed the amount of the fovereign's revenue, by fettling the portion of lands that belonged to him. It was found in the extremely fmall number and moderate nature of the wants of the people, which, being eafily gratified, rendered them happy and attached to the government. It was found in the influence of their religious opinions, which made the obfervation of the laws a matter of confcience. Thus was the defpotifm of the Incas founded on a mutual confidence between the fovereign and the people; a confidence which refulted from the beneficence of the prince, from the conftant protection he granted to all his fubjects, and from the evident intereft they had to continue in obedience to him.

A fpirit of pyrrhonifm, which hath fucceeded to a blind credulity, and hath been fometimes carried to unjuftifiable lengths, hath for fome time endeavoured to raife objections to what has been juft related of the laws, manners, and happinefs of ancient Peru. This account hath appeared to fome philofophers as chimerical, and formed only by the naturally romantic imagination of a few Spaniards. But among the deftroyers of this diftinguifhed part of the New World, was there a fingle ruffian fufficiently enlightened to invent a fable fo confiftent in all its parts? Was there any one among them humane enough to wifh to do it, had he even been equal to the tafk? Would he not rather have been reftrained by the fear of increafing that hatred, which fo many cruelties had brought on his country throughout the whole world? Would not the fable have been contradicted by a multitude of witneffes, who would have feen the contrary of what was publifhed with fo much pomp? The unanimous teftimony of cotemporary writers, and of their immediate fucceffors, ought to be regarded as the ftrongeft hiftorical demonftration that can poffibly be defired.

Let us therefore no longer confider, as the offspring of a wild imagination, this account of a fucceffion of wife fovereigns, and of a feries of generations among mankind exifting without reproach. Let us rather deplore the fate of thefe people, and not envy them the fad remembrance of this honour. It is enough to have deprived them of the advantages which they enjoyed, without adding the bafenefs of calumny to the meannefs of avarice, the outrages of ambition, and the rage of fanaticifm. It is to be wifhed that this beautiful era may be renewed, fooner or later, in fome quarter of the globe.

We fhall not juftify, with the fame confidence, thofe accounts which the conquerors of Peru publifhed concerning the grandeur and magnificence of the monuments of all kinds that they had found there. The defire of adding greater luftre to the glory of their triumphs might poffibly miflead them. Perhaps, without being convinced themfelves, they ftudied to impofe on their own country and on foreign nations. The firft teftimonies, and thofe even were contradictory, have been invalidated by fucceeding accounts, and at length totally deftroyed, when men of enlightened underftandings had vifited this celebrated part of the New Hemifphere.

We muft, therefore, confider as fabulous the report of that prodigious multitude of towns built with fo much labour and expence. If there were fo many fuperb cities in Peru, why do none exift except Cufco and Quito, befide thofe the conqueror built? Whence comes it that we fcarce find anywhere, except in the valleys of Capillas and of Pachacamac, the ruins of thofe of which fuch exaggerated defcriptions have been publifhed? The people muft therefore have been difperfed over the country; and indeed it was impoffible it fhould have been otherwife in a region where there were neither tenants, nor artifts, nor merchants, nor great proprietors, and where tillage was the fole or the principal occupation of all men.

We muft confider as fabulous the account of thofe

majeſtic palaces, deſtined for the accommodation of the Incas, in the place of their reſidence and on their travels. As far as it is poſſible to judge through thoſe heaps of ruins which have been ſtirred up ſuch an in-finite number of times by the hand of avarice, in ex-pectation of finding treaſures among them, the royal manſions had neither majeſty nor ornament. They differed only in extent and thickneſs from the ordi-nary buildings, which were conſtructed with reeds, with wood, with compacted earth, and with rough ſtones without any cement, according to the nature of the climate, or the vicinity of the materials.

We muſt conſider as fabulous the relation of thoſe fortified places which defended the frontiers of the empire. There were undoubtedly ſome of theſe. The Lower Peru ſtill preſents us with the ruins of two of them ſituated upon mountains, the one conſtructed with earth, the other with the trunks of trees. It is ſuppoſed that they were furniſhed with ditches, and with three walls, one commanding the other. This was ſufficient to contain the conquered people, and to check the incurſions of neighbours that were not very formidable. But theſe means of defence could be of no avail againſt the valour and the arms of the Eu-ropeans. Neither were the fortreſſes of the Upper Peru, though built of ſtone, better calculated for this purpoſe. M. de la Condamine, who viſited, with that ſcrupulous attention that diſtinguiſhed him, the fort of Cannar, which is the beſt preſerved, and the moſt con-ſiderable after that of Cuſco, found it to be of very ſmall extent, and only ten feet high. A people who had nothing but their arms to aſſiſt them in carrying or dragging the moſt bulky materials, and who were ignorant of the uſe of levers and pulleys, could not poſſibly execute any greater deſigns.

We muſt conſider as fabulous the hiſtory of thoſe aqueducts and reſervoirs that are ſaid to have been comparable to the moſt magnificent monuments of the ſame kind tranſmitted to us from the ancients.

Neceſſity had taught the Peruvians to dig trenches
round the mountains, and upon the ſlopes of hills,
and canals and ditches in the valleys, in order to make
their lands fruitful which were not fertilized by the
rains, and to bring water for their own uſe, when
they had never thought of conſtructing wells for this
purpoſe : but theſe works of earth or dry ſtone had
nothing remarkable in them; nothing that could imply the ſlighteſt knowledge of hydraulics.

We muſt alſo conſider as fabulous the diſplay of
thoſe ſuperb roads which rendered communication ſo
eaſy. The great roads of Peru were nothing more
than two rows of ſtakes diſpoſed in a line, and intended for no other purpoſe but to point out the way
to travellers. There was no road of any conſequence,
except that which bore the name of the Incas, and
which traverſed the whole empire. This, which was
the moſt beautiful monument of Peru, was entirely
deſtroyed during the civil wars of the conquerors.

We muſt alſo conſider as fabulous what has been
ſaid of thoſe · bridges which are ſo much boaſted of.
How could the Peruvians, who were ignorant of the
method of conſtructing arches, and knew not the uſe
of lime, raiſe ſtone bridges? It is certain, however,
that the traveller was continually ſtopped in his paſſage by a great number of torrents he met with among
theſe regions. To overcome this great obſtacle, it was
contrived to put together ſeven or eight cables, or even
a greater number, made of oſier, to faſten them with
other ſmaller cords, to cover them with the branches
of trees and with earth ; and to fix them ſtrongly to
the oppoſite banks. Rivers that were larger and leſs
rapid, were croſſed in ſmall ſailing-boats which tacked
about with celerity.

We muſt alſo conſider as fabulous, the wonders related of the *quipos*, which were, among the Peruvians,
a ſubſtitute to the art of writing that was unknown
to them. Theſe were, as it hath been ſaid, regiſters
made of cords, in which different kinds of knots and
various colours, pointed out the facts, the remem-

brance of which it was either important or agreeable B o o k VII. to preferve ; thefe records were kept by depofitaries of confidence appointed by public authority. It might perhaps be rafh in us to affirm, that thefe kinds of hieroglyphics, of which we have never had any but obfcure defcriptions, could not poffibly throw any light upon paft events. But, when we obferve the many errors that infinuate themfelves into our hiftories, notwithftanding the great facility of avoiding them, we fhall fcarce be inclined to think, that annals of fo fingular a nature-as thofe we have been mentioning, could ever merit much confidence.

The Spaniards do not deferve more credit, when they tell us of thofe baths that were made of filver and gold, as well as the pipes that fupplied them ; of thofe gardens full of trees, the flowers of which were of filver, and the fruit of gold, and where the eye, being deceived, miftook art for nature ; of thofe fields of maize, the ftems of which were of filver, and the ears of gold ; of thofe baffo-relievos, in which the herbs and plants were fo admirably exhibited, that whoever faw was tempted to gather them ; of thofe dreffes covered over with grains of gold more delicate than the feed of pearl, and the workmanfhip of which the ableft artifts of Europe could not have equalled. We fhall not fay, that thefe works were not worthy to be preferved, becaufe they never have been. If the Greek ftatuaries in their compofitions had only employed precious metals, it is probable that few of the capital productions of Greece could have reached us. But, if we may judge of what hath perifhed by what ftill remains, we may be certain that the Peruvians had made no progrefs in drawing. The vafes, which have efcaped the ravages of time, may ferve as a fignal proof of the patience of the Indians ; but they will never be confidered as monuments of their genius. Some figures of animals, and of infects, in maffive gold, which were long preferved in the treafury of Quito, were not more perfect. We cannot any longer judge of them ; for they were melted down in 1740, in order to furnifh succours for Carthagena, that was then befieged by the Englifh; and there was not found in all Peru-a Spaniard curious enough to purchafe a fingle piece at the bare weight.

From what hath been faid, it appears clearly, that the Peruvians had made fcarce any advances in the abftract fciences. Moft of them depend on the progrefs of the arts, and thefe again on accidents which nature produces only in a courfe of feveral centuries, and of which the greateft part are loft among people who have no intercourfe with enlightened nations.

If we reduce all thefe accounts to the fimple truth, we fhall find that the Peruvians had arrived at the art of fufing gold and filver, and of working them. With thefe metals they made ornaments, moft of which were very thin, for the arms, for the neck, for the nofe, and for the ears; and hollow ftatues, all of one piece, which, whether they were carved or caft in a mould, had no greater degree of thicknefs. Vafes are feldom made of thefe rich materials. Their ordinary vafes were of very fine clay, eafily wrought, and of the fize and figure adapted to the purpofes for which they were deftined. Weights were not known among them, and fcales are difcovered from time to time, the bafons of which are of filver, and which are in the fhape of an inverted cone. Two kinds of ftone were ufed as looking-glaffes; the one was foft, the other hard; one was entirely opaque, the other had a fmall degree of tranfparency; one was black, the other of a lead colour: it had been contrived to give them a fufficient polifh to reflect objects. Wool, cotton, and the barks of trees, were woven by thefe people into a cloth more or lefs compact, and more or lefs coarfe, which was ufed for wearing-apparel, and of which houfehold furniture was even made. Thefe ftuffs and cloths were dyed black, blue, and red, by means of the arnotto, by different plants, and by a kind of wild bean that grows in the mountains. Their emeralds were cut in all forts of forms. Thofe that have been often taken out of the tombs, moft of which are in elevated fituations, where citi-

zens of diftinction were buried with whatever they **B O O K**
poffeffed that was rare, prove that thefe precious ftones **VII.**
were more perfect here than they have been found to
be anywhere elfe. Sometimes, by fortunate chance,
pieces of workmanfhip are difcovered in red and yellow copper, and others which partake of both colours;
from whence it hath been concluded, that the Peruvians were acquainted with the art of mixing metals.
One more important matter is, that this copper never
rufts, and never collects any verdigrife; which feems
to prove, that the Indians mixed fomething in the preparing of it, which had the property of preferving it
from thefe fatal inconveniences. It is to be regretted
that the ufeful art of tempering it in this manner has
been loft, either from want of encouraging the natives
of the country, or from the contempt which the conquerors had for every thing that had no concern with
their paffion for riches.

But with what inftruments were thefe works executed, among a people who were unacquainted with
iron, which is looked upon with reafon as the foundation of all the arts? Nothing has been preferved in
the private houfes, nor hath any thing been difcovered among the public monuments, or in the tombs,
which can give information fufficient to folve this problem. Perhaps the hammers and mallets that were
ufed were made of fome fubftance that time may have
either deftroyed or disfigured. If we will not admit
of this conjecture, we muft conclude, that all the
workmanfhip was executed with thofe hatchets of copper, which alfo ferved the people for arms in battle.
In this cafe, labour, time, and patience, muft have
fupplied among the Peruvians the deficiency of tools.

It was alfo, perhaps, with hatchets of copper or
flint, and by inceffant friction, that they contrived to
cut ftones, to fquare them, to make them anfwer to
each other, to give them the fame height, and to join
them without cement. Unfortunately thefe inftruments had not the fame effect on wood as they had
upon ftone. Thus it happened that the fame men

B O O K who shaped the granite, and who drilled the emerald,
VII. never knew how to join timber by mortises, tenons,
and pins; it was fastened to the walls only by rushes.
The most remarkable buildings had only a covering of
thatch, supported by poles, like the tents of our armies.
They had but one floor, and no light except by the
entrance, and they consisted only of detached apart-
ments, that had no communication with each other.

The sub-   But whatever were the arts which the Spaniards
jection of found in the country of Peru, these barbarians were
Peru is the
epocha of no sooner masters of this vast empire, than they dif-
the most puted the spoils of it with all the rage which their
bloody con-
tests be- first exploits announced. The seeds of these divisions
tween its had been sown by Pizarro himself, who, when he
conquerors. went into Europe to prepare for a second expedition
into the South Seas, had prevailed upon the ministry
to give him a great superiority over Almagro. The
sacrifice of what he had obtained from a temporary
favour, had contributed to reconcile him with his colleague, who had been justly incensed at this perfidy;
but the division of Atabalipa's ransom irritated again
these two haughty and rapacious robbers. A dispute,
which arose concerning the limits of their respective
governments, completed their animosity, and this extreme hatred was attended with the most deplorable
consequences.

Civil wars usually originate in tyranny and anarchy.
In a state of anarchy the people divide themselves into
small parties. Each petty faction hath its demagogue;
each hath its pretensions, be they wise or extravagant,
unanimous or contradictory, without their being known.
A number of confused clamours arise. The first stroke
is followed by a thousand others; and the people destroy each other without listening to reason. Private
interests and personal animosities prolong the duration
of the public troubles; and men do not come to expla-
nations till after they are tired with carnage. Under
the influence of tyranny, there are scarce ever more
than three parties, that of the court, that of the opposition, and that of indifferent persons : these are in-

deed lukewarm citizens, but fometimes of great fer- vice by their impartiality, and by the ridicule they caft upon the other two parties. In a ftate of anarchy, when tranquillity is reftored, the life of every individual is fafe ; under that of tyranny, tranquillity is followed by the death of feveral individuals, or of one only.

Though the interefts which divided the chiefs of the Spaniards were not of fuch importance, yet their effects were equally terrible. After fome negotiations, difhoneft at leaft on one part, and confequently ufelefs, recourfe was had to the fword, in order to determine which of the two competitors fhould govern the whole of Peru. On the 6th of April 1538, in the plains of Salines, not far from Cufco, fate decided againft Almagro, who was taken prifoner and beheaded.

Thofe of his partifans who had efcaped the carnage, would willingly have reconciled themfelves with the conquering party. But whether Pizarro did not choofe to truft the foldiers of his rival, or whether he could not overcome a refentment that was too deeply rooted, it is certain that he always fhowed a remarkable averfion for them. They were not only excluded from all the favours that were profufely lavifhed upon the acquifition of a great empire ; but they were alfo ftripped of the rewards formerly granted for their fervices; they were perfecuted, and expofed to continual mortifications.

This treatment brought a great number of them to Lima. There, in the houfe of the fon of their general, they concerted in filence the deftruction of their oppreffor. Nineteen of the moft intrepid went out, fword in hand, on the 26th of June 1541, in the middle of the day, which in hot countries is the time devoted to reft. They penetrated, without oppofition, into the palace of Pizarro ; and the conqueror of fo many vaft kingdoms was quietly maffacred in the centre of a town that he had founded, and the inhabitants of which were compofed of his creatures, his fervants, his relations, his friends, or his foldiers.

Thofe who were judged moft likely to revenge his
death, were murdered after him : the fury of the affaffins fpread itfelf, and every one who ventured to appear in the ftreets and in the fquares was regarded as
an enemy, and put to the fword. Inftantly the houfes
and temples were filled with flaughter, and prefented
nothing but mangled carcafes. The fpirit of avarice,
which induced them to confider the rich merely as
partifans of the old government, was ftill more furious
than that of hatred, and rendered it more active, more
fufpicious, and more implacable. The reprefentation
of a place taken by affault by a barbarous nation,
would communicate but an imperfect idea of that
fpectacle of horror which thefe ruffians now exhibited,
who wrefted from their accomplices the booty of which
they had fruftrated them.

This cruel maffacre was followed by enormities of
another kind. The foul of young Almagro feems to
have been formed for tyranny. Every one who had
been in employment under the adverfary of his family was inhumanly profcribed. The ancient magiftrates
were depofed. The troops were put under the command of new officers. The royal treafury, and the
wealth of thofe who perifhed or were abfent, were feized upon by the ufurper. His accomplices, attached to
his fortune by being partakers of his crimes, were forced to give their fupport to undertakings which filled
them with horror. Thofe among them who fuffered
their uneafinefs at thefe proceedings to tranfpire, were
either put to death in private, or perifhed on a fcaffold.
During the confufion, in which a revolution fo unexpected had plunged Peru, feveral provinces fubmitted
to this monfter, who caufed himfelf to be proclaimed
governor in the capital : and he marched into the heart
of the empire, to complete the reduction of every place
that oppofed, or hefitated to acknowledge him.

A multitude of ruffians joined him on his march.
His army breathed nothing but vengeance and plunder : every thing gave way before it. If the military
talents of the general had equalled the ardour of his

troops, the war had ended here. Unhappily for Al-magro, he had loſt his conductor, John de Herrada. His inexperience made him fall into the ſnares that were laid for him by Pedro Alvares, who had put him-ſelf at the head of the oppoſite party. He loſt, in at-tempting to unravel his rival's plots, that time which he ought to have employed in fighting. In theſe cir-cumſtances, an event, which no one could have fore-ſeen, happened to change the face of affairs.

The licentiate Vaſco di Caſtro, who had been ſent from Europe to try the murderers of old Almagro, ar-rived at Peru. As he was appointed to aſſume the go-vernment in caſe Pizarro was no more, all who had not ſold themſelves to the tyrant, haſtened to acknowledge him. Uncertainty and jealouſy, which had for too long a time kept them diſperſed, were no longer an obſtacle to their re-union. Caſtro, who was as reſolute as if he had grown old in the ſervice, did not ſuffer their impatience to languiſh, but inſtantly led them againſt the enemy. The two armies engaged at Chapas on the 16th of September 1542, and fought with in-expreſſible obſtinacy. Victory, after having wavered a long time, at the cloſe of the day decided in favour of the government party. Thoſe among the rebels who were moſt guilty, dreading to languiſh under diſ-graceful tortures, provoked the conquerors to murder them, crying out, like men in deſpair, *It was I who killed Pizarro.* Their chief was taken priſoner, and died on the ſcaffold.

Theſe ſcenes of horror were juſt concluded, when Blaſco Nunnez Vela arrived in 1544 at Peru, with the title and powers of viceroy. The court had thought to inveſt their repreſentative with a ſolemn dignity, and with very extenſive authority, in order that the decrees he was commiſſioned to eſtabliſh, ſhould meet with leſs oppoſition. Theſe decrees were intended to leſſen the oppreſſion under which the Indians were ſunk, and more particularly to render theſe immenſe conqueſts uſeful to the crown: let us examine whe-ther they were judiciouſly contrived for this purpoſe.

They declared that some of the Peruvians should
be free from that moment, and the rest at the death of
their oppressors: that, for the future, they should not
be compelled to bury themselves in the mines; and
that no kind of labour should be exacted from them
without payment: that their public labours and tributes should be regulated: that the Spaniards who
travelled through the provinces on foot, should no
longer have three of these wretched people to carry
their baggage; nor five when they went on horse-
back: that the Caciques should be freed from the obligation of providing the traveller and his suite with
food.

By the same regulations, all the departments or
commanderies of the governors, of the officers of justice, of the agents of the treasury, of the bishops, of
the monasteries, of the hospitals, and of all persons
who had been concerned in the public troubles, were
to be annexed to the domains of the state. The few
lands that might belong to other proprietors, were to
be subject to the same law, after the present possessors
had ended their days, let their life be long or short;
and their heirs, their wives, or their children, were to
have no claim upon any part of them.

Before so great a revolution had been attempted,
would it not have been more proper to have softened
the ferocious manners of these people, to have gradually bent to the yoke men who had always lived in a
state of independence, to have brought back to principles of equity injustice itself, to have connected to
the general interest those who had been hitherto influenced by private interests only, to have made citizens of adventurers, who had, as it were, forgotten the
country from whence they sprang; to have established
properties where the law of the strongest had before
universally prevailed; to have made order arise from
the midst of confusion; and, by a striking contrast to
the evils which had just been occasioned by anarchy,
to have conciliated attachment and reverence to a
well-regulated government? But without any of these

preliminary fteps, how could the court of Madrid expect fuddenly to attain the end they propofed?

Even fuppofing the matter public, did they employ
a proper agent to effect it? At any rate, it would
have been a work of patience, and of a conciliatory
difpofition which would have required all the talents
of the moft confummate negotiator. Did Nunnez
poffefs any of thefe advantages? Nature had only
given him integrity, courage, and firmnefs; and he
had added nothing to her gifts. With thefe virtues,
which were almoft defects in his fituation, he began to
fulfil his commiffion, without any regard to place, to
perfons, or to circumftances. To the aftonifhment
with which the people were at firft feized, fucceeded
indignation, murmurs, and fedition.

Civil wars affume the character that diftinguifhes
the caufes from whence they fpring. When an abhorrence of tyranny, and the natural love of liberty,
ftimulate a brave people to take up arms, if they prove
victorious, the tranquillity that follows this tranfitory
calamity is an era of the greateft happinefs. The vigour which hath been excited in the foul of every individual, manifefts itfelf in his manners. The fmall
number of citizens who have been witneffes and inftruments of fuch troubles, poffefs more moral ftrength
than the moft populous nations. Abilities and power
are united; and every man is aftonifhed to find that
he occupies that very place which nature had marked
out for him.

But when diffenfions proceed from a corrupt fource;
when flaves fight about the choice of a tyrant; when
the ambitious contend, in order to opprefs, and robbers quarrel for the fake of fpoil; the peace which ter-
minates thefe horrors is fcarcely preferable to the war
which gave them birth. Criminals affume the place
of the judges who had difgraced them, and become
the oracles of thofe laws which they had infulted.
Men ruined by their extravagances and debaucheries,
infult, with an overbearing pomp, thofe virtuous citizens whofe patrimony they have invaded. In this

ftate of utter confufion, the paffions only are attended
to. Avarice feeks to grow rich without any trouble,
vengeance to gratify its refentments without fear, licentioufnefs to throw off every reftraint, and difcontent to occafion a total fubverfion of affairs. The
frenzy of carnage is fucceeded by that of debauchery.
The facred bed of innocence or of marriage is polluted
with blood, adultery, and brutal violence. The fury
of the multitude rejoices in deftroying every thing it
cannot enjoy; and thus, in a few hours, perifh the
monuments of many centuries.

If fatigue, an entire laffitude, or fome fortunate accidents, fufpend thefe calamities, the habit of wicked-
nefs and murder, and the contempt of laws, which neceffarily fubfifts after fo much confufion, is a leaven
ever ready to ferment. Genera.s who no longer have
any command, licentious foldiers without pay, and the
people, fond of novelty, in hopes of changing their
ftate for a better; this fituation of things, and thefe
means of confufion, are always in readinefs for the firft
factious perfon who knows how to avail himfelf of
them.

Such was the difpofition of the Spaniards in Peru,
when Nunnez attempted to carry into execution the
orders he had received from the old hemifphere. He
was immediately degraded, put in irons, and banifhed
to a defert ifland, where he was to remain till he was
conveyed to the mother-country.

Gonzales Pizarro was then returned from a hazardous expedition, which had carried him as far as the
river of the Amazons, and had employed him long
enough to prevent him from taking a part in thofe revolutions which had fo rapidly fucceeded each other.
The anarchy he found prevailing at his return, infpired
him with the idea of feizing the fupreme authority.
His fame and his forces made it impoffible that this
fhould be refufed him; but his ufurpation was marked
with fo many enormities, that Nunnez was regretted.
He was recalled from exile, and foon collected a fufficient number of forces to enable him to take the field.

Civil commotions were then renewed with extreme fury by both parties. No quarter was afked or given on either fide. The Indians were forced to take part in this, as they had done in the preceding wars; fome ranged themfelves under the ftandard of the viceroy, others under the banners of Gonzales. They dragged up the artillery, levelled the roads, and carried the baggage. After a variety of advantages for a long time alternately obtained, fortune at length favoured the rebellion under the walls of Quito, in the month of January in the year 1545. Nunnez, and the great- eft part of his men, were maffacred on that day.

Pizarro took the road of Lima, where they were de- liberating on the ceremonies with which they fhould receive him. Some officers wifhed that a canopy fhould be carried for him to march under, after the manner of kings. Others, with adulation ftill more extravagant, pretended that part of the walls of the town, and even fome houfes, muft be pulled down; as was the cuftom at Rome, when a general obtained the honours of a triumph. Gonzales contented him- felf with making his entrance on horfeback, preceded by his lieutenants, who marched on foot. Four bi- fhops accompanied him; and he was followed by the magiftrates. The ftreets were ftrewn with flowers, and the air refounded with the noife of bells and vari- ous mufical inftruments. This homage totally turned the head of a man naturally haughty, and of confined ideas. He fpoke and acted in the moft defpotic man- ner.

Had Gonzales poffeffed judgment, and the appear- ance of moderation, it would have been poffible for him to render himfelf independent. The principal perfons of his party wifhed it. The majority would have viewed this event with indifference, and the reft would have been obliged to confent to it. Blind cru- elties, infatiable avarice, and unbounded pride, altered thefe difpofitions. Even the perfons whofe interefts were more connected with thofe of the tyrant, wifhed for a deliverer.

An aged
prieſt at
length puts
an end to
the effuſion
of Spaniſh
blood.

Such a deliverer arrived from Europe in the perſon of Pedro de la Gaſca. He was a prieſt advanced in years, but prudent, diſintereſted, firm, and eſpecially endowed with an acute diſcernment. He brought no troops along with him; but he had been intruſted with unlimited powers. The firſt uſe he allowed himſelf to make of them, was, to publiſh a general amneſty without diſtinction of perſons or crimes, and to revoke the ſevere laws that had rendered the preceding adminiſtration odious. This ſtep alone ſecured to him the fleet, and the mountainous provinces. If Pizarro, to whom the amneſty had been particularly offered with every teſtimony of diſtinction, had accepted of it, as he was adviſed to do by the moſt enlightened of his partiſans, the troubles would have been at an end. The habit of commanding would not ſuffer him to deſcend to a private ſtation; and he had recourſe to arms, in hopes of perpetuating his memory. Without loſing a moment, he advanced towards Cuſco, where La Gaſca was aſſembling his forces. On the 9th of April 1548, the battle was begun at the diſtance of four leagues from this place, in the plains of Saeſahuana. One of the rebel general's lieutenants, ſeeing him abandoned at the firſt charge by his beſt ſoldiers, adviſed him, but in vain, to throw himſelf into the enemy's battalions, and periſh like a Roman; but this weak head of a party choſe rather to ſurrender, and end his life on a ſcaffold. Nine or ten of his officers were hanged round him. - A more diſgraceful ſentence was pronounced againſt Carvajal.

This confidant of Pizarro, who, in all the accounts, is accuſed of having maſſacred with his own hand four hundred men, of having ſacrificed, by means of his agents, more than a thouſand Spaniards, and of having deſtroyed more than twenty thouſand Indians through exceſs of labour, was one of the moſt aſtoniſhing men ever recorded in hiſtory. At a time when the minds of all men were elevated, he diſplayed a degree of courage which could never admit of a compariſon. He remained always faithful to the cauſe he had engaged in, although the cuſtom of changing ſtandards according to circumſtances was then univer-ſally prevalent. He never forgot the moſt trifling ſer-vice that had been rendered him; while thoſe who had once conferred an obligation upon him, might af-terwards affront him with impunity. His cruelty was become a proverb; and in the moſt horrid executions he ordered, he never loſt any thing of his mirth. Strongly addicted to raillery, he was appeaſed with a jeſt; while he inſulted the cry of pain, which appear-ed to him the exclamation of cowardice or weakneſs. His iron heart made a ſport of every thing. He took away or preſerved life for a nothing, becauſe life was a nothing in his eſtimation. His paſſion for wine did not prevent the uncommon ſtrength of his body, and the dreadful vigour of his ſoul, from maintaining them-ſelves to the moſt advanced time of life. In extreme old age, he was ſtill the firſt ſoldier, and the firſt com-mander in the army. His death was conformable to his life. At the age of eighty-four, he was quartered, without ſhowing any remorſe for what was paſt, or any uneaſineſs for the future.

Such was the laſt ſcene of a tragedy, every act of which hath been marked with blood. Civil wars have always been cruel in all countries and in all ages; but at Peru they were deſtined to have a peculiar charac-ter of ferocity. Thoſe who excited them, and thoſe who engaged in them, were moſt of them adventurers without education, and of mean birth. Avarice, which had brought them into the New World, was joined to other paſſions which render domeſtic diſſen-ſions ſo laſting and ſo violent. All of them, without exception, conſidered the chief whom they had choſen merely as a partner in their fortune, whoſe influence was only to extend to the guidance of their hoſtilities. None of them accepted any pay. As plunder and confiſcation were to be the fruits of victory, no quar-ter was ever given in action. After the engagement was over, every rich man was expoſed to informations; and there were nearly as many citizens who periſhed

B O O K by the hands of the executioner, as by thofe of the
  VII.   foldiers in battle. The gold that had been acquired
by fuch enormities, was foon exhaufted by the meaneft
kind of intemperance, and the moft extravagant luxury ; and the people returned again to all the exceffes
of military licence that knows no reftraint.

Fortunately for this opulent part of the New Hemifphere, the moft feditious of the conquerors, and of
thofe who followed their fteps, had perifhed miferably
in the feveral events that had fo frequently fubverted
it. Few of them had furvived the troubles, except
thofe who had conftantly preferred peaceable occupations to the tumult and dangers of great revolutions.
What ftill remained of that commotion that had been
raifed in their minds, infenfibly fank into a calm, like
the agitation of waves after a long and furious tem-
peft. Then, and then only, the Catholic kings might
with truth ftyle themfelves the fovereigns of the Spaniards fixed in Peru. But there was one Inca ftill remaining.

This legitimate heir of fo many vaft dominions, lived in the midft of the mountains in a ftate of independence. Some princeffes of his family, who had
fubmitted to the conquerors, abufed his inexperience
and youth, and prevailed upon him to come to Lima.
The ufurpers of his rights carried their infolence fo far
as to fend him letters of grace, and affigned to him
only a very moderate domain for his fubfiftence. He
went to hide his fhame and his regret in the valley of
Yucay, where, at the expiration of three years, death,
though ftill too tardy, put an end to his unfortunate
career. An only daughter, who furvived him, married
Loyola; and from this union are fprung the houfes of
Oropefa and Alcannizas. Thus was the conqueft of
Peru completed towards the year 1560.

When the Caftilians had firft made their appearance
in this empire, it had an extent of more than fifteen
thoufand miles of coaft upon the South Sea ; and in
its depth, it was bounded only by the higheft of the
Cordeleirias mountains. In lefs than half a century,

thefe turbulent men pufhed on their conquefts eaft-ward from Panama to the river Plata, and weftward from the Chagre to the Oroonoko. Although the new acquifitions were moft of them feparated from Peru by terrible deferts, or by people who obftinately defended their liberty, yet they were all incorporated with it, and fubmitted to the fame law, even down to thefe latter times. Let us take a review of thofe which have preferved or acquired fome degree of importance; and we fhall begin with the Darien.

B O O K VII.

This narrow flip of land, which joins South and North America together, is fortified by a chain of high mountains, fufficiently folid to refift the attacks of the two oppofite feas. The country is fo barren, fo rainy, fo unwholefome, and fo full of infects, that the Spaniards, in all probability, would never have thought of fixing there, had they not found at Porto-Bello, and at Panama, harbours well calculated for eftablifhing an eafy communication between the Atlantic and the Southern Ocean. The reft of the ifthmus had fo little attraction for them, that the fettlements of Saint Mary and of Nombre de Dios, which had at firft been formed there, were foon annihilated.

Notions concerning the province of Darien. whether that country be of importance enough to excite divifions among the nations?

This neglect determined, in 1698, twelve hundred Scotch to go there. The Company, united for this enterprife, intended to gain the confidence of the few favages whom the fword had not deftroyed; to arm them againft a people whofe ferocity they had experienced; to work the mines, which were thought more valuable than they are; to intercept the galleons by cruifes fkilfully conducted; and to unite their forces with thofe of Jamaica, with fufficient management to acquire the fway in this part of the New World.

A project fo alarming difpleafed the court of Madrid, which feemed determined to confifcate the effects of all the Englifh, who traded with fo much advantage in their dominions. It difpleafed Louis XIV. who offered to a power already too much exhaufted, a fleet fufficient to fruftrate the defign: it difpleafed the Dutch, who were afraid that this new company

BOOK would one day divide with them the smuggling trade
VII. which they monopolized in these latitudes: it was even
displeasing to the British ministry, who foresaw that
Scotland, growing rich, would wish to emerge from
that kind of dependence to which its poverty had hitherto reduced it. This violent and universal opposition determined king William to revoke a permission
which his favourites had extorted from him. It then
became necessary to evacuate the golden island upon
which this colony had been placed.

But the mere apprehension the Spaniards had felt
of having such a neighbour, determined them to pay
more attention themselves to a country which they had
always hitherto disdained. Their missionaries succeeded in forming nine or ten villages, each of which contained from one hundred and fifty to two hundred savages. Whether from the unsettled disposition of the
Indians, or from the oppression of their guides, these
rising settlements began to fall off in 1716: and in
our days, there are no more than three of them remaining, defended by four small forts and by a hundred soldiers.

Extent, cli-   The province of Carthagena is bordered on the
mate, soil,   West by the river Darien, and on the East by that
fortifica-
tions, har-   of Magdalena. The extent of its coast is fifty-three
bour, popu-   leagues, and of the inland countries eighty-five. The
lation, man-
ners, and   arid and extremely high mountains that occupy the
trade of   greatest part of this vast space, are separated by large
Cartha-
gena.   valleys, well watered and fertile. The dampness and
excessive heat of the climate prevent, indeed, the corn,
the oils, the wines, and the fruits of Europe from thriv-
ing there: but rice, cassava, maize, cacao, sugar, and
all the productions peculiar to America, are very common. But cotton is the only article cultivated for exportation; and even the wool of this is so long, and
so difficult in working, that it is only sold for the low-
est price in our markets, and is rejected by most of the
manufactures.

Bastidas was the first European, who, in 1502, appeared in these unknown latitudes. La Cosa, Guerra,

Ojeda, Vefputius, and Oviedo, landed there after him: but the people whom thefe plunderers meant to en-flave oppofed them with fuch firmnefs, that they were obliged to give up all thoughts of forming a fettlement there. At length Pedro de Heridia appeared in 1527, with a force fufficient to reduce them. He built and peopled Carthagena.

In 1544, fome French pirates pillaged the new town. Forty-one years after, it was burnt by the celebrated Drake. Pointis, one of the admirals of Louis XIV. took it in 1697; but, by his cruel rapacity, he dif-graced the arms which his ambitious mafter wifhed to render illuftrious. The Englifh were difgracefully obliged, in 1741, to raife the fiege of it, though they had undertaken it with twenty-five fhips of the line, fix fire-fhips, two bomb-ketches, and as many land forces as were fufficient to conquer a great part of America. The mifunderftanding between Vernon and Wentworth; the cabals which divided the army and the fleet; a want of experience in moft of the com-manders, and of fubordination in the fubalterns: all thefe caufes united to deprive the nation of the glory and advantage it had flattered itfelf with, from one of the moft brilliant armaments that had ever been dif-patched from the Britifh ports.

After fo many revolutions, Carthagena now fubfifts in fplendour in a peninfula of fand, which is joined to the continent only by two narrow necks of land, the broadeft of which is not thirty-five toifes. Its fortifi-cations are regular. Nature has placed, at a little di-ftance, a hill of a tolerable height, on which the cita-del of St. Lazarus hath been built. Thefe works are defended by a garrifon, more or lefs numerous, as cir-cumftances require. The town is one of the beft built, the moft regular, and beft difpofed, of any in the New World. It may contain twenty-five thoufand fouls. Of this number the Spaniards form the fixth part; the Indians, the Negroes, and feveral races compofed of mixtures of an infinite variety, make up the remainder.

Thefe mixtures are more common at Carthagena

BOOK than in moſt of the other Spaniſh colonies. A multi-
VII. tude of vagabonds without employment, without fortune, and without recommendations, are continually
reſorting to this place. In a country where they are
totally unknown, no citizen can venture to repoſe any
confidence in their ſervices ; they are deſtined to ſub-
ſiſt wretchedly on the alms of the convents, and to lie
in the corner of a ſquare, or under the portico of ſome
church. If the afflictions they experience in this miſerable ſtate ſhould bring ſome violent diſeaſe upon
them, they are commonly aſſiſted by the free negro
women, whoſe care and kindneſs they requite by marrying them. Thoſe who have not the happineſs of
being in a ſituation dreadful enough to excite the
compaſſion of the women, are obliged to take refuge
in the country, and to devote themſelves to fatiguing
labours, which a certain national pride, and ancient
cuſtoms, render equally inſupportable. Indolence is
carried ſo far in this country, that men and women
who are wealthy ſeldom quit their hammocks, and that
but for a little time.

The climate muſt be one of the principal cauſes of
this inactivity. The heat is exceſſive, and almoſt continual, at Carthagena. The torrents of water, which
are inceſſantly pouring down from the month of May
to November, have this peculiarity, that they never
cool the air, which, however, is ſometimes a little tem-
pered by the north-eaſt winds in the dry ſeaſon. The
night is as hot as the day. An habitual perſpiration
gives the inhabitants the pale and livid colour of ſick-
ly perſons. Even when they are in perfect health,
their motions partake of the ſoftneſs of the climate,
which evidently relaxes their fibres. This indolence
manifeſts itſelf even in their words, which are always
uttered ſlowly, and with a low voice. Thoſe who
come hither from Europe preſerve their freſh com-
plexions and plumpneſs three or four months ; but
they afterwards loſe both.

This decay is the forerunner of an evil ſtill more
dreadful, but the nature of which is little known. It

is conjectured that fome perfons are affected with it
from catching cold, others from indigeftion. It manifefts itfelf by vomitings, accompanied with fo violent a delirium, that the patient muft be confined, to
prevent him from tearing himfelf to pieces. He often
expires in the midft of thefe agitations, which feldom
laft above three or four days. A lemonade made of
the juice of the opuntium, or Indian fig, is, according
to Godin, the beft fpecific that has been found againft
fo fatal a difeafe. Thofe who have efcaped this danger at firft, run no rifk for the future. We are affured
from the teftimony of men of underftanding, that, even
upon their return to Carthagena, after a long abfence,
they have nothing to fear.

The town and its territory exhibit the fpectacle of a
hideous leprofy, which indifcriminately attacks both
the inhabitants and ftrangers. The philofophers who
have attempted to afcribe this calamity to the eating
of pork, have not confidered that nothing of a fimilar
kind is feen in the other parts of the New World,
where this kind of food is not lefs common. To prevent the progrefs of this diftemper, an hofpital has been
founded in the country. Perfons who are fuppofed to
be attacked with it, are fhut up here, without diftinction of fex, rank, or age. The benefit of fo wife an
eftablifhment is loft through the avarice of the governors, who, without being deterred by the danger of
fpreading the difeafe, fuffer the poor to go in and out
to beg. Thus it is that the number of the fick is fo
great, that the enclofure of the dwelling is of an immenfe extent. Every one there enjoys a little fpot of
ground that is marked out for him on his admiffion.
There he builds an abode fuitable to his fortune,
where he lives in tranquillity to the end of his days,
which are often long, though unhappy. This diforder
fo powerfully excites that paffion which is the ftrongeft of all others, that it has been judged neceffary to
permit marriage to fuch as are afflicted with it. This
is, perhaps, increafing the paffion, by increafing the
means of fatisfying it. Thefe defires appear to be ir-

ritated by the very gratification of them ; they increafe by their very remedies, and are reproduced by
each other. The inconvenience of beholding this ardent difeafe, which infects the blood, perpetuated in
the children, hath given way to the dread of other diforders, that are, perhaps, chimerical.

Let us be allowed to form a conjecture. There are
fome people in Africa that are fituated nearly under
the fame latitude, who have a cuftom of rubbing the
body with an oil that is exprefled from the fruit of a
tree refembling the palm. This oil is of a difagreeable
fmell : but befide the property it has of keeping off
infects which are very troublefome under this burning
fky, it ferves to make the fkin pliable, and to preferve,
or reftore to that organ fo effential to life, the free exercife of the office for which nature has defigned it ;
it alfo quiets the irritation which drynefs and aridity
muft bring on upon the fkin, which then becomes fo
hard, that all kind of perfpiration is intercepted. If a
fimilar method were tried at Carthagena, and if the
cleanlinefs which the climate requires were added to
it, perhaps this leprofy might be reftrained, or even
totally abolifhed.

Notwithftanding this difgufting diftemper, the various defects of an inconvenient and dangerous climate,
and many other difagreeable circumftances, Spain hath
always fhown a great predilection for Carthagena, on
account of its harbour, one of the beft that is known.
It is two leagues in extent, and hath a deep and excellent bottom. There is not more agitation there
than on the moft calm river. There are two channels
that lead up to it. That which is called Bocca Grande,
and which is from feven to eight hundred toifes in
breadth, had formerly fo little depth, that the fmalleft
canoe could with difficulty pafs through it. The ocean
hath gradually increafed its depth fo much, that in
fome parts twelve feet of water may be found. If the
revolutions of time fhould bring about greater alterations, the place would be expofed. Accordingly, the
attention of the court of Madrid is ferioufly engaged

in considering the means of preventing so great an
evil. Perhaps, after much reflection, no simpler or
more certain expedient will be found, than to oppose
to the enemy's fleets a dyke formed of old ships filled
with stones and sunk in the sea. The channel of Bocca Chica hath been hitherto the only one practicable.
This is so narrow, that only one vessel can enter at
once. The English, in 1741, having destroyed the
fortifications that defended this passage, they have
been since restored with greater skill. They were no
longer placed at the entrance of the gullet, but further
up the channel, where they will secure a better defence.

At the time that these countries were supplied with
provisions, by the well known method of the galleons,
the vessels which set out from Spain all together, sailed to Carthagena before they went to Porto Bello,
and visited it again on their return to Europe. In the
first voyage, they deposited the merchandise that was
necessary for the supply of the interior provinces, and
received the price of them in the second. When single ships were substituted to these monstrous armaments, the city served for the same kind of staple. It
was always the point of communication between the
Old Hemisphere and great part of the New. From
the year 1748 to 1753, this staple was only visited
with twenty-seven ships from Spain: these, in exchange for the merchandise they had brought, received every year 9,357,806 livres [389,908l. 11s. 8d.] in
gold, 4,729,498 livres [197,072l. 8s. 4d.] in silver, and
851,765 livres [35,490l. 14s. 2d.] in the produce of
the country; in all, 14,939,069 livres [622,461l. 13s.
4d.].

The article of the produce of the country was composed of four thousand eight hundred and fourscore
quintals of cacao, the value of which in Europe was
509,760 livres [21,240l. 10s.]; of five hundred and
eighty quintals of bark, of the value of 200,880 livres
[8370l.]; of seventeen quintals of vicuna wool, of the
value of 12,474 livres [519l. 15s.]; of one quintal and

BOOK
VII.

a half of vanilla, of the value of 11,988 livres [499l. 10s.]; of seven quintals of tortoife-fhell, of the value of 4698 livres [195l. 15s.]; of fifteen quintals of mother-of-pearl, of the value of 1701 livres [71l. 7s. 6d.]; of fixteen quintals of balfam, of the value of 18,900 livres [787l. 10s.]; of two thoufand and thirty quintals of a fpecies of Brafil wood, of the value of 29,295 livres [1220l. 12s. 6d.]; of two thoufand one hundred fkins, with the hair on, of the value of 34,020 livres [1417l. 10s.]; of forty-two quintals of dragon's blood, of the value of 2389 livres [99l. 10s. 10d.]; of fix quintals of balfam of capivi, of the value of 2700 livres [113l.]; of feven quintals of farfaparilla, of the value of 972 livres [40l. 9s.]; of one quintal of ivory, of the value of 388 livres [16l. 3s. 4d.]; and laftly, of one hundred and eighty-eight quintals of cotton, of the value of 21,600 livres [900l. 10s.].

In thefe returns, where there was nothing for government, and where all was for trade, the territory of Carthagena furnifhed only to the amount of 93,241 livres [3885l. 10d.]. That of Saint Martha was ftill lefs profitable.

Caufes of the oblivion into which the province of Saint Martha is fallen.

This province, the extent of which, from eaft to weft, is eighty leagues, and one hundred and thirty from north to fouth, was unfortunately difcovered, as were all the neighbouring regions, at the difaftrous period when the kings of Spain, folely intent upon their aggrandizement in Europe, required only from thofe of their fubjects, who went into the New World, the fifth part of the gold which they collected in their plunders. Upon this condition, thefe robbers, who were ftimulated by the love of novelty, by an inordinate paffion for wealth, and even by the hopes of meriting heaven, were left to be the fole arbiters of their actions. Without dread of punifhment or of cenfure, they might wander about from one country to another, preferve or abandon a conqueft, improve a territory, or deftroy it, and maffacre the people, or treat them with humanity, as they thought proper. Every thing fuited the court of Madrid; provided they were

supplied with plenty of riches, the source from which
they came always appeared honest and pure.

Ravages and cruelties, that cannot be expressed,
were the necessary consequence of these abominable
principles; and universal desolation prevailed. The
fatal vestiges of it are still to be traced in all parts, but
more especially at Saint Martha. After these destroy-
ers had spoiled the colonies of the gold which they
had picked up in their rivers, and of the pearls which
they had fished upon their coasts, they disappeared.
The few among them who settled themselves there,
raised one or two towns, and some villages, which remained without intercourse with each other, till it was
opened by some indefatigable Capuchin missionaries,
who, in our days, have contrived to collect, in eight
hamlets, three thousand one hundred and ninety-one
Motilones, or Evagiras, the most ferocious of the savages who opposed it. Here their despicable posterity
vegetates, fed and waited upon by some Indians or
Negroes. The mother-country hath never sent one
single vessel into this district, and hath never received
any kind of production from it. The industry and activity of this place consists only in a fraudulent trade
of cattle, and especially mules, carried on with the
Dutch, or with the other cultivators of the neighbouring islands, who give in exchange clothing, and some
other objects of little value. Superstition keeps up
this fatal indolence. It prevents the people from dis-
cerning that it is not by ceremonies, by flagellations,
or by *autos da fé*, that the divinity is to be honoured;
but by the sweat of man's brow, by the clearing of
land, and by useful labours. These proud men persuade themselves that they are greater in a church, or
at the feet of a monk, than in the fields or the work-
shop. The tyranny of their priests hath kept away
from them that knowledge which might have undeceived them. Even this work, written purposely to
enlighten them, they will never be acquainted with.
If some fortunate event should put it into their hands,
they would have an abhorrence of it, and would con-

BOOK fider it as a criminal production, the author of which
VII. would deferve to be burnt.

Alphonfo Ojeda was the firft who reconnoitred, in
1499, the country called Venezuela, or Little Venice,
a name that was given to it, becaufe fome huts were
feen there, fixed upon ftakes, to raife them above the
ftagnant waters that covered the plain. Neither this
adventurer, nor his immediate fucceffors, thought of
forming any fettlements there. Their ambition was
only to make flaves, that they might convey them to
the iflands which their ferocity had depopulated. It
was not till 1527 that John d'Ampuez fixed a colony
upon this coaft, and promifed to his court a region
abounding in metals. This promife gave rife, in the
following year, to an arrangement fingular enough to
attract our attention.

Charles V. who had united fuch a number of crowns
upon his head, and concentrated fo much power in
himfelf, was engaged, by his ambition, or by the jealoufy of his neighbours, in endlefs difputes, the expences of which exceeded his refources. In his neceffities, he had borrowed confiderable fums of the Welfers of Augfbourg, who were then the richeft merchants in Europe. That prince offered them in payment the province of Venezuela, and they accepted it
as a fief of Caftile.

It was to be fuppofed that merchants, who had acquired their fortune by the buying and felling of territorial productions, would eftablifh plantations in their
domains. It was to be fuppofed that Germans, who
had been brought up in the midft of mines, would
work thofe which were upon the fpot that was granted to them. But thefe expectations were entirely
fruftrated. The Welfers only fent into the New
World four or five hundred of thofe fierce foldiers,
whom their country began to fell to whoever would
and could pay for their blood. Thefe bafe hirelings
carried along with them beyond the feas that propenfity for pillaging which they had contracted in the
different wars in which they had ferved. Under the

guidance of their chiefs, Alfinger and Sailler, they overran an immenfe tract of country, putting the favages to the torture, and ripping them open, to extort from them where the gold was to be found. Some Indians, dragged along, and laden with provifions, who were put to death as foon as they fank under the laffitude, followed this favage band. Hunger, fatigue, and poifoned arrows, fortunately delivered the earth of this odious burden. The Spaniards refumed poffeffion of a foil which the Welfers would no longer have any concern with; and their conduct was not very different from that which had juft excited fo much horror. Their commander Carvajal, indeed, forfeited his life for thefe enormities : but this punifhment did not recal from the grave the victims that had been precipitated into it. From their afhes arofe, in procefs of time, a few productions, of which the cacao was the principal.

The cacao tree, which is of a middling fize, generally throws out five or fix trunks from its root. The wood of it is brittle and white; its root reddifh, and rather rugged. As it grows up it throws off fome inclined branches, which do not fpread far. Its leaves are alternate, oval, and terminated in a point. The largeft of them are from eight to nine feet in length, and three in breadth. They are all fixed upon fhort petals, flattened, and furnifhed at their bafis with two membranes or ftipulæ. The flowers arife in fmall bunches along the ftems and the branches. Their calix is greenifh, and hath five deep divifions. The five petals that compofe the corolla are fmall, yellow, inflated at their bafe, lengthened out into a kind of ftrap, which is folded up in a circular form, and widened at its extremity. Thefe petals are fixed to a fpatha, formed by the affemblage of ten threads, five of which bear ftamina. The five other intermediate ones are longer, and in the fhape of a tongue. The piftil, which is placed in the centre, and furmounted with one ftyle only, becomes an oviform capfula, almoft of a ligneous texture, fix or feven inches in length, and

The cacao hath always fixed the attention of the Spaniards upon Venezuela.

two in breadth; uneven upon its furface, marked with ten coftæ, and feparated internally by membranous partitions into five cells. The kernels which it contains, to the number of thirty, or more, are covered with a brittle fhell, and furrounded with a whitifh pulp.

Thefe kernels are the bafis of the chocolate, the goodnefs of which depends upon the oily part they contain, and confequently upon their perfect maturity. The capfula is gathered, when, after having changed fucceffively from green to yellow, it acquires a dark mufk colour. It is flit with a knife, and all the kernels, furrounded with their pulp, are taken out and heaped up in a tub, in order that they may ferment. This operation deftroys the principle of vegetation, and removes the fuperfluous moifture from the kernels, which are afterwards expofed to the fun upon hurdles, in order to complete the drying of them. The cacao, thus prepared, keeps for a confiderable time, provided it be in a dry place; but it is not proper to keep it too long, becaufe it lofes, with age, part of its oil and of its properties.

The cacao tree grows readily, from feeds that are fown in holes ranged in a ftraight line, and at the diftance of five or fix feet from each other. Thefe feeds, which muft be frefh, foon vegetate. The tree grows up tolerably faft, and begins to reward the labours of the cultivator at the end of two years. Two crops are gathered every year, which are equal in quality and quantity. This tree requires a rich and moift foil, which hath not been employed for any other kind of culture. If it fhould want water, it would produce no fruit, wither, and die. A fhade, to fhelter it continually from the heat of the fun, is not lefs neceffary to it. The fields in which the cacao trees are planted, are alfo liable to be deftroyed by the hurricanes, unlefs care be taken to fkirt them with ftronger trees. The culture which the tree further requires is neither laborious nor expenfive. It is fufficient to pull up the weeds that grow round it, and which would deprive it of its nourifhment.

The cacao tree is cultivated in feveral parts of the
New World; in fome of them it even grows naturally.
Neverthelefs, its fruit is nowhere fo plentiful as at'
Venezuela; and nowhere of fo good a quality, if we
except Soconufco.

But for the fpace of two centuries, the labours of
the colony did not turn out to the profit of the mother-country. The national trade was fo much overburdened with taxes, and fo much embarraffed with
formalities, that the province found a confiderable advantage in receiving from the hands of the Dutch of
Curaçoa all the merchandife they wanted, and in giving them for payment the produce of their foil, which
thefe indefatigable neighbours fold for an immenfe
profit to part of Europe, and even to the nation that
was proprietor of the territory in which it was collect-,
ed. This fmuggling intercourfe was fo brifk and fo
conftant, that from the year 1700 to the end of 1727,
only five fhips were fent out from the ports of Spain
to Venezuela, and they, all of them without exception, made a voyage more or lefs ruinous.

Such was the fituation of affairs, when fome merchants of the province of Guipufcoa imagined, in 1728,
that it would be advantageous to them to unite in a
body in order to undertake this navigation. Their
views were approved and encouraged by government.
The principal conditions of the grant were, that the
Company fhould pay for every thing they might choofe
to fend out, and for every thing they might receive,
the taxes that were already fettled, and that they
fhould entertain, at their own expence, a fufficient
number of guarda coftas, to prevent the inhabitants
from fmuggling.

*The pro-
vince of
Venezuela
is fubjected
to a mono-
poly. Pro-
fperity of
the Com-
pany.*

Some alterations were fucceffively made in the adminiftration of this fociety. At firft they were only
permitted to fit out two fhips every year; but in 1734
they obtained leave to fend as many as they thought
proper.

In the beginning, the Company had not the privilege of an exclufive charter. The government grant-

ed it to them in 1742, for the department of Caraccas;
and ten years after for that of Maracaibo, two territories, the union of which forms the province of Venezuela, extending four hundred miles along the coaft.

Till the year 1744, the fhips, on their return from
the New World, were all to depofit their whole cargo
in the port of Cadiz.   After this period, they were only obliged to carry there the cacao neceffary for the
fupply of Andalufia and of the neighbouring diftricts.
They were allowed to difembark the reft at Saint Sebaftian, the place of the rife of the Company.

It was in this town that the general meeting of the
proprietors was originally holden.   In 1751, it was
transferred to the capital of the empire, where fome
one of the moft efteemed members of the council of
the Indies prefides over it every two years.

The merchandife was at firft delivered to the higheft bidder.   The Court was then informed that a general difcontent prevailed; that a fmall number of rich
affociates fhould monopolize the cacao, which is confidered in Spain as an article of primary neceffity, and
fhould afterwards fell it at what price they chofe.
Thefe murmurs occafioned, in 1752, a regulation, that
without fuppreffing the magazines at Saint Sebaftian,
at Cadiz, and at Madrid, new ones fhould be eftablifhed at Corunna, at Alicant, and at Barcelona; and that
in all of them the cacao fhould be retailed to the inhabitants at the price fettled by the miniftry.

The Company obtained, in 1753, that their fhares
fhould be confidered as a real eftate, that they might
be perpetually entailed, and formed into thofe unalienable and indivifible *majorafcos*, or inheritances fettled upon the eldeft heir, which are in general fo flattering to the pride of the Spaniards.

It was decreed, in 1761, that the Company fhould
advance, to the members who might wifh for it, the
value of fixteen fhares; that thefe fhares fhould be
put in truft, and that they might be fold, if after a
ftipulated period the proprietor did not withdraw them.
The intent of this prudent arrangement, was to fuc-

cour such of the proprietors whose affairs might be B O O K
somewhat embarrassed, and to maintain the credit of VII.
the Company by honest means.

According to regulations made in 1776, the operations of the Company are to extend to Cumana, to
the Oroonoko, to the islands of the Trinity and St.
Margaret. These countries, indeed, have not been
subjected to its monopoly : but the favours it has received are equivalent to an exclusive privilege.

During these changes, the number of freemen and
of slaves were increasing at Venezuela. The seven
hundred and fifty-nine plantations, distributed in six-
ty-one villages, were emerging from their languid state,
and others were forming. The former cultures were
improved, and new ones established. The cattle penetrated more and more into the inland parts of the
country. But it was chiefly in the district of Caraccas
that the improvements were most conspicuous. The
town which bears this name, contained four and twenty thousand inhabitants, most of them in easy circumstances. The Guayra which served for the purpose of
its navigation, though it afforded nothing more than
an indifferent anchorage, surrounded with a small number of huts, was gradually becoming a considerable colony, and even a tolerable harbour, by means of a large
pier constructed with skill.

At Puerto Cabello, which had been entirely abandoned, though one of the best ports of America, three
hundred houses were raised. Let us endeavour to in-
vestigate the causes of this singular prosperity, under
the shackles of a monopoly.

The Company understood from the first, that their
success was inseparable from that of the colony ; and
they therefore advanced to the inhabitants as far as
3,240,000 livres [135,000l.], without interest. This
debt was to be discharged in commodities ; and those
who did not fulfil their engagements were summoned
to the tribunal of the king's representative, whose province it was solely to judge, whether the causes of delay were, or were not, reasonable.

BOOK   The magazines of the Company were conftantly
VII.   fupplied with every thing that might be of ufe to the
country, and always open to receive every thing the
country could pour into them. By this method, the
labours were never languid for want of means, or of a
market.

The value of what the Company were to fell, or
to buy, was not left to the rapacity of their agents.
The government of the province always fixed the price
of what came from Europe; and a meeting compofed
of the directors, colonifts, and factors, always regulated the price of the productions of the foil.

Such of the inhabitants of the New World as were
not fatisfied with thefe regulations, were allowed to
fend into the Old one, upon their own account, the
fixth part of their crops, and to receive the value in
merchandife; but thefe affairs were always to be tranfacted by the fhips of the Company.

By thefe arrangements the cultivator was better rewarded for his labours, than he had been at the time
of the contraband trade. The new difpofition of
things was in reality fatal only to a few fcheming,
turbulent, and adventurous men, who collected in
their hands, at a low price, the productions of the
country, in order to deliver them afterwards to foreign navigators of the fame character as themfelves.

The new kingdom of Grenada, Mexico, fome of
the American iflands, and the Canaries, were in the
habit of drawing from Venezuela part of the cacao
confumed by their inhabitants. Thefe colonies continued to enjoy this right without reftraint. They
even purfued it with greater advantage, becaufe the
production which they wanted to procure, became
more plentiful, and was obtained at a cheaper rate.

Formerly Venezuela furnifhed nothing to the trade
of the mother-country. The Company, fince their
eftablifhment, have always fupplied it with productions, the quantity of which hath fucceffively increafed. From the year 1748 to 1753, the Company
conveyed annually into the colony to the value of

3,197,327 livres [132,221l. 19s. 2d.], in merchandise.
They drew from thence annually to the amount of
239,144 livres [9964l. 6s. 8d.], in silver; thirty-seven thousand quintals of cacao, which they sold for
5,332,000 livres [222,166l. 13s. 4d.]; two thousand
five hundred quintals of tobacco, sold for 178,200 livres
[7425l.]; one hundred and fifty-seven quintals of indigo
sold for 198,990 livres [8291l. 5s.]; twenty thousand
skins, with the hair on, sold for 356,400 livres [14,850l.];
and some *dividi*, sold for 27,000 livres [1125l.]; so that
their returns amounted to 6,821,734 livres [284,646l.
1s. 8d.]. The apparent profit was therefore, 3,634,407
livres [151,433l. 12s. 6d.]. We call it apparent, because the expences and the customs absorbed 1,932,500
livres [80,590l. 16s. 8d.] of this sum; so that the real
profit of the Company was only 1,701,897 livres
[70,922l. 7s. 6d.].

All these branches of commerce have been increased except that of the *dividi*, which it hath been necessary to give up, since it hath been found that it
was not fit to be substituted to the Aleppo nut in dyeing, as it hath been rather inconsiderately imagined.
The extension would have been still greater, had it
been possible to put an end to smuggling. But notwithstanding the vigilance of ten cruizers, with eighty-
six guns, one hundred and ninety-two swivels, and
five hundred and eighteen men on board; notwithstanding twelve posts, with ten or twelve soldiers in
each, established along the coast, and notwithstanding
the annual expence of 1,400,000 livres [58,333l. 6s.
8d.], the contraband trade hath not been entirely eradicated; and it is chiefly at Coro that it is carried
on.

The nation has profited equally by the establishment of the Company. It does not pay them for the
cacao more than half the price which the Dutch used
to charge. The quintal, which is now bought in
Spain for 160 livres [6l. 13s. 4d.], used formerly to
cost 320 [13l. 6s. 8d.].

The advantages which accrue to the government

from the eſtabliſhment of the Company are not leſs
evident. Before this period, the revenues of the crown
at Venezuela, were never ſufficient to defray the expences of ſovereignty. They have ſince increaſed conſiderably, not only becauſe the citadel of Puerto Cabello has been conſtructed, which hath coſt 1,620,000
livres [67,500l.], but alſo, becauſe a greater number of
regular troops are maintained in the country. The
treaſury, however, hath ſome ſuperfluous caſh, which
it diſtributes at Cumana, at St. Margaret's, at Trinity iſland, and on the Oroonoko. This is not the
whole. In Europe, the productions of the country
pay annually to the ſtate more than 1,600,000 [66,666l.
13s. 4d.], and the navigation they give riſe to forms
fifteen hundred ſailors for it, or keeps them in conſtant
employment.

But hath the Company itſelf been equally proſper-
ous? There was every reaſon to doubt, in the beginning, whether it would maintain itſelf. Although the
coloniſts were allured to become members of it, they
refuſed at firſt to deliver their productions to it. In
Spain, where a commercial aſſociation was a novelty,
no great eagerneſs was ſhown to become a member
of it, notwithſtanding the example ſet by the monarch,
by the queen, by the infant Don Lewis, and by the
province of Guipuſcoa. It was neceſſary to reduce
the number of ſhares to fifteen hundred, which it had
been reſolved to carry on to three thouſand; and the
capital, intended to be ſix millions [250,000l.], was
reduced to three [125,000l.]. Theſe difficulties did
not prevent conſiderable dividends from being paid
to the proprietors, even in the very firſt years. The
ſums in reſerve were, however, ſufficient, in 1752, to
double the original funds, and in 1766 to treble them,
with a regular intereſt of five per cent, excluſive of the
extraordinary dividends. On the firſt of January 1772,
the Company's debts, even including the value of the
ſhares, which had riſen to 1,000,000 livres [375,000l,],
amounted to no more than 15,198,618 livres 12 ſols
[633,275l. 15s. 6d.], and they were in poſſeſſion of

21,153,760 livres 4 fols [881,407l. 3s. 6d.]. Confe-quently, they had 5,955,141 livres 12 fols [248,150l. 18s.] above what they owed.

The improper fpirit that generally prevails in ex-clufive focieties, hath not affected that of Caraccas fo much as others. It hath never been led aftray from its fyftem by abfurd enterprifes. Its integrity hath preferved it from every kind of law, and even from the flighteft conteft. That its deftiny might not be expofed to the caprices of the ocean, or to the rifks of war, its cargoes have been all of them infured. Its engagements have been fulfilled with inviolable fide-lity. And laftly, in a country where moft of the land-ed eftates are entailed, and where there are few good vents for money, the Company hath obtained all that it wanted, at two and a half per cent.

In order to conciliate to itfelf the good wifhes of the nation, which are generally denied in all parts to a monopoly, the Company hath always been defirous of appearing animated with a public fpirit. From the year 1735, it took upon itfelf the care of the manu-factures of Placentia, which fcarce ufed to furnifh eight thoufand firelocks per annum; and which, at prefent, without reckoning fome other kinds of arms that have begun to be fabricated there, fupplies fourteen thou-fand four hundred, with the fcutcheons of their locks, which it was before neceffary to bring from Liege. Though during the fhort war of 1762, fix of the Com-pany's veffels, richly laden, fell into the hands of the Englifh, it ftill devoted to government all the credit and influence it poffeffed. Wood for the building of fhips was perifhing in the province of Navarre, fo that it became neceffary to cut it down. Roads were alfo to be made to bring it down to the borders of the Vi-daffoa, and this uncertain river was to be put in a ftate fit to carry this wood to its mouth, after which it was to be conducted to the important harbour of Ferrol. Since the year 1766, all thefe things are executed by the Company to the great advantage of the military branch of the navy.

B O O K
VII. This Company ſtill continues to announce other enterprifes uſeful to the ſtate ; but it is a matter of doubt
whether it will be allowed time to execute them. The
refolution which the Court of Madrid feems to have
taken, to open its ports of the New World to all its
fubjects of the Old, muſt neceſſarily excite a preſump-
tion that the province of Venezuela will, ſooner or
later, ceaſe to be under the reſtraints of a monopoly.
It is however a problem, whether the diſſolution of the
Company will be productive of good or evil ; and it
can only be ſolved by the nature of the meaſures that
ſhall be adopted by the Spaniſh miniſtry.

The Court
of Madrid
gives up
Cumana to
the care of
Las Cafas.
Ineffectual
attempts of
this cele-
brated man
to render
this diſtrict
flouriſhing. The coaſt of Cumana was diſcovered in 1498 by
Columbus. Ojeda, who had embarked with this great
navigator, landed there the next year, and even made
ſome exchanges peaceably with the ſavages. It appeared more convenient to the adventurers who fucceeded him, to ſtrip theſe feeble men of their gold or
of their pearls ; and this kind of robbery was as common in this region as in the other parts of America,
when Las Cafas undertook to put a ſtop to it.

This man, ſo famous in the annals of the New
World, had accompanied his father at the time of
the firſt diſcovery. The mildneſs and ſimplicity of
the Indians affected him ſo ſtrongly, that he made
himſelf an eccleſiaſtic, in order to devote his labours
to their converſion. But this ſoon became the leaſt
of his attentions. Being more a *man* than a *prieſt*,
he felt more for the cruelties exerciſed againſt them
than for their ridiculous ſuperſtitions. He was continually hurrying from one hemiſphere to the other,
in order to comfort thoſe for whom he had conceived
ſuch an attachment, or to ſoften their tyrants. The
inutility of his efforts convinced him, that he ſhould
never do any good in ſettlements that were already
formed ; and he propoſed to himſelf to eſtabliſh a colony upon a new foundation.

His coloniſts were all to be planters, artificers, or
miſſionaries. No one was to be allowed to mix with
them without his conſent. A particular dreſs, orna-

mented with a crofs, was to prevent them from being B O O K
thought to belong to that race of Spaniards which VII.
had rendered itfelf fo odious. He reckoned, that
with thefe kinds of knights, he fhould be able, without war, violence, or flavery, to civilize the Indians,
to convert them, to accuftom them to labour, and
even to employ them in working the mines. He afked no affiftance from the treafury at firft, and he was
afterwards fatisfied with the twelfth of the tributes
which he fhould fooner or later bring into it.

The ambitious, who govern empires, confider the
people as mere objects of trade, and treat as chimerical every thing that tends to the improvement and
happinefs of the human fpecies. Such was at firft the
impreffion which the fyftem of Las Cafas made upon
the Spanifh miniftry. He was not difcouraged by de-
nials, and at length fucceeded in having the diftrict of
Cumana ceded to him, to put his theory in practice.
This man of ardent genius immediately went through
all the provinces of Caftile, in order to collect men accuftomed to the labours of the field, and to thofe of
manufactures. But thefe peaceful citizens had not fo
eager a defire to leave their country as foldiers or failors have. Scarce could he prevail upon two hundred
of them to follow him. With thefe he fet fail for
America, and landed at Porto-Rico in 1519, after a
fortunate voyage.

Although Las Cafas had only quitted the New Hemifphere two years before, yet he found a total alteration in it at his return. The entire deftruction of the
Indians in the iflands fubject to Spain, had excited the
refolution of going to the continent in fearch of flaves,
to replace the unfortunate men who had perifhed from
oppreffion. This cruelty difgufted the independent
minds of the favages. In the height of their refentment, they maffacred as many of the Spaniards as fell
into their hands by chance; and two miffionaries, who
probably came to Cumana with a laudable defign,
were the victims of thefe juft retaliations. Ocampo

B O O K immediately went from St. Domingo, to punifh an
VII.   outrage committed, as it was faid, againft Heaven it-
          felf; and after having deftroyed all by fire and fword,
he built a village upon the fpot, which he called Toledo.

It was within thefe weak palifades that Las Cafas
was obliged to place the fmall number of his companions who had refifted the intemperance of the climate, and the attempts made to feduce them from
him. Their refidence was not long here. Moft of
them were pierced with the darts of an implacable
enemy; and thofe who efcaped, were forced, in 1521,
to feek an afylum fomewhere elfe.

Some Spaniards have fince fettled at Cumana; but
the population of this diftrict hath always been much
confined, and hath never extended to any diftance
from the coafts. During the courfe of two centuries,
the mother-country had not any direct intercourfe
with this fpot. It is but lately, that one or two fmall
fhips have been fent there annually, which, in exchange for the liquors and merchandife of Europe, receive cocoa and fome other productions.

Of the river   It was Columbus, who, in 1498, firft difcovered the
Oroonoko.   Oroonoko, the borders of which have fince been named Spanifh Guiana. This great river takes its fource
among the Cordeleirias mountains, and difcharges itfelf into the ocean by forty openings, after it hath
been increafed throughout an immenfe track by the
afflux of a prodigious number of rivers more or lefs
confiderable. Such is its impetuofity, that it ftems
the ftrongeft tides, and preferves the frefhnefs of its
waters to the diftance of twelve leagues from that vaft
and deep channel within which it was confined. Its
rapidity, however, is not always the fame, which is
owing to a circumftance perhaps entirely peculiar.
The Oroonoko, which begins to fwell in April, continues rifing for five months, and during the fixth remains at its greateft height. From October, it begins
gradually to fubfide till the month of March, through-

but the whole of which it remains in the fixed ftate of B O O K
its greateft diminution. Thefe alternate changes are VII.
regular, and even invariable.

This phenomenon feems to depend much more on
the fea than on the land. In the fix months that the
river is rifing, the hemifphere of the New World prefents nothing but feas, at leaft but little land, to the
perpendicular action of the rays of the fun. In the
fix months of its fall, America exhibits nothing but
dry land to the planet by which it is illuminated. The
fea at this time is lefs fubject to the influence of the
fun, or, at leaft, its current towards the eaftern fhore
is more balanced, more broken by the land, and muft
therefore leave a freer courfe to the rivers, which not
being then fo ftrongly confined by the fea, cannot be
fwelled but by rains, or by the melting of the fnows
from the Cordeleirias. Perhaps, indeed, the rifing of
the waters of the Oroonoko may depend entirely on
the rainy feafon. But to be thoroughly acquainted
with the caufes of fo fingular a phenomenon, it would
be neceffary to confider the connection between the
courfe of this river, and that of the Amazons by Rio
Negro, and to know the track and direction both of
the one and the other. From the difference of their
pofition, their fource, and their opening into the fea,
it is not improbable that the caufe of fo remarkable a
difference in the periods of their flux and reflux might
be difcovered. All things are connected in this world
by fyftem. The courfes of the rivers depend either
on the diurnal or annual revolutions of the earth.
Whenever enlightened men fhall have vifited the
banks of the Oroonoko, they will difcover, or at leaft
they will attempt to difcover, the caufes of thefe phenomena : but their endeavours will be attended with
difficulties. This river is not fo navigable as it might
be prefumed from its magnitude; its bed is in many
places filled up with rocks, which oblige the navigator, at times, to carry both his boats and the merchandife they are laden with.

B O O K   Before the arrival of the Europeans, the people who
VII.   border on this river, but little diftant from the burn-
Former and ing equator, knew not the ufe of clothes, nor the reprefent   ftraints of police; neither had they any form of go-
condition of
the women vernment. Free under the yoke of poverty, they lived
on the   chiefly by hunting and fifhing, and on wild fruits.
banks of the
Oroonoko. But little of their time or labour could be fpent on
agriculture, where they had nothing but a ftick to
plough with, and hatchets made of ftone to cut down
trees; which, after being burned or rotted, left the
foil in a proper ftate for bearing.

The women lived in a ftate of oppreffion on the
Oroonoko, as they do in all barbarous regions. The
favage, whofe wants engage his whole attention, is employed only in providing for his fafety and his fubfiftence. He hath no other allurement to partake of the
pleafures of love, than that mere natural inftinct which
attends to the perpetuity of the fpecies. The intercourfe between the two fexes, which is generally cafual, would fcarce ever be followed by any permanent
confequences, if paternal and maternal tendernefs did
not attach the parents to their offspring. But before
the firft child can provide for itfelf, others are born,
which call for the fame care. At length the inftant
arrives, when this focial reafon exifts no more: but
then the power of long habit, the comfort of feeing
ourfelves furrounded by a family more or lefs numerous, the hopes of being affifted in our latter years by
our pofterity; all thefe circumftances expel the idea
and the wifh of a feparation. The men are the perfons who reap the greateft advantages from this coha-
bitation. Among people who hold nothing in eftimation but ftrength and courage, tyranny is always exercifed over weaknefs, in return for the protection that
is afforded it. The women live in a ftate of difgrace.
Labours, confidered as the moft abject, are their portion. Men, whofe hands are accuftomed to the hand-
ling of arms, and to the management of the oar, would
think themfelves degraded, if they employed them in

fedentary occupations, or even in the labours of agriculture.

Among a people of fhepherds, who having a more
certain exiftence, can beftow rather more attention
upon making it agreeable, the women are lefs wretched. In the eafe and leifure which they enjoy, thefe
people can form to themfelves an idea of beauty; they
can indulge their tafte in the object of their affections;
and, to the idea of natural pleafure, can add that of a
more noble fenfation.

The connections between the two fexes are ftill further improved, as foon as the lands begin to be cultivated. Property, which had no exiftence among favages, and was of little confequence among a people
of fhepherds, begins to acquire a degree of importance
among a people engaged in agriculture. The inequa-
lity which foon introduces itfelf among the fortunes of
men, muft occafion fome in the confideration they
hold. The ties of marriage are then no longer formed
by chance, but according to conditions in life that are
fuitable to each other. A man, in order to be accepted, muft make himfelf agreeable; and this neceffity
brings on attentions to the women, and gives them a
degree of dignity.

They receive additional importance from the eftablifhment of the arts and of commerce. Bufinefs is
then increafed, and connections are complicated.
Men, who are often obliged, from more extenfive affairs, to quit their manufactures and their home, are
under the neceffity of adding to their talents the vigilance of their wives. As the habit of gallantry, luxury, and diffipation, hath not yet entirely difgufted
them of folitary or ferious occupations, they devote
themfelves, without referve, and with fuccefs, to functions with which they think themfelves honoured.
The retirement which this kind of life requires, renders the practice of all the domeftic virtues dear and
familiar to them. The influence, the refpect, and the
attachment of all thofe that are about them, are the
reward of a conduct fo eftimable.

BOOK
VII.

At length the time comes, when men grow difgufted of labour, from the increafe of their fortunes.
Their principal care is to prevent time from hanging
heavy on their hands, to multiply their amufements,
and to extend their enjoyments. At this period, the
women are eagerly fought after, both on account of
the amiable qualities they hold from nature, and of
thofe they have received from education. Their connections become more extenfive, fo that they are no
longer fuited for a retired life, but required to fhine in
a.more brilliant fcene. When introduced upon the
ftage of the world, they become the foul of every
pleafure, and the primum mobile of the moft important affairs. Supreme happinefs confifts in making
one's felf agreeable to them; and it is the height of
ambition to obtain fome diftinction from them. Then
it is, that the freedom which exifts between the two
fexes in a ftate of nature is revived, with this remarkable difference, that, in polifhed cities, the hufband is
often lefs attached to his wife, and the wife to her hufband, than in the midft of the forefts; that their offspring, trufted, at the inftant of their birth, to the
hands of mercenaries, are no longer a tie; and that
infidelity, which would be attended with no fatal confequences among moft favage people, affects domeftic
tranquillity and happinefs among civilized nations,
where it is one of the principal fymptoms of general
corruption, and of the extinction of all decent affections.

The tyranny exercifed againft the women upon the
banks of the Oroonoko, ftill more than in the reft of
the New World, muft be one of the principal caufes
of the depopulation of thefe countries that are fo much
favoured by nature. Mothers have contracted the
cuftom of deftroying the daughters they bring forth,
by cutting the umbilical cord fo clofe to the body,
that the children die of an hæmorrhage. Chriftianity
itfelf hath not even been able to put a ftop to this
abominable practice. The fact is confirmed by the
Jefuit Gumilla; who being informed that one of his

converts had been guilty of fuch a murder, went to B O O K her, in order to reproach her of her crime in the ftrong- VII. eft terms. The woman liftened to the emiffary, without fhowing the leaft figns of emotion. When he had finifhed his remonftrance, fhe defired leave to anfwer him, which fhe did in the following manner:

" Would to God, O Father! Would to God, that,
" at the inftant of my birth, my mother had fhowed
" love and compaffion enough for her child, to fpare
" me all the evils I have endured, and thofe I fhall
" ftill fuffer, to the end of my life! Had my mother
" deftroyed me at my birth, I fhould have died, but
" I fhould not have been fenfible of my death; and
" fhould have efcaped the moft miferable of condi-
" tions. How much have I already fuffered; and who
" knows what I have ftill to undergo!

" Reprefent to thyfelf, O Father, the troubles that
" are referved for an Indian woman among thefe In-
" dians. They accompany us into the fields with
" their bow and arrows; while we go there, laden
" with an infant, whom we carry in a bafket, and an-
" other, who hangs at our breaft. They go to kill
" birds, or to catch fifh; while we are employed in
" digging the ground, and after having gone through
" all the labours of the culture, are obliged alfo to
" bear thofe of the harveft. They return in the even-
" ing without any burthen; and we bring them roots
" for their food, and maize for their drink. As foon
" as they come home, they go and amufe themfelves
" with their friends; while we are fetching wood and
" water to prepare for their fupper. When they have
" eaten, they fall afleep; and we pafs almoft the
" whole night in grinding the maize, and in preparing
" the chica for them. And what reward have we for
" thefe labours? They drink; and when they are in-
" toxicated, they drag us by the hair, and trample us
" under foot.

" O Father, would to God that my mother had de-
" ftroyed me at the inftant of my birth! Thou know-
" eft thyfelf that our complaints are juft; thou haft

" daily inftances before thine eyes of the truth of my
" affertions. But the greateft misfortune we labour
" under it is impoffible thou fhouldft know. It is a
" melancholy circumftance for a poor Indian woman
" to ferve her hufband as a flave in the fields, oppreff-
" ed with fatigue, and at home deprived of tranquil-
" lity: but it is a dreadful thing, when twenty years
" are elapfed, to fee him take another woman, whofe
" judgment is not formed. He attaches himfelf to
" her. She beats our children; fhe commands us,
" and treats us as her fervants; and, if the leaft mur-
" mur efcape us, a ftick raifed . . . . Oh! Fa-
" ther, how is it poffible that we fhould bear this con-
" dition? What can an Indian woman do better than
" to prevent her child from living in a ftate of flavery
" infinitely worfe than death? Would to God, O Fa-
" ther! I repeat it, that my mother had conceived af-
" fection enough for me to bury me when I was born!
" My heart would not have been thus afflicted, nor
" would mine eyes have been accuftomed to tears."

State of the
Spanifh co-
lony form-
ed on the
banks of
the Oroo-
noko.

The Spaniards, who could not pay attention to all
the regions they difcovered, loft fight of the Oroonoko. They did not attempt to fail up this river again
till the year 1535, when, not having found there the
mines they were in fearch of, they neglected it. Neverthelefs, the few who had been thrown upon this
fpot, devoted themfelves with fo much affiduity to the
culture of tobacco, that they delivered a few cargoes
of it every year to the foreign veffels which came to
purchafe it. This contraband trade was prohibited by
the mother-country; and this weak fettlement was
twice plundered by enterprifing pirates. Thefe difaf-
ters occafioned it to be forgotten. It was recalled to
mind again in 1753. The commodore Nicholas de
Yturiaga was fent there. This prudent man eftablifhed a regular fyftem of government in the colony that
had formed itfelf infenfibly in this part of the New
World.

In 1771, thirteen villages were feen upon the banks
of the Oroonoko, which contained four thoufand two

hundred and nineteen Spaniards, Meftees, Mulattoes, B O O K VII.
or Negroes; four hundred and thirty-one plantations;
and twelve thoufand eight hundred and fifty-four
oxen, mules, or horfes.

At the fame period, the Indians, who had been prevailed upon to quit their favage life, were diftributed
in forty-nine hamlets.

The five of thefe which had been under the direction of the Jefuits, computed fourteen hundred and
twenty-fix inhabitants, three hundred and forty-four
plantations, and nine hundred and fifty heads of cattle.

Eleven of them, which are under the direction of
the Francifcan Friars, reckoned nineteen hundred and
thirty-four inhabitants, three hundred and five plantations, and nine hundred and fifty heads of cattle.

Eleven others, which are under the direction of the
Capuchins of Arragon, computed two thoufand two
hundred and eleven inhabitants, four hundred and feventy plantations, and five hundred and feven heads
of cattle.

The two and twenty which are under the direction
of the Capuchins of Catalonia, reckoned fix thoufand
eight hundred and thirty inhabitants, fifteen hundred
and ninety-two plantations, and forty-fix thoufand
heads of cattle.

This amounted in the whole to fixty-two colonies,
fixteen thoufand fix hundred and twenty inhabitants,
three thoufand one hundred and forty-two plantations,
and feventy-two thoufand three hundred and forty-
one heads of cattle.

Till thefe laft mentioned times, the Dutch of Cu-
raçao were the only perfons who traded with this fettlement. They fupplied its wants, and were paid with
tobacco, hides, and cattle. The bargains were all concluded at St. Thomas, the capital of the colony. The
Negroes and the Europeans managed their own affairs; but they were the miffionaries alone who treated for their converts. The fame arrangement of things
ftill fubfifts, although for fome years paft the competi-

B O O K tion of the Spanish ships hath begun to keep away the
VII.   smuggling vessels.

It is pleasing to entertain a hope that these vast and
fertile regions will at length emerge from the state of
obscurity into which they are plunged, and that the
seeds which have been sown there will produce, sooner or later, abundant fruits. Between a savage life
and a state of society, there is an immense desert to
pass ; but from the infancy of civilization to the full
vigour of trade, there are but a few steps to take.
Time, as it increases strength, shortens distances. The
advantage that might be obtained from the labour of
these new colonies, by procuring them conveniences,
would bring riches to Spain.

Short de-   Behind these very extensive coasts of which we have
scription of
the New   been speaking, and in the inland part of the country,
kingdom of is found what the Spaniards call the New kingdom of
Grenada.
Grenada. Its extent is prodigious. Its climate is more
or less damp, more or less cold, more or less hot, and
more or less temperate, according to the direction of
the branches of the Cordeleirias mountains, which in-
tersect the different parts of it. Few of these mountains are susceptible of cultivation : but most of the
plains and valleys that separate them exhibit a fertile
soil.

Even before the conquest the country was very little inhabited. In the midst of the savages that wandered over it, a nation had, however, been formed,
which had a religion, a form of government, and which
practised cultivation. This nation, though inferior to
the Mexicans and Peruvians, had raised itself much
above the other people of America. Neither history
nor tradition inform us in what manner this state had
been created ; but we must suppose that it hath existed, although there be no traces remaining of its civilization.

This kingdom, if we may be allowed to call it so,
was called Bogota. Benalcazar, who commanded at
Quito, attacked it in 1526, on the south side ; and

Quefada, who had landed at Saint Martha, attacked it on the north. It was to be fuppofed that men, united among themfelves, accuftomed to fight together, and led on by an abfolute chief, would make fome refiftance. This they accordingly did; but were at length obliged to yield to the valour, the arms, and the difcipline of the Europeans. The two Spanifh captains had the glory, fince it is one, of adding one large poffeffion to thofe with which their fovereigns had fuffered themfelves to be overloaded in this New Hemifphere. In procefs of time, the provinces more or lefs diftant from this central point were partly fubjected. We fay partly, becaufe fuch is the natural difpofition of the country, that it was never poffible to fubdue all its inhabitants ; and that thofe among them who had fubmitted to the yoke, broke it as foon as they had the courage to determine refolutely about it. It is not even improbable that moft of them would have taken this refolution, had they been employed in thofe deftructive labours which have caufed fuch ravages in the other parts of the New World.

Some writers have fpoken with almoft unexampled enthufiafm of the riches which were at firft derived from this new kingdom. They make them amount to a fum capable of aftonifhing the minds of thofe who are moft eager of the marvellous. Never, perhaps, was exaggeration carried fo far. If the reality had only approached near to the fabulous accounts, this remarkable profperity would have been recorded in the public regifters, as well as the ftate of all the colonies that are really important. Other monuments could have perpetuated the remembrance of it. Thefe treafures have never, therefore, exifted at any time, except under the pen of a few writers, naturally credulous, or who fuffered themfelves to be feduced by the hope of adding to the fplendour with which their country already fhone.

What the New kingdom of Grenada hath been, what it is, and what it may become.

The New kingdom furnifhes at prefent the emerald, a precious ftone, which is tranfparent, and of a green

B O O K colour, and which hath no greater degree of hardnefs
   VII.   than the rock cryftal.

Some countries of Europe furnifh emeralds ; but
they are of a very imperfect kind, and in little eftimation.

It was for a long time believed that emeralds of a
bright green came from the Eaft Indies, and it is on
this account that they have been called oriental. This
opinion hath been rejected, fince thofe who fupported
it have not been able to name the places where they
were found. It. is now certain that Afia hath never
fold us any of thefe jewels, except what fhe herfelf
had received from the New Hemifphere.

Thefe beautiful emeralds, therefore, belong certainly to America alone. The firft conquerors of Peru
found a great quantity of them, which they broke on
anvils, from an opinion which thefe adventurers entertained, that they would not break if they were fine.
This lofs became the more fenfibly felt through the
impoffibility of difcovering the mine from whence the
Incas had drawn them. The kingdom of New Grenada foon fupplied this deficiency. This diftrict fends
at prefent a lefs quantity of thefe jewels, whether it be
that they are become more fcarce, or that they are
lefs in fafhion in our climate than they were. But
gold comes from thence in greater plenty, and it is
fupplied by the provinces of Popayan and Chaco. It
is obtained without much rifk, and at no confiderable
expence.

This precious metal, which in other parts muft be
digged out of the entrails of rocks, mountains, and
precipices, is here found almoft at the furface of the
earth. It is mixed with it, but eafily feparated by
wafhings, more or lefs frequently repeated. The negroes, who are never employed in mines of any depth,
becaufe experience hath fhown that the cold in thefe
mines deftroyed them very faft, are the only perfons
burdened with thefe troublefome labours. The cuftom is, that the flaves fhould bring to their mafters a

certain quantity of gold. All they can collect above this quantity belongs to themfelves, as alfo what they find upon the days confecrated to reft by religion, but under the exprefs condition that they fhall provide for their fubfiftence during thefe holidays. By thefe arrangements, the moft laborious, the moft frugal, and the moft fortunate among them, are able, fooner or later, to purchafe their liberty. Then they raife their eyes towards the Spaniards; then they mix their blood with that of thefe proud conquerors.

The court of Madrid was diffatisfied that a region, the natural advantages of which were continually extolled, fhould furnifh fo few articles, and fo little of each. The diftance of this immenfe country from the centre of authority, eftablifhed at Lima for the government of all South America, muft have been one of the principal caufes of this inactivity. A more immediate fuperintendance was accordingly given to it, in order to communicate more motion to it, and to make that motion more regular. The vice-royalty of Peru was divided into two parts. That which was eftablifhed in 1718, in the New kingdom of Grenada, was formed upon the North Sea, of all that fpace that extends from the frontiers of Mexico to the Oroonoko; and upon the South Sea of that fpace which begins at Veragua and ends at Tombez. In the inland parts of the country Quito was alfo incorporated in it.

This new arrangement, though prudent and neceffary, did not at firft produce the great advantages that were expected from it. Much time is required to form good directors; and more ftill, perhaps, to eftablifh order, and to reftore to labour whole generations, enervated by continuing for two centuries in a ftate of idlenefs and libertinifm. The revolution hath, however, begun to take place; and Spain already receives fome benefit from it.

Half of the gold collected in the colony was fmuggled to foreigners; and it was chiefly by the rivers Atrato and de la Hache that this clandeftine trade was carried on. The government have made themfelves

masters of the course of these rivers, by forts properly situated. Notwithstanding these precautions, the
smuggling will still continue, as long as the Spaniards
and their neighbours shall find their interest in it; but
it will diminish. The harbours of the mother-country
will send a greater quantity of merchandise, and will
receive more metals.

The communication between one province, one city,
and even one village and another, was difficult or impracticable. Every traveller was more or less exposed
to be plundered or massacred by the independent Indians. These enemies, who were formerly implacable,
yield, by degrees, to the invitations of the missionaries
who have the courage to go in search of them, and to
the marks of benevolence which have at length succeeded to the cruelties so generally practised in the
New World. If this mild spirit should be continued,
the savages of this region may one day become all civilized, and have a fixed residence.

Notwithstanding the known goodness of great part
of the territory, several of the provinces forming the
New kingdom used to draw their subsistence from Europe or from North America. At length the government have been able to prohibit the importation of
foreign flour throughout the extent of the vice-royalty, and even to furnish Cuba with some. When the
means shall no longer be wanting, private plantations
will be established in the New World along the coasts;
but the difficulty and the dearness of transport will never allow the inland parts of their country to extend
their harvests beyond what is required for local consumption. The chief wish of the people who inhabit
these parts is generally confined to the extension of
the mines.

Every thing announces that these mines are in a
manner innumerable in the New kingdom. The quality of the soil points them out. The almost daily
earthquakes that happen there are owing to them. It
is from them that the gold must flow, which the rivers
habitually carry along with them; and it is from them

that the gold came, which the Spaniards, at their firft B o o k arrival in the New World, took from the favages on VII. the coafts in fuch great quantities. Thefe are not mere conjectures at Maraquita, at Mufo, at Pampeluna, at Tacayma, and at Canaverales. The great mines that are found there are going to be opened; and it is hoped they will not be lefs abundant than thofe of the valley of Neyva, which for fome time paft have been worked with fo much fuccefs. Thefe new treafures will all unite themfelves to thofe of Chaco and Popayan in Santa Fè de Bogota, the capital of the vice-royalty.

The city is fituated at the foot of a fteep and cold mountain, at the entrance of a vaft and fuperb plain. In 1774, it contained feventeen hundred and feventy houfes, three thoufand two hundred and forty-fix families, and fixteen thoufand two hundred and thirty-three inhabitants. Population muft neceffarily increafe there, fince it is the feat of government, the place where the coin is ftricken, the ftaple of trade; and laftly, fince it is the refidence of an archbifhop, whofe· immediate jurifdiction extends over thirty-one Spanifh villages, which are called towns; over one hundred and ninety-five Indian colonies, anciently fubdued; and over eight and twenty miffions, eftablifhed in modern times. This archbifhop hath likewife, as metropolitan, a fort of infpection over the diocefes of Quito, of Panama, of Caraccas, of Saint Martha, and of Carthagena. It is by this laft place, though at the diftance of one hundred leagues, and by the river Magdalena, that Santa Fè keeps up its communication with Europe. The fame route ferves for Quito.

This province is of immenfe extent; but the greateft part of this vaft fpace is full of forefts, moraffes, and deferts, in which we meet with nothing but a few wandering favages, at great intervals of diftance. The only part that can properly be faid to be occupied, and governed by the Spaniards, is a valley of fourfcore leagues in length, and fifteen in breadth, formed by two branches of the Cordeleirias.

Remarkable fingularities in the province of Quito.

This is one of the fineſt countries in the world. Even in the centre of the torrid zone ſpring here is perpetual. Nature hath combined, under the line that covers ſo many ſeas and ſo little land, every circumſtance that could moderate the ardent heat of that beneficent conſtellation which is the cauſe of univerſal fertility : theſe are, the elevation of the globe in this ſummit of its ſphere ; the vicinity of mountains of immenſe height and extent, and always covered with ſnows ; and continual winds which refreſh the country the whole year, by interrupting the force of the perpendicular rays of heat. Nevertheleſs, after a morning which is uſually delightful, vapours begin to ariſe about one or two o'clock in the forenoon. The ſky is covered with gloomy clouds, which are changed into ſtorms. Then the whole atmoſphere is illuminated, and appears to be ſet on fire by lightning ; and the thunder makes the mountains reſound with a terrible noiſe. To theſe dreadful earthquakes are ſometimes added : at other times, rain or ſunſhine prevails without intermiſſion for fifteen days together ; and then there is an univerſal conſternation. The exceſs of moiſture ſpoils what is ſown, and drought produces dangerous diſeaſes.

But, if we except theſe unhappy accidents, which are extremely rare, the climate is one of the moſt wholeſome. The air is ſo pure, that thoſe nauſeous inſects are there unknown which infeſt almoſt the whole of America. Though licentiouſneſs and neglect render venereal complaints here almoſt general, the people ſuffer very little from them. Thoſe who have inherited this contagious diſtemper, or who have acquired it, grow old equally without danger and without inconvenience.

The moiſture and the action of the ſun being continual, and always ſufficient to unfold and ſtrengthen the ſhoots, the agreeable picture of the three moſt beautiful ſeaſons of the year is continually preſented to the eye of the inhabitants. In proportion as the graſs withers, freſh graſs ſprings up ; and the enamel of the meadows is hardly paft, but it appears afrefh. The trees are inceffantly covered with green leaves, adorned with odoriferous flowers, and always laden with fruit ; the colour, form, and beauty of which are continually varying in all their feveral progreffive ftates, from their firft appearance to their maturity. The corn advances in the fame progreffion of fertility that is always renewing. At one view one may behold the new-fown feed fpringing up, fome that is grown larger and fpiked with ears, fome turning yellow, and fome under the reaper's fcythe. The whole year is paffed in fowing and reaping, within the compafs of the fame horizon. This conftant variety depends on the diverfity of the expofures.

B O O K VII.

Accordingly, this is the moft populous part of the continent of America. There are ten or twelve thoufand inhabitants at St. Michael d'Ibarra. Eighteen or twenty thoufand at Otabalo. Ten or twelve thoufand at Latacunga. Eighteen or twenty thoufand at Riobamba. Eight or ten thoufand at Hambato. From five-and-twenty to thirty thoufand at Cuença. Ten thoufand at Loxa, and fix thoufand at Zaruma. The country places do not afford a lefs number of men than the towns,

Reafons why the country of Quito is fo populous as it is. Labours of its inhabitants.

Population would certainly be lefs confiderable, if, as in many other places, the people had been buried in the mines. Numberlefs writers have blamed the inhabitants of this diftrict for not having continued to work the mines that were opened at the time of the conqueft, and for having neglected thofe that have been fucceffively difcovered. This reproach appears to be ill-founded to enlighten perfons, who have an opportunity of examining nearly into thefe matters. Their opinion in general is, that the mines of this diftrict are not fufficiently plentiful to defray the neceffary expences of working them. We fhall not pretend to decide upon this difpute. Neverthelefs, if we do but juft confider the paffion which the Spaniards have always fhown for the kind of wealth, which, without any labour on their parts, cofts nothing more than the blood of their flaves, we fhall be induced to think, that nothing but a total impoffibility, evinced by repeated experience, can have determined them to refift their natural propenfity, and the urgent folicitations of the mother-country.

In the country of Quito, the manufactures keep thofe perfons employed, who in other parts are enervated by the mines. Many hats, cottons, and coarfe woollen cloths, are fabricated there. With the produce of the quantity of thefe articles, confumed in the different countries of South America, Quito paid for the wines, brandy, and oils which it was not allowed to procure from its own foil; for the dried and falt fifh that came from the coafts; for the foap, made of goats greafe, that was fupplied by Piura and Trufcillo; for the crude or wrought iron that was wanted for its manufactures; and for the fmall quantity that it was poffible it fhould confume of the merchandife of our hemifphere. Thefe refources have been confiderably leffened, fince manufactures of the fame kind have been eftablifhed in the neighbouring provinces; and efpecially fince the fuperior cheapnefs of the European cottons and linens hath extended the ufe of them in a fingular manner. Accordingly, the country is fallen into the moft extreme ftate of mifery.

It will never emerge from this fituation by its provifions. Not but that its fields are in general covered with fugar-canes, with all forts of corn, with delicious fruits, and with numerous flocks. It would be difficult to find a foil fo fertile, and cultivated with fo little expence; but nothing that it furnifhes can fupply foreign markets. Its natural riches muft be confumed upon the fame territory that hath produced them. The bark is its only production which it has hitherto been poffible to export.

The bark comes from the province of Quito. Reflections upon this remedy.
The tree which yields this precious remedy hath a ftraight ftem, and rifes to a confiderable height when left to itfelf. Its trunk and its branches are proportioned to its height. The leaves, which are oppofite, and connected at their bafe by an intermediary mem-

brane or ftipula, are of an oval figure, fpread out at the lower part, and acute at their apex; they are very fmooth and of a beautiful green. From the axillæ of the upper leaves, which are fmaller, arife clufters of flowers, refembling, at firft fight, thofe of the lavendar. Their calix, which is fhort, hath five divifions. The corolla forms an elongated tube, bluifh on the outfide, and red within; it is filled with five ftamina, fpread out at the upper part, and divided into five lobes finely dentated. It bears upon a piftil, which being furmounted with a fingle ftyle occupies the fundus of the calix, and becomes with it a dry fruit, truncated at the upper extremity, and divided longitudinally into two half-pods full of feeds, and lined with a membranous expanfion.

This tree grows upon the flope of mountains. The only precious part of it is the bark, known by its febrifuge qualities, and which requires no other preparation than that of drying. The thickeft was preferred, till repeated analyfes and experiments had fhown, that the thinneft poffeffed moft virtue.

The inhabitants diftinguifh three fpecies, or rather three varieties of bark. The yellow and the red, which are in equal eftimation, and differ only in the depth of their colour; and the white, which being of a much inferior quality, is not in great requeft. It is diftinguifhed by its leaf being lefs fmooth and rounder, its flower whiter, its feed larger, and its bark white on the outfide. The bark of the good fpecies is generally brown, brittle, and rough on its furface, with cracks upon it.

Upon the borders of the river Maragnon, the country of Jaën furnifhes a great deal of white bark: but it was imagined, for a long time, that the yellow and the red were found nowhere but upon the territory of Loxa, a town founded in 1546 by Captain Alonzo de Mercadillo. The moft efteemed was that which grew at the diftance of two leagues from this place, upon the mountain of Cajanuma; and no longer than fifty years ago, the merchants ufed to endeavour to prove

BOOK by certificates, that the bark which they fold came
VII. from that celebrated fpot. In endeavouring to increafe the quantity collected, the old trees were deftroyed, and the new ones were not fuffered to come
to their complete growth ; fo that the talleft of them
are at prefent fcarce three toifes high. This fcarcity
occafioned the trees to be fearched for in other places.
At length the fame tree was difcovered at Riobamba,
at Cuença, in the neighbourhood of Loxa, and ftill
more recently at Bogota in the New Kingdom.

The bark was known at Rome in 1639. The Jefuits, who had brought it there, diftributed it gratis to
the poor, and fold it at an exorbitant price to the
rich. The year following, John de Vega, phyfician
to a vice-queen of Peru, who had experienced the falutary effects of it, eftablifhed it in Spain at a hundred crowns a pound [12l. 10s.]. This remedy foon
acquired great reputation, which it maintained till the
inhabitants of Loxa, not being able to fupply the demands that were made on them, thought of mixing
other barks with that for which there was fo much demand. This fraud diminifhed the confidence that had
been placed in the bark. The meafures taken by the
court of Madrid to remedy fo dangerous an impofition,
were not entirely fuccefsful. The late difcoveries have
been more effectual than authority, in putting a ftop
to this adulteration. Accordingly, the ufe of the remedy hath become more general, efpecially in England.

It is a generally received opinion, that the natives
of the country were very anciently acquainted with
the bark, and that they had recourfe to its virtues in
intermittent fevers. It was fimply infufed in water,
and the liquor given to the patient to drink, free of the
refiduum. M. Jofeph de Juffieu taught them to make
the extract from it, the ufe of which is much preferable to that of the bark in kind.

This botanift, the moft intelligent of thofe whom
their zeal for the improvement of natural hiftory hath
carried into the Spanifh poffeffions in the New World,
had formed a much more extenfive plan. He went

over moſt of the mountains of South America with incredible fatigues, and was juſt going to enrich Europe with the valuable diſcoveries he had made, when his papers were ſtolen from him. An excellent memory might partly have repaired this misfortune; but he was alſo deprived of this reſource. There was great want of a phyſician and an engineer in Peru. M. de Juſſieu poſſeſſed all the knowledge which theſe two profeſſions required, and the government of the country called upon him to employ his talents in this double capacity. Theſe new employments were accompanied with ſo many contradictions, ſo much diſguſt and ingratitude, that this excellent man could not bear up againſt them. His mind was totally deranged, when, in 1771, he was embarked, without fortune, for a country which he had quitted ſix-and-thirty years. Neither the government which had ſent him to the other hemiſphere, nor that which had detained him there, condeſcended to take any care of his future deſtiny; which would indeed have been deplorable, had it not been for the tenderneſs of a brother, as reſpectable for his virtues as celebrated for his knowledge. The worthy nephews of M. Bernard de Juſſieu have inherited their uncle's attention to this unfortunate traveller, who died in 1779. May this conduct of a family, whoſe name is illuſtrious in the ſciences, ſerve as a model to all thoſe who, either for their happineſs or their misfortune, apply themſelves to the cultivation of literature!

M. Joſeph de Juſſieu, who found that the people had received with docility the inſtructions he had given them reſpecting the bark, endeavoured alſo to perſuade them to improve, by conſtant and regular attention, the wild cochineal which the country itſelf ſupplied their manufactures with, and the coarſe cinnamon which they drew from Quixos and Macas: but his advice hath hitherto had no effect, whether it be that theſe productions have not been found ſuſceptible of any improvement, or whether no pains have been taken to bring it about.

The laſt conjecture will appear the moſt probable to thoſe who have a proper idea of the maſters of the country. Still more generally than the other Spaniſh Americans, they live in a ſtate of idleneſs from which nothing can rouſe them, and in debaucheries which no motive can interrupt. Theſe manners are more particularly the manners of the perſons, whoſe reſidence, from birth, employments, or fortune, is fixed in the city of Quito, the capital of the province, and very agreeably built upon the declivity of the celebrated mountain of Pitchincha. Fifty thouſand Meſtees, Indians, or negroes, allured by theſe ſeducing examples, alſo infeſt this ſpot with their vices, and in particular carry their paſſion for rum, and for gaming, to an exceſs that is unknown in the other great cities of the New World.

Digreſſion upon the formation of mountains. But, in order to relieve our imagination from ſuch a number of diſtreſſing pictures, which, perhaps, have too much engaged our attention, let us for a moment quit theſe bloody ſcenes, and let us enter into Peru, fixing our contemplation upon thoſe frightful mountains, where learned and bold aſtronomers went to meaſure the figure of the earth. Let us indulge ourſelves in thoſe ſenſations which they undoubtedly experienced, and which every traveller, learned or ignorant, muſt experience, wherever nature preſents him with ſuch a ſcene. Let us even be allowed to throw out ſome general conjectures reſpecting the formation of mountains.

At the ſight of thoſe enormous maſſes, which riſe to ſuch prodigious heights above the humble ſurface of the earth, where almoſt all mankind have fixed their reſidence; of thoſe maſſes, which on one ſpot are crowned with impenetrable and ancient foreſts, that have never reſounded with the ſtroke of the hatchet, and which preſent, on another, nothing more than a barren and dreary ſurface; which in one country reign in ſedate and ſilent majeſty, that ſtops the cloud in its courſe, and breaks the impetuoſity of the wind; while in another, they keep the traveller at a

diſtance from their ſummits by ramparts of ice that
ſurround them, from the centre of which volleys of
flame iſſue forth ; or frighten him who attempts to aſ-
cend them, with horrid and concealed caverns digged
on each ſide : maſſes, ſeveral of which give vent to
impetuous torrents deſcending with dreadful noiſe from
their open ſides, or to rivers, ſtreams, fountains, and
boiling ſprings ; all of them ſpreading their refreſhing
ſhade over the plains that ſurround them, and affording them a ſucceſſive ſhelter againſt the heat of the
ſun, from the moment that luminary gilds their tops
at the time of its riſing, till that of its ſetting : at this
aſpect, I ſay, every man is fixt with aſtoniſhment, and
the inquirer into nature is led into reflections.

He aſks himſelf, who it is that hath given birth here
to Veſuvius, to Ætna, to the Appenines, and here to
the Cordeleirias? Theſe mountains, are they as old as
the world, have they been produced in an inſtant, or
is the ſtony particle that is detached from them more
ancient than they are? Can they be the bones of a
ſkeleton, of which the other terreſtrial ſubſtances are
the fleſh? Are they diſtinct maſſes ; or do they hold
together by one great common trunk, of which they
are ſo many branches, and which ſerves as a foundation to themſelves, and as a baſis for every thing that
covers them?

If we agree with one philoſopher : " The centre of
" the earth being occupied by an immenſe reſervoir of
" waters, the ſubſtance that contained them ſuddenly
" burſt. The cataracts of the ſky were immediately
" opened, and the whole globe was confounded and
" ſunk under water. The fabulous account of chaos
" was renewed ; and the earth did not begin to extri-
" cate itſelf from this ſtate, till the time when the dif-
" ferent materials precipitated, according to the laws
" of gravity, by which they were ſucceſſively impel-
" led ; the layers of theſe ſeveral heterogeneous ſub-
" ſtances were heaped one upon another, and raiſed
" their ſummits above the ſurface of the waters, which
" went to dig a bed for themſelves in the plains."

Another philosopher obferves: " That thefe caufes
" are infufficient to explain this phenomenon, without
" the intervention and approach of a comet, which he
" calls forth from the vaft regions of fpace where
" thefe bodies lofe themfelves. The column of wa-
" ters, he fays, which this comet drew along with it,
" was joined by thofe which rofe from the fubterra-
" nean abyfs, and thofe which defcended from the at-
" mofphere. The action of the comet made them rife
" above the higheft mountains, which were already
" exifting ; and from the fediment of this deluge they
" were reproduced."

A third writer treats all thefe opinions as idle
dreams, and fays : " Let us caft our eyes around us,
" and we fhall fee the mountains rifing from the very
" element that deftroys them. It is fire which hardens
" the foft layers of the earth ; it is that which, affift-
" ed in its expanfion by air and by water, throws
" them up, and drives their fummits into the clouds ;
" it is that which burfts them, and forms their im-
" menfe caldrons. Every mountain is a volcano,
" which is either preparing, or hath ceafed."

Thefe opinions are again contradicted by a moft
eloquent modern writer, the charms of whofe language, while I liften to it, fcarce leave me at liberty
to judge of his opinion. He fays : " In the beginning
" there were no mountains. The furface of the globe
" was uniformly covered with waters, which were not,
" however, in a ftate of reft. The action of the fatel-
" lite that accompanies the earth agitated them, even
" to their greateft depth, with the motion of ebb and
" flow which we now fee impreffed upon them. At
" each ofcillatory motion, thefe waters dragged along
" with them a portion of fediment, which they depo-
" fited upon a preceding portion. It is upon thefe de-
" pofits, continued through a long feries of ages, that
" the layers of the earth have been formed ; and the
" enormous maffes that aftonifh us, are thefe layers
" accumulated. Time is nothing to nature ; and the
" flighteft caufe, acting uninterruptedly, is capable of

" producing the greateſt effects. The imperceptible B O O K
" and continued action of the waters hath therefore ___VII.___
" formed the mountains; and it is the ſtill more im-
" perceptible, and not leſs continued, action of a va-
" pour that ſoftens them, and of a wind that dries
" them up, which lowers them from day to day, and
" will at length reduce them to a level with the
" plains. Then the waters will again be ſpread uni-
" formly over the equal ſurface of the earth. Then
" the firſt phenomenon will be renewed; and who
" knows how often the mountains have been deſtroy-
" ed and reproduced?"

At theſe words the obſerver Lehmann ſmiles, and,
preſenting to me the book of the Jewiſh Legiſlator,
together with his own, ſays to me : " Reſpect this
" book, and condeſcend to caſt thine eyes upon mine."
Lehmann hath explained, in his third volume of his
Art of Mines, his ideas upon the formation of the layers of the earth, and upon the productions of mountains. His ſyſtem is founded on conſtant and repeated
obſervations made by himſelf, with a very uncommon
degree of ſagacity, and with a labour, the aſſiduity of
which we can ſcarce conceive. They comprehend
the ſpace from the frontiers of Poland to the borders
of the Rhine. The analogy which renders them applicable to ſeveral other regions, recommends the
knowledge of them to men who are ſtudious of natural hiſtory; and although he attributes the formation
of the layers of the earth to a deluge, the facts with
which he ſupports his arguments are not the leſs certain, nor his diſcoveries the leſs intereſting.

He diſtinguiſhes three kinds of mountains. The
antediluvian, or primitive; the poſtdiluvian, and the
modern. The firſt, which are of different elevation,
are the higheſt. They are ſeldom found diſtinct, but
are uſually formed into chains. The declivity of them
is ſteep. They are ſurrounded on all ſides by the poſtdiluvian mountains, or ſuch as are compoſed of layers.
The ſubſtance of them is more homogeneous; the
portions of them leſs different; their beds are always

perpendicular, and thicker. Their roots defcend to a depth which is ftill unknown. The ores they contain run in the longitudinal direction of the mountain. Thofe in the poftdiluvian mountains are difpofed in layers, which are formed of different fubftances. The laft of thefe, or that which is at the bafis, is always of coal. The firft, or that which is neareft the fummit, always furnifhes falt fprings. The mountains never fail to terminate in the former. They fupply copper, lead, quickfilver, iron, and even filver, but in leaves, and capillaceous. But they would deceive our avidity, if we expected to find gold in them. The mountains which produce this metal are the work of a deluge.

The modern mountains, produced by fire, by water, and by an infinite number of various and recent accidents, exhibit, in their internal parts, nothing but broken layers, a confufed mixture of all kinds of fubftances, and all the marks of fubverfion and diforder.

It is in vain that nature had concealed the precious metals in the midft of thefe hard and moft compact maffes : our cupidity hath broken them. This circumftance, however, would not call for our cenfure, if we could fay of the men employed in thefe dreadful labours, what we read of them in Caffiodorus: " They " go down poor into the mines, and come out of them " wealthy. They enjoy a kind of riches which no " man dares to take away from them. They are the " only perfons whofe fortune is neither fullied by ra- " pine or meannefs."

Europeans, reflect upon what this judicious writer adds : " To acquire gold by facrificing men, is a crime. " To go in fearch of it acrofs the perils of the fea, is " a folly. To amafs it by corruption and vices, is " bafe. The only profits that are juft and honeft, are " thofe that are acquired without injury to any per- " fon; and we never can poffefs, without remorfe, " what we have obtained at the expence of other " men's happinefs."

And you, in order to have gold, you have gone

across the seas. In order to have gold, you have invaded other countries. In order to have gold, you
have maffacred the greateft part of the inhabitants.
In order to have gold, you have precipitated into the
bowels of the earth thofe whom your daggers had
fpared. In order to have gold, you have introduced
upon the earth the infamous trade of mankind and
flavery. In order to have gold, you repeat the fame
crimes every day. May the chimerical idea of Lazar-
ro Moro be realized; and may fubterraneous flames
fet on fire at once all thofe mountains of which you
have made fo many dungeons, where innocence expires, for feveral ages paft!

This curfe would firft fall upon the Cordeleirias, or, Natural or-ganization of Peru, properly fo called.
Andes, which cut almoft the whole of America
through its length, and the different branches of
which extend themfelves irregularly in its breadth. It
is particularly under the Line, and at Peru, that thefe
mountains awe us by their majeftic appearance.
Through the enormous heaps of fnow that cover the
moft confiderable of them, it may eafily be difcerned
that they formerly were volcanos. The clouds of
fmoke, and gufts of flame, which ftill iffue from fome
of them, cannot allow us to have the leaft doubt refpecting the eruptions. Chimboraco, the higheft of
them, and which is near three thoufand two hundred
and twenty toifes above the level of the fea, is more
than one third higher than the Peak of Teneriff, the
loftieft mountain of the ancient hemifphere. The Pitchincha and the Caraçon, which have principally ferved for taking the obfervations upon the figure of the
earth, have only two thoufand four hundred and thirty, and two thoufand four hundred and feventy toifes;
and it is, however, at this height, that the moft intrepid travellers have been obliged to ftop. Eternal fnows
have hitherto rendered fummits of greater height inacceffible.

A plain, which is from thirty to fifty leagues in
breadth, and is raifed one thoufand nine hundred and
forty-nine toifes above the level of the ocean, ferves

BOOK as the bafis to thefe aftonifhing mountains. Part of
VII. this vaft fpace is occupied by lakes more or lefs confiderable. That of Titicaca, which receives ten or
twelve large rivers, and feveral fmall ones, is feventy
toifes in depth, and fourfcore leagues in circumference.
In the midft of it there rifes an ifland, where the legiflators of Peru pretended to have received their birth.
They owed it, as they faid, to the Sun, who had prefcribed to them to eftablifh his worfhip, to raife mankind from a ftate of barbarifm, and to give them beneficent laws. This fable rendered the fpot venerable;
and one of the moft auguft temples in the empire was
conftructed upon it. Pilgrims reforted to it in crowds
from the provinces, with offerings of gold, filver, and
jewels. It is a tradition generally received in the
country, that, at the arrival of the Spaniards, the priefts
and the inhabitants threw all thefe riches into the waters, as they had before done at Cufco, in another lake,
fix leagues to the fouth of that celebrated capital.
From moft of the lakes there are torrents iffuing;
which, in procefs of time, have digged ravines of a tremendous depth. At the fummit of them the mines
are ufually found in a foil generally arid. It is a little
below this that the corn grows, and the cattle feed:
in the bottom, the fugar, the fruits, and the maize, are
cultivated.

The coaft, which is of an immenfe length, and from
eight to twenty leagues in breadth, which extends
from the plain we have been fpeaking of to the fea,
and which is known to us by the name of the Valleys,
is nothing but a heap of fand. Solitude and eternal
barrennefs feem as if they were intended to belong to
this ungrateful foil.

Nature varies, and in a very remarkable manner, in
this uneven territory. The moft elevated places are
perpetually covered with fnow. After this come the
rocks and naked fands. Beneath thefe fome moffes
begin to fhow themfelves. Lower down is the Icho,
a plant which they burn, fomewhat refembling rufhes;
and which grows longer and ftronger in proportion as

one defcends. At length the trees make their appearance, to the number of three fpecies, particular to
thefe mountains; and which, all of them, announce,
in their ftructure and their foliage, the feverity of the
climate that produces them. The moft ufeful of thefe
trees is the caffis. It is weighty, hath fome fubftance,
and is lafting; and thefe qualities have occafioned it
to be deftined to the labours of the mines. Thefe
large vegetable productions are not to be met with
under a milder fky, and they are only replaced by a
fmall number of others of a different quality. There
would not even be any one fpecies in the valleys, if
fome had not been conveyed there, which have become naturalized.

In this region, the air hath an evident influence upon the conftitution of the inhabitants. Thofe of the
moft elevated diftricts are fubject to afthmas, pleurifies,
to pulmonary complaints, and to rheumatifms. Thefe
difeafes, which are dangerous to all individuals that
are feized with them, are commonly mortal to any one
that hath contracted venereal maladies, or is addicted
to ftrong liquors; and this is unfortunately the ufual
ftate of thofe who are born in thefe climates, or have
been led into them by avarice.

*Circum-
ftances in
which the
mountains,
plains, and
valleys of
Peru differ
from each
other.*

Thefe calamities do not affect the inferior mountains; but other fcourges, ftill more fatal, are fubftituted to them. Putrid and intermittent fevers, unknown in the countries we have been mentioning, are
habitual there. They are fo eafily caught, that travellers are afraid to come near the places that are in
fected with them. They are frequently fo contagious,
that not a fingle man would efcape the infection, if
the inhabitants did not abandon their villages, in order
to return to them again when a frefh feafon hath purified them. It was not thus in the time of the Incas.
But fince the Spaniards have introduced the fugar
canes into the narrow gorges of the mountains, where
the air circulates with difficulty, there arife, from the
moiftened foil which this cultivation requires, infec-

tious vapours, which, being heated by the rays of the burning fun, become fatal.

The tertian, and other intermittent fevers, are fcarce lefs common or lefs obftinate in the valleys than in the gorges of the mountains: but they are infinitely lefs dangerous: they are feldom attended with fatal confequences, except in the country places where no helps are to be had, and where precautions are neglected.

Another general malady in this part of the New World, is the fmall-pox, which was brought there in 1588. It is not habitual, as in Europe; but it occafions, at intervals, inexpreffible ravages. It attacks, indifferently, the white men, the Negroes, the Indians, and the mixed races. It is equally deftructive in all the climates. Much advantage is to be expected from the practice of inoculation, introduced two years fince at Lima, and which will undoubtedly foon become general.

There is another fcourge prevailing here, againft which human invention will never find a remedy. Earthquakes, which in other countries are fo rare, that whole generations frequently fucceed each other without beholding one, are fo common in Peru, that they have there contracted an habit of reckoning them as a feries of epochas, fo much the more memorable, as their frequent return does not diminifh their violence.

This phenomenon, which is ever irregular in its fudden returns, is, however, announced by very perceptible omens. When the fhock is confiderable, it is preceded by a murmur in the air, the noife of which is like that of heavy rain falling from a cloud that fuddenly burfts and difcharges its waters. This noife feems to be the effect of a vibration of the air, which is agitated in different directions. The birds are then obferved to dart in their flight. Neither their tails nor their wings ferve them any longer as oars and helm to fwim in the fluid of the fkies. They dafh themfelves in pieces againft the walls, the trees, and

the rocks; whether it be that this vertigo of nature B o o к
dazzles and confuses them, or that the vapours of the VII.
earth take away their ftrength and power to command
their movements.

To this tumult in the air is added the rumbling of
the earth, the cavities and deep receffes of which re-
echo each other's noifes. The dogs anfwer thefe previous tokens of a general diforder of nature, by howl-
ing in an extraordinary manner. The animals ftop,
and, by a natural inftinĉt, fpread out their legs that
they may not fall. Upon thefe indications, the inhabitants inftantly run out of their houfes, and fly to
fearch, in the enclofures of public places, or in the
fields, an afylum from the fall of their roofs. The
cries of children, the lamentations of women, the fudden darknefs of an unexpeĉted night; every thing
combines to aggravate the too real evils of a dire calamity, which fubverts every thing, by the excruciat-
ing tortures of the imagination, which is diftreffed and
confounded, and lofes, in the contemplation of this
diforder, the thought and courage to remedy it.

The diverfity of afpeĉts under which volcanos have
prefented themfelves to one of our moft indefatigable
and intelligent obfervers, hath pointed out to him different periods, feparated from each other by intervals
of time fo confiderable, that the firft formation of our
planet is thrown back by them to a degree of antiquity at which our imagination is ftartled. At the firft
of thefe periods, the volcanos throw out from their
fummits fire, fmoke, and afhes, and pour out torrents
of lava from their fides that are laid open. At the fecond, they are all of them extinguifhed, and exhibit
nothing but an immenfe caldron. At the third, the
air, the rain, the wind, the cold, and the lime, have
deftroyed the caldron, or crater, and nothing but a
hillock remains. At the fourth period, this hillock,
deprived of its covering, difcovers a kind of nidus,
which, being deftroyed by time, leaves nothing but
the place where the mountain and volcano have exifted; and this ftate conftitutes a fifth period. From the

centre of this place caufeways of lava are extended to a diftance; and thefe caufeways, whether entire or broken, or reduced into feparate fragments, are ftill as many other periods, between each of which we may infert as many years, as many ages, or as many thoufands of ages as we choofe. One thing, however, is certain, that one of thefe periods, whichever of them we may choofe, is not connected, in the memory of man, with that which fucceeds it in the courfe of nature. The principle, therefore, that from nothing nothing can be produced; and the deftruction of be-ings, which, by being changed into others, fhow us that nothing is annihilated, feem to announce an eter-nity which hath preceded, an eternity which will fol-low, and the co-exiftence of the Great Architect with his wonderful work.

The climate exhibits fome very remarkable fingula-rities in the Upper Peru. The inhabitants experience on the fame day, fometimes in the fame hour, and al-ways in a very fhort fpace of time, the temperature of the two oppofite zones. Thofe who come there from the valleys, are pierced on their arrival with fevere cold, which they cannot get the better of either by fire, by motion, or by adding to their clothing; but the impreffion of which ceafes to be difagreeable, af-ter a refidence of a month or three weeks. The voy-agers who come there for the firft time, are tormented with the fymptoms of fea ficknefs, with more or lefs violence, in proportion as they have fuffered from it on the ocean. But, whatever may be the reafon of it, men are not expofed to this accident in all parts; for not one of the aftronomers who meafured the figure of the earth upon the mountains of Quito, were attacked with it.

Our aftonifhment is equally, if not more, excited in the valleys. This country, though very near the equa-tor, enjoys a delicious temperature. The four feafons of the year are evidently marked, and yet neither of them can be called troublefome. The winter feafon is the moft fenfibly felt. This hath been attempted to be accounted for from the winds of the fouth pole, which carry the effects of the fnows and ice over which they have paffed. They preferve it only in part, be-caufe they blow under the influence of a thick fog, which at that time covers the earth. Thefe grofs va-pours do not indeed rife regularly till about noon; but it is feldom they are diffipated. The fun gene-rally remains fo much clouded, that its rays, which fometimes make their appearance, can only mitigate the cold in a very flight degree.

Whatever may be the caufe of fo conftant a winter under the torrid zone, it is certain that it never rains, or that it rains only every two or three years, in the Lower Peru.

Natural philofophy hath exerted its efforts to difco-ver the caufe of a phenomenon fo extraordinary. May it not be attributed to the fouth-weft wind, which pre-vails there the greateft part of the year; and to the prodigious height of the mountains, the fummit of which is covered with eternal ice?

The country fituated between both, being continu-ally cooled on one fide, and continually heated on the other, maintains fo equal a temperature, that the clouds which rife can never be condenfed fo far as to be dif-folved into water.

Rains, however, and even daily rains, would be ne-ceffary to communicate fome degree of fertility to the coafts which extend from Tumbez to Lima, that is, throughout a fpace of two hundred and fixty-four leagues. The fands are in general fo barren, that there is not a fingle herb to be feen, except in parts which it is poffible to water, and thefe do not often occur. There is not a fingle fpring throughout the whole of Lower Peru; rivers are not frequent there; and thofe which we do meet with have, for the moft part, water in them only for fix or feven months in the year. They are torrents iffuing from the lakes, of greater or lefs magnitude, that are formed in the Cordeleirias, which only flow over a fmall fpace, and are dried up during the fummer. In the times of the Incas, thefe

B O O K precious waters were carefully collected, and, by the
VII.   affiftance of feveral canals, difperfed over a large furface, which they fertilized. The Spaniards have availed themfelves of thefe labours. Their villages and
towns have been erected on the places where the huts
for the Indians were, which, perhaps for this reafon,
were lefs numerous in the Lower Peru than on the
mountains. The valleys which lead from the capital
of the empire to Chili, have a great refemblance with
thofe we have fpoken of ; but they are in fome places
more fufceptible of cultivation.

The few   Notwithftanding thefe defects of natural organiza-
Peruvians
who have   tion, the region we have been defcribing hath feen a
efcaped the flourifhing empire arife in the midft of it. Its popula-
fword or
tyranny of tion cannot reafonably be called in queftion, when we
the con-   behold felf-evident proofs that this happy people had
querors, are
fallen into covered with their colonies all the provinces that they
the moft   had conquered ; when we attend to the aftonifhing
degraded
and brutal number of men engaged in the fervice of government,
ftate.   and deriving their fubfiftence from the ftate. Such a
variety of hands and levers employed in moving the
political machine, neceffarily imply a confiderable degree of population, that may be enabled to maintain,
with the productions of the earth, a very numerous
clafs of the inhabitants, who are not themfelves concerned in agriculture.

By what fatality, then, hath it happened that Peru
is now fuch a defert ? By tracing things to their origin, we find that thofe who conquered the coaft of the
South Sea, being ruffians, without birth, education,
and principle, originally committed greater enormities
than the conquerors of Mexico. The mother-country
was a longer time before fhe checked their ferocity,
which was continually fomented by thofe long and
cruel civil wars that fucceeded the conqueft. A more
heavy and regular fyftem of oppreffion was afterwards
eftablifhed than had prevailed in the other countries
of the New World lefs diftant from Europe.

Univerfal difcouragement was the neceffary confequence of this abominable conduct. Accordingly, the

natives of the country grew difgufted of the ftate of
fociety, and of the fatigues it brings along with it.
They continue in the fame difagreeable difpofitions,
and would not even give themfelves the leaft trouble
to cultivate fubfiftence for themfelves, were they not
compelled to it by the government. This compulfion
influences their behaviour. All the inhabitants of one
community, men, women, and children, unite themfelves to till and fow a field. Thefe labours, which
are interrupted every inftant by dancing and feafting,
are carried on by the found of various inftruments.
The harveft of the maize, and of the other grain, is
gathered with the fame carelefsnefs, and accompanied
with the fame pleafures. Thefe people are not more
anxious to procure themfelves clothes. In vain hath
it been attempted to infpire them with better difpofitions, and more fuitable to the good of the empire.
Authority hath been unavailing againft cuftoms which
its tyranny had given rife to, and which were kept up
by its injuftice.

The Peruvians, all of them without exception, are
an inftance of that profound ftupidity into which it is
in the power of tyranny to plunge men. They are
fallen into a liftlefs and univerfal indifference. Can it
be poffible that thefe people fhould have any kind of
attachment, whofe religion once elevated the foul, and
from whom the moft abjeft flavery hath taken away
every fentiment of greatnefs and glory ? The riches,
which nature hath fcattered at their feet, do not tempt
them; and they are even infenfible to honours. They
are whatever one choofes, without any ill humour,
or choice, vaffals or caciques, or *mitayos*, the objeſts
of diftinſtion or of public derifion. The fpring of all
their paffions is broken. That of fear itfelf hath often
no effeſt on them, through the little attachment they
have to life. They intoxicate themfelves, and dance;
thefe are all the pleafures they have, when they are
able to forget their mifery. Indolence is their predo-
minant habit. *I am not hungry*, they fay to the perfon
who would pay them for their labour.

The void that had been made in the population of Peru, and the indolence of the few men that remained there, determined the conquerors to introduce a foreign race; but this mode of fubftitution, which was dictated by the refinement of European barbarity, was more prejudicial to Africa than ufeful to the country of the Incas. Avarice did not derive from thefe new flaves all the advantages it had flattered itfelf with. The government, ever intent on laying taxes upon vices and virtues, upon induftry and idlenefs, upon good and bad projects, upon the liberty of exercifing oppreffions, and the permiffion of being exempted from them, made a monopoly of this bafe traffic. It was neceffary to receive the Negroes from the hands of a rival or an enemy, to carry them to the place of their deftination, through immenfe feas and unwholefome climates, and to defray the expences of feveral very dear markets. Neverthelefs, this fpecies of men hath multiplied more at Peru than at Mexico. There is alfo a much greater number of Spaniards there, for the following reafons:

At the time when the firft conquefts were made, when emigrations were moft frequent, the country of the Incas had a much greater reputation for riches than New Spain; and, in reality, for half a century, much more confiderable treafures were brought away from it. The defire of partaking of them muft neceffarily draw thither, as was really the cafe, a greater number of Caftilians. Though they almoft all went over there with the hope of returning to their country to enjoy the fortune they might acquire, yet the majority of them fettled in the colony. They were induced to this by the foftnefs of the climate, and the goodnefs of the provifions. They alfo fuppofed they fhould enjoy a great fhare of independence in a region fo remote from the mother-country.

We muft now examine to what degree of profperity Peru hath been raifed by the united labours of fo many different people.

The immenfe coaft that extends from Panama to

Tombez, and which, in 1718, was detached from Peru to be incorporated in the New Kingdom, is one of the most miserable regions of the globe. A great part of it is occupied by spacious and numerous morasses. The part that is not covered with these is deluged for six months in the year with rains that fall down in torrents. From the midst of these stagnating and unwholesome waters forests arise, that are as ancient as the world, and so much choked up with *lianes*, or osiers, that the strongest and most intrepid man cannot penetrate into them. Thick and frequent fogs throw a dark veil over these hideous countries. None of the productions of the Old Hemisphere can grow in this ungrateful soil, and those even of the New Hemisphere do not thrive much. And, indeed, there is but a small number of savages to be seen here, and those for the most part wandering; and so few Spaniards, that it might almost be said there were none. The coast is fortunately terminated by the Gulf of Guayaquil, where nature is in a less degenerate state.

The second town which the Spaniards built in Peru was raised upon this river, in 1533. The Indians did not long suffer this monument, erected against their liberty, to subsist; but it was rebuilt four years after by Orellana. It was not placed in the Bay of Charopte as it had been at first. The back of a mountain, at the distance of five or six hundred toises from the river, was preferred. The exigencies of commerce afterwards determined the merchants to fix their dwellings upon the side of the river itself. The space which separated them from their former habitation hath been gradually filled up; so that at present the two quarters of the town are entirely united. The houses are in general built of wood, both in the lower and in the upper town. Formerly they were all covered with thatch; but this practice hath been abolished gradually by the orders of government, who have thought this regulation necessary, to prevent the accidents of fire, so common in these countries. Guayaquil was lately an entirely open place. It is at present defended by three forts, guarded only by the inhabitants. These are large beams difposed in palifades. Upon this foil, which is always damp, and under water a great part of the year, a fort of wood, which never rots, is preferable to the beft conftructed works either in earth or in ftone.

It is a circumftance well known at prefent, that, on the coaft of Guayaquil, as well as on that of Guatimala, are found thofe fnails which yield the purple dye fo celebrated by the ancients, and which the moderns have fuppofed to have been loft. The fhell that contains them is fixed to rocks that are watered by the fea. It is of the fize of a large nut. The juice may be extracted from the animal in two ways. Some perfons kill the animal after they have taken it out of the fhell; they then prefs it from the head to the tail with a knife; and, feparating from the body that part in which the liquor is collected, they throw away the reft. When this operation, repeated upon feveral of the fnails, hath yielded a certain quantity of the juice, the thread that is to be dyed is dipped in it, and the bufinefs is done. The colour, which is at firft as white as milk, becomes afterwards green, and does not turn purple till the thread is dry.

Thofe who do not choofe this method, draw the animal partly out of its fhell, and by preffure oblige it to difcharge its liquor. This operation is repeated four different times, but at each time with lefs advantage. If it be continued, the animal dies, from the lofs of that fluid which was the principle of its life, and which it hath no longer the power to renew.

We know of no colour that can be compared to the one we have been fpeaking of, either in luftre or in permanency. It fucceeds better with cotton than with woollen, linen, or filk.

It is little more than an object of curiofity; but Guayaquil fupplies the neighbouring provinces with oxen, mules, falt, and fifh. It furnifhes a great quantity of cacao to Mexico and to Europe. It is the univerfal dock-yard of the South Sea, and might partly

become that of the mother-country. We know of no
spot upon the earth more abundant in wood for masts
and for ship-building. The hemp and the pitch, which
it is destitute of, is procured from Chili and from Guatimala.

This town is the necessary staple of all the trade
which the Lower Peru, Panama, and Mexico, keep
up with the country of Quito. All the commodities
which these countries exchange pass through the hands
of its merchants. The largest of the ships stop at the
island of Puna, six or seven leagues distant from the
place. The others can go thirty-five leagues up the
river, as far as Caracol.

Notwithstanding these several means of prosperity,
Guayaquil, the population of which consists of twenty
thousand souls, is far from being wealthy. The fortunes of its inhabitants have been succeffively destroyed nine times, by fires, and by pirates, who have twice
sacked the town. Those fortunes which have been
acquired since these fatal periods, have not continued
in the country. A climate where the heat is intole-
rable the whole year, and the rains incessant for six
months ; where dangerous and noisome insects do not
allow any tranquillity ; where distempers, prevailing
in the most opposite degrees of temperature, appear to
be united ; where one lives in perpetual dread of losing one's sight : such a climate is by no means proper
to fix the residence of its inhabitants. Such persons
are only seen here as have not acquired sufficient
wealth to enable them to remove elsewhere, and spend
their days in indolence and pleasure.

On quitting the territory of Guayaquil, we enter
into the valleys of Peru. They occupy four hundred
leagues of the coast ; and upon this extent there are a
great number of bad harbours, among which chance
hath placed one or two that are tolerably good.
Throughout this vast space, there is not the vestige of
a single road ; and it is necessary to travel over it upon mules in the night-time, because the reverberation
of the sun renders these sands unpassable in the day

At the intervals of thirty or forty leagues, we find the small towns of Piura, of Peyta, of Santa, of Pisco, of Nascar, of Ica, of Moquequa, and of Arica, and in the intermediate space a small number of hamlets and villages. Throughout this whole extent there are but three places worthy of being called towns; Truxillo, which hath nine thousand inhabitants; Arequipa, which hath forty thousand; and Lima, which hath fifty-four thousand. These several settlements have been formed wherever there was the least appearance of land fit for cultivation, and wherever the waters were capable of fertilizing a slime naturally barren.

The country produces the fruits peculiar to the climate, and most of those in Europe. The culture of maize, of pimento, and of cotton, which was found established there, was not neglected: and that of wheat, barley, cassava, potatoes, sugar, and of the olive and vine, was set on foot there. The goat hath thriven very well; but the sheep have degenerated, and their wool is extremely coarse. Throughout the whole of the valleys there is but one mine, which is that of Huantajaha.

In the Upper Peru, at the distance of one hundred and twenty leagues from the sea, stands Cusco, built by the first of the Incas, on a very uneven territory, and upon the declivity of several hills. It was at first only a small village, which in process of time became a considerable city, divided into as many quarters as there were nations incorporated with the empire. Each of these nations were allowed to follow their ancient customs; but they were all of them obliged to worship the brilliant constellation that fertilizes the globe. There was no edifice that had any grandeur, elegance, or convenience, because the people were ignorant of the first elements of architecture. Even the temple of the sun itself could not be distinguished from the other public or private buildings, unless by its extent, and by the profusion of metals with which it was ornamented.

To the north of this capital was a kind of citadel,

built with much care, labour, and expence. The Spa-
·niards long fpoke of this monument of Peruvian induftry with a fpirit of admiration that impofed upon
all Europe. The ruins of this fortrefs have been feen
by enlightened perfons, and the marvellous hath difappeared. It hath been found, that this fortification
had fcarce any advantage over the other works of the
fame kind erected in the country, except that of being
built with ftones of a more confiderable fize.

At the diftance of four leagues from the city are the
country-houfes of the great, and of the Incas, in the
wholefome and delicious valley of Yucai. There it
was that they went to recover their health, or to relax
from the fatigues of government.

After the conqueft, the place fcarce preferved any
thing but its name. There were other edifices, other
inhabitants, other occupations, other manners, other
prejudices, and another religion. Thus the fatality
which fubverts the earth, the fea, empires, and nations; which throws fucceffively upon all parts of the
globe the light of the arts and the darknefs of ignorance; which changes the refidence of men, and transfers their opinions from one place to another, as marine productions are pufhed upon the coaft by the impulfe of the winds and the currents: that impenetrable
and fingular deftiny, I fay, ordained that Europeans,
with all the appendages of their crimes, and monks,
with all the prejudices of their faith, fhould come to
reign and repofe in thofe walls, where the virtuous
Incas had for fo long a time promoted the felicity of
mankind, and where the fun was fo folemnly adored.
Who, therefore, can forefee what kind of race, or form
of worfhip, will one day arife upon the ruins of our
kingdoms and our altars? Cufco reckons twenty-fix
thoufand inhabitants under its new mafters.

In the midft of thefe mountains other towns are ftill
to be feen. Chupuifaca, or La Plata, which hath thirteen thoufand fouls; Potofi, twenty-five thoufand;
Oropefa, feventeen thoufand; La Paz, twenty thou-

ſand; Guancavelica, eight thouſand; and Huamanga, eighteen thouſand five hundred.

But let it be well obſerved, that none of theſe towns were erected in regions which preſented a fertile ſoil, copious harveſts, excellent paſtures, a mild and ſalubrious climate, and all the conveniences of life. Theſe places, which had hitherto been ſo well cultivated by a numerous and flouriſhing people, were now totally diſregarded. Very ſoon they exhibited only a deplorable picture of a horrid deſert; and this wildneſs muſt have been more melancholy and hideous than the dreary aſpect of the earth before the origin of ſocieties. The ſight of confuſion is not always diſpleaſing; it ſometimes aſtoniſhes: that of deſtruction afflicts us. The traveller, who was led by accident or curioſity into theſe deſolate plains, could not forbear abhorring the barbarous and bloody authors of theſe devaſtations, while he reflected that it was not owing even to the cruel illuſions of glory, and to the fanaticiſm of conqueſt, but to the ſtupid and abject deſire of gold, that they had ſacrificed ſo much more real treaſure, and ſo numerous a population.

This inſatiable thirſt of gold, which neither attended to ſubſiſtence, ſafety, nor policy, was the only motive for eſtabliſhing new ſettlements, ſome of which have been kept up, while ſeveral have decayed, and others have been formed in their ſtead. The fate of them all hath correſponded with the diſcovery, progreſs, or decay of the mines to which they were ſubordinate.

Fewer errors have been committed in the means of procuring proviſions. The natives had hitherto lived ſcarcely on any thing elſe but maize, fruits, and pulſe, for which they had uſed no other ſeaſoning except ſalt and pimento. Their liquors, which were made from different roots, were more diverſified; of theſe the *chica* was the moſt uſual; it is made from maize ſoaked in water, and taken out of the veſſel when it begins to ſprout. It is dried in the ſun, then parched a little, and at laſt ground. The flour, after it

has been well kneaded, is put with water into large
pitchers. The fermentation may be expected in two
or three days, and muſt not continue longer. The
great inconvenience of this drink, which, when uſed
immoderately, infallibly intoxicates, is, that it will not
keep more than ſeven or eight days without turning
ſour. Its taſte is nearly that of the moſt indifferent
kind of cyder.

All the cultivations eſtabliſhed in the empire, were
ſolely intended to ſupply articles of primary neceſſity.
The only thing cultivated for luxury was the coca;
this is a ſhrub which ramifies much, and ſeldom grows
higher than three or four feet. Its leaves are alternate,
oval, entire, and marked in their longitudinal direction with three coſtæ, two of which are not very apparent. The flowers collected in cluſters along the
ſtems, are ſmall, compoſed of a calix, with five diviſions, and five petals, furniſhed at their baſe with a
ſcale. The piſtil, ſurrounded with ten ſtamina, and
ſurmounted with three ſtiles, is changed into a ſmall,
reddiſh, oblong berry, which as it dries becomes triangular, and contains one nut filled with a ſingle ker-
nel.

The leaf of the coca was the delight of the Peruvians. They chewed it, after having mixed it with
an earth of a light grey colour, and of a ſaponaceous
quality, which they called *Toura;* it was, in their opinion, one of the moſt ſalutary reſtoratives they could
take. Their taſte for the coca hath ſo little altered,
that, if thoſe among them who are buried in the mines
were to be deprived of it, they would ceaſe to work,
whatever ſeverities might be employed to compel them
to it.

The conquerors were not ſatisfied either with the liquors or with the food of the people they had ſubdued.
They naturalized freely, and with ſucceſs, all the corn,
all the fruits, and all the quadrupeds of the ancient
hemiſphere, in the new one. The mother-country,
which had propoſed to ſupply its colonies with wine,
oil, and brandy, wiſhed, at firſt, to forbid the culture

of the vine and of the olive tree : but it was foon found, that it would be impoffible to convey regularly to Peru articles liable to fo many accidents, and of fo confiderable a bulk ; and they were permitted to multiply them there as much as was confiftent with the climate and their wants.

After they had provided for a better and a greater choice of fubfiftence, the next care of the Spaniards was to have a drefs more commodious and more agreeable than that of the Peruvians. Thefe were, however, better clothed than any other American nation. They owed this fuperiority to the advantage which they alone poffeffed, of having the lama and the pacos, domeftic animals, which ferve them for this ufe.

Singularities refpecting the lama, the pacos, the guanco, and the vicuna.
The lama is an animal four feet high, and five or fix in length; of which its neck alone takes up one half. Its head is well made, with large eyes, a long fnout, and thick lips. Its mouth hath no incifors in the upper jaw. Its feet are cloven like thofe of the ox, but furnifhed with a fpur behind, which enables it to faften itfelf on the fides of fteep places, where it delights to climb. Its wool, which is fhort on its back, but grows long on its fides and under the belly, conftitutes part of its ufefulnefs. Though very falacious, thefe animals copulate with great difficulty. In vain the female proftitutes herfelf to receive the male, and invites him by her fighs; they are fometimes a whole day groaning, grumbling, and ineffectually attempting enjoyment, if men do not help them to fulfil the defire of nature. Thus feveral of our domeftic animals, that are confined, broken, forced, and reftrained in all their freeft motions and fenfations, lofe, through ineffectual efforts, the principles of generation while they are confined in ftables, if care and attention do not fupply the place of that liberty of which they have been deprived. The females of the lama have only two dugs, never more than two young, commonly but one, which follows the dam immediately after its birth; it is of a very quick growth, and its life of a fhort du-

ration. At three years old it propagates its species, preferves its vigour till twelve, then decays, and dies about the age of fifteen.

The lamas are employed as mules, in carrying on their backs loads of about a hundred weight. They move with a flow but firm pace at the rate of four or five leagues a-day, in countries that are impracticable to other animals; defcending through gullies, and climbing up rocks, where men cannot follow them. After four or five days journey, they reft of their own accord for twenty-four hours.

Nature hath formed them for the people of that climate where they are produced, mild, regular, and phlegmatic, like the Peruvians. When they ftop, they bend their knees and ftoop their body in such a manner as not to difcompofe their burden. As foon as they hear their driver whiftle, they rife with the fame care, and proceed on their journey. They browfe on the grafs they find in their way, and chew the cud at night, even when afleep, reclining on their breaft, with their feet doubled under their belly. They are neither difpirited by fafting nor drudgery, while they have any ftrength remaining; but when they are totally exhaufted or fall under their burden, it is to no purpofe to harafs and beat them : they will continue obftinately ftriking their heads againft the ground, till they kill themfelves. They never defend themfelves either with their feet or their teeth ; and in the height of their indignation content themfelves with only fpitting in the face of thofe who infult them.

The pacos is to the lama what the afs is to the horfe, a fubordinate fpecies, fmaller in fize, with fhorter legs, and a flat fnout ; but of the fame difpofition, the fame manners, and the fame conftitution, as the lama ; made, like the lama, to carry burdens, but more obftinate in its caprices, perhaps becaufe it is weaker.

Thefe animals are fo much the more ufeful to man, as their fervice cofts him nothing. Their thick fur fupplies the place of a pack-faddle. The little grafs which they find along the road fuffices for their food, and furnishes them with a plentiful and fresh saliva, which exempts them from the necessity of drinking.

In the times of the Incas, the people showed a great attachment to these useful animals, and this spirit of benevolence hath been continued. Before they are employed in the labours for which they are adapted, the Peruvians assemble their relations, friends, and neighbours. As soon as the company are met, dancing and festivals begin, which last two days and two nights. From time to time the guests pay a visit to the lamas and the pacos, speak to them in the most affectionate terms, and bestow upon them all the caresses they would upon the person that was most dear to them. They then begin to make use of them, but do not strip them of the ribbands and bands with which their heads are ornamented.

Among the lamas, there are some of a wild species called guanacos, which are stronger, more sprightly, and more nimble, than the domestic lamas; running like the stag, and climbing like the wild goat, covered with short wool, and of a fawn colour. Though free, they like to collect in herds, to the number sometimes of two or three hundred. If they see a man, they survey him at first with an air of greater astonishment than curiosity; then snuffing up the air and neighing, they run all together to the summit of the mountains. These animals seek the North, travel on the ice, and fix themselves above the height of the snow; they are vigorous, and appear in vast numbers on the tops of the Cordeleras; but small in size, and seldom met with at the bottom of the mountains. When they are hunted for their fleece, if they gain the rocks, neither hunters nor dogs can ever catch them.

The vicunas, a species of wild pacos, delight still more in the cold, and on the summits of mountains. They are so timid, that their fear itself makes them an easy prey to the hunter. Men surround them and drive them into narrow defiles, at the end of which they have fufpended pieces of cloth or linen, on cords, that are raifed three or four feet from the ground. Thefe rags, being agitated by the wind, ftrike fuch terror into them that they ftand crowded and fqueezed one againft another, fuffering themfelves to be killed rather than fly. But if there happens to be, among the vicunas, a guanaco, which, being more adventurous, leaps over the cords, they follow it and efcape.

All thefe animals belong fo peculiarly to South America, and efpecially to the higheft Cordeleras, that they are never feen on the fide of Mexico, where the height of thefe mountains is confiderably diminifhed. Attempts have been made to propagate the breed in Europe, but they have all failed. The Spaniards, without reflecting that thefe animals, even in Peru itfelf, fought the coldeft parts, have tranfported them to the burning plains of Andalufia. They might poffibly have fucceeded on the Alps or the Pyrenees. This conjecture of M. de Buffon, to whom we are indebted for fo many ufeful and profound obfervations on animals, is worthy the attention of ftatefmen, whofe fteps ought always to be guided by the lights of philofophy.

The flefh of the lamas and pacos may be eaten when they are young. The fkin of the old ones ferves the Indians for fhoes, and the Spaniards for harnefs. The guanacos may alfo ferve for food. But the vicunas are only fought after for their fleece, and for the bezoar they produce.

The wool of thefe animals is not equally good. That of the lama and the pacos, which are domeftic animals, is much inferior to that of the guanaco, and ftill more to that of the vicuna. There is even a great difference in the fame animal. The wool of the back is commonly of a clear, light colour, and of moderate quality; under the belly it is white and fine, and white and coarfe upon the thighs. Its price, in Spain, is from four to nine livres [from 3s. 4d. to 4s. 2d.] a pound, according to its quality.

Thefe fleeces were ufefully employed at Peru, before the empire had fubmitted to a foreign yoke.   The
inhabitants of Cufco made tapeftry of them for the
ufe of the court.   This tapeftry was ornamented with
flowers, birds, and trees, which were tolerably well
imitated.   It ferved alfo to make mantles which were
worn over a fhirt of cotton.   It was cuftomary to tuck
them up, in order to have the arms free.   The principal people faftened them with gold and filver clafps;
their wives with pins made of thefe metals, ornamented at the top with emeralds; and the common people with thorns.   In hot countries, the mantles of
perfons in office were made of fine cotton, and dyed
with various colours.   The common people in the
fame climate had no clothing at all, except a girdle
that was compofed of the filaments of the bark of a
tree, and ferved to cover thofe parts which nature intended fhould be concealed.

The pride and the habits of the conquerors, which
generally made inconvenient or contemptible to them
all the cuftoms eftablifhed in the countries upon which
their avarice or their fury was exerted, would not allow them to adopt the drefs of the Peruvians.   They
required from Europe every thing that country could
furnifh moft complete and moft magnificent in linens
and cottons.   In procefs of time, the treafures that
had been at firft pillaged, were exhaufted; and it was
not poffible to acquire more, without making confiderable advances, and without entering upon labours,
the profit of which was doubtful.   Then thefe ex-
travagancies diminifhed.   The ancient manufactures
of cotton, which a fyftem of oppreffion had reduced
almoft to nothing, were revived.   Others were fet on
foot of a different kind; and their number hath fucceffively increafed.

With the wool of the vicuna they make, in feveral
provinces, ftockings, handkerchiefs, and fcarfs.   This
wool, mixed with that of the fheep imported thither
from Europe, which hath exceedingly degenerated,
ferves for carpets, and makes alfo tolerably good cloth.

This laſt kind alone is employed to make ſerges and other coarſe ſtuffs.

The manufactures ſubſervient to luxury are eſtabliſhed at Arequipa, Cuſco, and Lima. From theſe three large towns come all the jewels and diamonds, all the plate for the uſe of private perſons, and alſo for the churches. Theſe manufactures are but coarſely wrought, and mixed with a great deal of copper. There is ſeldom more taſte or perfection diſcovered in their gold, ſilver, and other laces and embroideries, which their manufactures alſo produce.

Other hands are employed in gilding leather, in making, with wood and ivory, pieces of inlaid work and ſculpture, and in drawing figures on the marble that hath been lately found at Cuença, or on linen imported from the Old Hemiſphere. Theſe productions of imperfect art ſerve for ornaments for houſes, palaces, and temples : the drawing of them is not abſolutely bad, but the colours are neither exact nor permanent. This ſpecies of induſtry belongs almoſt excluſively to the Indians ſettled at Cuſco, who are leſs oppreſſed, and leſs degenerated upon this firſt ſcene of their glory, than throughout the reſt of the empire. If theſe Americans, to whom nature hath denied the genius of invention, but who are excellent imitators, had been ſupplied with able maſters and excellent models, they would have become good copyiſts. At the cloſe of the laſt century, ſome works of a Peruvian painter, named Michael de St. Jaques, were brought to Rome ; and the connoiſſeurs diſcovered marks of genius in them.

Theſe deſcriptions excite the complaints of ſome of my readers. I hear them ſay, How can we be intereſted in theſe idle details, with which you have troubled us ſo long ? Speak to us of the gold and of the ſilver of Peru. In this ſo diſtant region of the New World, *I have never conſidered, and ſhall never conſider, any thing but theſe metals.* Whoever thou mayeſt be that doſt addreſs thyſelf to me in this manner, avaricious mortal, and deſtitute of taſte, who, when conveyed to Mexico and Peru, wouldſt neither ſtudy the manners nor the cuſtoms, who wouldſt diſdain to caſt a look upon the rivers, the mountains, the foreſts, the fields, the diverſity of climate, and the varieties of fiſh and inſects; but who wouldſt only aſk, where are the golden mines? where are the places in which the gold is wrought? I ſee that thou haſt entered upon the reading of my work with the ſame ſpirit as the fero-cious Europeans entered upon theſe rich and unhappy countries; I ſee that thou wert worthy to accompany them, becauſe thy propenſities are the ſame as theirs. Deſcend then into the mines, and meet with thy de-ſtruction by the ſide of thoſe who work them for thee; and if thou doſt come out of them again, make thy-ſelf at leaſt acquainted with the criminal ſource of theſe fatal treaſures which thou doſt covet; and may-eſt thou never poſſeſs them hereafter without feeling the pangs of remorſe. May the gold change its co-lour, and appear to thine eyes as if it were dyed with blood.

Deſcription of the mines of Peru, and parti-cularly thoſe of platina and quickſilver.
In the country of the Incas are found mines of cop-per, tin, ſulphur, and bitumen, which are generally ne-glected. Extreme neceſſity hath occaſioned ſome at-tention to be paid to thoſe of ſalt. This foſſil is cut into large pieces, proportioned to the ſtrength of the lamas and pacos, deſtined to convey it in all the pro-vinces of the empire diſtant from the ocean. This ſalt is of a violet colour, and is ſtreaked with veins of red like the jaſper. It is ſold neither by weight nor mea-ſure, but in pieces nearly of equal ſize.

A new ſubſtance has been diſcovered lately in theſe regions: this is the platina, ſo called from the Spaniſh word *plata*, from whence the diminutive *platina*, or little ſilver, is made.

This is a metallic ſubſtance, which hath hitherto been brought from the New World into the Old, on-ly in the form of ſmall, pointed, triangular, and very irregular gravel, like the coarſe filings of iron. Its co-lour is that of a white between that of ſilver and iron, partaking a little of the tenacity of lead.

M. Ulloa is the firſt who has ſpoken of the platina, B o o k in the account he publiſhed, in 1748, of a long voyage ^{VII.} to Peru, from whence he was juſt returned. He informed Europe that this extraordinary ſubſtance, and which may be conſidered as an eighth metal, came from the gold mines of America, and was particularly found in thoſe of the new kingdom.

The year following, Wood, an Engliſh metallurgiſt, brought ſome ſpecimens of it from Jamaica to Great Britain. He had received them eight or nine years before from Carthagena, and was the firſt perſon who made experiments upon them.

Some very ſkilful chemiſts have ſince employed themſelves in experiments and inquiries upon the platina; in England, Mr. Lewis; in Sweden, M. Scheffer; in Pruſſia, M. Margraff; and in France, M. M. Macquer, Beaumé, De Buffon, De Morveau, De Sickengen, and De Milly. The united labours of theſe ſeveral chemiſts have ſo much improved our knowledge upon this article, that we do not ſcruple to ſay, there are few metallic ſubſtances, the nature of which is better known to us at preſent than the platina. That which comes into France is never entirely pure. It is uſually mixed with rather a conſiderable quantity of ſmall black ſand, which is as ſtrongly affected by the loadſtone as the beſt iron, but which is indiſſoluble in acids, and cannot be melted without great difficulty; and laſtly, particles of very fine gold are ſometimes obſerved in it.

This mixture, which is almoſt always found, of the native platina with gold and with iron, had raiſed a ſuſpicion that it might be nothing more than a combination of theſe two metals; and accordingly, on melting together gold and iron, or rather gold and magnetic ſand, ſimilar to that which is found mixed with the platina, a combination is obtained, which hath ſome apparent affinities with this metallic ſubſtance: but a more ſtrict examination ſeems to have deſtroyed this opinion, and the experiments of M. M. Macquer and Beaumé, and particularly thoſe of M. le

Baron de Sickengen, appear to have fhown that the
platina is a peculiar kind of metal, which is not formed by the union of any other, and which hath properties belonging to itfelf.

The little information which chemifts have hitherto
obtained refpecting the natural hiftory of the platina,
and the fmall quantity they have had in their poffeffion, hath not yet allowed them to apply the proceffes
of metallurgy to it at large; but the methods they
have given an account of, and particularly thofe for
which we are indebted to the Baron de Sickengen,
are fufficient for chemical accuracy. Nothing remains
now but to make them more fimple and lefs expenfive.

The firft operation to be performed on the platina
confifts in feparating from it the gold, the iron, and
the magnetic fand, with which it is united. In order
to do this, it is diffolved with the affiftance of a little
heat, in an aqua regia, compofed nearly of equal parts
of the nitrous and marine acid. The magnetic fand,
which is indiffoluble, remains at the bottom of the veffel; and, by pouring off the liquor, a folution is obtained, which contains gold, iron, and platina. To
feparate, in the firft inftance, the gold, a fmall portion
of the vitriolum martis is added to the folution. The
gold immediately precipitates, while the platina continues united to the folvent. Laftly, to get rid of the
iron, fome alkali, which hath been previoufly calcined
with ox's blood, is poured *guttatim* into the fame liquor. The iron is inftantly precipitated, under the
colour of Pruffian blue, and nothing more remains in
the folution than the platina, perfectly pure, and combined with the aqua regia.

The platina being thus purified, the next bufinefs is
to feparate it from the folvent; and this is to be done
by the addition of fal ammoniac. This fubftance precipitates the platina under a yellow colour; and this
precipitate being expofed to a great heat, foftens, and
even diffolves; and, by forging it with a hammer, the
platina is obtained very pure and malleable. It appears from what we have been able to collect from the

Baron de Sickengen's Memoir, which hath been communicated to the Academy of Sciences, but not yet
published, that the rough platina, worked by itself,
and heated with an intense fire, becomes sufficiently
soft to be forged and made into bars; and this circumstance naturally indicates the method to be pursued for the management of it in large works.

The metal obtained by these several processes is
nearly of the same specific weight as gold; it is of an
intermediate colour between that of iron and silver;
it can be forged and extended into thin plates; it may
also be worked into thread; but it is not near so duc-
tile as gold; and the thread obtained from it is not, in
equal diameter, able to support so great a weight without breaking. When dissolved in aqua regia, it may
be made to assume, by precipitation, an infinite diver-
sity of colours; and Count Milly hath succeeded in
varying these precipitates so much, that he hath had
a picture painted, in the colouring of which there is
scarce any thing but platina made use of.

Gold is susceptible of combination with all the metals, and platina hath in like manner this property;
but when too great a proportion of it enters into the
combination, it renders the metal brittle. When allied with yellow copper, it forms a hard and compact
metal, which will take the finest polish, which will not
tarnish in the air, and which would consequently be
very fit for making the mirrors of telescopes.

It doth not appear that mercury hath any effect upon platina; and therefore Mr. Lewis had proposed to
amalgamate it with mercury, as a proper method of
separating it from the gold with which it might have
been united; but this method hath been considered
by modern chemists as uncertain and defective; and
there are others at present more to be depended upon:
such are those we have been mentioning at the commencement of this article.

This new metal displays some properties infinitely
interesting to society. It cannot be affected by any
simple acid, nor by any known solvent, except the

aqua regia; it will not tarnifh in the air, neither will
it ruft; it unites to the fixednefs of gold, and to the
property it hath of not being fufceptible of deftruction, a hardnefs almoft equal to that of iron, and a
much greater difficulty of fufion. In a word, from
confidering the advantages of the platina, we cannot
but conclude, that this metal deferves, at leaft, from
its fuperiority to all others, to fhare the title of king
of the metals, of which gold hath fo long been in poffeffion.

It were undoubtedly to be wifhed that a metal fo
precious might become common, and that it might be
employed for culinary utenfils, in the arts, and in the
laboratory of the chemift. It would unite all the advantages of veffels of glafs, of porcelain, and of ftone
ware, without partaking of their fragility. A prejudice of the Spanifh miniftry, and which hath for a
long time been adopted by all chemifts, deprives us of
this advantage. They have perfuaded themfelves that
the platina might be allied with gold in fuch a manner
as that it could not be feparated from it by any means,
and they have confequently thought proper to forbid
the extraction and tranfportation of a fubftance that
might be productive of fo much mifchief in the hands
of avaricious men. But at prefent, that we are acquainted with methods as fimple and eafy to feparate
gold from platina, as to feparate filver from gold; at
prefent, that the chemifts have taught us, that, when
thefe two metals are diffolved in aqua regia, we may
precipitate the gold by the addition of the vitriolum
martis, or the platina by the addition of fal ammoniac, and that in both thefe cafes the two metals are
perfectly diftinct; at prefent, in a word, that the rulers
of nations can eafily obtain information by confulting
the academies, it cannot be doubted but that the Spanifh government will haften to avail itfelf of a treafure
of which it feems hitherto to have been the only pof-
feffor, and of which fo advantageous a ufe may be
made for the nation and for fociety in general.

Nature hath not formed any mines of gold or filver

in what are called the Valleys of Peru, except one. B O O K
The large maſſes of theſe precious metals which we VII.
ſometimes find there, have been conveyed by ſubter-
raneous fires, by volcanos, and by earthquakes, as well
as by the revolutions which America hath experienced, and doth ſtill experience every day. Theſe detached maſſes are ſometimes found in other parts.
About the year 1730, a piece of gold, weighing ninety marks, was found near the town of La Paz. It was
a compoſition of ſix different ſpecies of this precious
metal, from eighteen to three and twenty carats and a
half. There are but few ores, and thoſe of baſe alloy,
in the hillocks bordering upon the ſea. It is only in
very cold or very high places that they are rich and
frequent.

Though the Peruvians were unacquainted with coin,
they knew the uſe of gold and ſilver, of which they
made toys and even vaſes. The torrents and rivers
furniſhed them with the firſt of theſe metals; but, in
order to obtain the ſecond, more labour and induſtry
was neceſſary. Moſt frequently the ground was opened, yet never to ſo great a depth but that the workmen themſelves could throw the ore on the borders of
the ditch which they had digged, or could at leaſt convey it there by paſſing it on from one perſon to another. Sometimes the ſides of the mountains were opened, and the different veins which chance might preſent
were followed, though always to very ſmall extent.
The two metals were melted and diſengaged from the
foreign materials that might be mixed with them by
the means of fire. Furnaces, in which a current of air
ſupplied the office of the bellows, an inſtrument entirely unknown in theſe countries, were employed to perform this difficult operation.

Porco, at a little diſtance from the ſpot where one
of the lieutenants of Pizarro founded, in 1539, the city
of La Plata, Porco was, of all the mines which the Incas cauſed to be worked, the moſt plentiful and the
moſt known. It was alſo the firſt which the Spaniards

B O O K worked after the conqueſt; and their labour was ſoon
   VII.   extended to a multiplicity of others.

All of them, without exception, were found to be
very expenſive in the working. Nature hath placed
them in regions deſtitute of water, wood, proviſions, and
all the neceſſaries of life, which muſt be conveyed at
a great expence acroſs immenſe deſerts. Theſe difficulties have been, and are ſtill, ſurmounted with more
or leſs ſucceſs.

Several mines, which have acquired ſome ſhare of
reputation, have been ſucceſſively abandoned. Their
produce, though equal to what it was originally, was
not ſufficient to defray the expences neceſſary to obtain it : this is a kind of revolution which many of the
reſt will experience.

It hath alſo been neceſſary to renounce ſome of the
mines which had given falſe hopes. Among this number was that of Ucantaya, diſcovered in 1703, ſixty
leagues to the ſouth-eaſt of Cuſco. This was only an
incruſtation of almoſt maſſive ſilver, which at firſt
yielded a conſiderable quantity, but was ſoon exhauſted.

Some very rich mines have been neglected, becauſe
the waters had invaded them. The declivity of the
ſoil, which from the ſummit of the Cordeleirias runs
continually ſhelving to the South Sea, muſt neceſſarily have rendered theſe events more common at Peru
than in other places. This miſchief hath ſometimes
been found irremediable; at other times it hath been
repaired; moſt frequently it hath been perpetuated,
for want of means, activity, or ſkill.

The gold mines were at firſt preferably attended to.
Wiſe men ſoon determined in favour of the ſilver
mines, which are generally more extenſive, more equal,
and, conſequently, leſs deceitful. Several of the former, however, are ſtill worked. A tolerably regular
ſeries of ſucceſs hath made thoſe of Lutixaca, of Ara-
ça, of Suches, of Caracava, of Lipoani, and of Cacha-
bamba, to be conſidered as the richeſt.

Among the filver mines which, in our days, are the B O O K
moft celebrated, we muft mention that of Huantaja- VII.
ha, which hath been worked forty or fifty years ago,
at two leagues diftance from the fea, near the harbour
of Iqueyqua. Upon digging five or fix feet in the
plain, we often find detached maffes, which at firft
might be taken only for a confufed mixture of gravel
and fand, and which, upon trial, yield two-thirds of
their weight in filver. Sometimes they are fo confiderable, that, in 1749, two of them were fent to the
court of Spain, one of which weighed one hundred
and feventy-five pounds, and the other three hundred
and feventy. In the mountains, the ore is difpofed in
veins, and is of two kinds. That which in the country is called *barra*, is cut with the rock, and is fent to
Lima, where it is wrought. It yields moft frequently
from one, two, three, four, and as far as five, parts of
filver, to one of ftone. The other fpecies is purified
by fire, in the country itfelf. If five of its quintals do
not produce a mark of filver, it is thrown among the
rubbifh. This negleƈt arifes from the exceffive dearnefs of provifions, from the neceffity of obtaining water fit for drinking fourteen leagues off, and from that
of grinding the ore at a very confiderable diftance.

At thirty leagues to the north-eaft of Arequipa
ftands Caylloma. Its mines were difcovered very early: they have been fince inceffantly worked, and their
produce is ftill the fame.

Thofe of Potofi were difcovered in 1545. An Indian, named Hualpa, as it is faid, purfuing fome deer,
in order to climb certain fteep rocks, laid hold of a
bufh, the roots of which being loofened from the earth,
brought to view an ingot of filver. The Peruvian had
recourfe to it for his own ufe, and never failed to return to his treafure every time that his wants or his
defires folicited him to it. The change that had happened in his fortune was remarked by his countryman
Guanca, to whom he avowed the fecret. The two
friends could not keep their counfel, and enjoy their
good fortune. They quarrelled; and the indifcreet

B O O K confidant difcovered the whole to his mafter Villaroell,
VII. a Spaniard who was fettled in the neighbourhood.

This difcovery foon inflamed the minds of the Spaniards. Several mines were immediately opened in a
mountain of a conical form, which is one league in
circumference, five or fix toifes in height, and is of a
dark red colour. In procefs of time, a lefs confiderable mountain, iffuing from the former, was alfo fearched, and with equal fuccefs. The treafures that were
derived from each of thefe mountains, were the origin
of one of the largeft and moft opulent cities in the
New World.

Nature never offered to the avidity of mankind, in
any country on the globe, fuch rich mines as thofe of
Potofi. Exclufive of what was not regiftered, and
was fmuggled away, the fifth part, belonging to
the government, from 1545 to 1564, amounted to
36,450,000 livres [1,518,075l.] *per annum*. But this
abundance of metals foon decreafed. From 1564 to
1585, the annual fifth part amounted to no more than
15,187,489 livres 4 fols [632,812l. 1s.]. From 1585
to 1624, it amounted to 12,149,994 livres 12 fols
[506,249l. 15s. 6d.]. From 1624 to 1633, to 6,074,997
livres 6 fols [253,124l. 17s. 9d.]. From this laft period, the produce of thefe mines hath fo evidently decreafed, that, in 1763, the fifth part, belonging to the
king, did not exceed 1,364,682 livres 12 fols [56,861l.
15s. 9d.].

In the firft inftance, each quintal of ore yielded fifty
pounds of filver. At prefent, fifty quintals do not
produce more than two pounds of filver. This is one
part inftead of twelve hundred and fifty.

If this diminution fhould be carried on a little further, this fource of riches muft neceffarily be given up.
It is even probable, that this event would already have
taken place, if the ore were not fo foft at Potofi, if
the waters were not fo favourably fituated for grinding
it, and if the expences were not infinitely lefs than at
any other place.

But while the mines of Potofi were gradually lofing

their celebrity, thofe of Oruro, not far diftant from them, were rifing into great reputation. Their profperity was even increafing, when the waters flowed into the richeft of them. At the period in which we are writing, it hath not yet been poffible to drain them, and all thefe treafures ftill remain under water. The mines of Popo, the moft confiderable of thofe that have efcaped this great difafter, are no more than twelve leagues diftant from the town of San Philip de Auftria de Gruro, which was built in this diftrict, formerly fo celebrated.

The labours of the miners, fettled to the eaft of La Plata, in the diftrict of Carangas, were never difturbed by any accident; thofe, however, whom chance had brought to Turco were conftantly the moft fortunate, becaufe this mountain always afforded them an ore incorporated, or, as it were, melted with the ftone, and confequently richer than all the reft.

In the diocefe of La Paz, and near to the fmall town of Puna, Jofeph Salcedo difcovered, about the year 1660, the mine of Laycacota. It was fo rich, that the filver of it was often cut with a chifel. Profperity, which debafes little minds, had fo elevated that of the proprietor of fo much opulence, that he permitted all the Spaniards who came to feek their fortune in this part of the New World, to work fome days for their own benefit, without weighing or meafuring the prefent he made them. This generofity attracted an infinite number of adventurers, whofe avidity induced them to take up arms. They attacked each other; and their benefactor, who had neglected nothing that might prevent or extinguifh their fanguinary contentions, was hanged as being the author of them. Such incidents might be fufficient to leffen in our hearts the inclination to benevolence; and it is with reluctance I have mentioned this.

While Salcedo was in prifon, the water got poffeffion of his mine. Superftition foon gave birth to the idea, that this was a punifhment for the outrage committed againft him. This idea of divine vengeance

B O O K was for a long time revered; but at length, in 1740,
VII.   Diego de Baena, and some other enterprising men, associated themselves, in order to turn away the springs
which had deluged so much treasure. In 1754, the
work was so far advanced, that some utility was already derived from it. We know not what hath happened since that period.

All the mines of Peru were originally worked by
means of fire. In most of them, mercury was substituted to this in 1571.

This powerful agent is found in two different states
in the bosom of the earth. If it be altogether pure,
and in the fluid form which is proper to it, it is then
denominated virgin mercury, because it hath not experienced the action of fire, in order to be extracted
from the mine. If it be found combined with sulphur,
it forms a substance of a red colour, which is more or
less vivid, called cinnabar.

Till the mine of virgin mercury, which was lately
discovered at Montpelier under the buildings of the
town itself, and which for that reason will probably
never be worked, there had been no others known in
Europe, except those of Udria in Carniola. These are
in a valley, at the foot of high mountains, which were
called by the Romans *Alpes Juliæ*. They were discovered by chance in 1497. They are about nine hundred feet deep. The descent into them is by pits, as
into all other mines. There are under ground an infinite number of galleries, of which some are so low, that
it is necessary to stoop, in order to pass along; and there
are places where it is so hot, that it is not possible to
stop without being in a profuse sweat: it is in these
subterraneous caverns that mercury is found, in a kind
of clay, or in stones. Sometimes even this substance
is seen running down like rain, and oozes so copiously
through the rocks which form the vaults of these subterraneous caverns, that one man hath often gathered
thirty-six pounds of it in a day.

There are some people so fond of the marvellous,
that they prefer this mercury to the other; which is a

mere prejudice. Experience fhows, that the beft mercury that can be ufed, either in medicine or in metallurgy, is that which hath been extracted from cinnabar. In order to feparate the natural combination of thefe two volatile fubftances, fulphur and mercury, recourfe muft neceffarily be had to the action of fire, to which fome intermediate fubftance muft be joined. This is either the filings of fteel or copper, or the regulus of antimony, or lime, or fome fixed alkaline falt. Europe is fupplied with this laft fpecies of mercury from Hungary, Sclavonia, Bohemia, Carinthia, Friuli, and Normandy. The quantity that Spain wants for Mexico comes from the mine of Almaden, which was famous even in the time of the Romans: but Peru hath found within itfelf, at Guança-Velica, a fufficient quantity for all its exigencies.

This ore, as it is faid, was known to the ancient Peruvians, who made no other ufe of it than to paint their faces. It was forgotten during the confufion into which the conqueft plunged this unfortunate region. It was found again in 1556, according to fome hiftorians, and in 1564, according to others; but Pedro Fernandez Velafco was the firft who, in 1574, thought of employing it in working the other mines: the government referved to itfelf the property of it. They even forbade, upon any pretence whatfoever, that other mines of the fame kind fhould be opened, left they fhould be defrauded of the duties they laid upon mercury.

The mine of Guança-Velica hath undergone feveral changes. At the time in which we are writing, its circumference meafures one hundred and eighty varas, its diameter fixty, and its depth five hundred and thirteen. It hath four openings, all of them at the top of the mountain, a fmall number of buttreffes, deftined to fupport the foil, and three vent-holes, which either let in air, or ferve to carry off the waters. It is worked by fome partners, moft of them without fortune, to whom the fovereign advances whatever they want, and who deliver the mercury to him at his ftipulated

BOOK price. The men employed in these labours were ge-
VII. nerally seized, formerly, with convulsive motions.
This malady is at present much less frequent; whether it be, that the mercury contained in the mine
hath lessened by more than one-half, or that some precautions have been taken, which had at first been neglected. Those who have the care of the furnaces,
are at present almost the only persons who are exposed
to this calamity: they are, however, easily cured. The
only thing necessary is to send them into a warm climate, or to employ them in cultivating the lands. The
mercury, which affected their limbs, is carried off by
perspiration.

The barrenness of Guança-Velica, and of the neighbouring lands, is remarkable. No fruit tree can be
naturalized there. Of all the species of corn that
have been sown, barley is the only one that hath
sprung up; and even that hath never come to maturity. Nothing but the potato has thriven.

The air is not more wholesome than the soil is fertile. Children, newly born, die of the tetanos still
more frequently than in the rest of the New World.
Those who have escaped this danger, are seized at the
end of three or four months with a violent cough, and
most of them perish in convulsions, unless care be tak-
en to convey them into a milder climate. This precaution, which is necessary for the Indians and for the
Mestees, is still more so for the Spaniards, who are less
robust. The extreme severity of the climate, the sul-
phureous vapours which cover the horizon, and the
generally vitiated constitution of the fathers and mothers, must be the principal causes of so great a calamity.

The very elevated mountains of Guança-Velica had
for a long time engaged the attention of men who are
greedy of riches, when, at length, they became interesting to philosophers.

The astronomers who were sent in 1735 to Peru, in
order to measure the degrees of the meridian, travelled
over a space of ninety leagues, beginning a little to the

north of the equator, and proceeding as far as the fouth B o o к
of the city of Cuenca, without difcovering any mark VII.
which could lead them to think that thefe mountains,
which were the higheft in the univerfe, had been ever
covered by the ocean. The banks of fhells that were
found out fome time after at Chili, did not prove the
contrary, becaufe they were upon eminences of no
more than fifty toifes. But fince Guança-Velica hath
furnifhed recent and petrified fhells, and both of them
in very great quantity, it is neceffary to retract, and
give up all the confequences that had been deduced
from this phenomenon.

It is not at Guança-Velica that the mercury is delivered to the public. The government fends it to the
provinces where the mines are. The places where it
is depofited are twelve in number. In 1763, Guança-
Velica itfelf confumed one hundred and forty-two
quintals; Taiya, two hundred and forty-feven; Pafca,
feven hundred and twenty-nine; Truxillo, one hundred and thirty-one; Cufco, thirteen; La Plata, three
hundred and fixty-nine; La Paz, thirty; Caylloma,
three hundred and feventy-four; Caranjas, one hundred and fifty; Oruro, twelve hundred and fixty-four;
and Potofi, one thoufand feven hundred and ninety-
two. This made, on the whole, five thoufand two
hundred and forty-one quintals.

Although the quality of the ore determines the
greater or lefs confumption of the mercury, yet it is
generally thought in the other hemifphere, where the
art of metallurgy is very imperfect, that, upon the
whole, the confumption of mercury is equal to the
quantity of filver obtained from the mines. In this
fuppofition, the twelve magazines which, from 1732
to 1763, delivered, one year with another, five thoufand three hundred and four quintals eighteen pounds
of mercury, fhould have received the fame quantity of
filver. Neverthelefs, they received no more than two
thoufand two hundred and fifty. Therefore, two thoufand feven hundred and fifty-four quintals eighteen
pounds were fecreted, in order to defraud the cuftoms.

B O O K
VII.

Subverfion
and re-
building of
Lima.
Manners of
this capital
of Peru.

Lima hath always attracted the greateſt part of theſe riches, whether they have eſcaped the vigilance of the treaſury or not.   This capital, built in 1535 by Francis Pizarro, and which hath ſince become ſo celebrated, is ſituated at two leagues from the ſea, in a delicious plain.   The proſpect from it on one ſide extends over a tranquil ocean, on the other it ſtretches as far as the Cordeleirias.   Its ſoil is nothing but a heap of flints, which the ſea hath undoubtedly in a ſeries of ages piled together, but they are covered with earth a foot below the ſurface, which the ſpring waters, that are every where found on digging, have brought from the mountains.

Sugar-canes, numberleſs olive trees, ſome vines, artificial meadows, paſtures full of ſalt which give meat an exquiſite taſte, ſmall grain appropriated to the feeding of fowls, fruit-trees of every kind, and certain other plantations, cover the ſurface of theſe fortunate plains.   Wheat and barley proſpered there for a long time ; but an earthquake happening about a century ago, cauſed ſuch a revolution, that the ſeeds rotted without ſprouting.   It was not till after forty years of barrenneſs, that the ſoil reſumed its former fertility. Lima, as well as the other towns of the valleys, owes its ſubſiſtence chiefly to the labours of the negroes.   It is ſcarce any where, except the inland parts, that the fields are cultivated by the Indians.

Before the arrival of the Spaniards, all the edifices in Peru were conſtructed without any foundations. The walls of the houſes of private perſons, as well as thoſe of the public buildings, were alike placed on the ſurface of the earth, of whatever materials they might be made.   Experience had taught theſe people, that in the country they inhabited this was the only way of dwelling in ſecurity.   Their conquerors, who had a ſovereign contempt for every thing which deviated from their habits, and who carried every where along with them their European cuſtoms, without conſidering whether they were ſuitable to the countries they were invading ; the conquerors departed, particularly

at Lima, from the manner of building which they BOOK
found generally eſtabliſhed. Accordingly, when the VII.
natives of the country ſaw them open deep trenches,
and make uſe of cement, they ſaid that their tyrants
were digging graves to bury themſelves in ; and, perhaps, it was ſome conſolation to the wretchedneſs of
the conquered to foreſee, that the earth would one day
take upon itſelf to avenge them of their deſtroyers.

The prediction hath been fulfilled. The capital of
Peru, after having been partially ſubverted by eleven
earthquakes, was at length totally deſtroyed by the
twelfth. On the 28th of October 1746, at half an
hour after ten at night, all, or almoſt all the buildings,
whether large or ſmall, were thrown down in the ſpace
of three minutes. Thirteen hundred perſons were cruſhed under the ruins. A much more conſiderable number were mutilated ; and moſt of them expired in horrid torments.

Callao, which ſerves as a harbour to Lima, was likewiſe overthrown ; but this was the leaſt of its misfortunes. The ſea, which had ſtarted back with horror
at the inſtant of this dreadful cataſtrophe, ſoon returned to invade with its impetuous waves the ſpace
it had quitted. It ſwallowed up the few houſes and
fortifications that had eſcaped the former danger. Of
the four thouſand inhabitants that were computed to
be in this celebrated port, there were only two hundred ſaved. It then contained three-and-twenty ſhips ;
nineteen of them were ſwallowed up, and the reſt
thrown very far in upon the land by the irritated
ocean.

The ravage extended itſelf all over the coaſt. The
few veſſels there were in theſe bad harbours were ſhat-
tered. The towns in the valleys ſuſtained in general
ſome damages ; ſeveral of them even were totally ſubverted. Among the mountains, four or five volcanos
threw out ſuch prodigious columns of water, that the
whole country was deluged by them.

The minds of men, which had been for a long time
in a ſtate of lethargy, were rouſed by this fatal cala-

mity; and it was Lima that firſt ſet the example of the change. The buſineſs was to clear away immenſe ruins heaped one upon another; and to get out prodigious treaſures that were buried in theſe ruins. It was neceſſary to bring from Guayaquil, and from a ſtill greater diſtance, every requiſite for the conſtruction of numberleſs edifices; and with all theſe materials, collected from theſe different regions, to raiſe a city ſuperior to that which had been deſtroyed. Theſe miracles, which were not to be expected from an indolent and effeminate people, were performed with great rapidity. Neceſſity inſpired them with activity, emulation, and induſtry. Lima, though, perhaps, leſs wealthy, is at preſent more agreeable than in 1682, when its gates preſented to the view of the Duke of Palata, the viceroy, on his entering, ſtreets paved with ſilver. It is alſo built with greater ſolidity, and for the following reaſon:

The vanity of having palaces, concealed for a long time from the inhabitants of the capital of Peru the dangers to which this abſurd oſtentation expoſed them. In vain had the earth ſwallowed up at different periods theſe enormous maſſes; the leſſon was never powerful enough to correct them. The laſt cataſtrophe hath at length opened their eyes. They have yielded to neceſſity, and have at laſt followed the example of other Spaniards ſettled in the valleys.

The houſes are at preſent very low, and have moſt of them no more than a ground-floor. For walls they have poſts placed at different diſtances. The intervals are filled up with reeds, nearly ſimilar to ours, but which have no cavity, which are very ſolid, which do not eaſily rot, and which are covered over with clay. Theſe ſingular edifices are topped with a wooden roof entirely flat, and alſo covered with clay, a ſufficient precaution in a climate where it never rains. The ſeveral parts of theſe buildings are faſtened together, and to the foundations with a ſtrong kind of oſier, which in the country is called chaglar. With this kind of conſtruction, the whole building readily yields to the motion communicated to it by the earthquakes. They may poffibly be damaged by the convulfive motions of nature, but they cannot be eafily thrown down.

Thefe houfes, however, are not deficient in appearance. The attention that is taken to paint the walls and cornices, fo as to refemble free-ftone, conceals the quality of the materials of which they are formed. They are even found to have an air of grandeur and folidity, which it would not be natural to expect. The defect of conftruction is ftill more concealed in the infide of the houfes, where all the ornaments are painted in a ftyle of greater or lefs elegance. The ordinary method of conftruction hath been but a little deviated from in the public buildings. Several of them are raifed to the height of ten feet, with bricks baked in the fun; fome of the churches even are raifed to the fame height in ftone. The reft of thefe monuments are in wood, painted or gilt; as well as the columns and ftatues which decorate them.

The ftreets of Lima are wide, parallel, and interfect each other at right angles. Its walls are continually wafhed and refrefhed by waters brought from the river of Rimac. The water that is not employed in this falutary purpofe, is advantageoufly diftributed for the convenience of the citizens, for the ufe of the gardens, and for fertilizing the fields.

The fcourges of nature, which have revived induftry to a certain degree in Lima, have had lefs influence on the manners of its inhabitants.

Superftition, which reigns throughout the whole extent of the Spanifh dominions, hath at Peru two fceptres at its command; one of gold, for the ufurping and triumphant nation; the other of iron, for the enflaved and pillaged inhabitants. The fcapulary and the rofary are all the tokens of religion which the monks require of the Spaniards of Peru. It is on the form and colour of thefe kinds of talifmans that the populace and the grandees found the profperity of their undertakings, the fuccefs of their amorous intrigues, and the hopes of their falvation. The monkifh habit,

BOOK assumed in the last moments, constitutes the security
VII. of opulent people who have lived ill; they are convinced, that when wrapt in this clothing, which is so
formidable to the devil, that avenging power of crimes
will not dare to descend into their graves and seize upon their souls. If their ashes repose near the altar, they
hope to.partake of the sacrifices of the pontiffs, much
more than the poor and the slaves.

Influenced by such fatal errors, what enormities will
they not commit to acquire riches, which secure their
happiness in this world and in the next? The vanity of
immortalizing their name, and the promise of eternal
life, secure to the monks a fortune, which can no longer
be enjoyed; and families are disappointed of an inheritance, whether acquired by honesty or fraud, by legacies which serve to enrich men who have discovered
the secret of escaping poverty by devoting themselves
to it. Thus it is that the order of sentiments, ideas,
and things, is subverted; and the children of opulent
fathers are condemned to misery by the pious rapaci-
ousness of a number of voluntary mendicants. The
English, the Dutch, and the French, lose their national prejudices by travelling; the Spaniard carries
his along with him throughout the whole universe;
and such is the madness of bequeathing legacies to the
church, that the ground of all the houses of Peru belongs to the priesthood, or pays them some share of
rent. The institution of monkish orders hath done at
Peru, what the law of the *Vacuf* will do, sooner or
later, at Constantinople. Here the people bequeath
their fortunes to a minaret, in order to secure it to
their heirs; there they deprive an heir of it, by leaving it to a monastery from the dread of being damn-
ed. The motives are a little different, but in the end
the effect is the same. In both countries the church
is the gulf, in which all the riches are absorbed; and
these Castilians, who were heretofore so formidable,
shrink before superstition, as Asiatic slaves do in the
presence of their despot.

These extravagances might induce one to suppose

thefe people totally ftupid; but this would be an injuftice. Since the beginning of the century, good
books are common enough at Lima; the people are
not entirely deftitute of knowledge; and we may be
allowed to fay, that the French navigators, during the
war for the fucceffion, implanted fome good principles
among them. Neverthelefs the ancient habits have
loft but little of their force. The Spanifh Creole lives
conftantly among courtezans, or amufes himfelf at
home in drinking the herb of Paraguay. He would
be afraid to diminifh the joys of love by confining it
within legitimate bonds. His inclination leads him
to marry in the country behind the church, that is an
expreffion, which fignifies living in a ftate of concu-
binage. In vain do the bifhops anathematize every
year, at Eafter, thofe perfons who are united in thefe
illicit bonds. But what power have thefe vain terrors
againft the impulfe of amorous defires, againft cuftom,
and efpecially againft the climate, which is continually ftruggling with, and at laft proves victorious over
all the civil and religious laws that oppofe its influence?

The charms of the Peruvian women are fuperior to
the terror which the fpiritual arms of Rome infpire.
The majority of them, efpecially the women of Lima,
have eyes fparkling with vivacity, a fair fkin, a complexion that is delicate, animated, full of fprightli-
nefs and life, and a flender and well-formed fhape; a
foot better turned and fmaller than that of the Spanifh women themfelves; thick and black hair, flowing as if by chance, and without ornament, over their
neck and fhoulders; which are extremely white.

Thefe various natural graces are heightened by every
improvement that art can add to them. The clothing
of the women is moft fumptuous, and they ufe an unbounded profufion of pearls and diamonds in every
kind of drefs in which it is poffible to introduce them.
It is even looked upon as a fort of grandeur and dignity, to fuffer thefe valuable articles to be miflaid or
loft. A woman even who hath no titles, and is not
ennobled, feldom appears in public without gold tiffues

and without jewels. She never goes out without being attended by three or four flaves, moft of them
Mulatto women, in liveries as the men are, and adorned with lace as their miftreffes.

Perfumes are in general ufe at Lima. The women
are never without amber; they fcent their linen and
their clothes with it, and even their nofegays, as if
there were fomething wanting to the natural perfume
of flowers. The amber is undoubtedly an additional
allurement to the men, and the flowers impart a new
attraction to the women. With thefe they adorn their
fleeves, and fometimes their hair like fhepherdeffes.

The tafte for mufic, which prevails throughout all
Peru, is converted into a paffion in the capital. The
walls refound with nothing but finging, and concerts
of vocal and inftrumental mufic. Balls are frequent.
The people dance here with furprifing lightnefs; but
they neglect the graces of the arms, to attend to the
agility of the feet, and efpecially to the inflections of
the body; as images of the true emotions of voluptuoufnefs.

Such are the pleafures which the women, who are
all dreffed rather with elegance than modefty, tafte
and diffufe at Lima. But it is particularly in thofe
delicious faloons where they receive company, that
they appear feducing. There, carelefsly reclined on
a couch, which is a foot and a half high, and five or
fix feet wide, and upon carpets and fuperb cufhions,
they pafs their days in tranquillity and in delicious
repofe. The men who are admitted to their conver-
fation, feat themfelves at fome diftance, unlefs their
adorers, from greater intimacy, be permitted to come
up to the couch, which is, as it were, the fanctuary of
worfhip and of the idol. Yet thefe goddeffes choofe
rather to be affable than haughty; and, banifhing ceremony, they play on the harp and guittar, and fing
and dance when they are defired.

The moft diftinguifhed citizens find in thofe *majorafcos*, or perpetual entails, tranfmitted to them by the
firft conquerors their anceftors, a fufficiency to anfwer

thefe profufions : but the landed eftates have not been
adequate to the expences of a great number even of
very ancient families. Moft of them have had recourfe
to trade. An employment fo worthy of man, and
which extends at once his activity, his knowledge, and
his power, hath never appeared to them to derogate
from their nobility ; and the laws have given a fanction to a mode of thinking fo rational and fo ufeful.
Their capitals, added to the remittances that are continually fent from the inland countries, have rendered
Lima the centre of all the tranfactions which the provinces of Peru carry on, either among themfelves, or
with Mexico and Chili, and of the more important
ones with the mother-country.

The Straits of Magellan appeared the only open
way to form this laft connection. The length of the
paffage, the terror infpired by ftormy and almoft unknown feas, the fear of exciting the ambition of other
nations, the impoffibility of finding an afylum in cafe
of unfortunate accidents, and other confiderations,
perhaps, turned the general views towards Panama.

This town, which had been the gate through which
an entrance had been gained into Peru, had rifen to
great profperity, when, in 1670, it was pillaged and
burnt by pirates. It was rebuilt on a more advantageous fpot, at the diftance of four or five miles from
the firft, and of three leagues from the harbour of Pe-
rico, which is formed by a great number of iflands,
and fufficiently fpacious to contain the moft numerous
fleets. It rules over the provinces of Panama, the Ve-
raguas, and Darien, regions without inhabitants, without culture, and without riches, and which were de-
corated with the great name of the kingdom of Terra
Firma, at a period when great expectations were entertained of their mines. Panama hath never furnifhed any thing to trade from its own produce, except
pearls.

The pearl fifhery is carried on in forty-three iflands
of the gulf. The greateft part of the inhabitants employ fuch of their Negroes in it as are good fwimmers.

BOOK
VI.

Panama
was for a
long time
the channel
of commu-
nication be-
tween Peru
and Spain.
Manner in
which this
trade was
carried on.

Thefe flaves plunge and replunge in the fea in fearch
of pearls, till this exercife hath exhaufted their ftrength
or their fpirits.

Every Negro is obliged to deliver a certain number
of oyfters. Thofe in which there are no pearls, or in
which the pearl is not entirely formed, are not reckoned. What he is able to find beyond the ftipulated
obligation is confidered as his indifputable property :
he may fell it to whom he thinks proper, but commonly he cedes it to his mafter at a moderate price.

Sea monfters, which abound more about the iflands
where pearls are found than on the neighbouring coafts,
render this fifhing dangerous. Some of thefe devour
the divers in an inftant. The manta fifh, which derives its name from its figure, rolls them under its body, and fuffocates them. In order to defend themfelves againft fuch enemies, every diver is armed with
a poniard. The moment he perceives any of thefe voracious fifh, he attacks them with precaution, wounds
them, and drives them away. Notwithftanding this,
there are always fome fifhermen deftroyed, and a great
number crippled.

The pearls of Panama are commonly of a very fine
water : fome of them are even remarkable for their
fize and figure. Thefe were formerly fold in Europe.
Since art hath imitated them, and the paffion for diamonds hath entirely fuperfeded or diminifhed the ufe
of them, they are all carried to Peru.

This branch of trade hath, however, infinitely lefs
contributed to give reputation to Panama than the
advantage which it enjoyed of being the ftaple of all
the productions of the country of the Incas that are
deftined for the Old World. Thefe riches, which were
brought hither by a fmall fleet, were carried, fome on
mules, others by the river Chagre, to Porto Bello, that
is fituated on the northern coaft of the ifthmus which
feparates the two feas.

Though the fituation of this town had been furvey-
ed and approved by Columbus in 1502, it was not
built till 1584, from the ruins of Nombre de Dios. It

is difpofed in the form of a crefcent, on the declivity of a mountain which furrounds the harbour. This celebrated harbour, which was formerly very well defended by forts, which Admiral Vernon deftroyed in 1740, feems to afford an entrance fix hundred toifes broad; but it is fo ftraitened by rocks that are near the furface of the water, that it is reduced to a very narrow canal. Veffels can only be towed into it, becaufe they always experience either contrary winds or a great calm. Here they enjoy perfect fecurity.

The intemperature of the climate of Porto Bello is fo notorious, that it hath been named the grave of the Spaniards. It hath been more than once neceffary to leave fhips here, becaufe all their crews had perifhed. The inhabitants themfelves do not live long, and have all a vitiated conftitution. It is rather a difgrace to refide here. Some Negroes and Mulattoes only are to be met with, with a fmall number of white people, fixed by the pofts they hold under government. The garrifon itfelf, though only confifting of a hundred and fifty men, doth not continue here more than three months at one time. Till the beginning of the prefent century no woman dared to lie-in here: fhe would have deemed it devoting both her child and herfelf to certain death. The plants that are tranfplanted into this fatal region, where the heat, the moifture, and the vapours are exceffive and continual, have never profpered. It is an eftablifhed opinion, that the domeftic animals of Europe, which have prodigioufly multiplied in all the parts of the New World, lofe their fruitfulnefs on coming to Porto Bello; and, if we may judge by the few that are now there, notwithftanding the abundance of paftures, we might be induced to believe that this opinion is not ill founded.

The badnefs of the climate prevented not Porto Bello from becoming at firft the centre of the moft extenfive commerce that ever exifted. While the riches of the New World arrived there, to be exchanged for the productions of the Old, the veffels that failed from Spain, known by the name of galleons, came hither, laden with all the articles of neceffity, convenience, and luxury, which could tempt the proprietors of the mines.

The deputies for tranfacting this commerce, on both fides, regulated on board the admiral's fhip the price of goods, under the infpection of the commander of the fquadron and of the governor of Panama. The eftimate was not adjufted by the intrinfic value of each article, but by its fcarcity or plenty. The ability of the agents confifted in forming their combinations fo judicioufly, that the cargo imported from Europe fhould abforb all the treafures that were come from Peru. It was regarded as a bad market, when there were found goods neglected for want of money, or money not laid out for want of goods. In this cafe only, the Spanifh merchants were allowed to go and complete the fale of their merchandife in the South Seas, and the Peruvian merchants were permitted to make remittances to the mother-country for their purchafes.

As foon as the prices were fettled, the traffic commenced. This was neither tedious nor difficult; it was carried on with the utmoft franknefs. Every thing was tranfacted with fo much honefty, that they never opened their chefts of piaftres, nor proved the contents of their bales. This reciprocal confidence was never deceived. There were found, more than once, facks of gold mixed among facks of filver, and articles which were not entered on the invoice. Thefe miftakes were rectified before the departure of the fhips, or on their return. There only happened, in 1654, an event which might have interrupted this confidence. It was found in Europe, that all the piaftres that were received at the laft fair had a fifth of alloy. The lofs was borne by the Spanifh merchants; but, as the coiners of Lima were known to be the authors of this fraud, the reputation of the Peruvian merchants incurred no difgrace.

The fair, the duration of which, on account of the noxious qualities of the air, was limited to forty days, was regularly holden. It is clear from the acts of

1595, that the galleons muſt have been diſpatched from Spain every year, or at the lateſt every eighteen months; and the twelve fleets that ſailed from the fourth of Auguſt 1628, to the third of June 1635, prove that this rule was ſtrictly obſerved. They returned after a voyage of eleven, ten, and ſometimes even eight months, laden with immenſe riches, in gold, ſilver, and merchandiſe.

This proſperity continued without interruption to the middle of the ſeventeenth century. After the loſs of Jamaica, a conſiderable contraband trade took place, which till that time had been trifling. The ſacking of Panama in 1670, by John Morgan the Engliſh pirate, was attended with ſtill more diſtreſsful conſequences. Peru, which ſent its ſtock beforehand into this city, now no longer tranſmitted it till after the arrival of the galleons at Carthagena. This alteration occaſioned delays and uncertainties. The fairs were not much frequented, and ſmuggling increaſed.

The elevation of a French prince to the throne of Charles V. excited a general war; and, at the very commencement of hoſtilities, the galleons were burnt in the port of Vigo, where the impoſſibility of gaining Cadiz had obliged them to take refuge. The communication of Spain with Porto Bello was then totally interrupted; and the South Sea had more than ever direct and regular connections with foreign powers.

The peace of Utrecht did not put an end to the miſchief. The unfortunate ſituation of circumſtances, made it impoſſible for the court of Madrid to diſpenſe with granting excluſively to an Engliſh Company the privilege of providing Peru with ſlaves. They were even obliged to grant to this encroaching Company the right of ſending to each fair a veſſel laden with the different merchandiſe that the country conſumed. This veſſel, which ought not to have been of more than five hundred tons burden, always carried more than a thouſand. It was neither furniſhed with water nor proviſions. Four or five veſſels, which followed it, ſupplied its wants; and frequently ſubſtituted new goods in the place of fuch as had been fold. The galleons, ruined by this competition, were ftill more completely fo by the fraudulent tranfactions carried on in all the ports to which the Negroes were conveyed. At laft, after the expedition of 1737, it was impoffible to fupport this commerce any longer ; and a ftop was put to thofe famous fairs envied by all nations, though they ought to have been regarded as the common treafure of all people.

From this period Panama and Porto Bello have aftonifhingly declined. Thefe two towns now only ferve to carry on a few branches of a languid trade. Affairs of greater importance have been turned into another channel.

The Spaniards have fubftituted the route through the Straits of Magellan and by Cape Horn to that of Panama.
It is well known that Magellan difcovered, in 1520, at the fouthern extremity of America, the famous ftrait which bears his name. He faw there, and they have been frequently feen fince, men who were about a foot higher than Europeans. Other navigators have only feen in the fame latitudes men of an ordinary ftature. During the courfe of two centuries, navigators have mutually accufed each other of ignorance, prejudice, and impofture. At length fome voyagers have been fortunate enough to meet with hordes of a common fize, and others of a more elevated ftature ; and they have concluded from this decifive event, that the perfons who had gone before them had been right in what they affirmed, and wrong in what they denied. Then only it occurred, that there were no fixed inhabitants in thefe uncultivated regions ; that the people came there from countries more or lefs diftant ; and that it was probable that the favages of one diftrict were taller than thofe of another. This conjecture hath been fupported by natural philofophy. It can never indeed be reafonably imagined, that nature deviates more from her principles, in producing thofe perfons whom we choofe to call giants, than in giving birth to thofe we call dwarfs.

There are giants and dwarfs in all countries. There are giants, dwarfs, and men of a common fize, born of

the fame father and the fame mother. There are gi-BOOK
ants and dwarfs in every fpecies of animals, trees, fruits, VII.
and plants; and whatever fyftem of generation we
may adopt, we have no greater reafon to be aftonifhed
at the difference of ftature between men of the fame
family, or of different families, than to fee fruits of a
different fize upon a neighbouring tree, or upon the
fame. The man who fhall explain one of thefe phenomena will explain them all.

The Strait of Magellan is one hundred and fourteen
leagues long, and in fome places lefs than a league in
breadth. It feparates the land of the Patagonians
from the Terra del Fuego, which, it is prefumed, were
formerly one and the fame continent. The conformity of their barren coafts, of their rough climate, of
their monftrous rocks, of their inacceffible mountains,
of their eternal fnows, of their favage inhabitants; every circumftance, in a word, tends to fuggeft the idea,
that this large channel of navigation is the effect of
one of thofe natural revolutions which fo often change
the face of the globe.

Though it was for a long time the only paffage
known into the South Sea, the dangers incurred there
caufed it almoft to be forgotten. The boldnefs of
Drake, the celebrated navigator, who failed by this
track to ravage the coafts of Peru, determined the
Spaniards, in 1582, to form a confiderable fettlement
there, deftined to preferve this rich part of the New
World from invafion. This new colony perifhed almoft entirely for want of provifions.

Pedro Sarmiento, who was charged with this important enterprife, fet out from Europe in 1581, with
twenty-three fhips, and three thoufand five hundred
men. The expedition was thwarted by fo many repeated calamities, that the admiral arrived the following year at the Strait with only four hundred men,
thirty women, and provifions for feven or eight months.
The deplorable remains of fo fine a colony were fettled
at Phillipeville, in a fafe, commodious, and fpacious
bay. But the misfortunes that had fo cruelly attacked

B O O K the Spaniards in their paſſage, obſtinately purſued them
VII. at the end of their voyage. No ſuccour was ſent to
them; the country furniſhed them no ſubſiſtence, and
they periſhed with miſery. Of the four-and-twenty
wretches who had eſcaped this terrible calamity, three-
and-twenty, whoſe fate hath always remained unknown, embarked for the river Plata. Fernando Go-
mez, the only one that remained, was taken up in
1587, by the Engliſh pirate Cavendiſh, who gave to
the place where he had found him the name of Port
Famine.

The loſs of this colony was not, however, attended
with ſuch conſequences as had been apprehended.
The Straits of Magellan ſoon ceaſed to be the road of
theſe pirates, who were urged by their mercenary
views to viſit theſe remote regions. In 1616, ſome
Dutch navigators having doubled Cape Horn, this became afterwards the road which the enemies of Spain
followed, who deſigned to paſs into the South Sea. It
was ſtill more frequented by French veſſels, during the
war which cauſed ſuch confuſion in Europe at the beginning of the preſent century. The impoſſibility
which Philip V felt of furniſhing his colonies himſelf
with proviſions, emboldened the ſubjects of his grand-
father to go to Peru. The want of every thing, which
the inhabitants then experienced, made the French to
be received with joy; and at firſt they got a profit of
eight hundred *per cent.* The merchants of Saint Malo, who had ſeized upon this commerce, did not acquire riches for themſelves alone. In 1709, they delivered them up to their country, which was exhauſted
by the inclemency of the ſeaſons, by repeated defeats,
and by an ignorant and arbitrary adminiſtration. A
navigation which allowed of ſuch noble ſacrifices, ſoon
excited an emulation that was too univerſal. The
competition became ſo conſiderable, and the goods
fell into ſuch diſrepute, that it was impoſſible to ſell
them; and ſeveral privateers burnt them, that they
might not be obliged to carry them back into their
country. The equilibrium was not long in re-eſta-

blifhing itfelf; and thefe foreign traders made advantages that were confiderable, when the court of Madrid, in 1718, took effectual meafures to remove them from thefe latitudes, which they had but too long frequented.

It was not, however, till 1740, that the Spaniards began themfelves to double Cape Horn. They employed fhips and pilots from Saint Malo in their firft voyages: but a little experience foon enabled them to go without thefe foreign affiftances; and thefe ftormy feas foon grew more familiar to their navigators, than they had ever been to their mafters in this career.

Till then, the high opinion that had been always Is Peru as rich as it was formerly? entertained, and for a long time with reafon, of the riches of Peru, had been kept up. The court of Spain accufed the fmuggling trade of having turned afide the greateft part of them; and they flattered themfelves that the new fyftem they adopted would bring them back into their ports in as great abundance as at the moft diftant periods. A demonftration, to which it was impoffible not to accede, convinced the moft incredulous perfons, that the mines of this part of the New World were no longer what they had been, and that the void they had left had not been filled up by any other objects.

From 1748 to 1753, Lima received from Spain, for all Peru, ten fhips, which brought back every year 30,764,617 livres [1,281,859l. 8d.]. This fum was compofed of 4,594,192 livres [191,404l. 13s. 6d.] in gold; of 20,673,657 livres [861,402l. 7s. 6d.] in filver; and of 5,496,768 livres [229,032l. 10s.] in various productions.

Thefe productions were thirty-one thoufand quintals of cacao, which were fold in Europe for 3,240,000 livres [135,000l.]. Six hundred quintals of bark, which were fold for 207,360 livres [8640l.]. Four hundred and feventy quintals of Vicuna wool, which were fold for 324,000 livres [13,500l.]. Ten thoufand eight hundred and fifty quintals of copper, which were fold for 810,108 livres [33,792l.]. Ten thoufand fix hundred quintals of tin, which were fold for 915,300 livres [38,137l. 10s.].

Of the gold and filver, 1,620,000 livres [67,500l.] belonged to the government; 19,422,671 livres [809,277l. 19s. 2d.] to trade; and 4,225,178 livres [176,049l. 1s. 8d.] to the clergy, and the civil and military officers.

Of the merchandife, there were 1,381,569 livres [57,565l. 7s. 6d.] for the crown; and 4,115,199 livres [171,466l. 12s. 6d.] for the merchants.

Time hath produced fome little change in affairs, but the improvement is not confiderable.

BOOK VIII.

Conqueft of Chili and Paraguay by the Spaniards. Account of the Events that have accompanied and followed the Invafion of thefe Countries. Principles on which Spain regulates her Colonies.

B O O K
VIII.
⎝⎯⎯⎯⎠
Have the
Europeans
had a right
to found
colonies in
the New
World? REASON and equity both allow the foundation of colonies; but they point out the principles from which we ought not to deviate in eftablifhing them.

Any number of men, however confiderable, coming into a foreign and unknown country, are to be confidered only as one fingle man. Strength increafes with numbers, but the right is ftill the fame. If one or two hundred men can fay, *this country belongs to us*, one man may fay the fame.

The country is either defert, or partly defert; and partly peopled, or it is entirely peopled.

If it be entirely peopled, I have no right to claim any thing but hofpitality, and the affiftance which one man owes to another. If I fhould be expofed to perifh with cold or hunger upon any fhore, I fhall make ufe of my weapon, I fhall take what I want by force, and I fhall kill any one who refifts me. But when I have obtained an afylum, fire and water, bread and falt, the people have fulfilled their obligations towards

me. If I require more, I become a thief and an affaſ- B O O K
fin. I have been, however, ſuffered to remain among VIII.
them, and have made myſelf acquainted with their
laws and manners. They ſuit my inclinations, and I
am deſirous of ſettling in the country. If the people
conſent, it is a favour they do me; if they refuſe, I
have no right to be offended. The Chineſe are, perhaps, bad politicians, when they ſhut the gates of their
empire againſt us; but they are not unjuſt. Their
country is ſufficiently populous, and we are gueſts of
too dangerous a nature.

If the country be partly deſert and partly occupied,
the deſerted part belongs to me; for I may take poſſeſſion of it by my labour. The former inhabitant
would be barbarous, if he came ſuddenly to overthrow
my hut, deſtroy my plantations, and pillage my fields.
I may repel his irruption by force. I may extend my
domain to the confines of his. The foreſts, the rivers,
and the ſhores of the ſea, are common to us both, unleſs the excluſive uſe of them ſhould be neceſſary to
his ſubſiſtence. All he can require of me further, is,
that I ſhould be a peaceable neighbour, and that my
eſtabliſhment ſhould have no threatening aſpect to
him. Every nation is authoriſed to provide for its future and preſent ſafety. If I make a formidable enclo-
ſure, if I collect arms, if I raiſe fortifications, its deputies will be wiſe, if they come to tell me, Art thou
our friend or our enemy? If a friend, what is the uſe
of all theſe warlike preparations? If an enemy, you
will give us leave to deſtroy them; and the nation will
act prudently, if at the inſtant they get rid of their
well-founded apprehenſions. With much greater reaſon may they expel and exterminate me, without offence to the laws of humanity and juſtice, if I ſeize
upon their wives, their children, or their property; if
I make any attempts againſt their civil liberty; if I
reſtrain them in their religious opinions; if I pretend
to give them laws; and if I wiſh to enſlave them. I
then become one wild beaſt more in their neighbourhood; and they owe me no more pity than they would

a tiger. If I have provisions which they want, and if they have some that are useful to me, I may propose exchanges. We are both of us at liberty to set what price we choose on what belongs to us. A needle is of more real value to a people reduced to the necessity of sewing the skins of the beasts which cover them with the bone of a fish, than their silver can be to me. A sabre, or a hatchet, will be of infinite value to him who supplies the place of these instruments with cutting stones, fixed in a piece of wood hardened in the fire. Besides, I have crossed the seas to bring these useful articles; and I shall cross them again to carry back into my country the things I have taken in exchange. The expences of the voyage, the averages, and the dangers, must therefore enter into the calculation. If I laugh within myself at the absurdity of the man who gives me up his gold for iron, he, in his turn, laughs at me, who give him up my iron, all the usefulness of which he knows, for his gold, which is of no service to him. We are both mutually imposed upon, or rather, indeed, there is no imposition on one side or the other. Exchanges ought to be perfectly free. If I want to take away by force what is denied me, or to compel by violence the acceptance of what is rejected, they have a legal right to confine me, or to drive me away. If I seize upon the foreign commodity without offering the price for it, or if I carry it away clandestinely, I am a thief, who may be killed without scruple.

A desert and uninhabited country is the only one we can appropriate to ourselves. The first discovery, being well ascertained, was a legitimate taking of possession.

From these principles, which appear to me founded in truth, let the European nations judge of themselves, and give themselves what name they deserve. Their navigators arrive in a part of the New World which is not occupied by any of the people belonging to the Old, and they immediately bury in the ground a small plate of metal upon which they have engraved these words: THIS DISTRICT BELONGS TO US. And why does it belong to you? Are you not as unjuft and as foolifh as favages, who, being thrown by chance upon your coafts, fhould write upon the fand of your fhore, or upon the bark of your trees: THIS COUNTRY BELONGS TO US? You have no right over the infenfible and brute part of the creation, over the foil where you land; and yet you arrogate one over man, who is your fellow-creature. Inftead of acknowledging in this man a brother, you confider him only as a flave, or beaft of burden. O my fellow-citizens! you think and you act in this manner, although you have notions of juftice, a fyftem of morality, a holy religion, and one common Parent with thofe whom you treat fo tyrannically. This reproach fhould be addreffed more particularly to the Spaniards; and it will unfortunately be ftill more juftified by the enormities they have committed in the country of Chili.

This region, fuch as it is poffeffed by the Spaniards, hath one common breadth of thirty leagues between the fea and the Cordeleirias, and nine hundred leagues of coaft, from the great defert of Atacamas, which feparates it from Peru, to the iflands of Chiloe, which divide it from the country of the Patagonians.

The Incas had prevailed upon part of the inhabitants of this vaft region to fubmit to their wife laws, and intended to fubdue the whole, had they not met with infuperable difficulties.

This important project was refumed by the Spaniards, as foon as they had conquered the principal provinces of Peru. In the beginning of 1535, Almagro fet out from Cufco with five hundred and feventy Europeans, and fifteen thoufand Peruvians. He traverfed at firft the country of Carcas, to which the mines of Potofi have fince given fo much celebrity. To go from this country to Chili, there were but two ways known, and they were both confidered as impracticable. The firft prefented along the borders of the fea nothing but burning fands, without water and without fubfiftence. To purfue the fecond, it was

BOOK VIII.

First irruptions of the Spaniards into Chili.

neceſſary to croſs very ſteep mountains of a prodigious
height, and covered with ſnows as old as the creation.
Theſe difficulties did not diſcourage the general; and
he determined upon the laſt of theſe, for no other reaſon than becauſe it was the ſhorteſt. His ambition
was the deſtruction of one hundred and fifty Spaniards,
and ten thouſand Indians: but at length he accom-
pliſhed his deſign, and was received with the greateſt
marks of ſubmiſſion by the nations that had been formerly under the dominion of the empire that had juſt
been ſubverted. The terror of his arms would, probably, have procured him greater advantages, had not
ſome concerns of a private nature brought him back
to the centre of the empire. His little army refuſed
to repaſs the Cordeleirias; and he was obliged to bring
it back by the way he had firſt neglected. It accidentally met with ſo many fortunate circumſtances, that it
ſuffered much leſs than had been expected. This good
ſucceſs enlarged the views of Almagro, and precipitat-
en him, perhaps, into thoſe enterpriſes which occaſioned his fatal end.

The Spaniards appeared again in Chili in 1541.
Valdivia, their leader, entered it without the leaſt oppoſition. The nations that inhabited it were no ſooner recovered from the aſtoniſhment with which they
had been ſeized at the view of the European arms and
diſcipline, than they wiſhed to regain their independence. The war continued inceſſantly for ten years.
If ſome diſtricts, diſcouraged by repeated loſſes, reſolved at laſt to ſubmit, many of them obſtinately perſiſted
in the defence of their liberty, though they were generally defeated.

An Indian captain, whoſe age and infirmities confined him to his hut, was continually told of theſe miſ-
fortunes. The grief of ſeeing his people always beaten
by a handful of ſtrangers, inſpired him with courage.
He formed thirteen companies of a thouſand men each,
arranged them in file, and led them againſt the enemy.
If the firſt company was routed, it was not to fall back
upon the next, but to rally, and be ſupported by it.

This order, which was ſtrictly obeyed, diſconcerted the B O O K VIII.
Spaniards. They forced through all the companies
one after another, without gaining any material advantage. As both the men and horſes wanted reſt,
Valdivia retreated towards a defile, where he judged
he could eaſily defend himſelf; but the Indians did
not allow him time ſufficient to ſecure his retreat thither. Their rear marched through bye-ways, and
took poſſeſſion of the defile; while their vanguard followed him with ſo much precaution, that he was ſurrounded and maſſacred, together with his hundred and
fifty men. It is ſaid, that the ſavages poured melted
gold down his throat, exclaiming with exultation, *glut
thyſelf with that metal thou art ſo fond of.* They availed
themſelves of this victory, to burn and deſtroy many
of the European ſettlements, which would all have
ſhared the ſame fate, had not the Spaniards been time-
ly aſſiſted by ſome conſiderable reinforcements from
Peru, which enabled them to defend their remaining
poſts, and to recover thoſe they had loſt.

These fatal hoſtilities have been renewed, in pro- The Spani-
portion as the uſurpers have wiſhed to extend their ards have
been obli-
empire, and frequently even when they did not enter- ged to be
tain this ambitious deſign. The engagements have continually
engaged in
been very bloody, and have ſcarce ever been inter- hoſtilities
rupted, except by truces of more or leſs duration. in Chili.
Manner in
Since the year 1771, however, tranquillity hath not which their
been diſturbed. enemies
make war.

The people of Arauco are the moſt common, the
moſt intrepid, and the moſt irreconcileable enemies the
Spaniards have in theſe regions. They are often joined by the inhabitants of Tucapel, and of the river Bio-
bio, and by thoſe who extend towards the Cordeleirias.
As their manners bear a greater reſemblance to thoſe
of the ſavages of North America, than to thoſe of the
Peruvians, their neighbours, the confederacies they
make are always formidable.

When they go to war, they carry nothing with
them, and want neither tents nor baggage. The ſame
trees from which they gather their food, ſupply them

with lances and darts. As they are fure of finding in one place what they had in another, they willingly refign any country which they are unable to defend. All places are equally indifferent to them. Their troops, free from all encumbrance of provifions and ammunition, march with furprifing agility. They expofe their lives like men who fet little value on them; and, if they lofe the field of battle, they are not at a lofs for magazines and encampments wherever there is ground covered with fruits.

Thefe are the only people of the New World who have ventured to try their ftrength with the Spaniards in the open field, and who have thought of the ufe of the fling to lance the ftroke of death from afar againft the enemy. They are fo bold, that they will attack the beft fortified pofts. They fometimes fucceed in thefe violent attacks, becaufe they are continually receiving fuccours, which prevent them from being fenfible of their loffes. If thefe be fo confiderable as to oblige them to defift, they retire to the diftance of a few leagues; and five or fix days after, they direct their attacks to another poft. Thefe barbarians never think themfelves beaten, unlefs they be furrounded. If they can reach a place of difficult accefs, they think themfelves conquerors. The head of a Spaniard, which they carry off in triumph, comforts them for the lofs of a hundred Indians.

Sometimes hoftilities are forefeen for a confiderable time before, and are concerted with prudence. Very frequently a drunken fellow wantonly calls to arms; the alarm is inftantly fpread, a chief is chofen, and war is determined. A certain night is immediately fixed upon, in the dead of which, the time they always choofe for the commencement of hoftilities, they fall upon the next village where there are Spaniards, and from thence proceed to others. They murder all the inhabitants, except the white women, whom they always take to themfelves. This is the origin of the many white and fair Indians that are to be met with.

As thefe Americans carry on war without expence

or inconvenience, they have nothing to apprehend B O O K VIII. from its continuance; and it is a conftant rule with them never to fue for peace. The pride of Spain muft always condefcend to make the firft overtures. When thefe are favourably received, a conference is holden. The governor of Chili and the Indian general, attended by the moft diftinguifhed captains on both fides, fettle the terms of accommodation, at a convivial meeting. Thefe meetings were formerly holden on the frontiers; but the two laft were in the capital of the colony. The favages have even been prevailed upon to keep conftantly fome deputies there, who are commiffioned to maintain harmony between the two nations.

Notwithftanding the violence and obftinacy of fo many engagements, feveral good fettlements have been formed at Chili, chiefly on the borders of the ocean. Settlements formed by the Spaniards at Chili.

Coquimbo, or La Serena, a town built in 1544, at the diftance of five or fix hundred toifes from the fea, to contain the Indians, and to fecure the communication between Chili and Peru, was never a place of importance. It became ftill lefs confiderable after having been pillaged and burnt by pirates. Notwithftanding the fertility of its territory, and although plentiful mines of the fineft copper have been difcovered in its neighbourhood, it hath never entirely got the better of this misfortune.

Valparaifo was at firft nothing more than a collection of huts, deftined to receive the merchandife coming from Peru, and the provifions that were to be fent there. By degrees the factors of this trade, which belonged entirely to the merchants of the capital, fucceeded in appropriating it to themfelves. Then this wretched hamlet, though in a very difagreeable fituation, became a flourifhing city. Its harbour runs a league into the land. The bottom of it is a tenacious and firm kind of mud. At the diftance of a thoufand toifes from the fhore, there are from thirty-fix to forty fathoms of water, and from fifteen to fixteen quite

B O O K clofe to the fhore. In the months of April and May,
VIII. the north winds would expofe the fhips to fome danger, if care were not taken to faften their anchors
ftrongly. The advantage which this port hath of being the neareft to the beft plantations, and to Saint
Yago, may relieve it from the apprehenfion of feeing
its profperity diminifh.

In 1550, the town of La Conception was built on
an uneven and fandy foil, a little raifed, upon the borders of a bay which is near four leagues in circumference, and which hath three ports, one of which only
is fafe. The town was at firft the capital of the colony : but the neighbouring Indians fo frequently made
themfelves mafters of it, that, in 1574, it was thought
proper to deprive it of this ufeful and honourable diftinction. In 1603, it was again deftroyed by an implacable enemy. Since that period, it hath received
very confiderable damages from feveral earthquakes.
Such, however, is the excellence of its territory, that it
ftill retains fome degree of fplendour.

At the diftance of feventy-five leagues from Conception ifland, and ftill on the borders of the Pacific
Ocean, ftands Valdivia, a town more important than
it is populous. Its harbour and fortrefs, which are
confidered as the key of the South Sea, were for a long
time under the immediate infpection of the viceroys of
Peru. It was at length found that this was too diftant
a fuperintendence ; and the place was incorporated
with the government of the province.

No one had yet thought of the iflands of Chiloe.
The good fortune which the Jefuits had had, of collecting and civilizing a great number of favages in the
chief of them, which is fifty leagues long, and feven
or eight broad, excited a defire of fettling in them.
In the centre are the converted Indians. On the eaftern coaft a fortification, named Chacao, hath been
built, where the garrifon neceffary for its defence is
maintained.

In the inland part of the country is Saint Yago,
haftily built in 1541, deftroyed in 1730 by an earth-

quake, and immediately after rebuilt, in a ſtyle ſo BOOK
pleaſant, and with ſuch conveniencies, as are very rare- VIII.
ly found in the New. World.   The houſes, indeed, are
low, and conſtructed with bricks hardened in the ſun :
but they are all white on the outſide, all painted within.   They have all large gardens, and are refreſhed
with running ſtreams.   This city reckons forty thouſand inhabitants ; and the number would be ſtill greater, were it not for nine convents of monks, and ſeven
of nuns, which have been erected there by ſuperſtition.

Among the number of unfortunate auſpices under
which the diſcovery of the New World was made,
we muſt not forget the importance which the prevailing ſpirit of ſuperſtition then gave to the monks ; an
importance which in ſome countries hath ſince been
conſiderably diminiſhed ; which ſeems to ſtruggle powerfully againſt the progreſs of ſcience in others ; which
ſtill prevails with imperious ſway in thoſe poſſeſſions
that are diſtant from Spain, and which would yet
leave traces as permanent as they are fatal, if even
they were from this moment counteracted by all the
authority of the miniſtry.

Saint Yago is the capital of the ſtate and the ſeat
of empire.   The commandant there is ſubordinate to
the viceroy of Peru in all matters relating to the government, to the finances, and to war : but he is independent of him as chief adminiſtrator of juſtice, and
preſident of the royal audience.   Eleven corregidors,
diſtributed in the province, are charged, under his orders, with the details of adminiſtration.

A population of four or five hundred thouſand
perſons hath ſucceſſively been formed in this diſtrict.
There are but few here of thoſe unfortunate ſlaves
that Africa ſupplies ; and moſt of them are devoted
to domeſtic ſervice.   The deſcendants of the firſt ſavages, who were ſubdued with ſo much difficulty by
a ſet of ferocious adventurers, have either taken refuge among inacceſſible mountains, or are confounded with their conquerors.   All the coloniſts are conſidered and treated as Spaniards.   The pride of this

B O O K descent hath not inspired them with that invincible
VIII. aversion for useful labour, which is so universal in their
nation. Most of these healthy, active, and robust men
live upon separate plantations, and cultivate, with their
own hands, a territory of greater or less extent.

Fertility of   They are encouraged in these commendable labours,
Chili, and
its present by a sky always pure, and always serene ; by a climate
state. the most agreeably temperate of any in the two he-
misspheres ; and still more by a soil, the fertility of
which astonishes all travellers. Upon this fortunate
land, the crops of the vine, of corn, and of the olive,
although little care hath been taken in the cultivation, are four times as much as those we obtain in Europe, with all our industry and with all our skill. None
of the fruits of the earth have degenerated. Several
of our animals have improved, and the horses, in particular, have acquired a speed and a spirit, which those
of Andalusia, from which they descend, never had.
Nature hath carried her favours still farther, in bestow-
ing upon this region an excellent kind of copper,
which is employed, with advantage, in the Old and
in the New World. Gold is likewise found here.

Before the year 1750, the treasury had not received
in any year, for its twentieth of this precious metal,
more than 50,220 livres [2092l. 10s.]. At this period
a mint was established in the colony ; and this innovation was attended with favourable consequences. In
1771, the royal duties amounted to 200,032 livres 4
sols [8334l. 13s. 6d.] ; and it must have increased considerably since. The alcavala, and the customs, did
not produce more than 324,000 livres [13,500l.], and
they now bring in 1,080,000 livres [45,000l.]. These
several branches of revenue are increased since 1753,
by the exclusive sale of tobacco.

Accordingly, Chili is no longer obliged to draw any
thing from the coffers of Peru for its public expences.
The most considerable of these is the maintenance
of the troops. It amounts to 490,125 livres 12 sols
[20,421l. 18s.], for the pay of a thousand infantry,
of two hundred and forty horse, and of two com-

panies of well-affected Indians; which, since 1754, form the establishment of the country. Exclusive of these forces, which are distributed in the islands Juan Fernandez, and of Chiloe, and in the ports of La Conception, and of Val Paraiso, upon the frontiers of the Andes, there is in Valdivia a particular garrison of seven hundred and forty-six soldiers, the maintenance of which costs 655,473 livres 12 sols [27,311l. 8s.]. These means of defence would be supported, if necessary, by a very numerous militia. Perhaps, the infantry of these forces would make but little resistance, notwithstanding the pains that have been lately taken to exercise them: but some exertions might reasonably be expected from the best horsemen there are, perhaps, on the globe.

Chili hath always had commercial connections with the neighbouring Indians on its frontiers, with Peru, and with Paraguay. Trade of Chili with the savages, with Peru, and with Paraguay.

The savages supply it chiefly with the Pancho. This is a woollen stuff, sometimes white, and generally blue, about three ells long, and two in breadth. The head is passed through a hole made in the middle, and it falls down on all the parts of the body. Except on occasions of some ceremonies that are very unfrequent, the men and women, the common people, and persons of a more elevated rank, use no other clothing. It costs from thirty to one thousand livres [from 1l. 5s. to 41l. 13s. 4d.], according to the degree of its fineness, and especially according to the borders, more or less elegant, and more or less rich, that are added to it. These people receive in exchange small looking-glasses, toys, and some other articles of little value. Whatever may be their passion for these trifles, when they are displayed before them, they would never go out of their forests and fields in search of them; it is therefore always necessary that they should be carried to them. The merchant who wishes to undertake this little trade, applies in the first instance to the heads of the families, who are the sole depositaries of the public authority. When he hath obtained permission to sell, he goes

through the habitations, and gives his merchandife indifcriminately to all the perfons who afk for it. Having finifhed this bufinefs, he gives notice of his departure, and every one who hath purchafed any thing of
him, brings, without delay, to the village where he firft
made his appearance, the goods agreed for between
them. There hath never been any inftance of difhonefty in this traffic. The merchant is allowed an efcort to
affift him in conducting the cloths and the cattle he hath
received in payment to the frontiers of the country.

It is not from what we find in the midft of forefts,
but from what we obferve in the centre of polifhed
focieties, that we learn to defpife and to miftruft mankind. If any of our merchants, in any one of our
fairs, were indifcriminately to diftribute his goods, without fecurity for the payment of them, to whomfoever
fhould come to receive them, is it to be imagined that
he would ever again fee the people return with the
price of the things they had purchafed? A favage, unreftrained by laws, would not be guilty of thofe things
which men who are under the influence of honour, and
the controul of civil and religious laws, would not
blufh to commit, to the difgrace of our religion, of
our policy, and of our morals.

Wine and brandy were fold, till the year 1724, to
thefe people, who, like moft other favages, are exceffively fond of them. When they were intoxicated
they ufed to take up arms, maffacre all the Spaniards
they met with, and ravage the country near their
dwellings. It is feldom that the corrupter doth not
receive his punifhment from the very perfon he hath
corrupted. Frequent inftances of this are feen in children with refpect to their fathers, who have neglected their education; in women towards their hufbands,
whofe morals are bad; in flaves, towards their mafters; in fubjects towards their fovereigns, when neglected by them; in a fubdued nation towards the
ufurpers. We ourfelves have been punifhed for the
vices we have transferred into the other hemifphere;
among ourfelves and among people of the New World,

whom we have fubdued ; among ourfelves, by the multitude of factitious wants we have created : among
them, in a variety of ways, and particularly by teach-
ing them the ufe of fpirituous liquors, which hath
often animated them with artificial fury, which they
have turned againft us. In whatever manner we proceed, whether by fuperftition, by patriotifm itfelf, or
by fpirituous liquors, in depriving man of his reafon,
it cannot be done without fatal confequences. If we
intoxicate him, whatever may be the nature of the
intoxication, it will foon go off, or it will be productive of mifchief.

Drunkennefs, or an habitual excefs in the ufe of
fpirituous liquors, is a coarfe and brutal vice, which
deprives the mind of its vigour, and the body of part
of its ftrength. It is an infringement of the law of
nature, which forbids man to forfeit his reafon, the
only advantage which diftinguifhes him from other
animals, who live on the furface of the globe.

This irregularity, though always blameable, is not
equally fo every where, becaufe it is not attended with
the fame inconveniences in all regions. Generally
fpeaking, it makes men furious in hot countries, and
only renders them ftupid in cold ones. It hath therefore been neceffary to forbid it with more ftrictnefs
in one climate than in another. From hence it hath
happened, that wherever a regular form of government hath been eftablifhed, this vice is become more
uncommon under the equator than towards the pole.

This is not the cafe among favage nations. Thofe
of the fouth not being more reftrained than thofe of
the north, by the magiftrate or by habit, they have
all devoted themfelves with equal fury to their paffion
for ftrong liquors. It hath been a part of the policy
of the Europeans, to fupply the favages with them,
either for the purpofe of ftripping or of enflaving them,
or even to induce them to employ themfelves in fome
ufeful labours. Thefe liquors have fcarce been lefs
deftructive to thefe people than our arms ; and we
cannot forbear to rank them among the number of

calamities with which we have loaded the other hemifphere.

Spain is to be commended for having at length ab-
ftained from felling to the inhabitants of Chili wine
and brandy. This prudent ftep hath evidently increafed the connections that were kept up with them:
but it is not poffible that they fhould for a long time
become fo confiderable as thofe that are maintained
with Peru.

Chili fupplies Peru with hides, dried fruit, copper,
falt meat, horfes, hemp, and corn, and receives in exchange, tobacco, fugar, cocoa, earthen ware, fome
manufactures made at Quito, and fome articles of luxury brought from Europe. The fhips fent from Callao on this traffic, which is reciprocally ufeful, were
formerly bound for Conception Bay, but now come
to Valparaifo. During the courfe of near a century,
no navigator in thefe tranquil feas would venture to
lofe fight of land; and then thefe voyages lafted a
whole year.

A pilot of the Old World having at length obferved the winds, performed the navigation in one month.
He was confidered as a wizard, and he was taken up
by order of the inquifition, whofe ignorance becomes
an object of ridicule, when its cruelty doth not excite our abhorrence. The journal he produced was
his vindication; and it plainly appeared that to perform the fame voyage, it was only neceffary to keep
clear of the coafts. His method was, therefore, univerfally adopted.

Chili fends to Paraguay wines, brandy, oil, and
chiefly gold; and receives in payment mules, wax,
cotton, the herb of Paraguay, negroes, and alfo much of
the merchandife of our hemifphere, before the merchants of Lima had obtained, either by bribery, or
by their influence, that this laft branch of commerce
fhould be prohibited. The communication between
the two colonies is not carried on by fea; it hath been
found more expeditious, fafer, and even lefs expenfive,
to go by land, though there are three hundred and fix-

ty-four leagues, from St. Jago to Buenos Ayres, and B O O K VIII. that more than forty of thefe are amidft the fnows and precipices of the Cordeleirias.

If the connections between thefe two eftablifhments fhould be multiplied or extended, they muft be kept up by the Straits of Magellan, or by Cape Horn. It hath been hitherto a matter of doubt which of thefe two ways was the beft; but the problem feems to be folved by the obfervations of the laft navigators. They almoft generally prefer the Straits, on account of a quantity of frefh water, wood, fifh, fhell-fifh, and the infinite number of plants, fpecific remedies againft the fcurvy, that are to be found there. But this preference can only take place from September to March, that is to fay, in the fummer months. During the fhort days of winter, it would be neceffary to fail only for a few hours, or to brave, in a channel moft commonly narrow, the violence of the winds, the rapidity of the currents, and the impetuofity of the waves, with an almoft moral certainty of being fhipwrecked. In this feafon of the year, the open fea, and confequently the doubling of Cape Horn, is to be preferred.

A number of combinations, palpably abfurd, have conftantly deprived Chili of every immediate connection with Spain. The little merchandife of our hemifphere which this country could confume came to it from Peru, which received them itfelf with difficulty, and at a great expence, by the road of Panama. The fate of Chili was not even changed when the failing by Cape Horn was fubftituted to that which was practifed by the ifthmus of Darien; and it was not till very late, that the fhips which ufed to coaft this country in their way to Lima, were permitted to leave fome fmall portion of their cargoes. At length, a more agreeable profpect hath opened itfelf to this beautiful country. Since the month of February 1778, all the ports of the mother-country are allowed to trade there at pleafure. This fortunate adoption of the true principles of commerce muft be attended with the greateft fuccefs;

and this innovation will have the fame influence over Paraguay.

This is an immenfe region, bounded on the north by Peru and the Brazils, on the fouth by the country bordering on the Straits of Magellan, on the eaft by the Brazils, and on the weft by Chili and Peru.

The Paraguay derives its name from a large river which all geographers have fuppofed to proceed from the lake Xarayes. The Spanifh and Portuguefe commiffioners, appointed in 1751 to regulate the limits of the two empires, were much furprifed to meet each other at the origin of this river, without having perceived this mafs of waters, which was faid to be immenfe. They afcertained, that what had been before taken for a prodigious lake, was nothing more than a very low portion of land, covered, from the fixteenth to the nineteenth degree of latitude, in the rainy feafon, by the overflowings of the river. Since that period, it is known that the Paraguay river takes its rife in the flat country called *Campo des Paracis*, in the thirteenth degree of fouthern latitude; and that towards the eighteenth degree, it communicates, by fome very narrow channels, with two great lakes in the country of the Chiquitos.

Before the arrival of the Spaniards, this immenfe country contained a great number of nations, moft of them confifting of a few families. Their manners muft have been the fame; and if there had been any difference in their characters, it would not have been perceived by the ftupid adventurers who had firft fhed the blood of this part of the New World. Thefe people lived upon hunting, fifhing, wild fruits, honey, which was commonly found in the forefts, and roots that grew fpontaneous. With a view of procuring greater plenty of wood, they were perpetually wandering from one diftrict to another. As the Indians had nothing to remove but a few earthen veffels, and as branches of trees could be found every where to build huts with, thefe emigrations were attended with few encum-

brances. Though they all lived in a ſtate of abſolute B O O K
independence, yet the neceſſity of mutual defence had VIII.
obliged them to connect their intereſts. Some individuals united under the direction of a leader of their
own choice. Theſe aſſociations, which were more or
leſs numerous, in proportion to the reputation and abilities of the chief, were as eaſily diſſolved as formed.

The diſcovery of the river Paraguay was made in
1515, by Diaz de Solis, a noted pilot of Caſtile. He
and moſt of his men were maſſacred by the natives,
who, to avoid being enſlaved, ſome years after alſo
deſtroyed the Portugueſe of Brazil.

The two rival nations, equally alarmed by theſe calamities, gave up all thoughts of Paraguay, and turned their avaricious views towards another place. The
Spaniards accidentally returned there in 1526.

Sebaſtian Cabot, who in 1496 had made the diſcovery of Newfoundland for the crown of England,
finding that kingdom was too much taken up with
domeſtic affairs to think of making ſettlements in a
new world, offered his ſervices to Caſtile, where his reputation made him be fixed upon to conduct an important expedition.

The *Victory*, celebrated for being the firſt ſhip that
ever ſailed round the world, and the only one of Magellan's ſquadron that returned to Europe, had brought
back from the Eaſt Indies a great quantity of ſpices.
The great profit that was made from the ſale of them,
occaſioned a ſecond expedition, the command of which
was given to Cabot. In purſuing the track of the
former voyage, he arrived at the mouth of the Plata.
Whether he was in want of proviſions neceſſary for a
longer voyage, or whether, which is more probable,
his men began to be mutinous, he ſtopped there. He
even ſailed up the river, gave it the name of *La Plata*,
becauſe, among the ſpoils of a few Indians, inhumanly
put to death, ſome ornaments of gold and ſilver had
been found, and built a kind of fortreſs at the entrance
of the river Riotecero, which comes down from the
mountains of Tucuman. The oppoſition he met with

B O O K from the inhabitants of the country, made him judge,
VIII. that, in order to form a folid eftablifhment, other means
were wanting fuperior to thofe he had ; and, in 1530,
he went to Spain in order to folicit them. Thofe of
his companions whom he had left in the colony were
moft of them maffacred, and the few who efcaped from
the arrows of the enemy foon followed him.

Some more confiderable forces, led by Mendoza,
appeared on the river in 1535, and laid the foundations of Buenos-Ayres. They were foon reduced to
the neceffity of perifhing with hunger within their pal-
lifades, or of devoting themfelves to certain death, if
they ventured to go out of them in order to procure
fubfiftence. A return into Europe feemed to be the
only way of relief from fo defperate a fituation : but
the Spaniards had perfuaded themfelves that the inland countries abounded in mines ; and this prejudice
induced them to perfevere. They abandoned a place
where they could no longer remain, and went to found,
in 1536, a colony on the ifland of Affumption, three
hundred leagues up the country, but ftill on the banks
of the fame river. By this change, they evidently removed further from the affiftance of the mother-country ; but they imagined it brought them nearer the
fource of riches ; and their avidity was ftill greater
than their forefight.

They were ftill, however, reduced to the neceffity
of perifhing, unlefs they could fucceed in diminifhing
the extreme antipathy the favages bore them. The
marriage of the Spaniards with the Indian women appeared calculated to effect this great change ; and it
was accordingly refolved upon. From the union of
two fuch different nations fprang the race of the Meftees, which, in procefs of time, became fo common in
South America. Thus it is the fate of the Spaniards,
in all parts of the world, to be a mixed race. The
blood of the Moors ftill flows in their veins in Europe,
and that of the favages in the other hemifphere. Perhaps this mixture may be of advantage, if it be a fact
that men, as well as animals, are improved by croffing

the breed.   It were indeed to be wished that the various races of mankind were lost in one, that there might be an end of those national antipathies, which only serve to perpetuate the calamities of war, and all the several passions that destroy the human species.   But discord seems to arise of itself between brothers ; can it therefore be expected that all mankind should become one family, the children of which sprung, as it were, from the same common parent, should no longer thirst after each other's blood ?   For is not this fatal thirst excited and maintained by that of gold ?

It was this shameful passion which kept up the cruelty of the Spaniards, even after the connections they had formed.   They seemed to punish the Indians for their own obstinacy in searching for gold where there was none.   Several ships, which were bringing them troops and ammunition, were lost, with all they had on board, by venturing too far up the river ; but even this circumstance could not prevent them from obstinately persisting in their avaricious views, though they had so long been disappointed in them ; till they were compelled, by repeated orders from the mother-country, to re-establish Buenos-Ayres.

This necessary undertaking was now become easy. The Spaniards, who had multiplied in Paraguay, were strong enough to restrain or destroy the nations that might oppose them.   Accordingly, as it had been expected, they met with little difficulty.   Juan Ortiz de Zarate executed the plan in 1580, and rebuilt Buenos-Ayres upon the same spot which had been forsaken for forty years.   Some of the petty nations in the neighbourhood submitted to the yoke.   Those which were more attached to their liberty, went to a greater distance, with a view of removing still further, in proportion as their oppressors should extend their establishments.   Most of them at last took refuge in Chaco.

This country, which is two hundred and fifty leagues in length, and one hundred and fifty in breadth, is reckoned one of the best in America ; and it is thought to be peopled with one hundred thousand savages.   They

Such of the Indians as will not submit to the yoke of Spain take

form, as in other parts of the New World, a great
number of nations, forty-fix or forty-feven of which
are very imperfectly known.

This region is traverfed by feveral rivers. The Pil-
comayo, more confiderable than all the reft, iffues from
the province of Charcas, and divides into two branches,
feventy leagues before it empties itfelf into the Rio de
la Plata. The courfe of this river appeared to be the
moft convenient way of eftablifhing fettled connections between Paraguay and Peru. It was not, however, till 1702, that an attempt was made to fail up it.
The people who dwelt upon the banks underftood
very well that they fhould fooner or later be enflaved
if the expedition were fuccefsful, and they prevented
this misfortune by maffacring all the Spaniards who
were engaged in it.

Nineteen years after, the Jefuits refumed this grand
project : but when they had advanced three hundred
and fifty leagues, they were forced to put back, becaufe they were in want of water to continue their
voyage. They were blamed for having undertaken
it in the months of September, October, and November, which, in thefe countries, are the dry feafons ;
and there is no doubt but that the enterprife would
be fuccefsful in the other feafons of the year.

This road of communication muft either have appeared lefs advantageous, or muft have prefented greater difficulties than were at firft conceived, fince no attempt hath fince been made to open it. The government, however, have not entirely given up their ancient project of fubduing thefe people. After incredible fatigues, and which were for a long time ufelefs,
fome miffionaries have at length fucceeded in fixing
three thoufand of thefe wanderers in fourteen villages,
feven of which are fituated on the frontiers of Tucuman, four on the fide of Santa Cruz de la Sierra, two
towards Taixa, and only one in the neighbourhood of
Affumption Ifland.

Notwithftanding the frequent incurfions of the inhabitants of Chaco, and the fury of fome other lefs

numerous colonies, Spain hath fucceeded in forming
three great provinces in this diftrict. That which is
called Tucuman is even, well watered, and wholefome. The cotton and the corn that is confumed in
the country is cultivated there with the greateft fuccefs ; and fome experiments have fhown that indigo,
and the other productions peculiar to the New World,
would thrive there as well as in any of the fettlements
which they have enriched for fo long a time. The
forefts are all filled with honey ; and there are not,
perhaps, better pafturages on the face of the globe.
Moft of the woods are of a fuperior kind. There is
one tree in particular, known by the name of Quebra-
cho, which is faid to be nearly as hard, as weighty,
and as durable as the beft marble, and which, on account of the difficulty of conveyance, is fold at Potofi
for as much as ten thoufand livres [416l. 13s. 4d.].
That portion of the Andes which is in this diftrict is
abounding in gold and copper, and fome mines have
been already opened there.

But it would require an infinite number of hands to
extract from this immenfe territory the riches it contains. Notwithftanding this, the perfons who give the
moft favourable accounts of its population do not reckon it to amount to more than one hundred thoufand
inhabitants, Spaniards, Indians, and Negroes. They
are collected in feven villages, of which Saint Yago
del Eftero is the principal, or are diftributed upon fcattered domains, fome of which have more than twelve
leagues in extent, and reckon as far as forty thoufand
horned cattle, and fix thoufand horfes, without including other herds of animals of lefs importance.

The province which is particularly called Paraguay
is much too damp, on account of the forefts, lakes,
and rivers, with which it is covered. Accordingly,
exclufive of the celebrated miffions of the fame name
which belong to it, it is not computed to contain more
than fifty-fix thoufand inhabitants. Four hundred only are at Affumption, the capital ; two other villages,
which alfo bear the names of towns, have ftill a lefs

BOOK
VIII.

founding
three large
provinces.
Peculiari-
ties in each
of them.

number. Fourteen colonies, governed upon the fame principle as thofe of the Guaranis, contain fix thoufand Indians. All the reft live in the country places, where they cultivate tobacco, cotton, and fugar, which are fent, with the herb of Paraguay, to Buenos-Ayres, from whence fome mercantile articles brought from Europe are received in exchange.

This country was always expofed to the incurfions of the Portuguefe on the eaftern fide, and to thofe of the favages on the north and on the weft. It was neceffary to adopt fome mode of driving back enemies that were moftly implacable. Forts were conftructed; lands were appropriated to the maintenance of them; and every citizen bound himfelf to defend them for a week in every month. Thefe arrangements, anciently made, ftill fubfift. If, however, this fervice fhould be difagreeable to any one, or fhould interfere with his bufinefs, he may be freed from it by paying from 60 to 100 livres [from 2l. 10s. to 4l. 3s. 4d.], according to his fortune.

The part which at prefent conftitutes the province of Buenos-Ayres was originally part of that of Paraguay. It was not feparated from it till 1621, and it remained for a long time in the greateft obfcurity. A fraudulent trade, which, after the peace of Utrecht, was opened with it by the fettlements of the Portuguefe at Saint Sacrament, and which enabled it to form fixed connections with Chili and Peru, imparted to it fome activity. The misfortune that happened to the fquadron under Pizarro, who in 1740 was commiffioned to protect the South Sea againft the forces of Great Britain, increafed its population and activity. They both received an addition of extenfion from thofe enterprifing men who fettled in this country, when the courts of Madrid and of Lifbon undertook to fix the too uncertain limits of their territory. At length the war carried on in 1776, between thefe two powers, with troops fent from Europe, contributed to give ftill greater folidity to the colony.

At prefent, the two banks of the river, from the

ocean to Buenos-Ayres, and from Buenos-Ayres to
Santa-Fé, are either covered with numerous flocks, or
tolerably well cultivated. Corn, maize, fruits, and
pulfe, every thing, in a word, which fupplies the ordinary wants of life, except wine and wood, grows there
in great abundance.

Buenos-Ayres, the capital of the colony, unites many advantages. The fituation is healthy and pleafant,
and the air temperate. It is regularly built. Its ftreets
are wide, and compofed of houfes that are extremely
low; but all of them are embellifhed with a garden
of greater or lefs extent. The public and private
buildings, which fifty years ago were all made of earth,
are more folid and commodious, fince the natives have
learned the art of making brick and lime. The number of inhabitants amounts to thirty thoufand. One
fide of the town is defended by a fortrefs, with a garrifon of fix or feven hundred men; and the reft is furrounded by the river. Two thoufand nine hundred
and forty-three militia, Spaniards, Indians, Negroes,
and free Mulattoes, are always ready to join the regulars.

The town ftands fixty leagues from the fea. The
fhips get to it by failing up a river that wants depth;
is full of iflands, fhoals, and rocks, and where ftorms
are more frequent and more dreadful than on the
ocean. It is neceffary to anchor every night on the
fpot they come to; and, on the moft moderate days,
a pilot muft go before in a boat to found the way for
the fhip. After having furmounted thefe difficulties,
the fhips are obliged to ftop at the diftance of three
leagues from the town, to put their goods on board
fome light veffels, and to go to refit, and to wait for
their cargoes, at Incenada de Barragan, fituated feven
or eight leagues below.

This is a kind of village, formed by fome huts built
with rufhes, covered with hides, and fcattered about
without order. Neither magazines nor fubfiftence are
to be found there; and the place is inhabited only by
a few indolent men, from whom fcarce any fervice is

BOOK
VIII.

Of the ca-
Pa-
raguay, and
of the dif-
ficulties
which na-
muft fur-
mount to
get there.

to be expected.   The mouth of a river, which is from
five to fix thoufand toifes broad, ferves it for a harbour.   No fhips that draw above twelve feet of water
can enter it.   Veffels that require more depth are obliged to take refuge behind a neighbouring point, where
the anchorage, fortunately, is more inconvenient than
dangerous.

The infufficiency of this afylum occafioned, in 1726,
the town of Montevideo to be built forty leagues below Buenos-Ayres, and upon a bay which is two
leagues in depth.   It is defended on the fide of the
land by a well-conftructed citadel, and protected on
the fide of the river by batteries judicioufly placed.
Unfortunately there are not more than four or five
fathoms of water, and the veffels are obliged to run
aground.   This is no great inconvenience for the merchantmen ; but the men of war perifh fpeedily upon
this mud, and are eafily warped.   Some experienced
navigators, on whom nature hath beftowed a fpirit of
obfervation, have obferved, that, with little labour and
expence, one of the fineft harbours in the world might
have been conftructed in the neighbourhood, on the
river Saint Lucia.   In order to effect this, the only
thing neceffary was to dig away the bank of fand
which renders the entrance of it difficult.   The court
of Madrid will fooner or later be obliged to adopt this
plan, fince Maldonado, which was their only hope, is
at prefent acknowledged to be one of the worft harbours in the world.

Of the herb
of Para-
guay, the
chief riches
of the co-
lony.
The richeft produce that comes from the three provinces is the herb of Paraguay.   It is the leaf of a
middle-fized tree, which hath not been defcribed or
obferved by any botanift.   The tafte is fimilar to that
of mallows, and in fhape it refembles an orange tree.
It is divided into three forts.   The firft, called *caacuys*,
is the bud when it juft begins to unfold its leaves.
This is far fuperior to the other two, but will not keep
fo long, and it is therefore difficult to export it to any
diftance.   The next, which is called *caamini*, is the
full-grown leaf ftripped of its ftalks.   If thefe be left

on, it is called *caaguaza*, which is the third fort. The leaves are firſt roaſted, and then kept in pits digged in the ground, and covered with bulls hides.

The mountains of Maracayu, at the eaſt ſide of Paraguay, furniſh the herb that is moſt eſteemed. The tree which produces it grows in the marſhy valleys that lie between the hills. The city of Aſſumption firſt brought this production, which was the delight of the ſavages, into repute. The exportation of it procured conſiderable riches to the town. But this advantage was not of long continuance, for all the Indians of that diſtrict were ſoon loſt in the long voyage they were obliged to take. The whole country became a deſert for forty leagues round the city; and the inhabitants were obliged to give up this trade, which was the only ſource of their wealth.

To this firſt mart ſucceeded that of Villa Rica, which was nearer to the production by thirty-ſix leagues. This alſo ſoon came to nothing, for the ſame reaſon as had occaſioned the fall of that to which it had ſucceeded.

At length, in the beginning of the century, Cunuguati was built, at the diſtance of a hundred leagues from Aſſumption, and at the foot of the mountains of Maracayu. It is at preſent the great market for the herb of Paraguay; but a competition hath lately riſen up againſt it, from a quarter where there was no reaſon to expect one.

The Guaranis, who at firſt gathered the herb only in ſufficient quantity for their own conſumption, collected it, in proceſs of time, for ſale. This employment, and the length of the voyage, kept them abſent from their colonies for a conſiderable part of the year. During this interval they were all deprived of inſtruction. Many of them periſhed by change of air and fatigue. Some grew weary of this laborious employment, and retired into the woods, where they reſumed their former way of life. Beſides, the miſſions, deprived of their defenders, were expoſed to the inroads of the enemy. Theſe evils were too numerous. To obviate them, the Jefuits procured feeds from Maracayu, and fowed them in thofe parts of the land that were moft analogous to the foil they were brought from. They grew up very rapidly, and have not degenerated, at leaft in any fenfible degree.

The produce of thefe plantations, added to that which grows fpontaneoufly, is very confiderable. Part of this remains in the three provinces. Chili and Peru confume annually twenty-five thoufand quintals of it, which coft them near two millions of livres [83,333l. 6s. 8d.].

This herb, which the Spaniards and other inhabitants of South America take fo much delight in, and to which they attribute fo many virtues, is in general ufe through this part of the New World. It is dried and reduced almoft to powder, then put into a cup with fugar, lemon-juice, and fweet-fcented pafte; boiling water is afterwards thrown upon it, and it is drunk off directly, before it hath time to turn black.

Connections of Paraguay with the neighbouring countries, and with Spain.
The herb of Paraguay is of no confequence to Europe, which doth not confume any of it; nor do we intereft ourfelves more about the trade which this diftrict carries on with the other regions of the New World in excellent mules.

This ufeful animal is generally multiplied upon the territory of Buenos-Ayres. The inhabitants of the Tucuman carry there woods for building, and wax, which they exchange every year for fixty thoufand mules of two years old, which formerly coft no more than three livres [2s. 6d.] each, but which now coft from eight to ten [from 6s. 8d. to 8s. 4d.]. They are kept fourteen months in the paftures of Cordova, eight in thofe of Salta, and are conducted through roads of fix, feven, and nine hundred leagues, by herds of fifteen hundred or two thoufand, into Peru, where they are fold near Oruro, Cufco, and Guanca-Velica, at the rate of feventy or a hundred livres [from 2l. 18s. 4d. to 4l. 3s. 4d.], according to the greater or lefs diftance they come from.

Befide this, the Tucuman furnifhes to Potofi fixteen

or eighteen thoufand oxen, and four or five thoufand
horfes, brought forth and reared upon its own territory. This diftrict would fupply twenty times as much
of both, if it were poffible to find a mart for them.

It will perhaps be a matter of more confequence to
our merchants to know the route the cargoes take
which they fend into this part of this hemifphere.

There is feldom any connection between the villages fcattered over this region, at a great diftance
from each other. Befide that it could not be kept up
without great fatigue and much danger, it would be
of little ufe to men who have not any thing, or who
have fcarce any thing, to offer or to require. Buenos-
Ayres alone was much interefted in finding a vent for
the merchandife it received from Europe, fometimes
openly, and fometimes fraudulently ; and it at laft
fucceeded in opening a tolerably regular trade with
Chili and with Peru. Originally the caravans, which
carried on this traffic, had recourfe to the ufe of the
needle to conduct them through the vaft deferts they
were obliged to traverfe ; but, in procefs of time, they
have travelled without this inftrument, which is fo neceffary for other purpofes of much greater importance.

At prefent carriages fet out from Buenos-Ayres for
their refpective deftinations. Several of them go together, in order to be able to refift the favage nations
which attack them on their march. They are all
drawn by four oxen, carry fifty quintals, and travel
feven leagues a day. Thofe which take the route of
Peru ftop at Jugey, after having gone over four hundred and fixty-feven leagues ; and thofe which are
deftined for Chili have no more than two hundred and
fixty-four to go over to reach Mendoza. The firft receive four piaftres, or twenty-one livres eight fols [17s.
10d.] per quintal ; and the fecond a price proportioned to the fpace they have travelled over. Thefe carriages are always followed by a herd of woolly and
horned cattle. The travellers who are tired or fatigued with the carriage ride upon the horfes ; the ox-

BOOK en ferve both for food, and alfo for change in the har-
VIII.   nefs.

The year 1764 was the fortunate period of another
ufeful inftitution. The miniftry had at length determined to difpatch, every two months, from Corunna,
a packet-boat for Buenos-Ayres. This was a ftaple
from which it was neceffary to fend the letters and
paffengers into all the Spanifh poffeffions in the South
Sea. The paffage was nine hundred and forty-fix
leagues to Lima, and three hundred and fixty-four to
Saint Yago; and a part of this vaft fpace was occupied
by immenfe deferts. An active and intelligent man
contrived, however, to eftablifh a regular poft from the
capital of Paraguay to the capitals of Peru and Chili,
to the great advantage of the three colonies, and confequently of the mother-country.

Paraguay fends feveral articles of greater or lefs importance to Spain; but they have all been brought
there from neighbouring diftricts. The only thing it
furnifhes from its own territory is hides.

When the Spaniards forfook Buenos-Ayres in 1539,
in order to go up the river again, they left in the
neighbouring fields fome horned cattle, which they
had brought over from their own country. They multiplied to fuch a degree, that, when the town was re-
eftablifhed, no one chofe to appropriate them. It
was afterwards found ufeful to knock them on the
head, in order to fell their hides in Europe. The
manner of doing this is remarkable.

A number of huntfmen on horfeback repair to fuch
places as are moftly frequented by the wild bulls. Each
huntfman purfues the bull he fixes upon, and ham-
ftrings him with a fharp iron cut in the fhape of a crefcent, and faftened to a long handle. When the animal falls down, the huntfman attacks others, and dif-
ables them in the fame manner. After fome days fpent
in this violent exercife, the huntfmen return in fearch
of the bulls they have difabled, which they flay, carry
away the hides, and fometimes the tongues and the

fat: the reft they leave to be devoured by wild dogs or vultures.

The price of hides was fo low at firft, that they coft no more than two livres [1s. 8d.]; though the buyers refufed thofe that had the leaft defect, becaufe they were fubject to the fame tax as others that were in the beft condition. In procefs of time, the number of them diminifhed fo much, that it was neceffary to give forty-three livres four fols [1l. 16s.] for the large ones; thirty-feven livres fixteen fols [1l. 11s. 6d.] for thofe of an intermediate fize; and thirty-two livres eight fols [1l. 7s.] for the fmall ones. The government, which faw with regret this branch of commerce gradually reduced to nothing, forbade the killing of the young bulls. Some active inhabitants collected a great number of heifers in immenfe parks; and fince thefe innovations have been made, the hides which have all the hair on, and which weigh from twenty to fifty pounds, have been lowered about a third in their price. They all pay eleven livres [9s. 2d.] to government.

From 1748 to 1753, Spain received annually from this colony 8,752,065 livres [364,669l. 7s. 6d.]. The gold that made part of this fum amounted to 1,524,705 livres [63,529l. 17s. 6d.]; the filver to 3,780,000 livres [157,500l.]; and the productions to 3,447,360 livres [143,640l.]. The laft article was compofed of three hundred quintals of Vicuna wool, which produced 207,360 livres [8640l.]; and of one hundred and fifty thoufand hides, which brought 3,240,000 livres [135,000l.]. All this was for the benefit of trade, and none of it belonged to the government.

The mother-country will foon receive from this region other articles of value; both becaufe the colony of Saint Sacrament, through which the riches ufed to flow, is now taken out of the hands of the Portuguefe, and becaufe the Paraguay hath acquired a ftate of greater importance than that which it enjoyed.

The immenfe empire which Caftile had founded in South America, was for a long time fubordinate to one fingle chief. The parts that were diftant from the A fortunate innovation, which muft improve

B O O K centre of authority, were then neceffarily abandoned
  VIII.   to the caprices, the inexperience, and the rapacity of a
the ftate of multitude of fubaltern tyrants. No Spaniard, and no
Paraguay. Indian, was mad enough to travel thoufands of miles,
in order to lay claim to juftice, which he was almoft
certain of not obtaining. The force of habit, which
fo often ftifles the voice of reafon, and which governs
ftates with ftill more abfolute fway than it does individuals, prevented men from difcerning the true caufe
of fo many calamities. At length the confufion became fo general, that what is called the New Kingdom of Granada was detached, in 1718, from this enormous extent of dominion. It ftill remained much too
confiderable ; and the miniftry have again confined it,
in 1766, by forming of part of the diocefe of Cufco, of
the whole of that of La Paz, of the archbifhopric of
La Plata, of the provinces of Santa Cruz de la Sierra,
of Cuyo, of Tucuman, and of Paraguay, another vice-
royalty ; the feat of which is at Buenos-Ayres. The
government will, undoubtedly, foon regulate the deftiny of thefe fingular miffions, which have been rendered equally celebrated by the praifes of their pane-
gyrifts, as by the fatires of their detractors.

Principles   America had been laid wafte during the courfe of a
on which
the Jefuits century, when the Jefuits conveyed there that indefa-
founded
their mif- tigable activity, which, from their firft origin, had made
fions in Pa- them fo fingularly remarkable. Thefe enterprifing men
raguay.
could not recal from the tomb the too numerous victims which had been unfortunately plunged into it by
a blind ferocioufnefs ; they could not drag out of the
bowels of the earth the timid Indians whom the avarice of the conquerors obliged daily to defcend there.
Their tender anxiety was turned towards the favages,
whom a wandering life had, till then, preferved from
the fword and from tyranny. The plan was to draw
them out of their forefts, and to collect them into a national body, but at a diftance from the places inhabited by the oppreffors of the New Hemifphere. Thefe
views were crowned with more or lefs fuccefs, in California, among the Moxos, among the Chiquitos, upon

the river Amazon, and in some other countries. Nevertheless, none of their institutions acquired so great a degree of splendour as that which was formed at Paraguay; because it had for its basis the maxims followed by the Incas in the government of their empire and in their conquests.

The descendants of Manco Capac used to march to their frontiers with armies, which at least knew how to obey, to fight, and to intrench themselves; and who, together with better offensive weapons than those of the savages, had also shields and defensive weapons, which their enemies had not. They proposed to the nation which they wanted to unite to their government, to embrace their religion, laws, and manners. These invitations were most commonly rejected. Fresh deputies were sent, who urged these matters more strenuously than the former. Sometimes they were murdered; and the savages fell suddenly upon those whom they represented. The troops that were attacked had generally the advantage; but they suspended the fight the instant they had gained the victory, and treated their prisoners so kindly, that they afterwards inspired their companions with an affection for a conqueror so humane. A Peruvian army seldom began the attack; and the Inca hath often been known to forbear hostilities, even after he had experienced the perfidy of the barbarians, and several of his soldiers had been murdered.

The Jesuits, who had no army, confined themselves to the arts of persuasion. They penetrated into the forests in search of the savages, and prevailed upon them to renounce their old customs and prejudices, to embrace a religion which they did not comprehend, and to enjoy the sweets of society, to which they were before strangers.

The Incas had another advantage over the Jesuits, which was the nature of their religion, calculated to strike the senses. It is a more easy matter to persuade men to worship the sun, which seems to announce its own divinity to mortals, than to adore an invisible God,

and to believe doctrines and mysteries which they cannot comprehend. Accordingly, the missionaries had
the prudence to civilize the savages in some measure,
before they attempted to convert them. They did
not pretend to make them Christians, till they had
made them men. As soon as they had got them together, they began to procure them every advantage
they had promised them, and induced them to embrace Christianity, when, by making them happy, they
had contributed to render them tractable.

They imitated the example of the Incas in the division of the lands into three shares; for religious purposes, for the public, and for individuals; they encouraged working for orphans, old people, and soldiers;
they rewarded great actions; they inspected or cen-
sured the morals of the people; they practised acts of
benevolence; they established festivals, and intermix-
ed them with laborious employments; they appointed
military exercises, kept up a spirit of subordination, invented preservatives against idleness, and inspired them
with respect for religion and virtue: in a word, whatever was valuable in the legislation of the Incas was
adopted, or even improved upon, at Paraguay.

The Incas and the Jesuits had alike established such
a system of regularity and order, as prevented the com-
mission of crimes, and removed the necessity of punishment. There was hardly such a thing as a delinquent
in Paraguay. The morals of the people were good,
and were maintained in this state of purity by still
milder methods than had been made use of in Peru.
The laws had been severe in that empire; they were
not so among the Guaranis. Punishments were not
dreaded there; and men feared nothing but the reproach of their own conscience.

After the example of the Incas, the Jesuits had established the theocratical government, with an additional
advantage peculiar to the Christian religion: this was
the practice of confession, which, in Paraguay, brought
the guilty person to the feet of the magistrate. There,
far from palliating his crime, remorse made him rather

aggravate it; and inftead of endeavouring to elude his B O O K puniſhment, he implored it on his knees. The more VIII. public and ſevere it was, the more did it contribute to quiet his conſcience. By theſe means, puniſhment, which in all other places is the terror of the guilty, was here conſidered as a ſource of conſolation to them, as it ſtifled the pangs of remorſe by the expiation of the guilt. The people of Paraguay had no civil laws, becauſe they knew of no property; nor had they any criminal ones, becauſe every one was his own accuſer, and voluntarily ſubmitted to puniſhment: their only laws were the precepts of religion. Theocracy would be the moſt excellent of all governments, if it were poſſible to preſerve it in its purity: but to effect this, it would be neceſſary that religion ſhould teach nothing but the duties of ſociety; that it ſhould conſider nothing as a crime but what violates the natural rights of mankind; that its precepts ſhould not ſubſtitute prayers in lieu of labour, vain ceremonies inſtead of works of charity, or imaginary ſcruples to juſt remorſe. This was not entirely the caſe at Paraguay. The Spaniſh miſſionaries had brought along with them too many of their monaſtic notions and practices. Perhaps, however, ſo much good had never been done to men, with ſo little injury.

There were more arts and conveniences in the republics of the Jeſuits, than there had been even in Cuſco itſelf, without more luxury. The uſe of coin was unknown there. The watchmaker, weaver, lockſmith, and taylor, all depoſited their works in public warehouſes. They were ſupplied with every neceſſary of life; and the huſbandman had laboured for them. The religious inſtitutors, aſſiſted by magiſtrates who were choſen by the people, attended to the ſeveral wants of the whole community.

There was no diſtinction of ſtations; and it is the only ſociety on earth where men enjoyed that equality which is the ſecond of all bleſſings; for liberty is undoubtedly the firſt.

The Incas and the Jefuits have both infpired men with a reverence for religion, by the dazzling pomp of external ceremonies. The temples of the fun were as well conftructed, and as well ornamented, as the imperfect ftate of the arts and of the materials would allow them to be; and the churches in Paraguay are really very beautiful. Sacred mufic, that awakened their fenfibility, affecting hymns, lively paintings, the pomp of ceremonies: every thing, in a word, confpired to attract and to detain the Indians in thefe places of divine worfhip, where they found pleafure blended with the exercifes of piety.

Reafons that have prevented the increafe of population in thefe celebrated miffions.
It fhould feem that men muft have multiplied confiderably under a government where none were idle, or fatigued with labour; where the food was equal in wholefomenefs, plenty, and quality for all the citizens; where every one was conveniently lodged and well clothed; where the aged and the fick, the widows and orphans, were affifted in a manner unknown in all other parts of the world; where every one married from choice and not from intereft, and where a number of children was confidered as a bleffing, and could never be burdenfome: where debauchery, the necef-fary confequence of idlenefs, which equally corrupts the opulent and the poor, never tended to abridge the term of human life; where nothing ferved to excite artificial paffions, or contradicted thofe that are regu-lated by nature and reafon; where the people enjoy-ed the advantages of trade, and were not expofed to the contagion of vice and luxury; where plentiful ma-gazines, and a friendly intercourfe between nations united in the bonds of the fame religion, were a fe-curity againft any fcarcity that might happen from the inconftancy or inclemency of the feafons; where pub-lic juftice had never been reduced to the cruel necef-fity of condemning a fingle malefactor to death, to ig-nominy, or to any punifhment of long duration; where the very names of a tax or a law-fuit, thofe two ter-rible fcourges which every where elfe afflict mankind,

were unknown; such a country muſt naturally be expected to have been the moſt populous in the world;
and yet it was far from being ſo.

This empire, which began in the year 1610, extends
from the river Parana, which runs into the Paragua under the 20th degree of ſouth latitude, to the Uragua
that falls into the ſame river towards the 34th degree.
On the banks of thoſe two great rivers, which deſcend
from the mountains near Brazil, in the fertile plains
that lie between them, the Jeſuits had already, in 1676,
ſettled twenty-two colonies; though no account hath
been given of their degree of population. In 1702,
there were twenty-nine, conſiſting in all of 22,761,
families, which amounted to 89,491 ſouls. No account, that can be depended upon, ever made the
number of villages amount to more than thirty-two,
nor that of the inhabitants to more than 121,168.

Theſe religious legiſlators have long been ſuſpected
of concealing the number of their ſubjects, with a
view of defrauding Spain of the tribute theſe people
had voluntarily ſubmitted to pay; and the court of
Madrid hath diſcovered ſome anxiety on that account.
An exact inquiry hath diſpelled thoſe injurious and ill-
grounded ſuſpicions. Can it with any probability be
ſuppoſed, that a ſociety, whoſe idol was always glory,
ſhould, for a mean and ſordid intereſt, ſacrifice a ſenſe
of greatneſs, adequate to the majeſty of an eſtabliſhment they were forming with ſo much care and pains?

Thoſe who were too well acquainted with the genius
of the ſociety, to charge it with ſuch injurious and illi-
beral accuſations, have pretended that the number of
the Guaranis did not increaſe, becauſe they periſhed by
working in the mines. This accuſation, urged above
a hundred years ago, hath been propagated by the
ſame ſpirit of avarice, envy, and malignity, that firſt
invented it. The greater pains the Spaniſh miniſtry
have employed in ſearch of theſe hidden treaſures, the
more they have been convinced that they were all
chimerical. If the Jeſuits had diſcovered any ſuch
treaſures, they certainly would have taken care to

conceal the difcovery; which, if known, would have
introduced every kind of vice; by which their empire
would foon have been fubverted, and their power totally deftroyed.

Others are of opinion, that the oppreffion of monkifh government muft have checked the population of
the Guaranis. But oppreffion confifts in impofing labour and exacting tribute by compulfion; in arbitrary
levies of men or money to fupply armies and fleets,
deftined for deftruction; in the violent execution of
laws made without the confent of the people, and
contrary to the remonftrances of the magiftrates; in
the violation of public, and the eftablifhment of private privilege; in the inconfiftency of the principles of an authority, which, under pretence of being
founded by divine will on the right of the fword,
lays claim to every thing by the one, and commands
every thing by the other; which makes ufe of force
to eftablifh religion, and of religion to influence the
decifions of juftice: this is oppreffion. But it can never exift, where every action is the refult of voluntary
fubmiffion, and proceeds from inclination founded on
conviction, and where nothing is done but from choice
and full approbation. This is that gentle fway of opinion, the only one, perhaps, that it is lawful for one
man to exercife over another, becaufe it makes thofe
people happy who fubmit to it. Such, undoubtedly,
was that of the Jefuits in Paraguay, fince whole nations came voluntarily to incorporate themfelves into
their government, and none have ever thrown off the
yoke. It cannot be pretended that fifty miffionaries
could have been able to compel a hundred thoufand
Indians to be their flaves, who had it in their power
either to maffacre their priefts, or to take refuge in
the deferts. This ftrange paradox would be equally
rejected by men of a fanguine or of a credulous difpofition.

Some perfons have fufpected that the Jefuits had
propagated that love of celibacy among their people,
which was fo prevalent in Europe in the dark ages of

ignorance, and is not yet entirely eradicated, notwith- ftanding it hath conftantly been urged how contrary it is to nature, reafon, and fociety. But this opinion is entirely without foundation. The miffionaries have never even given any idea to their converts of a fuper- ftition which was totally improper and inconfiftent with the climate; and would have been fufficient to preju- dice them againft their beft inftitutions, or to defeat the defign of them.

Politicians have further endeavoured to account for the want of population among the Guaranis, from their having no property. The idea under which we confider property, namely, as a fource of the increafe both of men and fubfiftence, is an unqueftionable truth; but fuch is the fate of the beft inftitutions, that our errors will of- ten threaten their deftruction. Under the law of pro- perty, when it is attended with avarice, ambition, lux- ury, a multitude of imaginary wants, and various other irregularities arifing from the imperfections of our go- vernments, and from the bounds of our poffeffions, ei- ther too confined, or too extended, prevent, at the fame time, both the fertility of our lands and the in- creafe of our fpecies. Thefe inconveniencies exifted not in Paraguay. All were fure of fubfiftence; con- fequently all enjoyed the great advantages of proper- ty, though deprived, in a ftrict fenfe, of the right to it. This privation cannot juftly be confidered as the reafon that hath impeded the progrefs of population among them.

A mercenary writer, or one who is blinded by his hatred, hath ventured to publifh, lately, in the face of the whole univerfe, that the territory occupied by the Guaranis could not fubfift more than the number of men who exifted upon it, and that their miffion- aries, rather than fuffer them to extend themfelves fo as to have an intercourfe with the Spaniards, had them- felves ftopped the progrefs of population, by perfuad- ing, as it is faid, their converts to let their children perifh, becaufe they would be fo many beings pre- deftined to falvation, and fo many protectors to them.

Man or devil! whichever thou art, haſt thou reflected
upon the atrociouſneſs and the extravagance of thy
accuſation? Haſt thou any idea of the inſult thou haſt
offered to thy rulers, and to thy fellow-citizens, in
ſuppoſing that thou ſhouldſt obtain their favour or
their eſteem by ſuch aſperſions? How much muſt thy
nation have degenerated from the dignity and genero-
ſity of its character, if it did not partake of my indignation upon this occaſion!

To the chimerical notions we have been refuting,
let us endeavour to ſubſtitute the real, or the probable
cauſes of this deficiency of population.

Firſt, the Portugueſe of St. Paul, in 1631, deſtroyed
twelve or thirteen communities in the province of
Guayra, bordering upon Brazil. Theſe ruffians, whoſe
number did not amount to more than two hundred
and ſeventy-five, could not indeed bring away more
than nine hundred of the twenty-two thouſand Guaranis
that compoſed this riſing colony: but ſeveral of them
were deſtroyed by miſery and by the ſword. Several
of them returned to their ſavage life. Scarce twelve
thouſand of them eſcaped upon the borders of the
Parana and of the Urugua, where it had been reſolved
to fix them.

The paſſion which the devaſtators had for making
ſlaves was not ſtifled by this emigration. They purſued their timid victims into their new aſylum; and,
in proceſs of time, would have diſperſed, enſlaved, or
aſſaſſinated all of them, unleſs the Indians could be
ſupplied with arms ſimilar to thoſe of their aggreſſors.

It was a nice matter to make this propoſal: for it
was a maxim with Spain not to introduce the uſe of
fire-arms among the ancient inhabitants of the other hemiſphere, in the apprehenſion that they might one day
uſe them themſelves to recover their primitive rights.
The Jeſuits approved of this precaution, as being neceſſary with nations whoſe ſubjection was compelled:
but they judged it to be uſeleſs with people, who were
freely attached to the kings of Spain by ſuch eaſy
bands, that they could be under no temptation of

breaking them. The arguments or the folicitations of the miffionaries prevailed over oppofition and prejudice. In 1639 fire-locks were given to the Guaranis, and this favour delivered them for ever from the greateft of dangers they could incur.

This caufe of deftruction was fucceeded by others of a more obfcure nature. The cuftom had prevailed, to fend annually, to the diftance of two or three hundred leagues from their frontiers, fome of the inhabitants of the villages to collect the herb of Paraguay, for which they were known to have an unfurmountable defire. In thefe long and fatiguing journeys, feveral of them perifhed with hunger and fatigue. Sometimes, during their abfence, their plantations, deprived of moft of their defenders, were laid wafte by wandering favages. Thefe defects were fcarce corrected before the miffions were afflicted with a new calamity.

An unfortunate concurrence of circumftances brought among them the fmall-pox; the baneful influence of which was more deftructive in this diftrict than in the reft of the New World. This contagion did not diminifh, and continued uninterruptedly to heap one victim upon another. Were the Jefuits ignorant of the falutary effects of inoculation upon the borders of the Amazon, or did they, from motives of fuperftition, decline to adopt a practice, the advantages of which are fo well afcertained?

But it was the climate which more particularly ftopped the progrefs of population among the Guaranis. The country they occupied, chiefly on the Parana, was hot, damp, and inceffantly covered with thick and immoveable fogs. Thefe vapours gave rife, in every feafon, to contagious diforders; and thefe calamities were aggravated by the propenfities of the inhabitants. Inheriting the voracious appetites which their fathers had brought with them from the midft of the foreft, they fed upon green fruit, and ate meat that was almoft raw, while neither reafon, nor authority, nor experience, could root out thefe inveterate habits. The mafs

B O O K
VIII.

Examina-
tion of the
reproaches
made to the
Jesuits con-
cerning
their mif-
fions.

of blood being thus corrupted by the air and by the food, it was impoffible that a numerous and long-lived offspring fhould be produced.

In order to enfure the felicity of the Guaranis, what-ever their number were, or might be, their inftitutors had originally fettled with the court of Madrid, that thefe people fhould never be employed in the labours of the mines, nor fubjected to any vaffalage. They foon found that this firft ftipulation was not fufficient to procure tranquillity to the new republics, and occa-fioned it to be decreed, that the Spaniards fhould be excluded from them, under whatever denomination they prefented themfelves. They forefaw, that if they were admitted as traders, or even as travellers, they would excite commotions in thofe peaceable retreats, and would introduce vice and every fpecies of cor-ruption. Thefe rapacious and deftructive conquerors were the more offended at thefe meafures, as they were approved by prudent men. Their refentment broke out in imputations, for which there was an apparent, and, perhaps, a real foundation.

The miffionaries traded for the nation. They fent to Buenos-Ayres wax, tobacco, hides, cotton both raw and fpun, and received in exchange, vafes and orna-ments for the temples; iron, arms, toys, fome Euro-pean commodities that were not manufactured in the colony; and metals defigned for the payment of the tribute due from the male Indians from twenty to fifty years of age. As far as it is poffible to judge, and penetrate into the myftery which hath always furround-ed thefe objects, the wants of the ftate did not abforb the entire profit of the fales. The reft was fecreted for the benefit of the Jefuits. Accordingly, they were traduced in all parts of the world as a fociety of mer-chants, who, under the veil of religion, attended only to their own fordid intereft.

This cenfure could not fall upon the firft founders of Paraguay. The deferts through which they travelled afforded neither gold nor mercantile commodities. In thefe they only met with forefts, ferpents, and mo-

raſſes; ſometimes they periſhed, or were expoſed to
the moſt ſevere torments, and always to exceſſive fatigue. The hardſhips they endured with much patience, and the pains they took to induce the ſavages to
quit their roving life, are not to be conceived. They
never entertained the idea of appropriating to themſelves the produce of a land, which their care only
prevented from being a haunt of wild beaſts. Their
ſucceſſors may probably have been actuated by leſs noble and diſintereſted views; probably they might ſeek
an increaſe of fortune and power, where they ought
to have only ſought the glory of Chriſtianity and the
good of mankind. It was certainly a great crime to
rob the people of America, in order to acquire conſequence in Europe, and to increaſe over the whole
world an influence already too dangerous. If any
thing could diminiſh our abhorrence of ſo great a
crime, it is, that the happineſs of the Indians was never affected by it. They never appeared to deſire any
thing beyond thoſe conveniences which they generally
enjoyed.

Thoſe who have not accuſed the Jeſuits of avarice
have cenſured their inſtitutions in Paraguay, as being
the effect of blind ſuperſtition. If our idea of ſuperſtition be the true one, it retards the progreſs of population; it devotes to uſeleſs ceremonies the time
that ſhould be employed in the labours of ſociety; it
deprives the laborious man of his property, to enrich
the indolent and dangerous recluſe; it promotes diſcord and civil wars for things of little moment; it
gives the ſignal for revolt in the name of God; it
frees its miniſters from obedience to the laws, and
from the duties of ſociety: in a word, it makes the
people miſerable, and arms the wicked againſt the virtuous. Have any of theſe calamities been found a-
mong the Guaranis? If their happy inſtitutions be the
effect of ſuperſtition, this is the only inſtance in which
it ever was beneficial to mankind.

Politicians, who are ever reſtleſs and ſuſpicious, ſeemed to be apprehenſive that the republics formed by the

Jefuits might one day detach themfelves from the power under the protection of which they had been raifed.
The inhabitants appeared to them as the beft difciplined foldiers of the New Hemifphere. They confidered them as obedient from a principle of religion,
added to the energy of their new manners, and as
fighting with the fame zeal that brought fo many mar-
tyrs to the fcaffold, and overthrew fo many empires
by the arms of the followers of Wodin and Moham-
med. But it was their form of government which
particularly excited their alarms.

In ancient forms of government, civil and religious
authority, which are derived from the fame fource, and
tend to the fame end, have always been united; or
the one hath been fo fubfervient to the other, that the
people could not venture to feparate them in idea, and
were equally kept in awe by both. Chriftianity introduced another kind of fpirit in Europe, and formed,
at its firft origin, a fecret rivalfhip between thefe two
powers, the one of arms, the other of opinion. This
difpofition manifefted itfelf particularly when the barbarous nations of the north made incurfions upon the
Roman empire. The Chriftians, perfecuted by the
heathen emperors, haftened to implore the affiftance of
thefe foreigners againft oppreffion. They preached to
thefe conquerors a new fyftem of religion, which enjoined to them as a duty to extirpate the eftablifhed
one; and they demanded the ruins of the temples, in
order to erect their own fanctuaries upon thefe magnificent fpoils.

The favages freely difpofed of what was not their
property; they facrificed to Chriftianity all its enemies
and their own; they feized upon the perfons of men
and upon their lands, and diftributed fome of them to
the church. They demanded tribute; but exempted
the clergy from it, becaufe they countenanced their
ufurpations. Noblemen became priefts, and priefts
obtained the rank of nobility. The great connected
the privileges of their birth with that of the priefthood which they embraced. The bifhops imprinted

the feal of religion on the domains they poffeffed. From B O O K this mixture and confufion of birth with high ftations, XVIII. of titles with eftates, and of perfons with things, fprang up a monftrous power, which, from the firft, endeavoured to eftablifh itfelf as diftinct from the only true authority, which is that of government; a power, which afterwards attempted even to raife itfelf above government; but having been unfuccefsful in the attempt, hath fince fubmitted to feparate itfelf from it, and to exert its authority in fecret over thofe who were willing to acknowledge it. Thefe two powers have been always fo much at variance, that they have conftantly difturbed the harmony of all ftates.

The Jefuits of Paraguay, who were well acquainted with this fource of divifion, have been warned by the mifchief their fociety hath often done in Europe, and have exerted themfelves to promote the real happinefs of America. They have united both powers in one; which gave them the entire difpofal of the thoughts, affections, and faculties of their converts.

Did fuch a fyftem of government render the legiflators formidable? Some perfons thought fo in the New World; and this opinion was much more prevalent in the Old one: but in all parts, the neceffary information was wanting to decide the point. The readinefs, perhaps unexpected, with which the miffionaries have evacuated what was called their empire, hath feemed to fhow that they were incapable of maintaining themfelves in it. They have even been lefs regretted there than it was thought they would be. It is not that thefe people had any caufe to complain of the negligence or feverity of their leaders. An indifference fo extraordinary, proceeded undoubtedly from the wearifomenefs which thefe Americans, apparently fo happy, muft have experienced, during the courfe of a life too uniform not to be languid, and under a government which, when confidered in its true point of view, refembled rather a religious community than a political inftitution.

How was it poffible that a whole nation fhould live

Whether the people were happy in thefe miffions, and whether they have regretted their legiflators?

without reluctance under the restraint of an austere law, which is not capable of subjecting a small number of men, although they may have put themselves under its controul from a spirit of enthusiasm, and from the most sublime motives, without inspiring them with melancholy, and without souring their tempers? The Guaranis were a species of monks; and there is not, perhaps, a single monk, who at some time or other hath not detested his habit. Their duties were tyrannically enforced, no fault escaped punishment, and order established its controul in the midst of pleasures. The Guaranis, whose conduct was closely inspected even in their amusements, could not give themselves up to any kind of excess. Noisy mirth and freedom were banished from these melancholy festivals. These manners were too austere. The state of equality to which these people were reduced, and from which it was impossible they should raise themselves, expelled every kind of emulation from among them. One Guaranis had no sort of motive to induce him to excel another. He had acted sufficiently well, when there was no cause of complaint against him, and when he could not be punished for having done ill. Did not also the privation of all property exert some influence over the most tender connections? It is not enough for the happiness of man that he should have what is sufficient for him; he must also have something to bestow. A Guaranis could not be a benefactor to his wife, his children, his relations, his friends, or his countrymen; neither could any of these do good for him. He felt no kind of appetency. If he was without vice, he was also without virtue; he neither loved nor was beloved. A Guaranis with passions would have been the most wretched of beings; and a man without them exists not, either in the midst of forests, in society, or in a cell. There is no passion but that of love, which, being irritated and increased by restraint, could possibly find its advantage in them. But can it be supposed that the Guaranis retained nothing of the sense of their savage state of liberty? Let

the reader take no account of what hath been written, B O O K
and reflect only upon the few lines I now shall add. VIII.
The Guaranis had never any thing but very confused
ideas of what they owed to the care of their legislators,
while they, in the most lively manner, were continually sensible of their despotism. At the time that they
were expelled, these people readily persuaded themselves that they should be free, and that their happiness would not be diminished by it. All kind of authority is more or less odious; and this is the reason
why all masters, without exception, are paid with ingratitude from their servants.

When the missions of Paraguay were taken out of Preliminary steps ta-
the hands of the Jesuits in 1768, they were arrived, ken by the
perhaps, to the highest degree of civilization to which court of
Spain for
it is possible to bring recent nations, and which was the govern-
certainly very superior to every thing that existed in ment of
these mis-
the rest of the New Hemisphere. The laws were ob- sions.
served; an exact police was established; the manners
were pure; and all the inhabitants were united by
brotherly love. All the arts of necessity were improved, and some of those of luxury were known. Plenty
was universal, and the public stores were filled. The
number of horned cattle amounted to seven hundred
and sixty-nine thousand three hundred and fifty-three,
that of mules and horses to ninety-four thousand nine
hundred and eighty-three, and that of sheep to two
hundred and twenty-one thousand five hundred and
thirty-seven, without reckoning other domestic animals.

Authority, which had been hitherto concentrated
in the same hands, was divided. A chief, to whom
three lieutenants were given, was charged with the
government of the country. Every thing that concerned religion was committed to the care of the
monks of the orders of Saint Dominic, Saint Francis,
and La Merci.

This is the only change that hath been hitherto
made in the former arrangements. The court of Madrid certainly wished to examine whether the order

BOOK
VIII.
that was eftablifhed was to be maintained or altered? Attempts have been made to perfuade them to withdraw the Guaranis from a diftrict rather unwholefome, and not fufficiently fertile, in order to people with them the uninhabited borders of the Rio Plata, from Buenos-Ayres to Affumption. If this plan be adopted, and that the people fhould refufe to quit the land of their forefathers, they will be reduced to the neceffity of difperfing themfelves; if they fhould accede to the views of Spain, they will no longer form a national body. Whatever may happen, the moft beautiful edifice that has been raifed in the New World will be overthrown.

But this is enough, and perhaps too much, upon the circumftances and revolutions, more or lefs important, which have agitated Spanifh America during the courfe of three centuries. It is time to afcend to the principles which directed the foundation of this great empire, and to trace, without malignity as without flattery, the confequences of a fyftem of which antiquity hath not left, and could not poffibly leave, any model. We fhall begin, by giving an account of the feveral fpecies of men which are at prefent collected in this immenfe region.

People who inhabit Spanifh America; and firft of the Chapetons. We fhall not reckon among the inhabitants of the New Hemifphere either the commanders who are commiffioned to give them laws, or the troops deftined to protect and contain them, or the merchants employed in fupplying their wants. Thefe feveral orders of men do not fettle in America, but return all of them to Europe after a fhorter or a longer ftay. Among the perfons fent by public authority, there are fcarce any, except a few magiftrates, and a few fubaltern directors, who fix themfelves in thefe diftant regions. The law prohibits every citizen from going there without the confent of government; but men who are known eafily obtain this permiffion, and obfcure perfons frequently go there clandeftinely. Individuals are powerfully ftimulated to this emigration, by the hope of making a large fortune, and fometimes alfo by the

certainty of acquiring a degree of confideration which B O O K
they would not have enjoyed in the place of their ori- VIII.
gin. It is fufficient to be born in Spain, to obtain diftinguifhed marks of refpect; but this advantage is not
tranfmitted. The children that are brought forth in
this other world are not honoured with the name of
Chapetons, as their fathers were; they are fimply called *Creoles*.

This is the name given to thofe who are of Spanifh The Cre--
iffue in the New Hemifphere. Many of them defcend oles.
from the firft conquerors, or their immediate fucceffors; and others have had illuftrious anceftors. Moft
of them have purchafed or obtained diftinguifhed titles; but few of them have directed the great fprings
of government. Whether the court thought them incapable of application, or whether they were apprehenfive they fhould prefer the intereft of their own to
that of the mother-country, they excluded them early
from places of truft, and feldom deviated from this
fyftem, whether it were a proper or an improper one.
This contempt, or this miftruft, difcouraged them, and
they loft, in the vices arifing from idlenefs, from the
heat of the climate, and from the abundance of all
things, the remainder of that elevation of mind, of
which fuch great examples had been left them. A
barbarous luxury, pleafures of a fhameful kind, a ftupid fuperftition, and romantic intrigues, completed the
degradation of their character. One road ftill remained open to the ambition of thefe colonifts, who are in
fome meafure profcribed upon their native land. The
court, the army, the courts of juftice, and the church,
are purfuits of greater or lefs eftimation in Spain, which
they are at liberty to follow. A very fmall number,
however, have entered into them, either becaufe their
minds are entirely corrupted, or becaufe the diftance
renders the accefs to them difficult. Some of lefs diftinguifhed birth have turned, even in America, their
activity and their faculties to the great operations of
trade; and thefe have been the moft prudent and the
moft ufeful.

B O O K   The fame fuperiority which the Chapetons affected
VIII.   over the Creoles, the latter affumed over the Meftees.
The Mef- Thefe are the race proceeding from a European with
tees.   an Indian woman. The Spaniards, who, at the firft
period of the difcovery, landed in the New World,
had no women with them. Some of the moft confiderable of them waited till women were fent from Europe. Moft of them plighted their faith to the moft
diftinguifhed or the moft agreeable girls of the country. Frequently even they became mothers without
being married. The law ordained, that thefe children,
legitimate or illegitimate, fhould enjoy the fame privileges as their fathers ; but prejudice placed them in a
lower rank. It is fcarcely till after three generations,
that is to fay, when their complexion differs in nothing
from that of the white men, who are all very dark,
that, in the ordinary courfe of civil life, they are treated as the other Creoles are. Before they can attain to
fo flattering an equality, thefe Meftees, who are every
where very numerous, and whofe fpecies is uninterruptedly renewed, were moftly employed in the me-
chanic arts, and in the minuter details of trade. When
they have acquired a greater fhare of dignity, they are
ftill obliged to continue the fame labours, till fome
fortunate alliance, or fome particular circumftance,
enables them to pafs their ufelefs days in pleafure and
idlenefs.

The Ne-   Scarce had the New World been difcovered, when
groes.   Negroes were brought into it, in 1503. Eight years
afterwards, a greater number of them was introduced,
becaufe experience had fhown that they were infinitely better calculated for all the labours than the natives
of the country. The government foon prohibited them,
from an apprehenfion that they would corrupt the
Americans, and incite them to revolt. Las Cafas, who
was deficient in proper notions concerning the rights
of mankind, but who was inceffantly employed in the
relief of the Indians, to whom he was attached, obtained the revocation of a law, which he thought
would be injurious to them. Charles V. permitted,

in 1517, that four thoufand of thefe flaves fhould be conveyed into the Spanifh colonies; and the Flemifh courtier, who had obtained the profit of this traffic, fold his privilege to the Genoefe.

At the expiration of this grant, this vile commerce ceafed almoft entirely; but the Portuguefe, having become fubjects of the court of Madrid, revived it. It fell again, after thefe people had fhaken off the yoke which they bore with fo much impatience, and did not recover any activity, till the two nations came to be upon better terms with each other. At length, the fubjects of the court of Lifbon engaged, in 1696, to furnifh, in five years time, twenty-five thoufand Negroes to their former tyrants; and they fulfilled this engagement with the affiftance of their fovereign, who advanced two-thirds of the funds required for an undertaking which was then fo confiderable.

The French, who had juft been giving a king to Spain, too lightly took upon themfelves, in 1702, the engagements of the Portuguefe. Being deficient in fettlements on the coaft of Africa, little fkilled in maritime operations, and having been unfortunate in the courfe of a long war, they did nothing of what they had fo boldly promifed.

This contract paffed into the hands of the Englifh at the peace of Utrecht. The South Sea Company, to whom the Britifh miniftry gave it up, engaged to deliver, each of the thirty years that their charter was to laft, four thoufand eight hundred Africans to the Spanifh fettlements. They were confined to this number during the five laft years of their grant; but all the reft of the time they were allowed to introduce as many as they could fell. They engaged to pay thirty-three piaftres and one-third, or one hundred and eighty livres [7l. 10s.], for each of the firft four thoufand Negroes; the other eight hundred were freed from this burdenfome tribute, in indemnity for 1,080,000 livres [45,000l.] advanced to the court of Madrid, and which were only to be reimburfed in the courfe of ten years. This tribute was reduced to half for all the flaves that were not required by the contract. Philip V. indemnified' himfelf for this facrifice, by referving the fourth part of the profits made by the Company. The execution of this treaty was only interrupted by the hoftilities which, in 1739, divided the two kingdoms. The peace of 1748 reftored to the crown of England all its rights ; but the Company which reprefented it were induced, by an indemnity that was offered to them, to give up the fhort remains of a grant, which they forefaw they fhould not bé allowed to enjoy without confiderable reftrictions.

Robert Mayne, a merchant of London, fucceeded, under a Spanifh name, to the Affociation. Such was the difhonefty or the negligence of the agents whom he had fettled at Buenos-Ayres, which was become the ftaple of the trade, that in 1752 he was ruined, and obliged to give up an undertaking, which, if more prudently managed, or more carefully attended to, ought to have yielded very confiderable profits.

The refolution was then taken to receive flaves at Porto Rico, which were to pay to government two hundred and fixteen livres [9l.] each, and which, after having defrayed this heavy tax, were freely admitted upon the continent and in the iflands. The Englifh, who had treated with the governor of Cuba, fulfilled their engagements punctually, when the court of Madrid thought a change of fyftem would be better calculated for their intereft.

In 1765, an affociation was formed between fome Spanifh, French, and Genoefe commercial houfes, fettled at Cadiz. This Company, which was ill ferved by its agents, and much loaded with debt, was going to be diffolved, when, in 1773, the miniftry thought it prudent and equitable to offer fome alleviation of the terms they had at firft impofed upon it. The charter was prolonged, and the taxes diminifhed ; and, from that period, the importation of flaves hath acquired frefh activity. They are bought indifcriminately in all places where they can be procured to the beft advantage.

Savage Europeans! ye doubted at firft whether the B o o k
inhabitants of the regions you had juft difcovered were VIII.
not animals which you might flay without remorfe,
becaufe they were black, and you were white. You
almoft envied them the knowledge of God, your common Father. Moft horrid thought! But when you
had permitted them alfo to raife their hands and eyes
to heaven ; when you had initiated them in your ceremonies and myfteries; made them join in your prayers and offerings, and in the hopes of a future ftate,
afforded by one common religion ; when you had acknowledged them to be your brethren; was not the
general horror redoubled, at feeing you trample under
foot the ties of this facred confanguinity? You have
put them more upon an equality with yourfelves ; and
yet you go to diftant parts in order to buy and fell
them ! You fell them, too, as you would a bafe herd
of cattle! In order to repeople one part of the globe,
which you have laid wafte, you corrupt and depopu-
late another. If death be preferable to flavery, are
ye not ftill more inhuman upon the coafts of Africa
than you have been in the regions of America? Englifh, French, Spaniards, Dutch, or Portuguefe, let me
fuppofe that I am converfing with one of you about a
treaty concluded between two civilized nations; and
that I fhould afk him, what kind of compenfation he
imagines may have been agreed upon in the exchange
you have made? He will think it to confift in gold,
provifions, privileges, a town, or a province ; while,
on the contrary, it confifts in a greater or lefs number
of your fellow-creatures, which the one gives up to
the other, to difpofe of at pleafure. But fuch is the
infamy of this unnatural contract, that it doth not
even prefent itfelf to the ideas of the contracting parties.

Every thing announces that the court of Spain
will fhake off the dependence they had upon foreign
nations for their flaves. This is the only view they
can poffibly have had, in requiring of Portugal, in

1771, the ceffion of two of their iflands on the African coaft.

   Laborious cultivations, and fome mines of a particular kind, have employed part of the flaves introduced upon the Spanifh continent in the New World.
The fervice of the rich hath been the deftiny of the
greater number. Thefe have foon become the confi-
dents of their mafters pleafures ; and by this infamous
employment they have gained their liberty. Their
defcendants have allied themfelves fometimes with the
Europeans, and fometimes with the Mexicans, and
have formed the vigorous and numerous race of the
Mulattoes, which, as that of the Meftees, but two or
three generations later, acquires the colour and the
rank of white people. Thofe among them who are
ftill in flavery have affumed a determined fuperiority
over the wretched and poor. This fuperiority they
owe to the favour granted to them by government.
For this reafon, the Africans, who, in the fettlements
of other nations, are the enemies of the white people, are become their defenders in the Spanifh Indies.

   But why fhould the favour of government be beftowed upon the flave that was bought, in preference
to the flave that was conquered ? It is, becaufe the
injury done to the latter was of more ancient date,
and greater than the injury done to the former ; that
the latter was accuftomed to the yoke, and that the
former was to be broken to it ; and that the flave of a
mafter, whom a fyftem of policy hath made mafter of a
flave, is brought, by this diftinction, to take part with
the common tyrant. If the African, who is the de-
fender of the white people in the Spanifh Indies, hath
been their enemy in all other parts, it is becaufe in all
other parts he hath always obeyed, and never commanded ; it is, becaufe he was not comforted in his
fituation by the fight of one more wretched than his
own. In the Spanifh Indies, the African is alternately flave and mafter ; in the fettlements of other nations, he is perpetually a flave.

The Indians form the laft clafs of inhabitants, in a B O O K VIII. country which belonged entirely to their anceftors. The misfortunes of thefe people began even at the era of the difcovery. Columbus diftributed lands at firft to thofe who accompanied him, and attached fome natives of the country to them in 1499. This arrangement was not approved of by the court, who, three years after, fent Ovando to St. Domingo, to reftore thefe wretched people to liberty. This new commander, barbarous as he was, complied with the will of his fovereigns: but the indolence of the Americans, and the complaints of the Spaniards, foon determined him to put thofe whom he had fet free again into chains, and to add ftill a greater number to them. But he decreed, that thefe flaves fhould reap fome advantage from their labour, whether they were employed in the culture of the lands, or the working of the mines. In 1504, this arrangement was confirmed by Ferdinand and Ifabella, with a provifo, that the ftipend fhould be regulated by government.

The Dominicans, who had juft arrived in the colony, were incenfed at an arrangement which overthrew all former principles. They refufed, in the confeffional chair, abfolution to thofe individuals who folicited, or even accepted, thofe gifts, which were indifcriminately ftyled repartitions, or commanderies. They thundered out excommunications from the pulpit againft the authors or promoters of thefe injuftices. The exclamations of thefe monks, fo much revered at that time, refounded throughout all Europe, where the cuftom, which they attacked with fo much inveteracy, was again difcuffed in 1510, and was again confirmed.

In 1516, the Indians found in Las Cafas a more zealous, more intrepid, and more active protector, than thofe who had preceded him. His folicitations determined Ximenes, who at that time governed Spain with fo much fplendour, to fend over to America three friars to determine upon this matter, which had already been twice decided. The decrees they pronounced were not fuch as were expected from their profeffion. They decided in favour of the commanderies, but excluded from them all the courtiers and favourites who did not refide in the New World.

Las Cafas, who had been declared the protector of the Indians by the minifter himfelf, and who, invefted with this honourable title, had accompanied the delegates, returned immediately into Spain, in order to devote to public indignation men of a pious profeffion, whom he accufed of having facrificed humanity to political views. He fucceeded in having them recalled, and Figueroa was fubftituted to them. This magiftrate took the refolution to collect, in two large villages, a confiderable body of Indians, whom he left entirely at their own difpofal. The experiment did not turn out in their favour. The government concluded, from their ftupidity and their indolence, that the Americans were children incapable of conducting themfelves; and their condition was not altered.

Neverthelefs, the clamours of many refpectable perfons were raifed on all fides againft thefe arrangements; and the ftates of Caftile themfelves demanded, in 1523, that they fhould be annulled. Charles V. yielded to all thefe folicitations. He forbad Cortez, who had juft conquered Mexico, to give any commanderies, and enjoined him to revoke thofe he might already have granted. When thefe orders arrived in New Spain, the repartitions were already fettled as in the other colonies, and the monarch's pleafure was not complied with.

From this, and all other countries fubject to Caftile, intelligence was conftantly received, that no real or ufeful labours would be carried on in the New World, if the people who were fubdued fhould for a moment ceafe to be at the difpofal of their conquerors. The apprehenfion of having made the difcovery of fo rich a hemifphere without advantage, made a great impreffion upon the miniftry: but, on the other hand, the idea of having invaded one half of the globe, merely to reduce the nations to flavery, was another

point of view which could not fail of exciting some B O O K
alarms in the government. In this uncertainty, com- VIII.
manderies were allowed or prohibited at hazard. At
length, in 1536, the government adopted the medium
of giving a fanction to them for two generations. Although they had been granted only for two years before this period, they were in reality perpetual, fince
there was not a fingle inftance of the grant's not being
renewed. The king continued to referve to himfelf
all the Indians fettled in the ports or in the principal
towns.

The protector of thefe wretched people grew in-
dignant at thefe ordinances. He fpoke, he exerted
himfelf, he fummoned his nation to the tribunal of the
whole univerfe, and made the two hemifpheres fhudder
with horror. O! Las Cafas! thou waft greater by thy
humanity, than all thy countrymen were by their conquefts. Should it happen in future ages, that thefe unfortunate regions which they have invaded fhould be
peopled again, and that a fyftem of laws, manners,
and liberty, fhould be eftablifhed among them, the
firft ftatue they would erect would be thine. We
fhould fee thee interpofing between the American and
the Spaniard, and prefenting thy breaft to the poniard
of the one, in order to fave the other. We fhould
read, at the bottom of this monument, IN AN AGE OF
BARBARITY, LAS CASAS, WHOM THOU SEEST, WAS A BE-
NEVOLENT MAN. In the meanwhile thy name will remain engraved upon every feeling heart; and when
thy countrymen fhall blufh at the barbarifm of their
pretended heroes, they will take pride in thy virtues.
May thefe fortunate times not be fo far diftant as we
apprehend they are!

Charles V. enlightened by his own reflections, or
prevailed upon by the impetuous eloquence of Las Cafas, ordered, in 1542, that all the commanderies which
fhould become vacant fhould be indifcriminately reunited to the crown. This decree was not in force in
Mexico and Peru, and occafioned a bloody and obftinate war. The government were obliged to annul it

three years after; but authority was eftablifhed with fufficient folidity in 1549, to bid defiance to all complaints, and to be no longer impeded by the fear of infurrections.

At this period, the Indians were freed from all perfonal fervices, and the tribute they were to pay to their commanders was regulated. The mafters, hitherto fo oppreffive, were forbidden to refide in the extent of their jurifdiction, and to fleep there more than one night. They were alfo prohibited from having any dwelling there, from leaving their families, from poffeffing any lands, from breeding any cattle, and from eftablifhing any manufactures. They were forbidden to intermix in marriage with their vaffals, and to take any of them into their fervice. The perfon commiffioned to collect their taxes muft have the fanction of the magiftrate, and muft give fecurity againft any vexations he fhould be guilty of.

The tax impofed upon the natives of the country, to make their conquerors fubfift with a degree of dignity, is not even merely a gratuitous favour. Thefe proud mafters are obliged to collect their fubjects in a village, to build them a church, and to pay the clergyman appointed to inftruct them. They are obliged to fix their refidence in the principal town of the province, in which their commandery is fituated, and to have always horfes and arms in readinefs to repel an enemy, whether foreign or domeftic. They are not permitted to abfent themfelves, till they have put a foldier, approved by government, in their place.

No material alterations were made in thefe regulations till 1568. It was then refolved, that the commanderies, which, for thirty-two years paft, had been granted for two lives, fhould continue to be given in the fame manner; but that thofe, the revenue of which exceeded ten thoufand eight hundred livres [450l.], fhould be fubject to penfions. All of them were in future to be proclaimed when they became vacant, and fuppofing the merit of the competitors equal, to be diftributed in preference to the heirs of the con-

querors, and, after them, to the defcendants of the firft B O O K
colonifts. The court, perceiving that thefe rewards VIII.
were more frequently diftributed by favour than by
talents, or the claim of an ancient origin, ordered, in
1608, that they fhould be annulled, if the favours
granted by the viceroys were not confirmed in fix
years for Peru, and in five for the reft of America.
The chief of the commandery, however, entered into
the enjoyment of his poft as foon as he was appointed.
It was only required of him to fecure the reftitution of
the fums he might have received, if the choice that
had been made of him were not ratified at the time
prefcribed by the ordinances.

At the beginning of the laft century, the government appropriated to themfelves the third part of the
revenue of the commanderies. Soon after this, they
took the whole of it into their hands, and forbade
their delegates to fill up thofe that fhould become vacant. At length, they were all fuppreffed in 1720,
except thofe that were given in perpetuity to Cortez,
and to fome hofpitals or religious communities. At
this period, fo remarkable in the annals of the New
World, the Indians were dependent only on the crown.

Was this fyftem the beft that could poffibly be a-
dopted for the intereft of Spain, and the felicity of the
other hemifphere? Who will be able to folve a problem, in which fo many circumftances are complicated? The rights of juftice; the fentiments of humanity; the private views of minifters; the fway of the
moment; the ambition of the great; the rapacioufnefs of favourites; the projects of fpeculative men; the
authority of the priefthood; the influence of the manners and of prejudice; the character of the diftant fubjects; the nature of the climate, of the foil, and of the
labours; the diftance of places; the tardinefs and contempt of the fovereign's orders; the tyranny of governors; the impunity of crimes; the uncertainty of accounts and of accufations; and fuch a multitude of
other different matters. We need not therefore be
furprifed at the long uncertainty of the court of Ma-

B O O K   drid ; when, in the centre of European nations, at the
VIII.   foot of the throne, under the immediate infpection of
the directors of the ftate, we fee abufes fubfifting, and
often increafing, on account of the abfurdity of meafures. The man, with whom they were furrounded,
was then taken for the model of the man at a diftance;
and it was imagined that the fame fyftem of legiflation
which fuited the one, was equally adapted to the other.
In former times, and, perhaps, even at prefent, we con-
found with each other, two beings feparated by immenfe differences, the favage and the civilized man ;
the man born in the centre of liberty, and the man
born in the fhackles of flavery. The averfion of the
favage for our cities, arifeth from the improper manner
in which we have introduced ourfelves into his forefts.

At prefent, the Indians who have not been fettled in
the towns, are all collected in villages, which they are not
permitted to quit, and where they form municipal af-
femblies, over which their cacique prefides. To each
of thefe villages a territory of greater or lefs extent is
attached, according to the nature of the foil, and the
number of its inhabitants. Part of it is cultivated in
common for the public neceffities, and the reft is diftributed to the families for their private ufe. The law
hath ordained that this domain fhould be unalienable ;
fome portions of it, however, are, from time to time,
allowed to be detached from it, in favour of the Spaniards ; but always with an annual charge upon it, for
the profit of the fellers, under the infpection of government. There is no inftitution which prevents the Indians from having lands belonging to them ; but they
have feldom the power or the inclination to make acquifitions.

As difgrace breaks down all the fprings of the mind,
one of the caufes of this poverty and of this difcouragement, muft be the obligation impofed upon thefe people, of being alone devoted to the public labours. The
law ordains that they fhould be paid for this humiliating labour; but the diftance from whence they may

be brought, and the time they may be detained, de- B O O K
pends upon the government of the spot. VIII.

Another duty imposed upon the Indians, is to be at
the disposal of all the citizens; but merely for the manufactures, and the cultures of primary necessity; and
this in rotation only, for eighteen days consecutively,
and for a salary settled by the ordinances.

They have still a more burdensome task, and that is
the working of the mines. The directors were originally the sole regulators of this task. It was afterwards
provided for by statutes, which were frequently varied.
At present, no Indians are called to the mines, except
to those of Guanca Velica, and of Potosi, which have
particular privileges, who live at the distance of more
than thirty miles: they are allowed four reals, or fifty-
four sols [about 2s. 3d.] per day; they are detained no
longer than six months, and the seventh part of a colony is only employed in them at Peru, and the twen-
ty-fifth part at Mexico. Frequently even there are a
less number, because libertinism, cupidity, the expectation of thieving, and, perhaps, other motives, attract
there a great number of Mestees, Mulattoes, and natives.

A tribute which the male Indians, from eighteen to
fifty years of age, pay to the government, completes
this multitude of calamities. This tax, which was originally paid in provisions, is not the same in all parts.
It is from eight to fifteen, twenty, thirty, and forty
livres, [from 6s. 8d. to 12s. 10d.—16s. 8d.—1l. 5s. and
1l. 13s. 4d.] according to the different periods when,
at the request of the persons who paid it, it was converted into coin. The custom which prevailed with
the government, of requiring always in money the value of the productions, the price of which varies with
time and place, introduced these disproportions, which
were greater, and consequently more destructive in
South, than they were in North America, where the
capitation is usually of nine reals, or six livres one sol
six deniers [rather more than five shillings]. The
fourth part of this tax is distributed to the clergyman,

B O O K to the cacique, and to the Spaniard, commissioned in
VIII.   each province to prevent the oppression of the Indians,
or kept for the purpose of assisting the community in
any of its misfortunes. Such is the legal condition of
the Indians : but no one can determine how much private injustice adds weight to a burden already too
heavy. That, among the vexations which hath most
attracted the notice of government, hath proceeded
from the officer, who is called an Alcade at Mexico,
and a Corregidor at Peru.

This is a magistrate charged, under the inspection of
the viceroy, or of the tribunals, with the administration
of justice ; with the management of the finances, of
war, of police, and of every thing that can concern
public order, throughout the space of thirty, forty, and
fifty leagues. Although the law prohibited him, as
well as the other depositaries of authority, from undertaking any trade ; yet, from the earliest times, he monopolized all that was possible to be carried on with
the Indians under his jurisdiction. As he only remained five years in office, he used to deliver, almost as soon
as he got in, the merchandise he had to sell, and employed the rest of his time in collecting in the payments. The oppression became general. The unfortunate natives of the country were always crushed
by the enormity of the prices, and frequently by being
obliged to take goods of no use to them, but which
the tyrant himself had sometimes been compelled to
receive from the merchants, who afforded him a long
and hazardous credit. Every thing, or almost every
thing, was refused to the poor, and those who enjoyed
any kind of ease in their circumstances were overburdened. When the payments became due, they were
exacted with barbarous severity, by a creditor who is at
once both judge and party ; and the most heavy penalties were inflicted upon the debtors, who failed either in the voluntary or compelled obligations they
had entered into.

The humane and equitable chiefs were sensibly affected with these enormities, which were more atro-

cious and more frequent in South, than they were in North America. They thought it, however, neceſſary to tolerate them, from an idea generally entertained, that if the chain which was formed was once to be broken, theſe indolent and thoughtleſs people would be in want of clothing, of inſtruments of agriculture, of cattle neceſſary for all the labours, and that they would immediately fall into a ſtate of inaction and extreme miſery. Some prudent men endeavoured to reconcile intereſts that were ſo oppoſite to each other; but none of their ideas were found to be practicable. A ſure method of leſſening the miſchief, would have been, to put the magiſtrates, who went to ſeek, in another hemiſphere, a fortune which their native country refuſed them, upon a better footing : but the miniſtry would never conſent to this increaſe of expence. Since the year 1751, the Alcades and the Corregidors are obliged to fix upon the place of their reſidence, the goods they have to ſell, and the price they mean to put upon them. If they deviate from this rate, which is approved of by their ſuperiors, they are to loſe their places, and to reſtore the quadruple of what they have purloined. This regulation, which is rather ſtrictly attended to, hath in ſome degree diminiſhed the depredations.

A form of government was wanting for the ſeveral people we have been ſpeaking of; and the court of Madrid adopted that which was the moſt abſolute. The Spaniſh monarchs took all the rights and all the powers into their own hands, and entruſted the exerciſe of them to two delegates, who, under the title of viceroys, were to enjoy the prerogatives of ſovereignty during all the time of their commiſſion. They were attended in their public functions, and even in their private life, with a degree of pomp, which ſeemed calculated to increaſe the reſpect and terror which was inſpired by authority. The number of theſe diſtinguiſhed offices hath ſince been doubled, without the leaſt derogation from their dignity. Their conduct, however, as well as that of the inferior agents, was

BOOK VIII.

Civil government eſtabliſhed by Spain in the New World.

subject to the censure of the Council for India ; a tribunal erected in Europe, to govern, under the infpection of the monarch, the conquered provinces in the
New World.

In thefe diftant countries were eftablifhed ten courts
of juftice, appointed to enfure the tranquillity of the
citizens, and to fettle any differences that might arife
among them. Thefe tribunals, known by the name
of Audiences, pronounced definitively upon criminal
matters : but caufes that were merely civil, and which
were for more than 10,156 piaftres, or 54,843 livres
[2285l. 2s. 6d.], might be carried, by appeal, to the
Council for India. The privilege granted to thefe
great bodies to make remonftrances to the depofitaries of the royal authority, and the ftill more confiderable prerogative given to thofe of the capitals to fill
the duties of the vice-royalty, whenever they were vacant, raifed them to a degree of importance, which, as
magiftrates, they would not have acquired.

Nature of
the ecclefi-
aftical go-
vernment
adopted in
America.
It feemed more difficult to regulate the ecclefiaftical form of government. At the period of the difcovery of the New World, all Europe was covered with
a veil of darknefs, woven, or thickened, by the prejudices which the court of Rome had inceffantly diffufed, fometimes openly, and fometimes with cunning.
Thefe fuperftitions were more deeply rooted, and more
general in Spain, where the infidels had for fo long a
time paft been the object of their hatred and of their
wars. The fovereigns of this kingdom, one would naturally imagine, would have eftablifhed beyond the
feas the bad principles of the pontiffs who gave them
another hemifphere ; but this was not the cafe. Thefe
princes, more enlightened, as it fhould feem, than
might be expected from the age they lived in, deprived the ruler of Chriftendom of the privilege of collat-
ing to the benefices of the church, and even of the
tithes, which the priefts had affumed to themfelves in
all parts. Unfortunately, the prudence that had dictated this fyftem, was not followed by their fucceffors,
who founded, or permitted to be founded, too great a

number of bifhopricks. Numberlefs churches were B O O K
conftructed, and convents of both fexes multiplied be- VIII.
yond every idea of excefs. Celibacy became the ruling paffion in a defert country. Metals, which fhould
have been employed in fertilizing the earth, were
thrown away upon the churches. The clergy, notwithftanding their ignorance and corruption, obtained
the reftoration of the greateft part of thofe oppreffive
tithes which had been drawn out of their avaricious
hands. America feemed now to have been conquered
but for them. In the meanwhile, the inferior clergy,
thofe who are in other parts fo mild and fo refpectable,
did not find themfelves fufficiently opulent. The Indian, whom they were appointed to inftruct and comfort, did not dare to appear before them without fome
prefent. They indulged him in fuch of his former fuperftitions as were of advantage to themfelves ; as, for
inftance, the cuftom of putting a great quantity of
provifions upon the tombs of the dead. They fet an
exorbitant price upon their functions, and had always
fome pious inventions, which gave them an opportunity of exacting frefh taxes. Such a conduct had rendered their tenets generally odious. Thefe people
went to mafs as they did to the labours of vaffalage,
execrating the barbarous ftrangers, who loaded their
bodies and their fouls with burdens equally weighty.

The fcandal became public, and almoft general. The
fecular and the regular clergy, who both of them fulfilled the fame miniftry, mutually accufed each other of
thefe vexations. The firft defcribed their rivals as a fet
of vagabonds, who had withdrawn themfelves from the
fuperintendence of their fuperiors, in order to follow
their libertinifm with impunity. The latter accufed
the other of their ignorance and indolence, and cenfured them for being wholly taken up with the education of their families. We acknowledge, with regret,
that there was reafon for thefe reproaches on both
fides. The court was for a long time difturbed by the
intrigues of thefe two cabals, which were inceffantly
renewed. At length they decreed, in 1757, that the

monks ſhould occupy the benefices they held during life, but that they ſhould not be ſucceeded in them by men of the ſame profeſſion. This determination, which brings matters again into their natural order, will probably be attended with favourable conſequences.

It was a great point, to have regulated, in the firſt inſtance, all the great ſprings of the new empire. It now remained to ſettle the deſtiny of thoſe who were to live in it. The ſovereign, who thought himſelf the legitimate poſſeſſor of all the lands of America, by right of conqueſt, and by the conceſſion of the pontiffs, cauſed ſome of them, at firſt, to be diſtributed among his ſoldiers, who had fought in the New World.

The foot ſoldier received a piece of ground of the length of one hundred feet, and of the breadth of fifty, to build upon; one thouſand eight hundred and eighty-five toiſes for garden-ground; ſeven thouſand five hundred and forty-three for his orchard; ninety-four thouſand two hundred and eighty-eight for the culture of European corn; and nine thouſand four hundred and twenty-eight for that of Indian corn; and all the extent of ground that was neceſſary to breed ten hogs, twenty goats, one hundred ſheep, twenty horned cattle, and five horſes. The cavalry man was allowed double the quantity of ground for his buildings, and the quintuple of all the reſt.

Soon after towns were conſtructed. Theſe were not left to the caprice of perſons who meant to inhabit them. The ordonnances required that they ſhould be in an agreeable ſituation, in a wholeſome air, on a fertile ſoil, abounding with waters. They regulated the poſition of the churches, the direction of the ſtreets, and the extent of the public ſquares. It was uſually ſome rich and active individual who undertook to build them, after they had obtained the ſanction of government. If the whole was not finiſhed at the ſtipulated time, he loſt all the money he had advanced, and was likewiſe indebted to the treaſury 5400 livres [225l.]. The other obligations impoſed upon him were, to find a clergyman for his church, and to ſupply him with all that was required to keep up the de-BOOK cency of a regular form of worſhip. He was alſo VIII. obliged to collect at leaſt thirty Spaniſh inhabitants, each of whom was to have ten cows, four oxen, one mare, one ſow, twenty ſheep, one cock, and ſix hens. When theſe conditions were fulfilled, the civil and criminal juriſdictions were granted to him in the firſt inſtance for two generations, the right of appointing the municipal officers, and four leagues ſquare of territory.

Part of this great ſpace was taken up in the placing of the city, by the commons, and by the perſon who undertook the buſineſs. The reſt was divided into equal portions, which were drawn for by lot, and none of which could be alienated till after five years cultivation. Every citizen was to have as many lots as he had houſes; but his property was never to exceed what Ferdinand had originally granted at Saint Domingo to three horſemen.

Thoſe perſons who had poſſeſſions in the towns that were already founded, were excluded by law from the new ſettlements : but this ſtrict regulation did not extend to their children. All the Indians who were not detained elſewhere by engagements which they could not break, were allowed to ſettle there as ſervants, as mechanics, or as labourers.

Excluſive of the lands which were ſecured to the troops, and to the founders of towns, the chiefs of the ſeveral colonies were authoriſed to diſtribute ſome to the Spaniards who were inclined to ſettle in the New Hemiſphere. This great privilege was taken from them in 1591. Philip II. whoſe ambition engaged him in perpetual wars, and whoſe obſtinacy would never allow him to put an end to them, was not able to anſwer ſo many expences. The ſale of the lands in America, which to this period had been given away, was one of the reſources that ſuggeſted itſelf to him. His law had, even in ſome ſort, a retroactive effect, in as much as it ordered the confiſcation of all that was poſſeſſed without a legitimate title, unleſs the uſurper

fhould confent to redeem thefe poffeffions. An arrangement fo ufeful in reality, or in appearance, to the
treafury, never received any modification at any period, nor hath it yet experienced any.

But it was a more eafy matter to beftow lands gratuitoufly upon fome adventurers, or to cede them to
fuch perfons at a low price, than to induce them to
make them fertile. This kind of labour was defpifed
by the firft Spaniards, whom their avidity had led into
the Indies. The flow, laborious, and expenfive mode
of cultivation, could fcarce tempt men, who, in the
hope of making an eafy, brilliant, and rapid fortune,
had braved the waves of an unknown ocean, and the
dangers of all kinds that awaited them upon unwholefome and barbarous coafts. They were in hafte to enjoy; and the moft expeditious way of doing this, was
to feize upon the minerals. An enlightened government would have endeavoured to rectify the ideas of
their fubjects, and to give, as much as poffible, another
bent to their ambition. But the direct contrary of this
took place; the error of individuals became the policy of the miniftry; they were blind enough to prefer
treafures that are merely fo by convention, the quantity of which could not fail of being diminifhed, and
which muft daily lofe fomething of their imaginary
price, to riches that are inceffantly fpringing up afrefh,
and the value of which muft gradually increafe in all
times. This illufion of the conquerors and of the fovereigns threw the ftate out of the road of profperity,
and formed the manners in America. Nothing was in
eftimation but gold or filver, accumulated by rapine,
by oppreffion, and by the working of the mines.

Regula-
tions made
at different
periods for
the work-
ing of the
mines. In the earlieft times of the conqueft, it was decreed,
that the mines fhould belong to the perfon who difcovered them, provided he had them registered in the
tribunal neareft to the fpot. The government had at
firft the imprudence to have the portion of this rich
foil, which they had referved for themfelves, fearched
on their own account; but they foon renounced this
ruinous error, and contracted the habit of ceding it to

the proprietor of the reft of the mine for a very mo- B O O K
derate fum. If thefe treafures were found in cultivated   VIII.
parts, which fcarce ever happened, the perfon who undertook the mine was to purchafe the extent of ground
he wanted, or to give up the hundredth part of the
ore. Upon barren mountains, the proprietor was more
than fufficiently indemnified for the little damage he
received, by the value which a new exertion gave to
the productions cultivated in the neighbourhood.

From the moft ancient times, the mines, of whatfoever nature they were, gave up to the treafury in Spain
the fifth of their produce. This cuftom was carried
into the New World ; but in procefs of time the government was obliged to confine itfelf to a tenth for
the gold, and even in 1735, for the filver in Peru.
They were alfo obliged, in general, to lower the price
of mercury. Till the year 1761, this neceffary agent
had been fold for 432 livres [18l.] the quintal. At
this period it coft no more than 324 [13l. 10s.], or
even 216 livres [9l.], for the mines that were not
abundant, or which were very expenfive in the working.

Every thing leads us to fuppofe, that the court of
Spain will be obliged, fooner or later, to make other
facrifices. In proportion as the metals grow more-
common in commerce, they decreafe in value, and
they reprefent fewer commodities. This degradation
muft one day make the beft mines be negleected, as
it hath fucceffively made the middling ones to have
been abandoned, unlefs the burden of thofe who
work them be alleviated. The time, perhaps, is not
far diftant, when the Spanifh miniftry muft be contented with two reals, or one livre feven fols [about
1s. 1½d.], which they receive per mark for the ftamp
and for the coinage.

The circumftance that might give great weight to
thefe conjectures is, that there are fcarce any men,
except thofe whofe affairs are in a doubtful or ruinous
fituation, who venture the taking of a part in the mines.
If it fhould fometimes happen, that a rich merchant

ſhould be ſtimulated to it by an unbounded avidity,
he doth it always under the veil of the moſt impenetrable ſecrecy. The bold ſpeculator may conſent to
expoſe his fortune, but never his name. He is well
aware, that, if his engagements were known, his reputation and his credit would be inevitably loſt. It is
not till his raſhneſs hath been crowned with the moſt
brilliant ſucceſs, that he can venture to avow the riſks
he hath run.

Taxes eſta-
bliſhed in
Spaniſh A-
merica. When the government ſhall be obliged to give up
the duties they yet receive from the metals, they will
ſtill have conſiderable revenues for the expences of ſovereignty. The principal of theſe ought to have been
the tithes, which Ferdinand had compelled the court
of Rome to give up to him : but Charles V. from motives which it is not eaſy to conjecture, deprived himſelf of them in favour of the biſhops, the chapters, the
rectors, the hoſpitals, the building of the churches; in
a word, in favour of men and of eſtabliſhments, which
were either too rich already, or ſoon became ſo. This
prince ſcarce tranſmitted the ninth part of them to his
ſucceſſors. It was neceſſary that a tribute extorted
from the Indians ſhould fill up a void ſo inconſiderate-
ly made in the public treaſure. The ſuperior claſſes
of ſociety were not treated with leſs management; all
the New World was ſubject to the Alcavala.

This is a tax levied only upon what is ſold by whole-
ſale, and which doth not extend to articles of daily
conſumption. It comes originally from the Moors.
The Spaniards adopted it in 1341, and ſettled it at the
rate of five *per cent.* It was afterwards carried up to
ten, and even to fourteen : but, in 1750, arrangements
were made, which brought it back to what it had been
in the firſt inſtance. Philip II. after the diſaſter of that
fleet, ſo well known by the pompous title of Invincible, was urged, in 1591, by his wants, to require this
aſſiſtance from his poſſeſſions in America. It was at
firſt only at two *per cent.*, and in 1627 it roſe to four.

Stampt paper, that mode ſo wiſely invented to ſecure the fortune of individuals, and which is become,

in all parts, one of the principles of their ruin in the B o o k
hands of the treasury : ftampt paper, I say, was in-   VIII.
troduced, in 1741, into all the Spanish provinces of
the New World.

The monopoly of tobacco began to diftress Peru in
1752, Mexico in 1754, and in the interval of these
two periods, all the other parts of the hemisphere dependent on Castile.

At divers times, the crown hath appropriated to itself, in the New as well as in the Old World, the monopoly of gunpowder, lead, and cards.

The most extraordinary of all imposts, however, is
the crusade. It took its rise in those ages of folly and
fanaticism, when millions of Europeans went to lose
their lives in the East for the recovery of Palestine.
The court of Rome revived it in favour of Ferdinand,
who, in 1509, wished to attack the Moors of Africa.
This tax still subsists in Spain, where it is never lower
than twelve sols six deniers [rather more than 6d.], and
never higher than four livres [3s. 4d.]. A greater sum
is paid for it in the New World, where it is only collected every two years, and where it rises from thirty-
five sols to thirteen livres [from about 1s. 7d. to 11s.
8d.], according to the rank and fortunes of the citizens. For this sum the people acquire the liberty of
obtaining absolution from their confessors, for such
crimes as are reserved for the absolution of the pope
and the bishops; they acquire the right of eating, upon days of abstinence, some kinds of prohibited food,
and a multitude of indulgences for sins already committed, or for those that may be committed in future.
The government do not strictly oblige their subjects
to take this bull: but the priests would refuse the
comforts of religion to those who should neglect or
disdain it; and there is not, perhaps, in all Spanish
America one man sufficiently bold, or sufficiently enlightened, to brave this ecclesiastical censure.

I will not, therefore, address myself to a set of foolish
mortals, whom we should in vain advise to shake off
the double yoke under which they are oppressed; and

I will not fay to them, What! do ye not conceive
that Providence, which watches over your prefervation, in prefenting you with food which is proper for
you, and in perpetuating inceffantly the appetency
you have for it, meant undoubtedly to allow you the
free ufe of it? If the Heavens were irritated when
you eat of it in a forbidden feafon, there is no power
on earth that could difpenfe with your obedience. Do
ye not fee that your ftupid credulity is impofed upon,
and that, by an infamous kind of traffic, a being who
is not greater than you are, a creature who is nothing
before the face of your common Mafter, arrogates to
himfelf the right of commanding you in his name, or
or of freeing you from the obfervation of his orders,
for a piece of money? This piece of money, doth he
take it for himfelf, or doth he give it to his God? Is
his God indigent? Doth he depend upon refources, or
doth he amafs treafures? If in the other life he be a
rewarder of virtue, and an avenger of crimes, neither
the gold which you have given, nor the abfolution
which you fhall have purchafed with that gold, will
have any effect upon the fcale. If his venal juftice
fhould admit of corruption, he would be as vile and
as contemptible as thofe who are feated in your tribunals. If his reprefentative had the fame power for
himfelf as he hath perfuaded you that he hath for you,
he might be the moft wicked of mankind with impunity, fince there is not any crime which he would not
have it in his power to pardon. Neither will I addrefs myfelf to the fubaltern minifters of this proud
chief, becaufe they have a common intereft with him ;
and that, inftead of anfwering me, they would light
up the ftake under my feet. But I will addrefs myfelf to the chief himfelf, and to the whole body over
which he prefides, and I will tell them :

It is time you fhould renounce this unworthy monopoly, which difgraces you, and which difhonours
both the God whom you preach, and the religion
which you profefs. Simplify your doctrine, and purge
it from abfurdities. Abandon, with a good grace, all

the posts from which you will be driven. The world is too enlightened to be any longer gulled with in-comprehensibilities that are repugnant to reason, or to give credit to miraculous falsehoods, being common to all religions, cannot be admitted as proofs for any one. Return to a practicable and social system of morality. Let the reformation of your theology be followed by that of your manners. Since you enjoy the privileges of society, partake of the burdens of it. Do not any longer plead your immunities against the efforts of an equitable ministry, who would wish to bring you back to the general condition of other citizens. Your spi-rit of intoleration, and the odious means by which you have acquired, and still continue to heap up riches upon riches, have done more injury to your opinions, than all the arguments of incredulity. Had you been the appeasers of public and domestic troubles, the ad-vocates of the poor, the support of the persecuted, the mediators between the husband and the wife, between fathers and children ; had you been, among citizens, the organs of the law, the friends of the throne, and co-operators with the magistrate; however absurd your tenets had been, mankind would have been silent. No one would have ventured to attack a class of men so useful and so respectable. But you have spread divi-sions over Europe for concerns of the most frivolous nature. All countries have been reeking with blood, and for reasons which at present we blush to think of. If you would restore to your ministry its former dig-nity, be humble, be indulgent, be even poor if it should be necessary : for so your Founder was. His apostles, his disciples, and their followers, who con-verted all the known world, were so likewise. Be nei-ther mountebanks nor hypocrites, nor simoniacal, nor dealers in things which you give out as holy. Endea-vour to become priests again ; that is to say, delegates from the Most High, to preach virtue to men, and to show them the example of it. And thou, Pontiff of Rome, call thyself no longer the servant of the ser-vants of God, unless thou wilt be so. Consider that

BOOK VIII.

the era of thy bulls, of thine indulgences, of thy
pardons, and of thy dispensations, is past. It is in
vain that thou wouldst sell the Holy Ghost, if no one
can be found to purchase it. Thy spiritual revenue
is continually decreasing, and, sooner or later, it must be
reduced to nothing. Whatever the subsidies may be, the
nations that pay them are naturally inclined to get rid
of them; and the slightest pretence is sufficient. Since
from a fisherman thou hast made thyself a temporal
prince, become, as all good sovereigns are, the pro-
moter of agriculture, of the arts, of manufactures, of
trade, and of population. Thou wilt then have no
occasion for a traffic that is scandalous. Thou wilt
restore to the labours of man the precious days which
thou hast deprived him of; and thou wilt recover our
veneration, which thou hast lost.

The finances of the Spanish continent of the other
hemisphere were for a long time a mystery to the ministry themselves. The chaos was in some measure
cleared up by M. de la Ensenada. Each of the twelve
years of his fortunate administration, the crown received from these countries, or from the duties they
collected at the departure and at the return of the
fleets, 17,719,448 livres 12 sols [738,310l. 7s. 2d.].
This resource of government hath since been much
increased, both from the value of the new taxes, and
from the strictness that hath been observed in the
collecting of the old ones. At present the public
revenue of Mexico amounts to 54,000,000 livres
[2,250,000l.]; that of Peru, to 27,000,000 livres
[1,125,000l.]; that of Guatimala, of the New Kingdom of Chili, and of Paraguay, to 9,100,000 livres
[379,166l. 13s. 4d.]. This amounts in all to 90,100,000
livres [3,754,166l. 13s. 4d. The local expences absorb
56,700,000 livres [2,362,500l.]; so that there remain
for the treasury 34,500,000 livres [1,437,500l.]. Add
to this sum 20,584,450 livres [857,585l. 8s. 4d.], which
they receive in Europe itself upon the articles sent to
the colonies, or which are brought from thence, and
it will be found that the court of Madrid draws annu-

ally 55,084,450 livres [2,295,185l. 8s. 4d.] from its
provinces in the New World. But all thefe riches do
not enter into the royal coffers of the mother-country.
Part of them is employed in the Spanifh iflands in A-
merica, for the expence of fovereignty, and for the
building of fhips, or for the purchafing of tobacco.

Spain had fcarce difcovered this other hemifphere,
when fhe conceived the idea of a fyftem unknown to
the people of antiquity, but which hath fince been a-
dopted by modern nations, that of taking into her
hands all the productions of her colonies, and the whole
care of fupplying them with provifions. In this view
the government were not fatisfied with forbidding thefe
new eftablifhments, under capital penalties, to hold any
foreign intercourfe; but they carried their ftrictnefs fo
far, as to render all communication between them impracticable, and to prohibit them from fending any of
their fhips to the country from which they originally
came. This fpirit of jealoufy foon betrayed itfelf in the
mother-country. The fhips, indeed, were at firft allowed to fet out from different ports; but they were
all obliged to return to Seville. The wealth which
this preference accumulated in this city, foon enabled
it to obtain, that the fhips fhould be difpatched from
its harbour, as well as they were compelled to return
to it. The river that wafhes its walls, not being afterwards found confiderable enough to receive the fhips,
which had gradually increafed to a certain fize, it was
the peninfula of Cadix which became the general
ftaple. All foreign merchants fettled in this port,
which was become famous, were forbidden to take a
direct part in a trade of fo lucrative a nature. In vain
did they reprefent, that as they confumed the provifions of the kingdom, as they paid the taxes, and as
they encouraged agriculture, induftry, and navigation,
they ought to be confidered as citizens. Thefe reafons
were never attended to in a court where cuftom was
the fupreme law. Thefe active, opulent, and enlightened men, who for a long time paft had alone kept
up the connections between the Ancient and the New

BOOK
VIII.

Deftructive
principles
upon which
Spain firft
founded its
connections
with the
New
World.

World, were always obliged, with more difguft and inconvenience than one would imagine, to cover their moft trifling tranfactions under a Spanifh name.

The liberty of undertaking voyages to the great fettlements that were forming on all fides in the other hemifphere, was even much reftrained with regard to the natives themfelves. The government took the refolution of regulating, every year, the number of fhips that it was thought proper to fend, and to fix the time of their fetting out. It entered into their fyftem of politics, to render thefe voyages very unfrequent, and the permiffion to fit out a veffel became a very fignal favour. In order to obtain it, the capital of the empire was filled with intrigues, and corruption was kept up in all the offices.

Under the pretence of preventing frauds, of eftablifhing an invariable order, and of procuring entire fafety to fhips that were richly laden, delays, vifitations, fearchings, failors, and formalities of every kind were multiplied to fuch a degree, both in Europe and America, that the ufelefs expences doubled the value of fome goods, and enhanced confiderably that of others.

The oppreffion of the cuftoms completed the ruin of every thing. The articles exported to the other hemifphere were fubjected to fuch duties as had never exifted in any age, or in any part of the globe. The price even that had been given for them was taxed. The gold, on its return, paid four *per cent.* and the filver nine.

Reafons why the court of Madrid perfevered in their erroneous fyftem.
But how was it poffible that the court of Madrid fhould be fo grofsly deceived with refpect to their interefts; or ftill more, how was it poffible they fhould perfift in their error? Let us endeavour, if we can, to find out the caufes of fo ftrange an infatuation.

The empire of the Spaniards over the New World was eftablifhed in an age of ignorance and barbarifm. All the principles of government were then forgotten; and we need not certainly be furprifed, that in the intoxication of their victories, a fet of proud conquerors

fhould not have reſtored knowledge, which had been
baniſhed from Europe for ten or twelve centuries paſt.

At this period of general infatuation, the court of
Madrid did not conjecture that the ſettlements they
were forming in another hemiſphere would only be
uſeful, in as much as they ſhould produce an encouragement of their agriculture, induſtry, and navigation.
Far from making the colonies ſubordinate to the mother-country, it was, in ſome meaſure, the mother-
country that was ſubordinate to the colonies. Every
political economy was either neglected or diſdained ;
and the grandeur of the monarchy was viewed only in
the gold and ſilver of America. The people were ſeized with the ſame ambition, and abandoned their native
country in multitudes, to go in ſearch of theſe metals.
Theſe immenſe and continual emigrations, left a void
in the population of the principal country, which was
not filled up by the reſort of foreigners, becauſe they
were inceſſantly driven from it by pride and the ſpirit
of intoleration.

Spain was confirmed, by ſucceſſes which were maintained rather for a long time, in the falſe road ſhe had
at firſt marked out for herſelf. An aſcendency, which
ſhe owed to circumſtances alone, appeared to her to
be a neceſſary conſequence of her adminiſtration and
her maxims.

The calamities which afterwards invaded this kingdom on all ſides might poſſibly have enlightened it.
An almoſt continued ſeries of wars, ſome more fatal
than others, deprived it of the tranquillity neceſſary
to examine into the defects of a ſyſtem which had
been uninterruptedly purſued with the greateſt ſecurity.

The knowledge ſucceſſively acquired, or diffuſed by
other nations, was very well calculated to refute and
diſſipate the errors of Spain. Whether from pride or
jealouſy, this nation obſtinately rejected the lights it
might have obtained from its rivals or its neighbours.
In default of foreign aids, the Spaniards, born with
a ſpirit of reflection, and with penetrating ſagacity,

might have difcovered many circumftances of confequence to their profperity. This kind of genius, which
was fit for every thing, unfortunately turned itfelf towards contemplations which could not but increafe
their miftakes.

To fill up the meafure of thefe misfortunes, the
court of Madrid had, from early times, impofed a law
upon themfelves, to fupport the meafures they had
followed, in order that they might not be fufpected of
having lightly taken a refolution. Events, however
difgraceful they were, did not difguft them of thefe
politics in their connections with America; and they
were confirmed in them, by the combined or feparate
fuffrages of a multitude of corrupt or difhoneft agents,
who enfured their own private fortune by the keeping
up of univerfal confufion.

Confe-
quences
which the
fatal combi-
nations of
the Spanifh
miniftry
were at-
tended with
even in the
mother-
country. The mifchief, however, was not felt from the firft,
although fome celebrated writers have afferted this
with confidence. According to their opinion, Spain,
feeing herfelf the miftrefs of America, voluntarily renounced her manufactures and her agriculture. Such
an extravagant idea never entered into the fyftem of
any nation. At the period when the other hemifphere was difcovered, Seville was celebrated for its
filk manufactures; the woollens of Segovia were e-
fteemed the fineft in Europe; and the ftuffs of Catalonia found an advantageous mart in Italy and in the
Levant. Other openings for trade gave frefh activity
to this induftry, and to the cultivation of the lands,
which is infeparable from it. Had it been otherwife,
how is it poffible that this monarchy could have invaded fo many provinces; fuftained fo many tedious
and bloody wars; paid fo many foreign and national troops; equipped fuch numerous and formidable
fleets; kept up divifion in the neighbouring ftates,
and purchafed traitors among them; fubverted all
nations by their intrigues; and given the impulfe to
all political events? How could they have been the
firft, and, perhaps, the only power of the univerfe?

But all thefe exertions occafioned an immenfe con-

fumption of men : feveral went over into the New B O O K
World : this other hemifphere, more wealthy and VIII.
more populous, required more merchandife ; and hands
were wanting for all the labours. Then Spain was
furnifhed with fubfiftence, and her colonies were fupplied with clothing, by foreign nations, where fpecie
was ftill fcarce, and, confequently, labour at a moderate price. In vain were they excluded from this
traffic by ftrict regulations. Whether they were friends
or foes, they carried it on without interruption, and
with fuccefs, under the name of the Spaniards, whofe
honefty always deferved the higheft encomiums. The
government thought to remedy what they imagined
to be an evil, but which was nothing more than the
neceffary confequence of the ftate of things, by renewing the ancient prohibition of exporting either
gold or filver. At Seville, and afterwards at Cadix,
fome bravoes, called *Metedores*, carried the ingots upon the ramparts, and threw them over to other Metedores, who were to deliver them to the boats that
came up to receive them. This clandeftine trade was
never difturbed by excifemen, or by guards, who were
all paid to fhut their eyes. More ftrictnefs would only
have ferved to increafe the price of the merchandife,
from the greater difficulty of obtaining the value of
it. If, in conformity to the rigour of the ordonnances,
any delinquent had been feized, tried, and condemned
to death, and his property confifcated, fuch an atrocious act, far from preventing the exportation of the
metals, would have increafed it ; becaufe the perfons
who had before been fatisfied with a moderate gratui-
ty, requiring a falary proportioned to the danger they
muft incur, would have increafed their profits by their
rifks, and would have made a great deal of money go
out, in order that they might have the more for themfelves.

Such was the ftate of Spain, when fhe herfelf voluntarily aggravated her calamities by the expulfion of
the Moors.

This nation had reigned for a long time almoft over

BOOK VIII.

the whole of the peninsula. From one post to another, they were successively driven to Granada; where, after a ten years continuance of a bloody war, they were again forced, in 1492, to submit to the yoke. By the terms of capitulation, they were to be allowed to follow their own form of worship; but the conqueror, under various pretences, soon wished to deprive them of this sacred right; and they took up arms in order to maintain it. Fortune declared itself against these unfortunate Mussulmen; and numbers of them perished by the sword. Others purchased the right of taking refuge in Africa; and the rest were condemned to appear Christians.

This apparent compliance, with which Ferdinand and Charles chose to be satisfied, did not meet with the approbation of Philip II. This persecuting prince required that the Infidels should be really of his religion. In the hope of engaging them to this more certainly, and in less time, he ordered, in 1568, that these people should renounce their idiom, their names, their habits, their baths, their customs, and every thing that could distinguish them from his other subjects. Despotism was carried so far, as to forbid them from changing their residence, without the consent of the magistrate; from marrying, without the leave of the bishop; from bearing arms, under any pretence whatever; and even from having any in their possession. An obstinate resistance must have been the consequence of so blind an act of tyranny. Unfortunately, men who had no leader, no discipline, and no means of carrying on the war, could make none but unavailing efforts against numerous armies, accustomed to carnage, and commanded by experienced generals. The inhabitants of the towns and country places, who had entered into the rebellion, were almost generally exterminated. Servitude became the lot of all the prisoners of both sexes. Those even of the Moors who had remained quietly at home, were conveyed into the interior provinces of the kingdom, where they met with nothing but insults and reproach.

This difperfion, and this humiliation, did not pro- B O O K
duce the effect that was expected. The cruelties, VIII.
which were inceffantly renewed by a fanguinary tribunal, were not more availing. It appeared to the
clergy, that the only way remaining was to expel from
the monarchy all thefe enemies who fo obftinately per-
fifted in their doctrines. This was accomplifhed in
1610, notwithftanding the oppofition of fome ftatefmen, and notwithftanding the ftill warmer folicitations
of the grandees, who kept in their palaces, or on their
domain, many flaves of the nation that was perfecuted
by fuperftition.

We find from all accounts, that this profcription
deprived Spain of a million of inhabitants. Some authentic pieces, collected by Bleda, a prudent and con-
temporary writer, fhow that this number muft be reduced to four hundred and twenty-nine thoufand three
hundred and fourteen. This was not the whole of the
Moors that had efcaped the fury of the wars and the
fanaticifm of the conquerors, or that remained from
the emigrations, fometimes tolerated and fometimes
clandeftine. The government retained the women
that were married to former Chriftians, whofe faith
was not fufpicious to the bifhops, and all the children
under feven years of age.

In the meanwhile the ftate loft the twentieth part
of their population, and the moft laborious part, as
the profcribed and perfecuted fects will always be.
Whatever were the occupations of thefe people ; whether their ftrength was employed in the fields, in the
manufactures, or in the meaneft offices of fociety, it is
certain that a great deficiency was made in the labours, as well as in the tributes collected. The burden
which had been borne by the infidels fell chiefly upon
the weavers. This additional weight drove many of
them into Flanders and into Italy ; while the reft,
without quitting the country, renounced their profeffion. The filks of Valencia, and the fine wool of Andalufia and Caftile, were no longer manufactured by
the Spaniards.

BOOK   The treafury having no more manufacturers to op-
VIII. prefs, now oppreffed the farmers. The taxes levied
upon agriculture were as ill-judged as they were various and exceffive. Befide general duties, there were
what the financiers call extraordinary duties, which
is a mode of levying money upon a particular clafs of
citizens ; a kind of tax unprofitable to the ftate, and
ruinous to thofe who are taxed, and which tends only
to enrich the perfon who hath contrived it. Thefe
refources proved inadequate to the urgent neceffities
of government, and the financiers were called upon to
advance confiderable fums. At this period they became mafters of the ftate, and were empowered to
farm out the feveral parts of their leafe. This introduced a multitude of agents, and with them numberlefs reftraints and oppreffions. The laws which thefe
rapacious men were allowed to enact, were only fo
many fnares to feduce the honeft and credulous. In
procefs of time, they ufurped the fovereign authority,
and found means to elude the royal tribunals, to choofe
judges for themfelves, and to pay them.

The owners of the lands that were oppreffed by
this tyranny, either threw up their eftates, or neglected the improvement of them. That fertile peninfula,
which, though fubject to frequent droughts, ftill afforded fubfiftence to thirteen or fourteen millions of
inhabitants before the difcovery of America, and had
formerly been the granary of Rome and of all Italy,
was foon overfpread with thorns and briars. The pernicious cuftom of fixing the price of corn was then
adopted ; and public granaries were eftablifhed in every province, which were confequently managed without either fkill, care, or honefty. Befides, what advantage could be expected to arife from fuch precarious refources? How could it poffibly enter into any
one's thoughts, to lay reftraints upon the price of corn,
in order to increafe the quantity of it ; to raife the
price of provifions, in order to make them cheaper ;
or to facilitate monopoly, in order to prevent it?

When once a nation hath begun to decline, it fel-

dom recovers itself. The loss of population, of the B O O K
manufactures, of trade, and of agriculture, was attend-   VIII.
ed with the greatest evils. While Europe was daily
improving in knowledge, and all nations were animated with a spirit of industry, Spain was falling into
a state of inaction and barbarism. The duties of the
former customs, which were still suffered to remain upon goods passing from one province to another, were
carried to such an excess, as to prevent all, communication between them. Even the conveyance of money from one province to another was prohibited. In
a short time, not the least sign of a road was to be
seen. Travellers were stopped at the crossing of rivers,
where there was neither bridge nor boats. There was
not a single canal, or one navigable river. People, the
most superstitious in the world, with regard to the observance of fast days, suffered their fisheries to decline,
and bought fish every year to the amount of twelve
millions [500,000l.]. Except a few ill-built vessels
destined for their colonies, they had not a single ship
belonging to government in their harbours. Their
coasts lay exposed to the depredations of the Barbary
corsairs. To avoid these, they were obliged to freight
upon foreign bottoms, even the *avisos* they sent to the
Canary islands and to America. Philip IV. possessed of
all the rich mines of America, at once found all his
gold changed into copper, and was reduced to the necessity of making his copper coin bear almost the same
value as that of silver.

These were not the greatest grievances of the monarchy. Spain, from an absurd and superstitious veneration for the age of her conquests, scornfully rejected whatever was not practised in those glorious days.
The Spaniards saw all other nations growing more enlightened, more exalted, and more powerful; but
thought it beneath them to copy after any one of
them. An absolute contempt for the improvements
and customs of their neighbours, formed the distin-
guishing character of this people.

The inquisition, that tremendous tribunal, which

B O O K was at firſt eſtabliſhed, in order to ſtop the progreſs of
VIII. Judaiſm and of the Coran, had entirely altered the
character of the Spaniards. It had accuſtomed them
to reſerve, to miſtruſt, and to jealouſy. And, indeed,
how ſhould it have been otherwiſe? When a ſon
could accuſe his father, a mother her child and her
huſband, a man his friend or his fellow-citizen; when
mutual accuſations were the bent of all the paſſions;
when a man might be ſeized upon in the midſt of his
children, and thrown into a dark dungeon, by the ſa-
tellites, either in the day, or in the night-time; when
the crime laid to a man's charge was concealed from
him; when a man was compelled to defend himſelf,
and, being in priſon for a fault which he had not committed, was afterwards detained and tried for a ſecret
fault which he had avowed; when the trial was carried on, and finiſhed, without confronting the witneſſes;
when ſentence was pronounced, without allowing the
accuſed perſon to ſay any thing in his defence: then
men accuſtomed themſelves to blood, and to the moſt
atrocious ſcenes: then their minds were filled with
that ſpirit of fanaticiſm which diſplayed itſelf ſo cruelly in both hemiſpheres. Religious diſputes occaſioned, indeed, no diſturbances or ravages in Spain; but
the nation remained in a ſtate of the moſt profound
ignorance. Such diſputes, though always abſurd in
themſelves, ſerve, however, to exerciſe the mind.
They induce men to read and reflect, to conſult antiquity, ſtudy hiſtory, and the ancient languages; hence
ariſes criticiſm, which is productive of true taſte. The
ſubject that firſt excited the exertion of the mind ſoon
becomes of no conſequence; books written on con-
troverſial points are neglected, but the knowledge
they have diffuſed remains. Religious matters are
like thoſe active and volatile particles that exiſt in all
bodies fit for fermentation. They firſt occaſion a cloud
in the liquor that was before clear, but ſoon put the
whole maſs in motion. In this ferment, they fly off,
or ſink to the bottom; and when the whole is depu-
rated, nothing remains but a ſoft, pleaſant, and nutri-

tive fluid. But in the general ferment of theological difputes, all the refufe ftill continued in Spain. Su-perftition had fo blinded the nation, that they even gloried in their infatuation.

Inftead of that energy which could alone animate the feveral parts of thofe wide dominions that lay too much fcattered, the Spaniards were fo flow in their motions, that all bufinefs was impeded. Such a variety of forms, precautions, and deliberations, were multiplied to prevent impofition, that they only put a ftop to every commercial tranfaction.

The wars in which the Spaniards were engaged were as ill conducted as their fyftem of politics. A population, which was hardly fufficient for the many garrifons they kept in Italy, in the Low Countries, in Africa, and in the Indies, rendered them incapable of raifing an army at home. At the firft breaking out of a war, they were obliged to have recourfe to foreign troops. The few Spaniards who were fent to fight along with thefe mercenaries, were fo far from being able to manage them, that their own allegiance was frequently fhaken by this intercourfe. They have often revolted together with the foreign troops, and ravaged the provinces that were committed to their protection.

A regular pay would infallibly have prevented, or foon put a ftop to this fpirit of fedition. But to provide for the payment of troops, and to keep them in that ftate of dependence and fubordination fo neceffary to good difcipline, government fhould have fuppreffed that multitude of ufelefs officers, who, by their falaries and their oppreffions, abforbed the greateft part of the public revenue; the moft ancient rights of the crown fhould not have been alienated for a trifling confideration, or fuffered to be invaded; nor fhould the royal treafures have been fquandered away, to entertain fpies, and to procure traitors in every country. But care fhould have been particularly taken, that the grandeur of the prince fhould not have been made to confift in granting penfions and favours to all who had no other claim, but that which they derived from their boldnefs in afking for them.

This noble and iniquitous way of receiving alms was become general. The Spaniard, naturally generous, having acquired a fpirit of pride, difdained the common occupations of life, and afpired after nothing but governments, bifhoprics, and the chief employments in the ftate.

Thofe who could not attain to thefe preferments, glorying in their proud infolence, ftill affumed the ftyle of the court, and maintained as much gravity in their idlenefs, as a minifter who was abforbed in ftate affairs.

Even the lower clafs of the people would have thought they defiled their victorious hands by proftituting them to ufeful labours. They employed themfelves carelefsly, even in thofe which were the moft creditable, and trufted all the reft to foreigners, who carried fortunes away with them, which ferved to fertilize or to enrich their own country.

Men born to no property, meanly preferring idle flavery to laborious liberty, eagerly folicited to be admitted into the number of domeftics that the great kept in their retinue, with that pomp which magnificently difplays the pride of the moft ufelefs, and the degradation of the moft neceffary clafs of men.

Thofe who had too much vanity remaining to live without fome diftinction, crowded into the convents, where fuperftitious men had long fince provided a convenient retreat for their indolence, and had carried their abfurdity fo far, as to lavifh marks of diftinction upon them.

Even the Spaniards who had competent fortunes, languifhed in a ftate of celibacy, choofing rather to give up all thoughts of pofterity, than to attend to the eftablifhment of it. If fome, induced by love and virtuous motives, chofe, in imitation of the great, to enter into marriage, they fent their fons, in their earlier years, to be educated in the fuperftitious manner of the colleges; and from the age of fifteen refigned them to the courtezans. The abilities and ftrength of thefe young men being thus vitiated, they were equally enervated by thefe infamous connections, which they did not even break off when they entered into the facred ties of matrimony.

Out of this degenerate race were chofen the men who were to hold the reins of government. Their adminiftration was anfwerable to their education, being a conftant fcene of idlenefs and corruption. They feldom difcovered any fenfe of virtue, or principles of equity, or the leaft defire of promoting the happinefs of their fellow-creatures. They thought only of plundering the provinces intrufted to their care, in order to diffipate in idlenefs and profufion at Madrid the fruits of their extortion. This conduct was always purfued with impunity, though it often occafioned feditions, infurrections, confpiracies, and fometimes revolutions.

Befide thefe misfortunes, the ftates that were united to Caftile by marriage or conqueft contributed to complete the ruin of the Spanifh monarchy. The Low Countries did not afford a fufficiency to pay the garrifons that were kept to defend them. Franche Compté fupplied nothing ; Sardinia, Sicily, and the Milanefe, were even burdenfome to government. The tributes of Naples and Portugal were mortgaged to foreigners. Arragon, Valencia, Catalonia, Rouffillon, the Balearic iflands, and Navarre, pretended they owed nothing to the monarchy but a free gift, which was always fettled by their deputies, but feldom to the fatisfaction of a rapacious court, exhaufted by abfurd liberalities.

While the mother-country was declining, the colonies could not poffibly flourifh. If the Spaniards had underftood their true intereft, they would perhaps, on the firft difcovery of America, have been content with eftablifhing an equitable intercourfe with the Indians, which would have fettled a mutual dependence and reciprocal profits between the two nations. The manufactures of the Old World would have been bartered for the produce of the mines of the New ; and wrought iron would have been exchanged for its weight of unwrought filver. A lafting union, the neceffary confequence of a peaceable traffic, would have been eftablifhed without bloodfhed or devaftation. Spain would equally have been miftrefs of Mexico and Peru; becaufe any nation that cultivates the arts, and does not communicate the method by which it carries them on, will always have an evident fuperiority over thofe to whom it fells its manufactures.

This method of reafoning was not adopted by the Spaniards. The eafe with which they had fubdued the Indians, the afcendant which Spain had affumed over all Europe, the natural pride of conquerors, their ignorance of the true principles of commerce; all thefe, and various other caufes, prevented them from eftablifhing in the New World a fyftem of government founded upon good principles.

The depopulation of America was the melancholy effect of this irregularity. The firft fteps of the conquerors were marked with ftreams of blood. Aftonifhed as much at their own victories as the favages were at their defeat, and intoxicated with their fuccefs, they refolved to extirpate the people they had plundered. Innumerable nations difappeared from the face of the earth at the arrival of thefe barbarians; and thefe horrid fcenes of cruelty have been afcribed to a thirft of gold, and to a fpirit of fanaticifm.

But the ferocious difpofition natural to man, unreftrained by the fear of punifhment, or by any fenfe of fhame, and unawed by the prefence of civilized men, might fo far conceal from the Spaniards the image of an organization fimilar to their own (a fimilarity which is the foundation of all moral duties), as to induce them to treat their new-difcovered brethren as they did the wild beafts of the other hemifphere, and to do it with as little remorfe: befides, that the cruelty arifing from military exploits increafes in proportion to the dangers the foldier hath gone through, to thofe he now endures, or to thofe he expects: Is he not of a more fanguinary difpofition in remote countries than at home; and do not the fentiments of humanity grow weaker, the more diftant we are from our native country? It may likewife be conjectured, that the Spaniards, who, on their firft landing, were taken for gods, might be afraid of being detected and maffacred; that they miftrufted the marks of kindnefs that were fhown them; that when once they had begun to fhed blood, they thought their own fafety required that they fhould not difcontinue; that their army, confifting only of a fmall number of men, being furrounded by an innumerable multitude of natives, whofe language they did not underftand, and whofe cuftoms and manners they were ftrangers to, was feized with a panic, either well or ill founded.

The Spaniards, the defcendants or flaves of the Vifigoths, like them, divided among themfelves the defert lands, and the men who had efcaped their fword. Moft of thefe wretched creatures did not long furvive, doomed to a ftate of flavery worfe than death. The laws that were occafionally eftablifhed in order to alleviate the hardfhips of their fervitude, afforded them but fmall relief. The favage, proud, and rapacious Spaniards paid as little regard to the commands of a monarch who was too far remote from them, as to the tears of the poor miferable Indians.

The mines proved ftill a greater caufe of deftruction. Ever fince the difcovery of America, the Spaniards had attended only to this fpecies of wealth. In vain did fome men of more enlightened underftanding exclaim againft this infatuation. Let the gold remain where it is, faid they, provided the furface of. the earth that covers it can but produce an ear of corn that will make bread, or a blade of grafs to feed your fheep. The only metal you really want is iron. Work it into faws, hammers, and ploughfhares, but not into weapons of deftruction. The quantity of gold requifite for the purpofes of exchange is fo inconfiderable, that it is unneceffary to accumulate any great ftock of it. It is very immaterial whether a hundred

B O O K ells of cloth, or one pound or twenty pounds of gold,
VIII. be given in exchange.   The Spaniards have acted like
the dog in the fable, that dropped the meat out of
his mouth, to bite at the image of it in the water, and
was drowned in attempting to get it.

Unfortunately the Indians were the victims of this
fatal error.   Thofe unhappy men were fent to work
at a very great depth under ground, where they were
deprived of day-light, of a free and wholefome air,
and of the comfort of mingling their tears with thofe
of their friends and relations ; and were doomed to
dig their own graves in thofe dark manfions, which
now contain more afhes of the dead than gold duft.
All the nations of the univerfe being incenfed at thefe
barbarities, the Spanifh writers endeavoured to prove,
that the working of the mines was not attended with
any danger : but the evidence of the fenfes teftified
the contrary.   It was well known that man could not
dwell in the obfcure caverns of the earth, without fuffering fome inconvenience with refpect to his eye-
fight ; that he could not breathe mercurial, fulphu-
reous, arfenical, and peftilential vapours, without injury to his lungs : that unwholefome air could not be
abforbed by the pores of the fkin, or fwallowed by
the mouth, without prejudice to the ftomach, and to
the humours of the body.   But men coming out of the
mines prefented the image of death under all its forms;
a tormenting cough, a hideous atrophy, a melancholy
marafmus, with convulfions, contractions, and diftor-
tions of the limbs.   The miners were obferved to have
wrinkles, debility, tremblings, and a declining life, at
the age of the moft vigorous health ; and confequently, far from giving any credit to the accounts of the
Spaniards, their deceit excited indignation, when their
ignorance was not an object of ridicule.

Numbers of the Americans, in order to efcape thefe
means of deftruction, and to withdraw themfelves from
other acts of European tyranny, took refuge in the
forefts, and among inacceffible mountains.   In thefe

rough and wild climates, they contracted a ferocious difpofition, which frequently diftreffed their mercilefs oppreffors, and was the caufe of much bloodfhed.

In fome diftricts, defpair was carried fo far, that the men, in order not to leave behind them any heirs of their misfortunes, refolved unanimoufly to have no connection with the women. This abftinence from the moft natural defire implanted in human nature, which is the only inftance of the kind ever recorded in hiftory, feems to have been referved to the era of the difcovery of the New World, as a perpetual monument of Spanifh tyranny. What more could the Americans oppofe to this thirft of deftruction, than the horrid vow of ceafing to perpetuate their pofterity? Thus the earth was ftained with the blood of the fathers, and deprived of the fucceeding generation.

From this period the country feemed to lie under a curfe with refpect to thefe barbarous conquerors. The empire they had founded began to tend to general deftruction. Profligacy and corruption made a rapid progrefs among them. The moft important fortreffes were fuffered to decay. The country was left without arms or magazines. The foldiers, who were neither exercifed, fed, nor clothed, became beggars or thieves. The firft principles of war and navigation were forgotten, as well as the very names of the inftruments made ufe of in thefe two neceffary arts.

Trade confifted only in the art of cheating. The gold and filver, which were to be brought into the king's coffers, were fraudulently diminifhed, and reduced to a fourth part of the fum they ought to have produced. All orders of men, corrupted by avarice, united their efforts to prevent a true ftate of things from being laid before the throne, or to fcreen thofe perfons who had rendered themfelves obnoxious to the law. The magiftrates of every rank and degree always unanimoufly exerted themfelves to fupport each other in their injuftice.

BOOK
VIII.

The fcene of confufion occafioned by thefe extortions introduced the fatal expedient of all ill governed ftates, that of numberlefs taxes : it feemed as if government had two objects in view, to put a ftop to
every kind of induftry, and to increafe oppreffion.

Ignorance kept pace with injuftice. Europe was
not then much enlightened. Even the knowledge
that began to diffufe itfelf in this quarter of the globe
was rejected by Spain. In the meanwhile, a thicker
cloud was fpread over America. The moft fimple notions, upon objects of the greateft importance, were
entirely obliterated there.

As ignorance is always favourable to fuperftition,
the minifters of religion, rather more enlightened than
the colonifts, affumed a fuperiority over them in the
management of all public affairs. Being more fecure
of impunity, they were always the moft forward to
break through the laws of juftice, and through all
rules of morality and decency. The leaft corrupt
among them became traders, and the reft availed themfelves of their ecclefiaftical power to extort from the
Indians all they were poffeffed of.

The hatred which arofe between the Spaniards born
in America, and thofe who came from Europe, completed their ruin. The court had imprudently laid
the foundation of thefe unhappy divifions. The Creoles had been falfely reprefented as little better than
barbarians, and nearly of the fame character as Indians. They thought they could not depend upon their
fkill, courage, or fidelity, and therefore determined to
exclude them from all places of truft and profit. This
injurious refolution irritated the Creoles. The Spaniards, who were invefted with authority over them,
were fo far from endeavouring to reconcile them, that
they ftudied, on the contrary, to exafperate them by
humiliating partialities. This produced an inveterate
hatred between thefe two orders of men, one of which
was loaded with favours, and the other ftigmatized
with difgrace. This animofity hath often broken out

in such a manner as to endanger the dominion of the
mother-country in the New World. This discord was
fomented by the clergy on both sides, who had also
been infected with the contagion of these disorders.

It is a pleasing task to us to be able to think, and
to write, that the condition of Spain is every day improving. No longer do the nobility affect those airs
of independence which sometimes embarrass the government. Men of no rank, but of ability, have risen
to the direction of public affairs, which, for too long a
time, was confined to persons of high birth. The
countries which are more populous and better cultivated, yield fewer briars and more harvests. From
the manufactures of Grenada, of Malaga, of Seville,
of Priego, of Toledo, of Talavera, and especially of
Valencia, silks are produced which are in some repute,
and which deserve it. The manufactures of Saint Il-
defonso furnish very beautiful mirrors; those of Gua-
dalaxara and of Escaray supply cloths and scarlets;
and those of Madrid, hats, ribands, tapestry, and porcelain. All Catalonia is filled with manufactures of
arms and toys, of silk stockings and handkerchiefs, of
printed cottons, of common woollen goods, and of
gold and silver and other lace. Communications are
beginning to be opened between the capital and the
provinces, and these magnificent roads are planted
with useful or agreeable trees. Canals for watering
or navigation are digged, the plan of which, suggested
by foreigners, had so long disgusted the pride of the
ministry and that of the people. Excellent manufactures of paper; printing executed with much taste;
and societies consecrated to arts of elegance and utility, and to the sciences, will sooner or later dispel
prejudice and ignorance. These wise establishments
will be seconded by the young men whom the ministry send for instruction into those countries, the glory
and prosperity of which hath been extended by their
knowledge. The erroneous system of tributes, so difficult to correct, hath already undergone very material
reformations. The national revenue, formerly so li-

BOOK VIII.

Spain be-
gins to re-
cover from
its lethargy.

B O O K mited, hath arifen, as it is faid, to 140,400,000 livres
VIII. [5,850,000l.]. If the terrier, which the court of Madrid is occupied in making fince the year 1749, be fettled on good principles, and if it be carried into execution, the treafury will again find its refources increafe, and the perfons who contribute will be relieved.

At the death of the emperor Charles V. the public
treafury was fo much burdened, that it was deliberated whether it would not be proper to annul fo many
fatal engagements. Thefe amounted to a thoufand
millions of livres [41,666,666l. 13s. 4d.], or perhaps
more, under the uneafy and turbulent reign of his fon
Philip. The intereft of the fums advanced to government, abforbed, in 1688, all the produce of the taxes;
and it then became neceffary to have recourfe to an
entire bankruptcy. The events fubfequent to this
great crifis were all of them fo unfortunate, that the
finances fell fuddenly into the fame ftate of confufion
from which a defperate but neceffary refolution had
extricated them. In the beginning of the century,
a more enlightened adminiftration eftablifhed a fyftem
of order in the recoveries, and a regularity in the expences, which would have liberated the ftate, had it
not been for the revolutions which fucceeded each
other, with a degree of rapidity which it is difficult to
trace. Neverthelefs, in 1759, the debts of the crown
amounted to no more than 160,000,000 of livres
[6,666,666l. 13s. 4d.], which Ferdinand left in his
coffers. His fucceffor employed half of this fum in
liquidating fome debts; the reft of it was confumed in
the war of Portugal, in the augmentation of the navy,
and in a multitude of expences that were neceffary to
roufe the monarchy from that languid ftate in which
it had been plunged during two centuries of ignorance
and inactivity.

The vigilance of the new government hath not confined itfelf to the fuppreffion of part of the evils which
contributed to the ruin of their poffeffions in Europe.
Attention hath alfo been paid to fome of the abufes
which impeded the profperity of their colonies. Their

governors have been chosen with more care, and bet- B O O K
ter superintended. Some of the vices that had insinu-   VIII.
ated themselves into the tribunals have been reformed ; all the branches of administration have been improved ; and even the fate of the Indians is become
less unhappy.

These first steps towards a reformation must be an Means that
inducement to the Spanish ministry to hope, that a good Spain ought to employ
form of government may be established, when the true to hasten
principles on which it is founded shall be once known, her prosperity in Eu-
and the proper means made use of to effect it. The rope and in
character of the nation is not an invincible obstacle to America.
this change, as it is too generally thought to be. Indolence is not so natural to the Spaniards as we imagine. If we look back to those times in which this
unfavourable prejudice was first entertained, we shall
find that this want of activity did not extend to every
thing ; and that if Spain was inactive at home, she was
not so abroad, but was incessantly disturbing the repose
of her neighbours. Her idleness proceeds in some degree from foolish pride. Because the nobility were
unemployed, the people imagined it was a mark of nobility to do nothing. They all wanted to enjoy the
same prerogative ; and the starved, half-naked Spaniard, carelessly sitting on the ground, looks with pity on
his neighbours, who are well clothed, live well, work,
and laugh at his folly. The one, from a motive of
pride, despises the conveniencies of life ; while the
other, from a principle of vanity, endeavours to acquire
them. The climate had made the Spaniard abstemi-
ous, and indigence hath rendered him more so. The
monkish spirit, to which he hath long been subject,
makes him consider poverty, which is occasioned by
his vices, as a virtue. As he hath no property, he co-
vets none ; but his aversion for labour is greater still
than his contempt for riches.

That poor and proud people have nothing left of
their ancient character, but an immoderate fondness
for every thing that hath the appearance of grandeur.
They must be flattered with chimerical ideas, and ani-

mated with the ſtrongeſt hopes of glory. The ſatisfaction they feel in depending on none but the crown, ſince the abaſement of the grandees, makes them receive all that comes from the court with reſpect and confidence. This powerful influence might be made ſubſervient to their happineſs. Some means might be contrived to perſuade them that labour is honourable, and the nation will ſoon become what it was before the diſcovery of America, in thoſe glorious times, when, without any foreign aid, Spain threatened the liberties of all Europe.

When the imagination of this people is once properly directed, and they are brought to be aſhamed of their haughty ſpirit of indolence, other evils muſt be attended to. The moſt deſtructive to the bulk of the nation is the want of population. Well-governed colonies will naturally increaſe the population of the mother-country, which on her part promotes the increaſe of theirs, by ſupplying them with advantageous marts for the produce of their induſtry. It is on this plan, alike intereſting to humanity and ſound policy, that the more enlightened nations of the Old Hemiſphere have formed their ſettlements in the New one. This wiſe and noble deſign hath been univerſally crowned with ſucceſs. Spain alone, which had formed her ſyſtem in a darker age, hath ſeen her population decreaſe at home, in proportion as her poſſeſſions increaſed abroad.

When the diſproportion between the extent of a territory and its inhabitants is not extreme, the balance may be gradually reſtored by activity, economy, great encouragements given to matrimony, and a long peace. Spain, which, according to the exact account taken in 1768, hath no more than nine millions three hundred and ſeven thouſand eight hundred and four inhabitants of every age and ſex, and which doth not reckon, in her colonies, the tenth part of the individuals that would be neceſſary to cultivate them, cannot remedy this evil either at home or abroad, without new and extraordinary efforts. To increaſe the laborious claſ-

fics of men, there muſt be a reduction of the clergy, B O O K
who enervate and deſtroy the ſtate. Two thirds of VIII.
her military force muſt be aboliſhed, and theſe ſoldiers
muſt be employed in the arts ; ſince the connection
with France, and the weakneſs of Portugal, no longer
render them neceſſary. The government muſt apply
itſelf to alleviate the burdens of the people, as ſoon as
its poſſeſſions in both hemiſpheres are extricated from
that confuſion and diſorder into which they had been
thrown, for theſe two centuries paſt, through the effects of indolence, ignorance, and tyranny. But it is
firſt abſolutely neceſſary that the infamous tribunal of
the inquiſition ſhould be aboliſhed.

Superſtition, whatever may be the reaſon of it, prevails among all nations, whether rude or civilized. It
proceeds undoubtedly from the fear of evil, and from
the ignorance of its cauſes, or of its remedy. At leaſt
this alone is ſufficient to imprint it in the minds of all
men. The calamities of nature, plagues, ſickneſs, unforeſeen accidents, deſtructive phenomena, all the latent cauſes of pain and death, are ſo univerſal on earth,
that it would be very ſurpriſing if man had not been
deeply affected with them in every country and in
every age.

But this natural fear muſt always have increaſed, or
have been magnified in proportion to ignorance and
ſenſibility. It muſt have given riſe to the worſhip of
the elements that are moſt deſtructive to the earth,
ſuch as manifeſt themſelves in inundations, conflagra-
tions, and plagues ; and to the worſhip of animals,
whether venomous or voracious, but always noxious.
Hence too muſt have ariſen the worſhip of men who
have done the greateſt injuries to mankind, of conquerors, of fortunate impoſtors, of the workers of prodi-
gies, apparently good or bad ; and the worſhip of inviſible and imaginary beings, ſuppoſed to lie concealed
in every inſtrument of deſtruction. Reflection, and the
ſtudy of nature, muſt have inſenſibly leſſened the number of theſe inviſible agents, and the human mind muſt
have riſen from idolatry to theiſm ; but this laſt ſimple

BOOK and fublime idea will always have remained imperfect
VIII. and confufed in the minds of the vulgar, and mixed
with a multitude of errors and fancies.

Revelation had confirmed and perfected the idea of
the doctrine of the unity of God ; and, perhaps, a more
pure religion would then have been eftablifhed, had
not the northern barbarians, who poured in upon the
feveral provinces of the Roman empire, brought along
with them their own facred prejudices, which could
not be difpelled but by other fables. Unfortunately,
Chriftianity was preached to men incapable of underftanding it thoroughly. They would not embrace it,
unlefs it were attended with that external pomp and
fhow in which ignorance delights. Interefted motives
burdened it, and debafed it more and more with other
obfervances, and conftantly invented new doctrines
and miracles, which were the more revered as they
were the lefs credible. The nations, engaged during
twelve centuries in dividing and contefting about the
feveral provinces of an univerfal monarchy, which one
nation had formed in lefs than two hundred years, admitted, without examination, all the errors which the
priefts, after much controverfy, had agreed to teach the
multitude. But the clergy, too numerous to maintain
any unanimity of opinion, had fomented the feeds of
divifion, which muft fooner or later be communicated
to the people. The time came, when the fame fpirit of
ambition and avarice that actuated the whole church,
exerted itfelf with great animofity againft many fuperftitions that were univerfally adopted.

As it was from cuftom that the people had received
all thofe puerile notions which they had fuffered themfelves to be deluded into, and that they were not attached to them from national principles or party fpirit, thofe who were moft interefted in fupporting them
were unable to defend them, when they were attacked
with that fteadinefs that was calculated to fix the attention of the public. But nothing fo much promoted
the reformation of Luther and Calvin, as the liberty
they granted to every one to examine and determine

finally upon the religious principles he had been taught. Though the multitude were incapable of undertaking this difcuffion, yet every man plumed himfelf upon having the privilege to determine on a fubject in which his moft valuable and moft important interefts were concerned. The commotion was fo univerfal, that the new opinions would in all probability have triumphed totally over the old, had not the magiftracy thought it their intereft to ftem the torrent. Implicit obedience was as neceffary for the fupport of the fupreme power, as for that of religion, and was the fureft foundation of its authority; that power began therefore to be alarmed, left thofe who had overturned the old and firm foundations of the Roman hierarchy might next proceed to examine into its own prerogatives. The republican fpirit which naturally fpread itfelf among the reformed contributed to increafe this diftruft.

The kings of Spain, more jealous of their power than other fovereigns, endeavoured to fupport it, by eftablifhing a more uniform fyftem of fuperftition. They were not fenfible that the opinions of men, concerning an unknown Being, cannot be all the fame. In vain did reafon expoftulate with thofe weak monarchs, alleging that no power had a right to prefcribe to men what they were to think; that fociety, in order to fupport itfelf, is under no neceffity of reftraining the freedom of the foul; that to compel men to fubfcribe to certain articles of faith, is to exact a falfe oath, which makes a man a traitor to his cofcience, in order that he may be a faithful fubject; and that a citizen who ferves his country is, in a political light, preferable to him who is orthodox to no purpofe. Thefe permanent and inconteftable principles were not attended to. They were overruled by the profpect of great advantage, and ftill more by the furious clamours of a multitude of fanatical priefts, who haftened to affume the fupreme authority. The prince, thus reduced to become their flave, was forced to abandon his fubjects to their caprices, to fuffer them to be op-

preffed, and to become an idle fpectator of the cruelties exercifed againſt them.   From that time, fuperftitious manners, beneficial only to the prieſthood, became prejudicial to fociety.   A people thus corrupt
and degenerate were the moſt cruel of any.   Their
obedience to the monarch was fubordinate to the will
of the prieſt, who oppreſſed every other power, and
was in fact the fovereign of the ſtate.

Inaction was the neceffary confequence of a fuper-
ſtition that enervated all the faculties of the foul.   The
project which the Romans formed from their earlieſt
origin, of becoming maſters of the world, ſhowed itfelf even in their religion.   It was Victory, Bellona,
Fortune, the genius of the Roman people, Rome herfelf, that were their gods.   A nation that endeavoured
to imitate their example, and thought of becoming
conquerors, adopted a monkiſh government, which
hath deſtroyed every profpect of fuccefs, and will effectually prevent their reſtoration either in Spain or
America, unlefs this kind of government be totally
fubverted, and every idea of the horror it excites obliterated with it.   The fuppreffion of the inquifition
muſt certainly haften this great change; and it is a
pleafing expectation to think, that if the court of Madrid will not determine upon this neceffary ſtep, they
will one day be compelled to it by a humane conqueror, who will infert it as the firſt article in a treaty
of peace, that *the Autos-da fé ſhall be aboliſhed in all the
Spaniſh dominions both in Europe and America.*

This ſtep, however neceffary it may be towards the
reſtoration of the monarchy, is not alone fufficient.
Though Spain hath employed more art to conceal her
weaknefs, than was neceffary to enable her to acquire
ſtrength, the world is not unacquainted with the diforders ſhe labours under.   They have taken fo deep a
root, and are of fo inveterate a nature, that they cannot be remedied without foreign aids.   If ſhe will but
fubmit to accept them, ſhe will foon fee her provinces
in both hemifpheres filled with new inhabitants, who
will bring with them numberlefs branches of induſtry.

The northern and fouthern nations, actuated by that
paffion for riches which is the characteriftic of the prefent age, will refort in multitudes to the regions that
are thrown open to excite their emulation. The riches
of the public will increafe in proportion to thofe of
individuals; and thofe which have been acquired by
foreigners will become a national wealth, if they be
permitted to enjoy them with that fecurity, fatisfaction, and diftinction, which may induce them to forget
their native country.

BOOK
VIII.

Spain would foon fee her population increafe to the
degree fhe would wifh, if fhe not only admitted perfons of her own perfuafion, but even encouraged, indifcriminately, all fects to fettle among them. This
might be done without injury to the principles of religion, and without deviating from the maxims of true
policy. Well-regulated governments are not difturbed
by the diverfity of opinions that prevail in them; neither doth Chriftianity, rightly underftood, profcribe a
liberty of confcience. The truth of thefe maxims
hath been fo clearly demonftrated, that they cannot
fail of being foon adopted as a rule to all nations that
are in any degree enlightened.

When the Spaniards have once procured a fufficient
number of men, they will then think of employing
them in the moft advantageous manner. The anxiety
they felt to fee the treafures of America pafs into the
hands of their rivals and enemies, made them imagine
that the revival of their manufactures was the only
method that could enable them to retain part of thofe
treafures at home. Such of their writers upon finance
as have infifted upon this fyftem, appear to us to be in
an error. As long as the people, who are in poffeffion
of thofe manufactures which ferve to fupply the demands of America, will attend to the prefervation of
them, thofe which may be attempted to be eftablifhed in other parts will fcarce be able to vie with them.
Thefe manufacturers may poffibly procure the materials and workmanfhip at as reafonable a rate: but
fome centuries muft pafs before they can be able to

B o o k attain to the fame degree of expedition and perfection
VIII. in the work. Nothing could effect this great change,
but fuch a revolution as would convey the beft foreign
workmen, and the moft fkilful artifts, to Spain. Till
this period fhall arrive, which does not feem very near,
any attempts that are made will not be fuccefsful.

We may proceed ftill further, and venture to affirm,
that though it fhould be in the power of Spain to procure a fuperiority in the manufactures refpecting articles of luxury, fhe ought not to do it. A tranfient
fuccefs would be productive of total ruin. Let us
fuppofe that Spain can furnifh all the commodities
that are wanted in her colonies; the immenfe treafures this trade will bring in, will all centre in home
circulation, and the confequence will be, that the coin
will fink in value. This plenty of fpecie will certainly occafion a dearnefs of provifions, and enhance
the price of labour. There will be no proportion between the price Spain muft require for her manufactures, and that which the neighbouring nations will
fell theirs for. Thefe, being able to afford their commodities cheaper, will oblige the Spaniards to take
them, becaufe an exorbitant profit will furmount every obftacle. The Spanifh artificers, deftitute of employment, will be reduced to the neceffity of feeking
for it in other places, and Spain will lofe both her induftry and her population.

Since then it is impoffible that the Spaniards fhould
keep the whole produce of the American mines in
their own hands, and fince they muft unavoidably
fhare it with the reft of Europe, they fhould exert
all their policy to preferve the greateft part of it, to
make the balance incline in their favour; and in order to render their advantages permanent, they muft
be fatisfied with fuch as are moderate. They will fecure to themfelves this kind of fuperiority by the practice of the neceffary arts, and the plenty and goodnefs of their natural productions.

The Spanifh miniftry have been fenfible of this truth,
but have been deceived in the opinion they entertain-

ed, that the manufactures were the chief promoters BOOK
of agriculture. It is certain, however, that they con VIII.
tribute to promote the culture of lands. They are
even necessary, wherever the expence of transport
puts a stop to the circulation and consumption of the
produce, so that the cultivator is at a loss how to dispose of his commodities. But in all other cases, the
farmer can succeed without the assistance of manufactures. If he can but dispose of his produce, he is
under no concern, whether it be for local consumption or for trade and exportation, and will go on with
his tillage.

Spain annually sells for exportation, in wool, silk,
oil, wine, iron, and kali, to the omount of above
eighty millions of livres [3,333,333l. 6s. 8d.]. These
exports, most of which cannot be replaced from any
soil in Europe, will admit of immense augmentation.
They will be sufficient, independent of what the Spaniards receive from the Indies, to pay for all the foreign goods that can be consumed in the nation. We
grant, that by thus sending their unwrought produce
to other countries, they will increase their population,
wealth, and power; but they will promote a more certain and more beneficial kind of industry at home.
Their political influence will soon claim a relative superiority, and the nation employed in agriculture will
soon become greater than that which confines itself to
manufactures.

America will greatly increase these advantages; and
will be beneficial to Spain, both by her gold and silver,
and by her commodities.

We have none but vague notions concerning the
quantity of metals and of provisions which the Old
World received from the New, in the early periods after the conquest. Our knowledge of those points increases, in proportion as we draw nearer to modern
times. At present, Spain receives annually, from the
continent of America, 89,095,052 livres [3,712,293l.
16s. 8d.] in gold or in silver, and 34,653,902 livres

B O O K [1,443,912l. 11s. 8d.], in productions; which makes,
VIII. in the whole, 123,748,954 livres [5,156,206l. 18s. 4d.].
Taking this calculation for a rule, it will be found that
the mother-country bath received from its colonies, in
the space of two hundred and eighty-seven years,
35,515,949,798 livres [1,479,831,242l. 1s. 6d.].

It must be acknowledged, that a less quantity of
productions was received formerly than is at present;
but, on the other hand, the mines were more plentiful. If we choose to reckon the metals only, Spain
will have received no more than 25,570,279,924 livres
[1,065,428,330l. 3s. 4d.]; and we shall then strike out
of the calculation the 9,945,669,874 livres [414,402,911l.
8s. 4d.] of productions.

There would be a possibility of increasing this mass
of metals and productions. For the first of these objects, it would be sufficient that the government should
send over to America some persons skilled in metallurgy, and make the conditions easier on which they
allow the working of the mines. But this would be
only a transient advantage, since it is undeniable that
gold and silver are not to be considered as riches, but
only as the representations of them. These signs are
indeed very durable, as they ought to be, to answer
their destination. But the more they are multiplied,
the more they lose of their value, because they serve
to represent fewer things. In proportion as they are
become more common since the discovery of America, every thing is increased in value twice, thrice, and
four times beyond what it was before. The produce
of the mines hath constantly decreased, and the expence of working them hath been continually greater.
The balance, which inclines more and more to the
losing side, may so far destroy the equipoise, that it
may be found necessary to drop this source of wealth.
But at all events, it will be advisable to render these
operations more simple, and to try every possible method to make this labour less destructive to the human
race than it hath been hitherto. There is another
source of prosperity for Spain, which will be so far

from decreasing, that it will daily gather new strength; and that is agriculture.

Such is the important end which the court of Madrid must endeavour to compass. If, by placing the metals in that inferior rank which belongs to them, they resolve to lay the foundation of the public felicity on the productions that may be derived from a fertile and immense territory, the New Hemisphere will emerge from that state of annihilation in which it was found, and in which it hath been left. The sun, which hath hitherto shone only on uncultivated deserts, will produce universal fertility.

To the number of productions which its rays, affisted with the labour and skill of man, shall bring forth there, we shall add those which at present enrich the islands of the New World, the consumption of which is daily increasing, and which, after having been for a long time objects of luxury, begin now to be considered as articles of indispensable necessity.

The aromatics and spices of Asia, which carry from ten to twelve millions of livres [from 416,666l. 13s. 4d. to 500,000l.] annually out of the monarchy, might be made to thrive there; and there is particular reason to expect this with regard to the cinnamon. It grows naturally in some of the valleys of the Cordeleirias; and by cultivation, perhaps, some of the qualities it wants might be imparted to it.

Several of the provinces of Mexico formerly produced excellent silks, which were manufactured with success in Spain. This source of wealth hath been lost, by the numberless obstructions it hath met with; but it might easily be revived and extended.

The Vicuna wool is in great repute among all nations. The quantity they are supplied with is nothing in comparison of the demands for it. The most certain method of increasing this precious wool would probably be, to let the animal that supplies it live, after having taken it away from him.

It would be impossible to enumerate the productions which regions so immense, climates so various,

BOOK
VIII.
and foils of fo different a nature, might fupply. Among
fuch a variety of cultivations, fome, perhaps, might be
found that would fuit the Indians, others might probably induce fome of the wandering nations to fix.
Thefe affociations, diftributed with fkill, might alfo
ferve to eftablifh communications between colonies
that are now feparated from each other by immenfe
and uninhabited fpaces. The laws, which always lofe
their force among men too far diftant from each other,
and from the magiftrate, would then be obferved.
Commerce, which is perpetually interrupted by the
impoffibility of conveying the merchandife to their
deftination, would then become more animated. In
cafe of war, the people would be warned of any approaching danger, and would give each other fpeedy
and effectual fuccours. It muft be acknowledged that
this new fyftem could not be eftablifhed without difficulty. Thefe falutary views would be thwarted by
indolence, by the climate, and by prejudices: but
knowledge prudently diftributed, encouragements well
managed, and marks of confideration properly beftowed, would overcome, in procefs of time, all obftacles.
The progrefs of cultivation would be much accelerated, by fuppreffing the practice now become general,
of thofe majorafcos, or perpetual fucceffions, which
occafion fuch a number of idle perfons in the country,
and which are productive of ftill greater mifchief in
the colonies. The firft conquerors, and thofe who
purfued their meafures, ufurped immenfe diftricts, or
obtained the gift of them. They converted them into an indivifible inheritance for their children; and
the younger ones were thus, in fome meafure, devoted
to celibacy, to the cloifter, or to the priefthood. Thefe
enormous poffeffions have remained uncultivated, and
will ftill continue fo, till fome fteady and prudent man
fhall take upon him to permit, or to order, the divifion
of them. Then the number of proprietors, which is
at prefent fo much confined, notwithftanding the great
extent of the territories, will be increafed, and productions will be multiplied with property.

The labours would advance more rapidly, if foreign- B O O K
ers were permitted to take a part in them. The Spa- VIII.
nifh Indies were indifcriminately fhut againft them all,
even at the period of the difcovery. The laws formally prefcribed, that the perfons who had penetrated
into them, in any manner whatever, fhould be fent
back into Europe. Philip II. urged by his wants, authorifed, in 1596, his delegates to naturalize the few
that had flipped in there, upon condition that they
fhould pay the ftipulated price for this adoption. This
kind of market has been frequently renewed, but rather in favour of artifts of neceffary utility to the country, than for merchants, who, it was fuppofed, would
one day retire with the wealth they had accumulated.
The number, however, both of the one and the other,
hath always been extremely confined, becaufe it is
prohibited to embark any in the mother country; and
that the colonies themfelves, whether from motives of
miftruft or jealoufy, reject them. The advancement
of knowledge gives us reafon to think that this unfo-
ciable fpirit will have an end. The government will
at length underftand what they have to expect from a
healthy and vigorous man, between five-and-twenty
and thirty years of age; what mifchief he doth to the
country which he quits, and how acceptable he is to
the foreign nations, among whom he transfers his
ftrength and his induftry. They will comprehend
how ftrangely ftupid it is to make the right of hofpitality be purchafed by the man who fhould come to
multiply by his ufeful labours, either the productions
of the foil, or the works of the manufactures. They
will difcern the deep policy of thofe people, who fhould
make a point of inviting the inhabitants of neighbouring regions to fettle in their towns, or in their country-
places, or to traverfe their provinces. They will find
out what fort of tribute fhould be impofed upon nations who might fupply them with workmen, with cultivators, and with confumers; how much the fpirit of
intoleration which banifhes is fatal; what funds of
wealth a nation derives from toleration; and how in-

different a circumstance it is to the value of commodities, whether they be produced from the labours of orthodox persons or of heretics, of Spaniards, or of Hollanders. But the greatest encouragements that could be given to the cultivation of the lands, and all the favours which it would be possible to add to them, would be of no effect, without the certainty of an easy and advantageous mart for the productions. M. de la Enfenada first discovered that the exportation of them would be impracticable, as long as the commerce of the New World should be conducted in the manner it had been. Accordingly, notwithstanding the opposition he met with, and notwithstanding the prejudices he had to combat, he substituted, in 1740, detached vessels to the parade so anciently established, and so highly revered, of galleons and fleets. He was meditating other changes still more advantageous, when an unexpected disgrace stopped him in the midst of his brilliant career.

One half of the good which this bold and able minister had done was annulled in 1756, by the re-establishment of the fleets : but this mischief was partly repaired eight years after, by the setting on foot of the packet-boats, which, from Corunna, were to carry, every month, to the Havannah, the letters destined for the northern colonies ; and every two months, to Buenos-Ayres, those that were destined for the southern colonies. These vessels, which were of no inconfiderable fize, were allowed to load at their departure with European merchandise, and, at their return, with American commodities.

The exportation of metals was forbidden under capital penalties. This absurd prohibition was made a jest of, because it was neceffary that foreign commerce should receive the value of the merchandise it had furnished. Ancient governments, which had for the laws the refpect they deserve, would not have failed to abrogate one, the observance of which had been shown to be chimerical. In our modern times, when empires are rather conducted by the caprices of the governors,

than regulated upon reafonable principles, Spain went
no further, in 1748, than to permit the exportation
of gold and filver, upon condition that a duty of three
per cent. fhould be paid to the treafury. Twenty years
after, this tax was increafed to four *per cent.* although
the government was warned by perpetual frauds, that
it was their intereft to lower it.

The year 1774 was the period of another fortunate
innovation. Till that time, every kind of intercourfe
between the feveral parts of the American continent
had been rigidly prohibited. Mexico, Guatimala, Peru, and the New Kingdom, were all compelled to be
ftrangers to each other. The action and reaction which
would have made them all partake of the advantages
nature had diftributed among them, were confidered
as crimes, and feverely punifhed. But what reafon
can be affigned why this profcription fhould not have
been extended from one town to another, or from one
dwelling to a neighbouring one in the fame diftrict,
from one family to another in the fame diftrict? Hath
nature traced upon the foil, which men inhabit, any
line of limitation? How doth it happen, that, under
the fame dominion, a place fituated at an equal diftance from two other places, fhould be allowed a free
exercife of a privilege towards the Eaft, which is refufed to it towards the Weft? Doth not fuch an edict,
properly interpreted, fignify, let us forbid every country to cultivate more than is neceffary for its own confumption, and every inhabitant from being in want
of any thing befide the productions of his own foil?
A free communication was at length opened between
thefe provinces : and the inhabitants were allowed to
think themfelves fellow-citizens, and to treat each o-
ther as brethren.

One law, of the month of February 1778, permits
all the ports of Spain to difpatch fhips to Buenos-
Ayres, and to the South Sea. In the month of October of the fame year, this liberty hath been granted
for the reft of the continent, except for Mexico, which
will undoubtedly foon enjoy the fame advantage. This

B O O K
VIII.

B O O K will be a confiderable ftep; but it will not be fufficient,
 VIII. as it is fuppofed, to put a ftop to the fmuggling trade,
which occafions fo many clamours.

All the people, whofe poffeffions have been near
the Spanifh fettlements, have endeavoured to appropriate to themfelves clandeftinely their treafures and
their commodities. The Portuguefe have turned their
views towards the river Plata; the French, the Danes,
and the Dutch, towards the coaft of Caraccas, Carthagena, and Porto-Bello. The Englifh, who knew and
frequented thefe roads, have found that the ceffions
made to them by the laft treaty have opened to them
other ways of obtaining a more confiderable fhare of
thefe rich fpoils. All thefe nations have fucceeded in
their attempts, by deceiving or bribing the guarda
coftas, and fometimes by fighting them.

The governors, far from remedying thefe diforders,
encouraged them as much as poffible. Several of them
had purchafed their pofts; moft of them were in hafte
to get fortunes, and wifhed to be paid for the dangers they had incurred by the change of climate.
There was not a moment to be loft, becaufe it was
feldom they were continued in their places more than
from three to five years. Among the leaft dangerous
modes they had of acquiring riches, was that of encouraging the contraband trade, or of carrying it on
themfelves. No perfon in America exclaimed againft
a conduct which was favourable to all.

If the complaints of fome European merchants
reached the court, they were eafily filenced by proper gratuities to confeffors, miftreffes, or favourites.
The delinquent not only fheltered himfelf from punifhment, but was alfo rewarded. Nothing was fo
well eftablifhed, or fo generally known, as this practice. A Spaniard juft returned from America, where
he had filled an important poft, was complaining to a
friend of the injurious reports that were fpread concerning the difcharge of his truft. *If you are flander-
ed,* fays his friend, *you are undone; but if your extortions are not exaggerated, you have nothing to do but to*

give up part of your plunder, and you will enjoy the re-
mainder peaceably, and even with credit.

The fraudulent trade will continue till it hath been made impoffible to bear the expences of it, or to brave the dangers to which it expofes ; and this can never be done but by lowering the duties with which the Spanifh ports have been fucceffively overburdened. Even fince the facrifices made by government in the regulations of 1778, the contraband trader hath an advantage of fixty-four *per cent.* over the fair dealer.

The revolution which a judicious fyftem of policy may bring about will occafion a deficiency, and a very confiderable one, in the public treafury : but the diftrefs that would refult from it would be no more than momentary. Immenfe riches would one day be produced from this long-expected arrangement of things.

According to the new fyftem, Spain, which hither-to hath furnifhed annually no more than one thoufand feven hundred and forty-one tons of wine and bran-dy, by which the cultivators had not got one million of livres [41,666l. 13s. 4d.], will now fend ten or twelve times as much. This exportation would fer-tilize an uncultivated territory, and would difguft Mexico, as well as fome other provinces of the New World, of the bad liquors they are ufed to confume, on account of the dearnefs of thofe that have croffed the feas.

The manufactures, which the impoffibility of pay-ing for thofe which came from the Old Hemifphere hath caufed to be eftablifhed, would not fupport them-felves. It would have been the higheft act of tyranny to put them down by authority, as fome inconfiderate, corrupt, and defpotic minifters have not fcrupled to propofe ; but nothing would be more reafonable than to bring them into difrepute with the perfons who now ufe them for clothing, by offering them, at a price fuitable to their circumftances, linens and ftuffs, that would be more agreeable to their tafte or to their va-nity. Then the confumption of European merchan-

BOOK
VIII.
dife, which doth not exceed annually fix thoufand fix hundred and twelve tons, would be doubly increafed, and in procefs of time much more.

The hands which are employed in manufacture would be transferred to agriculture, which is at prefent much confined. The ports, however, of all nations are open to their commodities. Several of them might perhaps object, that Spain fhould make the moft of her iflands, becaufe fuch an improvement would neceffarily occafion an evident injury to her colonies; but they are all defirous that fhe fhould bring more of the productions of her continent to market, becaufe moft of them are neceffary, and cannot be replaced by others.

This new arrangement of things would be equally favourable to the mines. Thofe which have been neglected, from their not being able to pay for the mercury and other articles, would be opened again. Thofe, the working of which hath not been interrupted, would be followed up with more activity, and with greater means. The plenty of metals would open frefh markets to induftry, which even the ableft men do not think of.

The Americans, become more rich and more happy, would have more confidence in government. They would readily confent to pay taxes, the nature and levying of which can only be properly regulated on the fpot, and from a mature confideration of the character and cuftoms of the people. Thefe tributes, however trifling they may be fuppofed to be, would do more than fill up the deficiency occafioned in the public coffers by the leffening of the duties.

The crown, enjoying a more confiderable revenue, would no longer abandon their provinces to the rapacioufnefs of their agents. They would leffen the number of them, pay thofe they retained in a proper manner, and compel them to refpect the rights of the people and the interefts of government. To think it impoffible that this fpirit of juftice fhould be eftablifhed, would argue an ignorance of the refources of a well managed authority. Campillo fucceeded in it, during his auftere miniftry, although the governors of America at that time had contracted the habit of plunder, and that their appointments were not fufficient to maintain the dignity which their rank feemed to require.

It muft be acknowledged, that the freedom of trade between all Spain and America, hath been reckoned a chimera. The harbours of this peninfula are, as it has been faid, fo poor, that whatever fteps may be taken, that of Cadix will remain in the fole poffeffion of this monopoly. This would undoubtedly happen, if the ancient fyftem fhould only be departed from in this point : but, if the new plan be directed by the principles already eftablifhed, and already practifed among commercial nations, it will be found that there are in moft of the ports of this kingdom funds fufficient for thefe undertakings. Thefe armaments will even foon be multiplied, becaufe the moderate rate of the freight, and of the duties, will allow them to fend common merchandife, and to receive in return commodities of fmall value. In procefs of time, the navigation of the mother-country, with its colonies on the continent, which at prefent employs no more than from thirty to thirty-two fhips every year, would receive fo great an increafe, that the boldeft fpeculators could not venture to fix the limits of it.

It hath been fuppofed, with more foundation, that as foon as the ports of America fhould be open to all the ports of the monarchy, and that no kind of oppreffion would exift in the cuftoms, trade, when freed from thefe fhackles, would occafion unlimited emulation. The avidity and imprudence of the merchants, give reafon to fufpect this confufion; which might perhaps turn out to advantage. The colonifts, encouraged by the cheapnefs, to the acquifition of enjoyments which they had been never able to procure, will have other wants, and confequently would devote themfelves to other labours. If even the excefs of the competition would be an evil, it could never be any thing more than a temporary one. To endeavour to prevent this commotion, by laws deſtructive of every good, is to attempt the prevention of a fortunate revolution, by a continual ſyſtem of oppreſſion.

But the objection which had been moſt thought of in the court of Madrid, hath been, it ſeems, that all the European nations would find their trade increaſe by theſe arrangements. This is certainly true. But would not Spaniſh induſtry be equally encouraged, ſince, when freed from the duty which foreign merchandiſe would continue to pay on entering the kingdom, it would preſerve all its advantages? Would not the government ſtill collect the duties they might have thought proper to leave upon theſe productions? Would not their navigators ſtill gain their freight? Would not their merchants be the agents of this commerce? Would not their ſubjects of the New World obtain at a cheaper rate every thing that is conveyed to them? It is, perhaps, a fortunate circumſtance for this power, to be obliged to ſhare with other people the ſupplying of its American poſſeſſions. If it were otherwiſe, the maritime powers would exert their utmoſt efforts to deprive it of them. Whether they would ſucceed or not, is a point which remains to be examined.

Inquiry
whether
the Spaniſh
empire be
founded
upon a ſolid
baſis in the
New
World. The Dutch were the firſt people who ventured to turn their arms againſt Peru. They ſent a ſmall ſquadron thither in 1643, which eaſily took Baldivia, the only fortified port of Chili, and the key to thoſe peaceful ſeas. Their navigators already poſſeſſed, in imagination, the treaſures of thoſe rich countries, till their expectations were diſappointed by the appearance of famine and diſeaſe. The death of their favourite chief increaſed their anxiety, and the troops that were ſent againſt them from Callao threw them into total deſpair. The idea of the diſtance they were at from their native country, deprived them of all their courage, and the fear of falling into the hands of a nation whoſe hatred they had ſo often experienced, determined them to reimbark. If their perſeverance had been greater, they would probably have preſerved their conqueſts

till the arrival of the fuccours that would have been B O O K
fent from the Zuyder Zee, when their firft fuccefs came   VIII.
to be known.

Such was the opinion of thofe Frenchmen, who, in
1595, united their riches and their efforts to go and
plunder Peru, and to form a fettlement on that part of
the coaft of Chili which had been neglected by the
Spaniards. This fcheme was approved by Lewis XIV.
who, to facilitate the execution of it, granted fix men
of war. The fquadron proceeded very fortunately,
under the command of the brave De Gènes, till it got
towards the middle of the Straits of Magellan. Suc-
cefs was thought to be near at hand, when the navigators, obftinately repulfed by contrary winds, and af-
failed with every poffible calamity, were obliged to return to Europe. Thefe adventurers, ftill thirfting after
riches and dangers, were intending to form a new affociation, when the courfe of events united the interefts
of the two crowns.

The Englifh had turned their attention with avidity
towards thefe countries, before other people. They
were tempted by the mines as early as the year 1624;
but the weaknefs of the prince who then reigned,
proved the ruin of a confiderable affociation formed
for this great purpofe. Charles II. refumed this important project, and fent Sir John Narborough to reconnoitre thofe latitudes that were fo little known,
and to endeavour to open fome communication with
the favages of Chili. That monarch was fo impatient
to know the fuccefs of the expedition, that when he
was informed of the return of his admiral to the Downs,
he got into his barge and went to meet him at Gravef-
end.

Though this firft attempt had been of no advantage, the Britifh miniftry were not difcouraged. The
elevation of the Duke of Anjou to the throne excited
a general ferment. England, which had put itfelf at
the head of the confederacy formed to deprive this
prince of the throne, was victorious in all parts, but
was obliged to purchafe this glory at a very dear rate.

The nation was groaning under the oppreffion of taxes,
while the treafury had contracted immenfe engagements. It feemed difficult to fulfil them, and at the
fame time to continue the war, when the idea was
fuggefted of a company which fhould have the exclufive privilege of trading to the South Seas, upon condition that they fhould liquidate the national debt.
Such was the opinion they entertained of the riches
of Peru, and of the great fortunes that might eafily
be made there, that foreigners, as well as the people
of the country, were eager to lend their money to this
undertaking. The direction of it was given to the
Lord High Treafurer Oxford, the author of the project, and he employed, in the expences of the ftate,
funds that were deftined for a very different purpofe.

Then the fhares of the new company fell into the
utmoft difrepute ; but they foon rofe again. At the
peace, the court of London obtained from that of
Madrid, that the South Sea Company fhould fulfil its
deftination. The trade of Peru was formally given
up to them. They were quietly enriching themfelves,
when a bloody war changed the fituation of affairs.
A fquadron under the command of Anfon was fent,
inftead of the fhips of thofe rapacious merchants which
frequented thefe feas. It is probable he would have
executed the whole of his terrible commiffion, had he
not been prevented by the misfortunes that befel his
fquadron, in being obliged, from ill concerted meafures, to double Cape Horn at an improper and dangerous feafon.

Since the laft peace, the French in 1764, and the
Englifh in 1766, have undertaken to form a fettlement
not far from the coaft of Patagonia, or in fifty-one degrees thirty minutes of fouthern latitude, in three
iflands, which the former have called Malouine, and
the latter Falkland Iflands. Spain, alarmed at feeing
foreign nations in thefe latitudes, eafily obtained from
the court of Verfailles the facrifice of their feeble colony : but the warmeft reprefentations produced no
effect upon the court of London, which had not the

fame motives of attention and complaifance. The miniftry on both fides grew warm. Port Egmont, recently occupied, was fuddenly attacked, and taken
without refiftance. The two hemifpheres were again
going to be deluged with blood, if the aggreffors had
not at length determined to reftore a poft, which they
ought not to have feized upon, at a time when negotiations were opened to examine into the rights of the
two crowns. England hath fince engaged, by a verbal
agreement of the 22d January 1771, to fuffer this feeble, ufelefs, and expenfive fettlement gradually to decay. Accordingly, in the month of May 1774, there
remained no more than five-and-twenty men upon it,
when it was evacuated, leaving an infcription to cer-
tify to pofterity, that thefe iflands had belonged, and
had not ceafed to belong, to Great Britain. Thefe
navigators, attentive to the dignity of their nation, infulted, at their departure, the rival power. It is from
motives of condefcenfion, and not of fear, that they
are willing to defift from their claims. But when they
promife eternal duration to their empire, they forget
that their grandeur may difappear as rapidly as it hath
rifen. Of all the modern nations, what remains will
there be in the annals of the world? The names only
of a few illuftrious perfonages, of a Chriftopher Columbus, of a Defcartes, and of a Newton. What a number of petty ftates, all ridiculoufly afpiring to the great
deftinies of Rome!

Without the affiftance of this ftaple, and indeed
without any, Anfon thought that the empire of the
Spaniards in the Pacific Ocean might be attacked with
advantage. According to the plan of this celebrated
navigator, twelve men of war, fent from Europe with
three or four thoufand troops, would direct their courfe
towards the South Sea. They would procure refrefh-
ments at Bahia, at Rio Janeiro, at St. Catherine's, and
throughout all the Brazils, where a ftrong defire prevails of humbling the Spaniards. The repairs that
might become neceffary, would be executed with fafety upon the defert and uninhabitable coaft of Pata-

gonia, at Port Defire, or St. Julian. The fquadron would double Cape Horn, or would go through the Straits of Magellan, according to the different feafons of the year. If they fhould chance to feparate, they would meet again at the defert ifland of Socoro, and then attack Baldivia with their united force.

This fortrefs, the only one that covers Chili, being carried by a fudden and impetuous attack, what fervice, for the defence of the country, could be expected from enervated and unexperienced citizens, againſt troops inured to difcipline and military exercifes? What could they do againſt the Araucos, and other favages, always difpofed to renew their cruelties and their ravages?

The coaſts of Peru would make ſtill lefs refiſtance. They are all defended only by Callao, where a bad garrifon of fix hundred men would foon capitulate. The reduction of this famous port would open the way to Lima, which is no more than two leagues off, and incapable of making any defence. The feeble fuccours that could be fent to the two cities from the inland parts, where there are no foldiers, would not fave them; and the fquadron would eafily intercept any that might come from Panama by fea. Panama itfelf, which is furrounded only by a wall, without a ditch or any outworks, would be obliged to furrender. The garrifon, continually weakened by detachments that muſt be fent to Chagre, to Porto-Bello, and to other poſts, would be unable to repulfe the moſt trifling force.

Anfon was of opinion, that the coaſts being once fubdued, the reſt of the empire would foon be obliged to fubmit. This idea was founded upon the effeminacy, cowardice, and ignorance of thefe people in the management of arms. According to his informations, a bold enemy would have had nearly as much advantage over the Spaniards, as they themfelves had over the Americans at the period of the difcovery.

Such were, thirty years ago, the ideas of one of the greateſt feamen England ever had. But we may ima-

gine that he would not talk in this ftyle at prefent.
The court of Madrid, roufed by the humiliations and
misfortunes of the laft war, have fent well-difciplined
troops into Peru, and have intrufted the fortified places
to experienced commanders. The fpirit of the militia
is entirely changed in this part of the New World.
What, perhaps, was poffible, is now no more fo. An
invafion would more particularly become a chimerical
idea, if, in that diftant region, the land forces were
fupported by proportionate maritime ftrength. We
fhall even venture to affirm, that the junction of thefe
two forces would infallibly expel the flag of all other
nations from thefe roads.

The operations of the fquadron fhould not be limited, either to the fighting of the enemy, or to the keeping of them at a diftance. The fhips of which it would
confift might be ufefully employed in producing, or in
collecting upon thefe coafts, the articles which either
do not grow there, or which are loft from the difficulty of exportation. Thefe encouragements would probably awaken the colonifts from the lethargic ftate in
which they have continued for three centuries. When
they were affured that the produce of their cultures
would reach Panama without expence, and would
there be embarked upon the Chagre, to be conveyed
into Europe, at a very moderate rate, they would feel
themfelves inclined to labours, the reward of which
would no longer be doubtful. This activity would increafe, if the court of Madrid would refolve to dig a
canal of five leagues, which would complete the communication between the two feas, already fo much advanced by a navigable river. The general good of nations, and the advantage of commerce, required, that
the Ifthmus of Panama and the Ifthmus of Suez fhould
be open to navigation, and fhould draw the limits of
the world nearer to each other. Oriental defpotifm,
and Spanifh indolence, have for too long a time deprived the globe of fo confiderable a benefit.

If from the South we go on to the North Sea, we
fhall find that the Spanifh empire is eftablifhed there,

B O O K from the Miffiffippi to the Oroonoko. There are,
VIII. throughout this immenfe fpace, many inacceffible
fhores, and a ftill greater number where it would be
ufelefs to land. All the ports that are confidered as
important, fuch as Vera Cruz, Chagre, Porto-Bello,
Carthagena, and Puerto-Cabello, are fortified, and
fome of them are fo upon good principles. Experience, however, hath fhown, that none of thefe places
are impregnable. They might, therefore, be forced
again : but of what fervice would this fuccefs be?
The conquerors, who would find it impoffible to penetrate into the inland countries, would be confined
in fortreffes, where an air, which is dangerous in all
feafons, and fatal during fix months of the year, to
men who are accuftomed to a temperate climate,
would fooner or later bring them to the grave.

If even, contrary to all probability, the conqueft
fhould be completed, can it be imagined that the Spanifh Americans, who from tafte, idlenefs, ignorance,
habit, and pride, have an exceffive attachment to their
religion and to their laws, would not break, at one
time or other, the chains that had been impofed upon
them? If, to prevent this revolution, it fhould be refolved to exterminate them, this cruel expedient would
be as great a folly in politics, as it would be horrible
in morality. The nation that had been guilty of this
excefs of barbarity could not reap any advantage from
its new poffeffions, without facrificing to them its population, its activity, its induftry, and, in procefs of
time, all its power.

Thefe various obftacles to the invafion of Spanifh
America, had, as it is faid, fuggefted in England, during the laft hoftilities, the idea of a fyftem aftonifhing to vulgar minds. The project of this power, which
was then miftrefs of all the feas, was to feize upon
Vera Cruz, and to fortify itfelf there in a very ftrong
manner. It would not have been propofed to Mexico
to fubmit to a foreign yoke, for which it was known
to have too great an averfion; but the plan was to
detach that region from the mother-country, to make

it the arbiter of its own deftiny, and to leave it at
liberty, either to choofe a fovereign of its own, or to
form itfelf into a republic. As there were no troops
in the country, the revolution was infallible; and it
would equally have taken place in all the provinces
of this vaft continent, which had the fame motives
for defiring it, and the fame facility of carrying it into execution. The efforts of the court of Madrid, to
recover its rights, would have been unavailing, becaufe Great Britain took upon herfelf to repel them,
upon condition that the new ftates fhould grant her
an exclufive trade, but upon terms infinitely lefs unfavourable than thofe by which they had for fo long a
time been oppreffed.

If it were true that fuch ideas had ever ferioufly engaged the attention of the cabinet of London, they
muft have renounced thefe ambitious views, fince the
court of Madrid have taken the refolution to keep regular and European forces in their poffeffions in the
New World. Thefe forces will contain the nations,
and repel the enemy, ftrengthened as they are at prefent with a refpectable navy.

As foon as the Spaniards had difcovered another
hemifphere, they thought of appropriating to themfelves every part of it. To give fome eclat to their adminiftration, the chiefs of the great fettlements already
formed, were continually undertaking new enterprifes;
and private perfons, paffionately purfuing the fame
kind of fame, generally followed thefe brilliant projects. The calamities infeparable from a career fo little known, had not yet altered this active and indefatigable courage, when fome bold and enterprifing
navigators ventured to direct their courfe towards regions, forbidden to every other nation, except that
which had conquered them. The fuccefs which attended this boldnefs, convinced Philip II. that it was
time to fet bounds to his ambition; and he renounced
acquifitions, which might expofe his arms or his fleets
to infults. This timid, or perhaps only prudent policy, was attended with more important confequences

BOOK
VIII.

BOOK
VIII.
than had been foreseen. The spirit of enthusiasm was at an end, and that of inactivity succeeded to it. A new race of men was formed in the Indies. The people sank into superb effeminacy, and those who governed them no longer attended to any thing but the accumulation of riches ; and the dignities that accompanied them, which had formerly been reserved to talents, to zeal, and to services, were now purchased. At this period a stop was put to navigation, both in America and in Europe.

A few vessels only, ill built, ill armed, ill fitted out, and ill commanded, were dispatched from the ports of the mother-country. Spain could not be awakened from its lethargy, either from the terrible blows which it received from its enemies, or with the ruinous extortions it experienced from its allies.

At length, after two centuries of total inactivity, the docks are again revived. The Spanish navy hath acquired real strength. It consists, at the time of our writing, of sixty-eight ships of the line, carrying from one hundred and fourteen to sixty guns, and five of these are upon the stocks; and of eighty other ships, carrying from fifty-six to twelve guns. There are fifty thousand seamen upon its lists, a great number of whom serve in the armaments fitted out by government. Many of them are also employed in the merchantmen of Biscay, of Majorca, and of Catalonia. Some are wanted for about a hundred small vessels, regularly destined for the American islands, where so few were formerly sent. They will multiply still more, when the voyages to the continent of the other Hemisphere shall be undertaken with all the freedom which the first regulations seem to announce. The seas, which separate the two Worlds, will be covered with robust, active, and intelligent men, who will become the defenders of their country's rights, and will render her fleets formidable.

Spanish monarchs, ye are intrusted with the happiness of the most brilliant parts of the two Hemispheres. Show yourselves worthy of so glorious a destiny. In fulfilling this august and sacred duty, ye will repair the injuries done by your predeceffors and by their subjects. They have depopulated a world which they had difcovered ; they have put millions of mankind to death. Their conduct hath been ftill more atrocious, not only in enflaving them, but alfo in reducing thofe whom their fword hath fpared to the condition of brutes. Thofe whom they have flain, have fuffered only for an inftant, while the wretches whom they have permitted to live, muft have often envied the fate of their murdered brethren. Pofterity will not forgive you, till harvefts fhall arife in thofe fields which you have manured with fo much innocent blood ; and till thofe immenfe fpaces which you have laid wafte fhall be covered with happy and free inhabitants. If ye would know the period in which you may perhaps be abfolved of all your crimes, it will be when you fhall revive, in idea, fome one of the ancient monarchs of Mexico and Peru, and placing him in the midft of his poffeffions, fhall be able to fay to him, BEHOLD THE PRESENT STATE OF YOUR COUNTRY, AND OF YOUR SUBJECTS ; INTERROGATE THEM, AND FORM YOUR JUDGMENT OF US.

B O O K
VIII.

BOOK IX.

Settlement of the Portuguefe in the Brazils. The Wars they have fuftained there. Produce and Riches of that Country.

A NATIONAL fpirit is the refult of a great number of caufes, fome of which are permanent, and others variable. This part of the hiftory of a people is perhaps the moft interefting, and the leaft difficult to inveftigate. The permanent caufes are to be found on the portion of the globe which they inhabit ; the variable ones are configned in their annals, and manifefted by the effects which they have produced. While thefe caufes act in oppofition to each other, the nation is in a ftate of infanity, and doth not begin to recover its

B O O K
IX.

Whether the Europeans have been well acquainted with the art of founding colonies.

BOOK
IX.

proper underftanding, till the time when its fpeculative principles coincide with the nature of its fituation.　Then it is, that it advances rapidly towards
that fplendour, opulence, and felicity, to which it
may be allowed to afpire from a free ufe of its local
refources.

But this national fpirit, which ought to prefide in
the counfels of the people, though it be not always
to be found there, fcarce ever regulates the actions
of individuals.　They have interefts of their own, and
paffions which torment and blind them; and there is
fcarce any one who would not raife his profperity upon the public ruin.　The capitals of empires are the
centre of the national fpirit, that is to fay, the places
where it difplays itfelf with the greateft energy in
words, and where it is the moft completely neglected
in actions.　I except only fome unfrequent inftances,
where the general fafety is at ftake.　In proportion
as the diftance from the capital increafes, this mafk
detaches itfelf; it falls off on the frontiers; and, between one hemifphere and another, is totally loft.

When a man hath croffed the line, he is neither an
Englifhman, a Dutchman, a Frenchman, a Spaniard,
or a Portuguefe.　He preferves nothing of his country,
except the principles and prejudices which give a fanction to his conduct, or furnifh him with an excufe for
it.　Servile when he is weak, and oppreffive when he
is ftrong; eager to acquire wealth, and to enjoy it;
and capable of all the enormities which can contribute
moft fpeedily to the completion of his defigns; he is
a domeftic tiger again let loofe in the woods, and who
is again feized with the thirft of blood.　Such have all
the Europeans indifcriminately fhown themfelves in
the regions of the New World, where they have been
actuated with one common rage, the paffion for gold.

Would it not have been a more humane, more ufeful, and lefs expenfive plan, to have fent into each of
thofe diftant regions fome hundreds of young men and
women?　The men would have married the women,
and the women the men of the country.　Confangui-

nity, the tie that is the moſt ſpeedily formed, and the ſtrongeſt, would ſoon have made one and the ſame family of the ſtrangers and of the natives.

In this intimate connection, the ſavage inhabitant would ſoon have underſtood that the arts and ſciences conveyed into his country were very conducive to the improvement of his deſtiny. He would have entertained the higheſt opinion of the perſuaſive and mild inſtructors brought to him by the ſea, and he would have given himſelf up to them without reſerve.

From this fortunate confidence peace would have ariſen, which would have been impracticable, if the new comers had preſented themſelves with the imperious and authoritative tone of maſters and uſurpers. Commerce is eſtabliſhed without difficulty among men who have reciprocal wants ; and they ſoon accuſtom themſelves to conſider as friends and as brethren thoſe whom intereſt or other motives have brought into their country. The Indians would have adopted the European form of worſhip, becauſe a religion becomes univerſal among all the inhabitants of an empire, when the government leaves it to itſelf, and when the folly and intolerant ſpirit of the prieſts doth not convert it into a principle of diſcord. In like manner, civilization follows from the propenſity which urges every man to improve his ſituation, provided there be no deſire to compel him to it by force, and that theſe advantages be not preſented to him by ſuſpicious ſtrangers.

Such would be the effects that would be produced in a riſing colony by the allurement of the moſt imperious of the ſenſes. Let there be no arms and no ſoldiers ; but a multitude of young women for the men, and numbers of young men for the women. Let us examine what the Portugueſe have done in Brazil by purſuing contrary methods.

Brazil is an immenſe continent, bounded on the north by the river of the Amazons, on the ſouth by the river Plata, on the eaſt by the ſea, and on the weſt

When, and by whom, Brazil was diſcovered.

by moraffes, lakes, torrents, rivers, and mountains, which feparate it from the Spanifh poffeffions.

If Columbus had continued his courfe to the fouth, when he came to the entrance of the Oroonoko in 1499, he could not poffibly have miffed the Brazils; but he chofe to fteer to the north-weft, that he might not go too far from St. Domingo, the only fettlement belonging to the Spaniards in the New World.

Peter Alvarez Cabral had the honour of difcovering the Brazils the following year by a fortunate chance.

How doth it happen that this is the cafe in almoft all difcoveries; and that chance hath always more fhare in them than ingenuity? It is becaufe chance is ever employed, while the human underftanding is checked by indolence, changes its objects through inconftancy, repofes itfelf through laffitude or tedium, and is thrown into a ftate of inactivity by a number of moral, natural, domeftic, or national caufes. Moft difcoveries are therefore owing to chance, or to that infinite number of men, who are always in motion, and whofe attention is conftantly engaged on all the objects that furround, or ftrike them, oftentimes without any defign of gaining information, or of making thofe difcoveries, but merely becaufe they make ufe of their fenfes.

To avoid falling in with the calms on the coaft of Africa, Cabral kept fo far out at fea, that he came within fight of an unknown land lying to weftward. He was driven thither by ftrefs of weather, and anchored on the coaft in the 15th degree of fouth latitude, at a place which he called Porto-Seguro. He took poffeffion of the country, but made no fettlement in it, and gave it the name of Santa Cruz, which was afterwards changed for that of Brazil, becaufe the Brazil wood was the moft valuable production of that country to the Europeans, who ufed it in dyeing.

As this country had been difcovered in going to India, and as it was doubtful whether it was not a part of that country, the fame name was given to it, be-

caufe the Spaniards had imagined that it might be referred to thofe countries they had previoufly difcovered.   All the Europeans, however, diftinguifhed them
by the appellation of Weft Indies.   This name was
afterwards extended to all the New World, and the
Americans were very improperly called Indians.

Thus it is that the names of places and things, accidentally given by ignorant men, have always per-
plexed philofophers, who have been defirous of tracing
the origin of thefe names from nature, and not from
circumftances merely incidental, and oftentimes quite
foreign to the natural properties of the things denoted
by them.   Nothing can be more ftrange, for inftance,
than to fee Europe tranfplanted into America, and
there regenerated, as it were, in the names and forms
of our European cities, and in the laws, manners, and
religion of our continent.   But fooner or later the climate will refume its influence, and reinftate things in
their proper order, and with their original names,
though with thofe veftiges of the change they have
undergone, which a great revolution always leaves
behind it.   Is it not probable, that, in three or four
thoufand years hence, the hiftory of America at this
prefent period will be as confufed, and as inexplicable
to its inhabitants, as the hiftory of Europe, previous
to the rife of the Roman republic, is obfcure to us?
Thus it is that men, the knowledge they have acquired, and the conjectures they have formed, either with
refpect to events that are paffed, or to future tranfactions, are all fubject to the laws and motions of nature,
which purfues her own courfe, without paying the leaft
regard either to our projects or to our opinions.

Nothing can afford us a more convincing proof of Account of
the firft in-
habitants
conveyed
by Portu-
gal into the
Brazils.
this great truth, than the imprudence and uncertainty
of all the defigns and actions of men even in their
moft important undertakings, the blindnefs with which
their inquiries are purfued, and more efpecially the
improper ufe they make of their difcoveries.   As
foon as the court of Lifbon had ordered a furvey to
be taken of the harbours, bays, rivers, and coafts of

Brazil, and was convinced that the country afforded
neither gold nor filver, they held it in fuch contempt,
that they fent thither none but condemned criminals
and abandoned women.

Two ſhips were fent every year from Portugal, to
carry the refufe of the kingdom to this New World,
and to bring home parrots, and woods for the dyers
and cabinetmakers. Ginger was afterwards added, but
was foon prohibited, left it ſhould interfere with the
fale of the fame article from India.

Afia was then the object that attracted all men. It
was the road to fortune, to power, and to fame. The
great exploits of the Portuguefe in India, and the
wealth they brought from thence, gave their nation
fuch a fuperiority in all parts of the world, that every
individual wifhed to partake of it. The enthufiafm
was general. No perfon, indeed, went over voluntarily to America ; but thofe unfortunate men, whom
the inquifition had doomed to deftruction, were added
to the convicts already tranfported thither.

There never was a ftronger and more inveterate hatred than that which the Portuguefe have always entertained againft the Spaniards. Notwithftanding this
national antipathy, which is of fo long a ftanding that
its origin cannot be traced, and fo confirmed that it
can never be expected to ceafe, they have borrowed
moft of their maxims from a neighbour, whofe power
they dreaded as much as they detefted its manners.
Whether from a fimilarity of climate and temper, or
from a conformity of circumftances, they have adopted the worft of its inftitutions, they could not imitate
any one more horrid than the inquifition.

This bloody tribunal, erected in Spain in 1482, by
a combination of policy and fanaticifm, under the
reign of Ferdinand and Ifabella, was no fooner adopted by John III. than it ftruck terror into every family. To eftablifh its authority, and afterwards to fupport it, no lefs than four or five hundred victims were
annually facrificed, a tenth part of which was burnt
alive, and the reft banifhed to Africa or to the Bra-

zils. The fury of this tribunal was particularly exerted againſt thoſe who were ſuſpected of ſodomy ; a
crime of later date in the kingdom, and almoſt unavoidable in hot climates, where celibacy prevails. It
alſo proſecuted forcerers, who, in thoſe times of ignorance, were as much dreaded as their number was multiplied, by the credulity, bigotry, and barbariſm that
prevailed all over Europe. The Mohammedans, though
greatly decreaſed ſince they had loſt the empire, were
alſo perſecuted by the inquiſition ; but more eſpecially the Jews, becauſe they were the richeſt.

It is well known, that when the Jews, who had long
been confined to a very ſmall ſpot upon the face of
the earth, were diſperſed by the Romans, many of
them took refuge in Portugal. There they multiplied
after the Arabs had conquered Spain, were ſuffered to
enjoy all the rights of citizens, and were not excluded
from public offices, till that country had recovered its
independence. This firſt act of oppreſſion did not
prevent twenty thouſand Jewiſh families from remov-
ing thither, when, after the conqueſt of Granada, the
Catholic kings compelled them to quit Spain, or to
change their religion. Each family paid twenty livres
[16s. 8d.] for the liberty of ſettling in Portugal. Superſtition ſoon induced John II. to aggravate the ſuf-
ferings of that perſecuted nation : He demanded of
them 20,000 crowns [2500l.], and afterwards reduced them to a ſtate of ſlavery. In 1496, Emanuel baniſhed all thoſe who refuſed to embrace the Chriſtian
religion ; thoſe who complied were reſtored to their
freedom, and ſoon engroſſed the Aſiatic trade, which
then began to be laid open to every one. The eſtabliſhment of the inquiſition, in 1548, proved a check
to their activity. Their miſtruſt was increaſed by the
frequent confiſcations made by that odious tribunal,
and by the taxes which government extorted from
them at different times. They were in hopes of pur-
chaſing ſome tranquillity, by furniſhing Sebaſtian with
250,000 livres [10,427l. 13s. 4d.] for his African expedition ; but, unfortunately for them, that impru-

B O O K dent monarch came to an untimely end. Philip II.
   IX.   who foon after extended his dominion over Portugal,
enacted, that fuch of his fubjects as were defcended
from a Jew or a Moor, fhould be excluded from all
ecclefiaftical or civil employments. This mark of infamy, with which all the new converts to Chriftianity
were branded, gave them fuch a difguft for a country,
where even the greateft opulence could not exempt
them from being ftigmatized, that they removed, with
their wealth, to Bourdeaux, Antwerp, Hamburgh, and
other towns, with which they had regular connections. This emigration was the occafion of a great
revolution ; it diverted the commerce, which till then
had centered in Spain and Portugal, into other countries, and deprived thofe two nations of the advantages the one derived from the Eaft, and the other
from the Weft Indies.

Before thefe laft periods, the Jews, who were unre-
mittingly perfecuted by the inquifition, were banifhed
in numbers to the Brazils. Though deprived of their
fortunes by thefe infatiable leeches, they fucceeded in
eftablifhing fome cultures. This fortunate beginning
convinced the court of Lifbon that a colony might
be ferviceable to the mother-country by other means
than by metals. They began, as early as the year
1525, to caft a lefs difdainful look on this immenfe
poffeffion, which chance had beftowed upon them,
and which had till then been confidered as the fink
into which all the filth of the monarchy was poured.

Brazil di-   The nation foon adopted the opinion of the miniftry,
vided be- and the noblemen efpecially were firft animated with
tween feve-
ral noble- this new fpirit. Government granted, fucceffively, to
men by the thofe among them who afked for it, a fpace of forty or
court of
Lifbon.   fifty leagues upon the coaft, with an unlimited extent
in the interior parts of the country. They were authorifed by their charter to treat the vanquifhed people in whatever manner they chofe. They had a right,
which moft of them exercifed, to difpofe of the territory they had invaded, in favour of any Portuguefe
who would cultivate it ; but they difpofed of it only

for three lives, referving alfo to themfelves fome rent-charges. Thefe great proprietors were to enjoy all the rights of fovereignty, except that of condemning to death, coining, and the tithes; prerogatives which the court kept in their hands. Thefe ufeful and honourable fiefs could only be forfeited by the neglecting to cultivate and defend them, by the deficiency of male iffue, or by the commiffion of fome capital crime.

Thofe who had folicited and obtained thefe provinces, expected to acquire the poffeffion of them without much expence, and without expofing their lieutenants to any great danger. Their hopes were chiefly founded upon the indolence of the fmall nations they were to conquer.

Man is undoubtedly formed for fociety; his wants and his weakneffes require it. But focieties of twenty or thirty millions of men, cities confifting of four or five hundred thoufand fouls, are fo many monftrous productions, which are fo far from being formed by nature, that fhe, on the contrary, is inceffantly ftudying to deftroy them. They are only fupported by conftant forefight, and by moft extraordinary efforts. They would foon be diffipated, if a confiderable portion of this multitude did not attend to their prefervation. The air is infected by them, the waters are corrupted; the land exhaufted to a great extent; the duration of life is fhortened among them; the fweets of plenty are but little felt, and the horrors of dearth are extreme. They are the fpot which gives birth to epidemic difeafes; they are the haunts of crimes, of vices, and of diffolute manners. Thefe enormous and fatal heaps of men are likewife one of the fcourges of fovereignty, fince cupidity invites around the throne, and perpetually increafes the herd of flaves, under an infinite variety of functions and denominations. Thefe unnatural affemblages of population, are fubject to ferment and to corrupt during peace; and if war fhould increafe the ferment, the fhock becomes dreadful.

Character and cuftoms of the people whom the Portuguefe wifhed to fubdue.

Societies, in a ftate of nature, are little numerous; they fubfift of themfelves. They feparate before a

B O O K fuperabundance of population becomes troublefome,
    IX.   Each divifion removes to convenient diftances. Such
was the primitive ftate of the New Countries; fuch is
that of the New Continent.

The Brazilians in general were of the fize of the Europeans, but not fo ftout. They were fubject to fewer
diftempers, and were long-lived. They wore no clothing; the women wore their hair extremely long, the
men cut theirs fhort; the women wore bracelets of
bones of a beautiful white, the men necklaces of the
fame; the women painted their faces, and the men
their bodies.

Every colony of this vaft continent had its own idi-
oms, but not one of them had any words to convey
general and abftract ideas. This poverty of language,
which is common to all nations of South America, is a
convincing proof of the little progrefs the human underftanding had made in thefe countries. The analogy between the words in the feveral languages of this
continent fhows, that the reciprocal tranfmigrations of
thefe favages had been frequent.

The food of the Brazilians was very fimple. In a
country deprived of domeftic animals, they lived upon
fhell-fifh by the fea fide; along the rivers, by fifhing;
and in the forefts, by hunting. When thefe precarious provifions failed, they fed upon the caffava and
other roots.

Thefe men were very fond of dancing. Their fongs
were but one tedious uniform tone, without any mo-
dulations, and commonly turned upon their loves or
their warlike exploits.

In polifhed ftates, dancing and finging are reckoned
among the arts. In the midft of the forefts they are
almoft the natural expreffions of concord and friendfhip, of tendernefs and pleafure. We are obliged to
have mafters to inftruct us to difplay our voices, and
to move gracefully. The favage hath no other in-
ftructor but his paffion, his heart and nature. He really feels what we affect to feel. Accordingly, the favage who fings and dances is always happy.

Their amufements are not interrupted by the worfhip of a Supreme Being, for they know of none ; nor
is their tranquillity difturbed by the dread of a future
ftate, of which they have no idea. They have, however, their magicians, who, by ftrange contortions, fo
far work upon the credulity of the people as to throw
them into violent convulfions. If the impoftures of
thefe magicians are detected, they are immediately put
to death, which ferves, in fome degree, to check the
fpirit of deceit.

Thefe atheifts are equally ftrangers to all notions of
fubordination and fubmiffion, which among ourfelves
are originally derived from the idea of a Supreme
Being. They cannot conceive that any perfon can
have the audacity to command, much lefs that any one
can be fo weak as to obey. But they fhow moft de-
ference to the man who has killed the greateft number
of his enemies.

The Brazilians, like moft other favages, fhowed no
particular attachment to their native place. The love
of our country, which is a ruling paffion in civilized
ftates; which in good governments rifes to enthufiafm.
and in bad ones grows habitual; which for feveral centuries together perpetuates in every nation its difpofition, cuftoms, and tafte : this love of our country is
but a factitious fentiment arifing from fociety, but unknown in the ftate of nature. The moral life of a favage is the very reverfe of that of the civilized man.
The latter enjoys the gifts of nature only in his infancy. As his ftrength increafes and his underftanding
unfolds itfelf, he lofes fight of the prefent, and is wholly intent upon the future. Thus the age of paffions
and pleafures, the time deftined by nature for enjoyment, is fpent in fpeculation and difappointment. The
heart denies itfelf what it wifhes for, laments the indulgences it has allowed itfelf, and is equally tormented
by its felf-denials and its gratifications. The civilized
man, inceffantly deploring his liberty which he hath
always facrificed, looks back with regret on his earlieft
years, when a fucceffion of new objects conftantly a-

BOOK
IX.

wakened his curiofity, and kept his hopes alive. He
recollects with pleafure the fpot where he paffed his
infant days; the remembrance of his innocent delights
endears them to his imagination, and forcibly attracts
him to his native fpot; whereas the favage, who enjoys all the pleafures and advantages peculiar to every
period of his life, and does not abftain from them in
expectation of greater indulgence in old age, finds
equally, in all places, objects fuited to his defires, and
feels that the fource of his pleafures is in himfelf, and
that his country is every where.

Though the tranquillity of the Brazilians was not
the refult of any laws, diffenfions were feldom heard of
in their little focieties. If drunkennefs, or fome unfortunate incident, occafioned a difpute, and fome life
was loft, the murderer was inftantly delivered up to the
relations of the deceafed, who immediately facrificed
him to their vengeance without hefitation; then both
the families met, and their reconciliation was fealed by
a joyous and noify feaft.

Every Brazilian took as many wives as he chofe, or
as many as he could get, and put them away when he
grew tired of them. When they violated their marriage vow, they were punifhed, according to a cuftom
almoft generally adopted, with death, and the hufband
did not become an object of ridicule on account of the
injury his wife had done him. When the women
laid in, they kept their bed but a day or two; then
the mother, hanging the child to her neck in a cotton
fcarf, returned to her ufual occupations without any
kind of inconvenience.

In general, the confequences of child-birth among
the favages, are not fo bad as they are among the
women of civilized countries, becaufe the firft always
fuckle their children, and becaufe the indolence of
the men condemns them to a laborious life, which
occafions the menftrual flux in them to be lefs plentiful, and renders the channels, through which this fuperfluous blood is to flow, fo much the more narrow.
A long reft after child-birth, far from being neceffary,

would become as fatal to them, as it would be among us to our women of the lower clafs. This is not the only circumftance in which we find a compenfation for the advantages of the feveral ranks of life. We feel the want of exercife, and go into the country in fearch of health. Our women begin to deferve the name of mothers, by fuckling their own children ; the children too are juft refcued from the fhackles of fwaddling clothes. What can thefe innovations be attributed to, but to the confcioufnefs that man cannot deviate imprudently from the laws of nature, without injury to his own happinefs? In all future ages, the favages will advance by flow degrees towards the civilized ftate ; and civilized nations will return towards their primitive ftate; from whence the philofopher will conclude, that there exifts in the interval between thefe two ftates, a certain medium, in which the felicity of the human fpecies is placed. But who is it that can find out this medium? and even if it were found, what authority would be capable of directing the fteps of man to it, and to fix him there ?

Travellers were received with diftinguifhed marks of civility in the Brazils. Wherever they came, they were furrounded with women, who wafhed their feet, and welcomed them with the moft obliging expreffions. Nothing was fpared for their entertainment ; but it would have been an unpardonable affront, had they left the family where they were firft entertained, in hopes of better accommodation in another. This fpirit of hofpitality is one of the moft certain indications that man was intended for fociety.

Hofpitality, the offspring of natural commiferation, was univerfally practifed in the earlieft times. It was almoft the only thing that attached nations to each other : it was the fource of the moft ancient, the moft lafting, and the moft refpected friendfhip, contracted between families who were feparated by immenfe regions. A man, perfecuted by his fellow-citizens, or guilty of any mifdemeanour, retired to diftant countries in queft of tranquillity or impunity. He prefent-

BOOK
IX.

ed himfelf at the entrance of a town, or of a village, and faid, " I am fuch a one, the fon of fuch a one, or " the grandfon of fuch a one, and I come for fuch " reafons." And then he related his ftory, or his invented tale, in the manner the moft marvellous, the moft pathetic, and the beft calculated to give an idea of his confequence. He was eagerly attended to ; and he added, " Receive me ; for, if you or your children, " or your children's children, fhould ever be driven " by any misfortunes to my country, they need only " name me, and my friends will receive them." He was immediately entreated to become their gueft, and the perfons with whom he preferred to live thought themfelves honoured by this diftinction. He took up his abode in their houfe, and was treated by them like one of the family ; fometimes he became the hufband, the ravifher, or the feducer of his hoft's daughter.

To fuch adventurers as thefe, who were, perhaps, the firft travellers, the origin of the demigods of paganifm, the offspring of hofpitality and licentioufnefs, may be afcribed. Moft of them owed their birth to paffengers, to whom a bed had been given, and who were never feen afterwards.

Let us be allowed to fay, that there is no occupation in the world fo immoral as that of a traveller. The traveller by profeffion is like a man who is in poffeffion of an immenfe houfe ; and who, inftead of fitting down with his wife, and in the midft of his children, fhould employ all his life in ranging about from one apartment to another. Tyranny, guilt, ambition, curiofity, a kind of reftlefs fpirit, the defire of acquiring knowledge, and of feeing things, tedium, and the difguft arifing from exhaufted felicity, have driven, and will at all times drive, men from their country.

But, in ages previous to civilization, to commerce, and to the invention of figns to reprefent riches, before intereft had prepared a habitation for the traveller, hofpitality fupplied its place. The favourable reception of a ftranger was confidered as a facred debt, which was often repaid after the lapfe of feveral cen-

turies, by the defcendants of the perfon who had been
the object of it; and who, upon his return into his own
country, took a delight in repeating the favours he had
received, the remembrance of which was conftantly
preferved in his family.

Thefe affecting inftances of humanity have decreafed, in proportion as the intercoufe between nations
hath been facilitated. Induftrious, rapacious, and interefted men have formed, in all par s, fettlements,
where the traveller alights, where he commands, and
where he difpofes of all the conveniences of life, as if
he were at home. The mafter, or the landlord, of the
houfe, is neither his benefactor, his brother, nor his
friend; he is only his upper fervant. The gold that
he fpends at his houfe entitles him to treat his hoft as
he choofes; he cares not for your refpect, but for your
money. When you quit his houfe, he thinks no more
of you; nor do you recollect him, any farther than as
you have been either difpleafed or fatisfied with him.
Hofpitality, that facred virtue which is extinguifhed
amongft all nations where civilization and focial inftitutions have made any progrefs, is no longer found
but among the favages, and more particularly in the
Brazils than in any other country.

Far from fhowing that indifference or weaknefs
which makes us fhun the dead, and makes us unwil-
ling to fpeak of them, or to remain in the places that
might recal their image to our minds, the Brazilians
beheld their dead with tender emotions, recounted
their exploits with complacency, and celebrated their
virtues with tranfport. They were buried upright in
a round grave; and if the deceafed was the head of a
family, his plumes, his necklaces, and his arms, were
interred with him. When a clan removed to another
place, which often happened, merely for the fake of
changing, every family fixed fome remarkable ftones
over the graves of their moft refpectable relations; and
they never approached thofe monuments of grief, without breaking out into dreadful outcries, not unlike the

fhouts with which they made the air refound when they were going to battle.

Motives of intereft or ambition never prompted the Brazilians to war. The defire of avenging their relations or friends was always the occafion of their moft fanguinary contefts. Their chiefs, or rather their orators, were old men, who determined the commencement of hoftilities, gave the fignal for marching, and exerted themfelves during the march, in repeated expreffions of implacable hatred. Sometimes even the march of the army was fufpended, to liften to thefe paffionate harangues, that lafted for many hours. This cuftom makes thofe long fpeeches we meet with in Homer, and in the Roman hiftorians, appear more probable; but in thofe days the noife of the artillery did not drown the voices of the generals.

The combatants were armed with a club of ebony, fix feet long, one foot broad, and an inch thick. Their bows and arrows were of the fame wood. Their inftruments of martial mufic were flutes made of the bones of their enemies. They were as well calculated to infpire courage as our drums, which ftifle our fenfe of danger, and as our trumpets, which give the fignal, and perhaps the fear, of death. Their generals were the foldiers who had diftinguifhed themfelves moft in former wars.

The firft attack was never made openly, but both armies endeavoured to take the advantage of a furprifal. Their courage feldom confifted in maintaining their ground. The ambition of the Brazilians was to make a great many prifoners, which were flain and eaten with folemnity. During the feaft, the old men exhorted the young to become intrepid warriors, that they might often procure themfelves fuch an honourable repaft. This inclination for human flefh was never fo prevalent as to induce the Brazilians to devour fuch of their enemies as had fallen in battle: they only ate thofe who had been taken alive.

The treatment of prifoners of war hath varied according to the degree of perfection human reason hath gradually attained. The most civilized nations ransom them, exchange or restore them at the conclusion of a war. Nations that are not yet completely civilized claim them as their property, and make them slaves. The common savages massacre them, without putting them to torture. The most savage people of all torture, kill, and eat them. This is their execrable law of nations.

This anthropophagy hath long been considered as a chimera in the opinion of some sceptical persons. They could not conceive, that any nation could have been reduced to the cruel necessity of feeding upon their fellow-creatures, to satisfy their own wants; and still less could they suppose, that any thing, except an absolute privation of every support of life, could have induced man to commit so atrocious a deed. Since the doubts of the most incredulous have been removed by a great number of facts, by testimonies of higher authority, and by more authentic accounts, some philosophers have attempted to justify this practice of several savage nations. They have still exclaimed with vehemence against the barbarity of the sovereigns who, to satisfy their own caprice, sent their unfortunate subjects to the slaughter-house of war. But they have imagined, that it was a matter of indifference, whether their carcases were devoured by men or by birds.

Perhaps, indeed, this custom hath not in itself any thing criminal, any thing that is repugnant to morality : but how pernicious would be the consequences arising from it? When man is once authorised to eat the flesh of man, if the taste of it should suit his palate, nothing will remain, but to make the stream of blood grateful to the nostrils of the tyrant. Let us then form an idea of these two phenomena, generally prevailing on the face of the globe, and let us fix our eyes upon the human species, if we can possibly bear the sight.

In the Brazils, the heads of the enemies slain in action, or sacrificed after the engagement, were very

B O O K carefully preferved, and fhown with oftentation to all
IX. ſtrangers, as monuments of valour and victory. The
heroes of thoſe favage nations bore their exploits imprinted on their limbs; by inciſions which enſured them
reſpect. The more they were disfigured, the greater
was their glory.

Aſcendant   Such manners had not diſpoſed the Brazilians to
of the miſ-   ſubmit patiently to the yoke that was intended to be
fionaries   impoſed upon them : but what could the ſavages op-
over the   poſe to the arms and diſcipline of Europe? A conſi-
natives of   derable number of them had ſubmitted, when, in
Brazil, and   1549, the court of Liſbon thought proper to ſend
over the   over a governor, to regulate an eſtabliſhment which
Portu-   till then had been left to the fury and the caprices of a
gueſe, at   ſet of banditti. Thomas de Souſa, indeed, by building
the firſt ex- San Salvador, gave a centre to the colony ; but the
iſtence of   honour of reſtoring it to any kind of tranquillity was
the colony.   reſerved to the Jeſuits who attended him. Thoſe intrepid men, who have always been prompted by mo-
tives of religion, or of ambition, to undertake great actions, diſperſed themſelves among the Indians. Such
of theſe miſſionaries as were murdered from hatred to
the Portugueſe name, were immediately replaced by
others, who were inſpired with none but ſentiments of
peace and charity. This magnanimity confounded
the barbarians, who had never had any idea of for-
giveneſs. By degrees they began to place ſome confidence in men who ſeemed to ſeek them only with a
view of making them happy. Their attachment to
the miſſionaries grew into a paſſionate fondneſs. When
a Jeſuit was expected in one of their nations, the young
people flocked to meet him, concealing themſelves in
the woods along the road. As he drew near, they ſal-
lied forth, played upon their pipes, beat their drums,
danced, and made the air reſound with joyful ſongs ;
and, in a word, omitted nothing that could expreſs
their ſatisfaction. At the entrance of the village, the
old men and chief inhabitants were aſſembled, who
expreſſed as much joy, but with more ſedateneſs. A
little further on, ſtood the women and young girls, ın

a refpectful pofture fuitable to their fex. Then they all joined, and conducted their father in triumph to the place where they were affembled. There he inftructed them in the fundamental doctrines of religion; exhorted them to a regularity of manners, to a love of juftice, to brotherly charity, and to an abhorrence for human blood; after which he baptized them.

BOOK IX

As thefe miffionaries were too few in number to tranfact all the bufinefs themfelves, they frequently deputed fome of the moft intelligent Indians in their ftead. Thefe men, proud of fo glorious an office, diftributed hatchets, knives, and looking-glaffes among the favages they met with, and reprefented the Portuguefe as a harmlefs, humane, and good fort of people. They never returned from their excurfions without bringing with them fome of the Brazilians, who followed them from motives of curiofity. When thofe favages had once feen the Jefuits, it was with difficulty that they ever quitted them. When they returned home, it was to invite their families and friends to come and fhare their happinefs, and to difplay the prefents they had received.

If any one fhould doubt thefe happy effects of kindnefs and humanity over favage nations, let him only compare the progrefs the Jefuits have made, in a very fhort time, in South America, with what the forces and navy of Spain and Portugal have not been able to effect in the fpace of two centuries. While multitudes of foldiers were employed in changing two great and civilized empires into deferts inhabited by roving favages, a few miffionaries have changed little wandering clans into feveral great and civilized nations. If thefe active and courageous men had been lefs infected with the fpirit of the church of Rome; if, when formed into a fociety in the moft intriguing and corrupt court in Europe, they had not infinuated themfelves into other courts, to influence all political events; if they had not difgufted, by their fpirit of intoleration, all moderate perfons, and all the tribunals by

BOOK their paffion for defpotifm; if an outrageous zeal for
IX. religion had not made them the fecret enemies to the
progrefs of knowledge, and the perfecutors of philofophy; if they had employed as much art in making themfelves beloved, as they did in making themfelves feared; if they had been as jealous of increafing the fplendour of their fociety, as of augmenting its power; if
the chiefs of the order had not made an ill ufe of the
very virtues of their members; the Old and New
World would ftill have reaped the advantage of the
occupations of a fet of men, who might have been
made ufeful, had they been prevented from being neceffary; and the eighteenth century would not have
had caufe to be afhamed of the enormities that have
attended the fuppreffion of the fociety. The whole
univerfe would continue to be fertilized by their labours, and by their undertakings.

The Brazilians had too much caufe of hatred againft
the Europeans, not to miftruft their kindnefs; but their
diffidence was in fome meafure removed by a fignal act
of juftice.

The Portuguefe had formed the fettlement of St.
Vincent on the fea-coaft, in the 24th degree of fouth
latitude. There they traded peaceably with the Cariges, the mildeft and moft civilized nation in all the
Brazils. The advantages they reaped from this connection could not reftrain them from feizing upon feventy men to make flaves of them. The perfon who
had committed the offence was condemned to carry
the prifoners back to the place from whence he had
taken them, and to make the proper excufes for fo
heinous an infult. Two Jefuits, who were appointed
to difpofe the Indians to accept this fatisfaction, which
would never have been offered but at their defire, gave
notice of it to Farancaha, the moft refpectable man of
his nation. He came out to meet them, and, embra-
cing them with tears of joy; " Fathers," faid he, " we
" confent to forget all that is paft, and to enter into a
" frefh alliance with the Portuguefe; but let them for
" the future be more moderate, and more obfervant

" of the rights of nations. Our attachment entitles B O Q K IX.
" us at leaſt to equitable proçeedings. We are called
" barbarians, yet we reſpeƈt juſtice and our friends."
The miſſionaries having engaged that for the future
their nation ſhould more religiouſly obſerve the laws
of peace and unity, Farancaha proceeded thus : " If
" you doubt the faith of the Cariges, I will give you
" proof of it. I have a nephew, for whom I have a
" great affeƈtion ; he is the hope of my family, and
" the comfort of his mother ; ſhe would die with grief
" if ſhe were to loſe her ſon. Yet I will deliver him
" to you as a hoſtage. Take him along with you ;
" cultivate his young mind ; take care of his educa-
" tion ; and inſtruƈt him in your religion. Let his
" manners be gentle and pure. I hope, when you
" return, you will inſtruƈt me alſo, and enlighten my
" mind." Many of the Cariges followed his example,
and ſent their children to St. Vincent's for education.
The Jeſuits were too artful not to take great advantage of this event ; but it does not appear that they
ever had any intention to deceive the Indians by in-
culcating ſubmiſſion. Avarice had not yet poſſeſſed
the minds of theſe miſſionaries ; and the intereſt they
had at court ſecured ſufficient reſpeƈt in the colony to
make the ſituation of their converts a fortunate one.

This time of tranquillity was improved. For ſome
years paſt, ſugar plants had been tranſplanted from
Madeira to Brazil, where the climate and the ſoil were
found favourable to this rich produce. The culture
of it was at firſt very inconſiderable ; but no ſooner
was the ſtrength of the Negroes ſubſtituted to the languid labours of the Indians, towards the year 1570,
than it received an increaſe. This progreſs was growing daily more conſiderable, becauſe this produƈtion,
which had·been hitherto only of uſe in medicine, became more and more an article of luxury.

This proſperity, which was viſible in all the markets Irruption
of Europe, excited the cupidity of the French. They of the French into
attempted to form three or four ſettlements at Brazil. the Brazils.
Their levity would not ſuffer them to wait the uſually

BOOK
IX.

flow progrefs of new undertakings ; and merely from inconftancy and impatience, they gave up profpects that were fufficient to have encouraged any, except fuch volatile minds, that are as eafily difcouraged as they are ready to undertake. The only valuable monument we have of their fruitlefs incurfions is a dialogue, which more particularly fhows the natural good fenfe of the favages, as it is written with that fimplicity of ftyle which diftinguifhed the French language two hundred years ago ; a fimplicity in which there were graces we cannot ftill but regret.

" The Brazilians," fays Lery, one of the interlocutors, " being very much aftonifhed to fee the French " take fuch pains to get their wood, one of their old " men once afked me this queftion : What can be the " reafon that you Frenchmen come fo far to get wood " for firing ? Is there none in your own country ? To " which I anfwered, Yes, and a great deal too, but " not fuch as theirs, which we did not burn, as he " thought ; but as they themfelves ufed it to dye " their ftrings and their feathers, our people employ- " ed it alfo in dyeing. He replied, Well ; but do " you want fo great a quantity ? Yes, faid I ; for in " our country there are fome merchants who have " more rugs and fcarlet cloths than you ever faw in " this country ; one of thefe will buy feveral cargoes " of this wood. Ha, ha ! fays the favage, thou telleft " me wonders. Then paufing upon what I had been " telling him, he faid, But this very rich man thou " talkeft of, is he never to die ? Yes, yes, faid I, as " well as others. Upon which, as they are great talk- " ers, he afked me again, So then, when he is dead, to " whom does all the wealth he leaves belong ? It goes, " faid I, to his children, or, if he hath none, to his " brothers, fifters, or next of kin. Truly, fays the old " man, now I fee that you Frenchmen are great fools ; " for, muft you work fo hard, and crofs the fea, to " heap riches for them that come after you, as if the " earth that had fed you was not fufficient to feed " them likewife ? We have children and relations

" whom we love, as thou feeſt ; but as we are ſure
" that, after our death, the earth that hath provided
" for our ſubſiſtence will equally provide for theirs,
" we are ſatisfied."

This mode of reaſoning, ſo natural to ſavages, whom
nature hath exempted from ambition, but ſo foreign
to civilized nations, who have experienced all the ill
effects of luxury and avarice, made no great impreſſion on the French. They could not withſtand the
temptation of riches, which all the maritime nations
in Europe thirſted after at that time. The Dutch,
who were become republicans by chance, and merchants from neceſſity, were more perſevering and more
ſucceſsful than the French in their attempts on the
Brazils. The nation they had to contend with was
not more conſiderable than their own, and, in imitation of them, was preparing to ſhake off the yoke of
Spain, though they ſtill ſubmitted to that of a regal
government.

Conqueſts
of the Dutch
in the Bra-
zils.

All hiſtorical accounts are full of the acts of tyranny and cruelty that excited the Low-Countries to riſe
againſt Philip II. The richeſt provinces were retained, or brought back under the yoke of a tyrannical
government, while the pooreſt, that were in a manner
ſunk under water, found means, by more than human
exertions, to ſecure their independence. When their
liberty was firmly eſtabliſhed, they attacked their enemy upon the remoteſt ſeas, on the Indus, on the Ganges, and as far as the Moluccas, which made a part of
the Spaniſh dominions, ſince Portugal had been includ-
ed in them. The truce of 1609 gave time to that enterpriſing and fortunate republic to bring her new projects to maturity. Theſe deſigns were manifeſted in
1621, by the eſtabliſhment of a Weſt India Company,
from which the ſame ſucceſs was expected in Africa
and America, that were both compriſed in the charter,
as the Eaſt India Company had experienced in Aſia.
The operations of the new ſociety began by the attack
of Brazil.

Precautions had been taken to procure the neceſſary

informations. Some Dutch ships had ventured thither in defiance of the law that prohibited the admittance of any strangers. As they greatly undersold, according to the custom of their country, the commodities that came from Spain, they met with a favourable reception. At their return, the contraband traders reported, that the country was in a kind of anarchy; that foreign dominion had stifled in the people the love of their country; that self-interest had corrupted their minds; that the soldiers were turned merchants; that they had forgotten the first principles of war, and that whoever should appear there with a competent force, would infallibly surmount the trifling obstacles that might be opposed to the conquest of that wealthy region.

The Company committed this undertaking to Jacob Willekins, in 1624. He went directly to the capital. San Salvador surrendered at sight of the Dutch fleet; and the rest of the province, although it was the most extensive and most populous of the colony, made little more resistance.

This was a terrible misfortune, but it did not give any pain to the Spanish council. Since that crown had subdued Portugal, they did not find the people as submissive as they wished them to be. A disaster which might render them more dependent, appeared to be a great advantage; and their ministers congratulated themselves, upon having at length found an opportunity of aggravating the yoke of their despotism.

Philip, without entertaining more equitable ideas, or more elevated sentiments, thought that the majesty of the throne required of him some outward appearance of decency. Accordingly, he wrote to the Portuguese of the first rank, exhorting them to make such generous efforts as the present exigencies required. This they were already inclined to. Self-interest, patriotism, the desire of throwing a damp upon the joy of their tyrants; all concurred to quicken their alacrity. The monied men lavished their treasures; others raised troops; all were eager to enter into the service. In three months time twenty-fix ships were fitted out, which failed in the beginning of the year 1626, in company with thofe from Spain, which the tardinefs and policy of that nation had made them wait for much too long.

The archbifhop of San Salvador, Michael de Texeira, had prepared matters fo as to facilitate their fuccefs. That martial prelate, at the head of 1500 men, had at firft ftopped the progrefs of the enemy. He had infulted, haraffed, beaten, driven, enclofed, and blocked them up in the town. The Dutch, reduced by hunger, fatigue, and want, compelled the governor to furrender to the troops which the fleet had landed on their arrival, and they were all carried to Europe.

The fuccefs of the Company by fea, made them amends for this lofs. Whenever their fhips came into port they were victorious, and loaded with the fpoils of the Spaniards and Portuguefe. They were fo profperous as to give umbrage even to the powers moft interefted in the welfare of Holland. The ocean was covered with their fleets. Their admirals endeavoured, by ufeful exploits, to preferve their confidence. The fubaltern officers afpired to promotion, by feconding the valour and fkill of their commanders. The foldiers and failors fought with unparalleled ardour, and nothing could difcourage thofe refolute and intrepid men. The fatigues of the fea, ficknefs, and repeated engagements, all feemed to inure them to war, and to increafe their emulation. The Company encouraged this ufeful fpirit, by frequently diftributing rewards. Exclufive of their pay, the failors were allowed to carry on a private trade, which was a great encouragement, and procured a conftant fupply of men. By this wife regulation, their intereft was fo immediately connected with that of their employers, that they wifhed to be always in action. They never ftruck to the enemy, nor ever failed to attack their fhips with that degree of fkill, intrepidity, and perfeverance which muft enfure victory. In the courfe of thirteen years, the Company fitted out eight hundred fhips, which coft ninety mil-

lions [3,750,000l.]. They took five hundred and forty-five of the enemy's fhips, which, with the goods on
board, fold for 180,000,000 livres [7,500,000l.]. The
dividend was never below twenty *per cent.* and often
rofe to fifty. This profperity, which was entirely owing to the war, enabled the Company to make a fecond
attack upon the Brazils.

Their admiral, Henry Lonk, arrived in the beginning of the year 1630, with forty-fix men of war, on
the coaft of Fernambucca, one of the largeft provinces
in thofe parts, and the beft fortified. He reduced it
after feveral obftinate engagements, in which he was
always victorious. The troops he left behind fubdued
the neighbouring countries in the years 1633, 1634,
and 1635. This was the moft cultivated part of Brazil, and confequently that which afforded moft commodities.

The Company were fo elated with the acquifition
of this wealth, which flowed to Amfterdam inftead of
Lifbon, that they determined upon the conqueft of all
the Brazils, and intrufted Maurice of Naffau with the
conduct of that enterprife. That general reached the
place of his deftination in the beginning of the year
1637. He found the foldiers fo well difciplined, the
commanders fuch experienced men, and fo much readinefs in all to engage, that he directly took the field.
He was fucceffively oppofed by Albuquerque, Banjo-
la, Lewis Rocca de Borgia, and the Brazilian Came-
ron, the idol of his people, paffionately fond of the
Portuguefe, brave, active, cunning, and who wanted
no qualification neceffary for a general, but to have
learned the art of war under able commanders. Thefe
feveral chiefs exerted their utmoft efforts to defend the
poffeffions that were under their protection ; but their
endeavours proved ineffectual. The Dutch completed the conqueft of all the coaft extending from San
Salvador to the Amazon.

Complaints
of a Por-
tuguefe
preacher
It was in thefe circumftances that an eloquent Jefuit, named Anthony Vieira, pronounced, in one of the
churches of Bahia, the moft vehement and moft ex-

traordinary difcourfe that hath perhaps ever been heard
in a Chriftian pulpit. The fingularity of this fermon
will probably plead my excufe for the long extract I
am going to give of it.

B O O K
IX.

upon the
fuccefs of a
heretic na-
tion.

Vieira took for his text that part of the Pfalms,
where the prophet, addreffing himfelf to God, exclaims,
" Awake, O Lord; wherefore haft thou flept? Where-
" fore haft thou turned thy countenance from us ?
" Wherefore haft thou forgotten our mifery and our
" tribulation? Awake, and come to our fuccour. Think
" on the glory of thy name, and fave us."

" It is in thefe words, full of pious firmnefs and of
" religious boldnefs; it is thus," faith the orator,
" that the king prophet, protefting rather than pray-
" ing, addreffeth himfelf to God. The times and cir-
" cumftances are the fame ; and I may alfo venture to
" fay, Awake, wherefore haft thou flept?"

Vieira repeated his text ; and, after having fhown
the conformity between the misfortunes of the Ifrael-
ites and the Portuguefe, he adds, " It is not, therefore,
" to the people that my difcourfe this day fhall be ad-
" dreffed. My voice and my words fhall be employ-
" ed upon a higher theme. I afpire, at this inftant, to
" penetrate even into the breaft of the Divinity. This
" is the laft day of the fortnight which is deftined, in
" all the churches of the mother-country, to prayer
" before the facred altars ; and, fince this day is the
" laft, it is proper to have recourfe to the fole and laft
" remedy. The preachers of the gofpel have in vain
" endeavoured to lead you to repentance. Since ye
" have been deaf, fince they have not converted you,
" it is thou, O Lord, whom I will convert ; and al-
" though we are the finners, it is thou who fhalt re-
" pent.

" When the children of Ifrael had committed the
" crime in the defert, in worfhipping the golden calf,
" thou didft reveal their fault to Mofes, and thou didft
" add, in thy wrath, that thou wouldft annihilate thofe
" ungrateful people. Mofes faid unto thee, Why doth
" thy wrath wax hot againft thy people ? Before thou

BOOK " punisheft, confider what is proper for thee to do.
IX.   " Shall the Egyptians accufe thee of having taken
      " them out of flavery for mifchief, and to flay them
      " in the mountains? Reflect on the glory of thy name.
      " Such was the reafoning made ufe of by Mofes,
      " and fuch fhall be mine. Thou didft repent thee of
      " the defign which thou hadft formed. Thou art ftill
      " the fame; and my arguments are ftronger than thofe
      " of the Jewifh legiflator. They will have the fame
      " effect upon thee; and, if thou haft taken the refo-
      " lution to deftroy us, thou wilt repent of it. Thou
      " canft not be ignorant that the heretic, inflated with
      " the fuccefs which thou haft given him, hath already
      " faid, that it is to the falfity of our worfhip he owes
      " thy protection and his victories. And what doft
      " thou think the Gentiles that furround us, the Tala-
      " pouin, who is yet unacquainted with thee, the in-
      " conftant Indian, and the ignorant and ftupid Egyp-
      " tian, but juft wafhed with the waters of baptifm, will
      " think of this? Are the people capable of fearching
      " into, and of adoring the depth of thy judgments?
      " Arife, therefore, and, if thou haft any care of thy
      " glory, fuffer not that arguments againft our faith
      " fhould be drawn from our defeats. Awake, and let
      " the ftorms which have difperfed our fleets difperfe
      " thofe of our common enemy. Let the peftilence,
      " and the difeafes which have wafted our armies, bring
      " deftruction among theirs; and, fince the councils of
      " men are fruftrated at thy pleafure, let darknefs and
      " confufion prevail in theirs.

      " Jofhua was more holy and more patient than we
      " are; yet his language was not different from mine,
      " and the circumftance was much lefs important. He
      " croffed the Jordan, he attacked the city of Ai, and
      " his troops were difperfed. His lofs was moderate,
      " and yet behold him rending his clothes, falling up-
      " on the earth, giving way to the moft bitter com-
      " plaints, and exclaiming, *Wherefore haft thou brought*
      " *us over Jordan to deliver us into the hands of the Am-*
      " *monites?* And I, when the intereft of an immenfe

"people, and in a vaſt extent of country, are concern- B O O K
"ed, ſhall I not exclaim, Haſt thou given us theſe re- IX.
"gions merely to deprive us of them again? If thou
"didſt deſign them for the Dutch, why didſt thou
"not invite them while they were yet uncultivated?
"Has the heretic rendered thee ſuch great ſervices,
"and are we ſo vile in thine eyes, that thou ſhouldſt
"have drawn us from our country merely to clear
"their lands for them, to build their cities, and to en-
"rich them with our labours? Is this the indemnity
"which thou haſt fixed upon in thine heart, for ſo
"many men ſlaughtered upon the earth, or loſt in the
"waters? Yet, if it be thy will, it muſt be ſo. But I
"perceive that thoſe whom thou rejecteſt, and whom
"thou doſt oppreſs to-day, thou wilt ſearch for in vain
"to-morrow.

" Job, when cruſhed with misfortunes, expoſtulated
"with thee. Thou doſt not expect that we ſhould be
"more inſenſible than he was. He ſaid to thee, *Since*
"*thou haſt reſolved upon my deſtruction, complete thy*
"*work; kill me, and annihilate me: but thou ſhalt ſeek*
"*me in the morning, and I ſhall not be. Thou ſhalt find*
"*Sabeans, Chaldeans, and blaſphemers of thy name; but*
"*Job, thy faithful ſervant, who worſhippeth thee, will no*
"*more be found.*

" I will ſay to thee, O Lord, with Job, burn, de-
"ſtroy, and conſume us all: but one day, but in the
"morning, thou ſhalt ſeek for Portugueſe, and thou
"ſhalt ſeek in vain. Will Holland furniſh thee, at
"thy call, with apoſtolic conquerors, who, at the riſk
"of their lives, will convey over the face of the whole
"globe the ſtandard of the croſs? Will Holland eſta-
"bliſh a ſeminary of apoſtolic preachers, who will be
"ready, for the intereſt of thy faith, to ſpill their blood
"in barbarous regions? Will Holland raiſe temples
"that are agreeable to thee? Will it conſtruct altars
"upon which thou wilt deſcend? Will it conſecrate
"true miniſters to thee? Will it offer up to thee the
"great ſacrifice? Will it worſhip thee in a manner
"worthy of thee? Yes—the worſhip thou wilt receive

" from her will be the same as that which she practif-
" eth daily at Amsterdam, at Middlebourg, at Flessing,
" and in the other districts of those damp and cold in-
" fernal regions.

" I know well, O Lord, that the propagation of thy
" faith, and the interests of thy glory, do not depend
" upon us ; and that if there were no men, thy power
" animating the stones might raise up children to
" Abraham.   But I also know, that, since the time of
" Adam, thou hast not created any mortals of a new
" species ; that thou dost make use of those that exist ;
" and that thou dost admit in thy designs those that
" are less good, only in default of the better.   Wit-
" ness the parable of the feast, *Bring in the blind and*
" *the lame*.   Such is the proceeding of Providence ;
" and wilt thou reverse it at present ? We have been
" invited, and we have not refused to come to the
" feast, and yet thou dost prefer to us the blind and
" the lame, Lutherans and Calvinists, blind in the
" faith, and lame in their works !

" If we be so unfortunate, as that the Dutch should
" make themselves masters of Brazil, the circumstance
" that I will represent to thee, with all humility, but
" with great earnestness, is, that thou wouldst consider
" well before the execution of thy decree.   Weigh
" with attention what may be the consequence of it ;
" and reflect while there is still time for it.   If thou
" art to repent, it is better that thou shouldst do it at
" present, than when the evil shall be without remedy.
" Thou perceivest the scope of my argument, and the
" reasons, deduced from thine own conduct, for the
" remonstrance I make to thee.   Before the time of
" the deluge, thou wert also much incensed against
" mankind.   In vain did Noah address his prayers to
" thee during a century.   Thou didst persist in thine
" anger ; and the cataracts of the heavens were at
" length burst, and the waters rose above the summits
" of the mountains.   The whole earth was overflown,
" and thy justice was satisfied.   But three days after
" this, when the bodies floated upon the waters, when

" thine eyes beheld the multitude of livid carcafes, B O O K
" when the furface of the fea prefented to thee the IX.
" moft melancholy and the moft hideous fight that
" had ever afflicted the angelic choir, what was the
" confequence? affected with the fight, as if thou
" hadft not forefeen it, thy bowels were moved with
" anguifh. Thou didft repent of having made the
" world. Thou didft regret the paft, and didft take
" refolutions for the future. Since fuch is thy difpo-
" fition, why doft thou not fpare thyfelf, in fparing
" us? Why doft thou perfift in thy prefent wrath,
" if it be afterwards to excite thy murmurs, and if
" thy mercy is to be affected by the decrees of thy
" juftice? Reflect upon it before thou doft begin,
" and confider the confequences of the new deluge
" thou haft defigned to produce. Let me be allowed
" to reprefent them to thee.

" Let us fuppofe Bahia, and the reft of Brazil, are
" become the prey of the Dutch. Behold them en-
" tering into the city with the fury of conquerors, and
" with the rage of heretics. Behold that neither age
" nor fex are fpared. Behold the blood ftreaming on
" all fides. Behold the guilty, the innocent, the wo-
" men and the children, all put to the fword, and
" maffacred one upon another. Behold the tears of
" the virgins, who weep for the injury they have fuf-
" fered. Behold the old men dragged by their hair.
" Liften to the mixed cries of the monks and of the
" priefts, who embrace thine altars, and who lift up
" their hands unto thee. Even thou thyfelf, O Lord!
" wilt not efcape their violence. Yes—thou wilt par-
" take of it. The heretics will force the gates of thy
" temples. The hoft, which is thine own proper bo-
" dy, will be trampled under foot. The vafes that
" have been filled with thy blood, will ferve for riot-
" ing and drunkennefs. Thine altars will be thrown
" down. Thy images will be torn to pieces. Sacri-
" legious hands will be laid upon thy mother.

" That thefe infults fhould be offered to thee, and
" that thou fhouldft fuffer them, is not a matter of

BOOK "aftonifhment to me, fince thou haft formerly fuffer
IX. "ed others ftill more cruel: but thy mother! O!
"where is filial piety? Didft thou not deprive Hofea
"of life, for having touched the ark? Didft thou not
"wither the arm that Jeroboam had raifed againft a
"prophet; and yet the heretics have thoufands of
"arms for more atrocious deeds? Thou didft de-
"throne, and didft caufe Balfhazzar to die, for having
"drunk out of facred veffels, although thy blood had
"not been confecrated in them; and yet thou doft
"fpare the heretic, and there are not two fingers and
"a thumb to trace upon the wall the fentence of their
"death.

"In a word, O Lord, when thy temples are fpoil-
"ed, thine altars demolifhed, thy religion extinct in
"Brazil, and thy worfhip annihilated, when the grafs
"fhall grow upon the avenues to thy churches, Chrift-
"mas-day fhall come round, and no one fhall recol-
"lect the day of thy birth. Lent and the holy week
"fhall come round, and yet the myfteries of thy paf-
"fion fhall not be celebrated. The ftones of our
"ftreets fhall cry out, as the ftones did in the folitary
"ftreets of Jerufalem. There will be no more priefts,
"no more facrifices, no more facraments. Herefy
"will arife in the pulpit of truth; and the children of
"the Portuguefe will be tainted with falfe doctrines.
"The children of my audience will be afked, *Little*
"*boys, what is your religion?* and they will anfwer, *We*
"*are Calvinifts. And you, little girls, what is yours?*
"and they will anfwer, *We are Lutherans.* Then thou
"wilt be moved with compaffion, and repent: but if
"thy repentance be to be awakened, why doft thou
"not prevent it?

"But tell me, what glory canft thou find in de-
"ftroying a nation, and in caufing it to be fupplanted
"by another? This is a power thou didft formerly
"intruft to a mean inhabitant of Anatho. In punifh-
"ing us, thou doft triumph over the weak; in par-
"doning us, thou doft triumph over thyfelf. Be mer-
"ciful for thine own glory, and for the honour of thy

" name. Let not thy wrath be prolonged for ever, B O O K
" nor even for one day. Thou wilt not fuffer that   IX.
" the fun fhould fet upon our anger ; and yet how
" often hath it not rifen, how often hath it not fet up-
" on thine? Doft thou require from us a moderation
" thou doft not poffefs? Doft thou give us the precept
" without the example?

" Forgive us, O Lord ! and put an end to our mif-
" fortunes. Holy Virgin, intercede for us ; entreat
" thy Son ; lay thy commands upon him. If he be
" angered with our offences, tell him that he muft for-
" give them, as it is enjoined us by his law to forgive
" thofe who have offended us."

We know not whether the Lord liftened to this
apoftrophe of the orator Vieira ; but a little while after the conqueft, the Dutch were interrupted by a revolution which all nations wifhed for, and which none
had forefeen.

The Portuguefe had never enjoyed happy times
fince they had fubmitted to the Spanifh yoke in 1581.
Philip II. an avaricious, cruel, defpotic, defigning, and
falfe prince, had endeavoured to vilify them, but concealed his intentions under honourable pretences. His
fon, who too clofely followed his maxims, and thought
it better to reign over a ruined nation than to be indebted to the good will of the people for their fubmiffion, had fuffered them to be deprived of a multitude
of conquefts, which had proved a fource of riches,
power, and glory to them, and which they had acquired by much effufion of blood. The fucceffor of
that weak prince, who had ftill lefs underftanding than
his father, openly and contemptuoufly attacked their
adminiftration, their privileges, their manners, and all
that they were moft attached to. At the inftigation
of Olivarez, he wanted to provoke them to revolt, that
he might acquire the right of plundering them.

Thefe repeated outrages united all the Portuguefe,
whom Spain had been labouring to divide. A confpiracy, that had been forming for three years, with
incredible fecrecy, broke out on the third of Decem-

B O O K ber 1640. Philip IV. was ignominiously banished, and
  IX. the duke of Braganza was placed on the throne of his
anceftors. The example of the capital was followed
by the whole kingdom, and by all that remained of
the fettlements formed in happier times in Afia, Africa, and America. No blood was fhed on this great
revolution, except that of Michael Vafconcellos, the
bafe and vile inftrument of tyranny.

The new king united his interefts and his refentments with thofe of the Englifh, the French, and all
the enemies of Spain. On the 23d of June 1641, he
in particular concluded an offenfive and defenfive alliance with the United Provinces for Europe, and a ten
years truce for the Eaft and Weft Indies. Naffau was
immediately recalled with moft of the troops, and the
government of the Dutch poffeffions in Brazil was
given to Hamel, a merchant of Amfterdam; to Baffis,
a goldfmith of Haarlem; and to Bulleftraat, a car-
penter of Middleburgh. The decifion of all affairs
was to be referred to this council; and thefe were now
fuppofed to be confined to the carrying on of a great
and advantageous trade.

A confiderable obftacle fruftrated their hopes. The
lands belonged to the Portuguefe, who had remained
under the government of the republic. Some of them
had never acquired fufficient means to form rich plantations; and others had loft their fortunes by the calamities which are infeparable from war. As foon as
this inability was known in Europe, the monied men
in the United Provinces haftened to fend the funds
neceffary for the carrying on of all the labours which
it was poffible to undertake. The face of affairs was
foon changed in thofe regions, every thing feemed
animated with new life; but edifices too magnificent
were erected, an infinite number of flaves perifhed by
a contagious diforder; and exceffive luxury was generally prevailing. Thefe faults and misfortunes difabled the debtors from fulfilling their engagements.
In order not to lofe all their credit, they were imprudent enough to borrow money at three and four *per*

cent. per month. This abfurd conduct foon rendered
them infolvent ; and the prifons were filled with unfortunate or guilty perfons. The Company were obliged to take the debts upon themfelves, in order to
preferve this beautiful fettlement from total ruin ; but
they required that the cultivators fhould give up the
entire price of their productions, till all the debts fhould
be liquidated.

Before this arrangement, the agents for the monopoly
had fuffered the fortifications to fall into ruin ; they
had fold the arms and the ammunition ; they had permitted every foldier who was defirous of it, to return
to the mother-country. This conduct had annihilated the public ftrength, and had induced the Portuguefe to hope that they might throw off a foreign
yoke. The ftipulation, which deprived them of all
the comforts of life to which they were accuftomed,
determined them to haften the revolution.

The boldeft of them united, in 1645, to take their
revenge ; their defign was, to maffacre all the Dutch
who had any fhare in the government, at an entertainment in the midft of the capital of Fernambucca,
and then to attack the people, who, fufpecting no
danger, would be unprepared. The plot was difcovered ; but the confpirators had time to get out of
town, and retire to a place of fafety.

Their chief was a Portuguefe of obfcure birth, named Juan Fernandez de Viera. From a common fervant he had rifen to be an agent, and afterwards a
merchant. His abilities had enabled him to acquire
a large fortune ; his probity had gained him univerfal
confidence ; and his generofity had made him an infinite
number of friends, who were inviolably attached to
his intereft. He was not difcouraged by the difappointment he had juft met with ; but he ventured,
without the confent or fupport of government, to com-
mence hoftilities.

His name, his virtues, and his projects, affembled
the Brazilians, the Portuguefe foldiers, and even the
colonifts, about him. He infpired them with his con-

BOOK fidence, his activity, and his courage.   They attended
IX.   him in battle, crowded about his person, and were determined to conquer or to die with him.   He triumphed,
but did not allow himself to slumber over his victories,
or give the enemy time to recover.   Some checks he
met with in the course of his successes only served to
display the firmness of his soul, the extent of his genius, and the elevation of his mind.   He assumed a
threatening aspect even after a misfortune, and appeared still more formidable by his perseverance than by
his intrepidity.   He spread such terror among his enemies, that they dared no longer keep the field.   At
this period of his glory, Viera received orders not to
proceed.

Since the truce, the Dutch had seized upon some places
in Africa and Asia, which they obstinately refused to
restore.   The court of Lisbon, intent upon matters of
greater importance, had not been able to do themselves
justice ; but their present inability had not lessened
their resentment.   In this disposition, they had rejoiced
to see the republic attacked in Brazil ; and had even
clandestinely encouraged those who had begun the
hostilities.   As they constantly disavowed these proceedings, and declared, both in Europe and America,
that they would one day punish the authors of the
disturbances, the Company imagined they would soon
subside ; but their avarice, which had been too long
amused with false and frivolous protestations, was at
length roused.   John IV. being informed that considerable armaments were preparing in Holland, and
fearing to be drawn into a war which he wished to
avoid, exerted himself in earnest to put an end to the
hostilities in the Brazils.

Viera, who had no resource for the completion of
his designs, but in his fortune, his interest, and his a-
bilities, did not even deliberate whether he should
obey.   " If the king," said he, " were but informed
" of our zeal and our success, and acquainted with
" his own interest, far from disarming us, he would
" encourage us to pursue our undertaking, and would

" fupport us with all his power." Then, left the ardour of his companions fhould abate, he determined
to haften his operations; and they continued to be
crowned with fuch fuccefs, that, with the affiftance of
Baretto, Vidal, and fome other Portuguefe, who were
able and willing to ferve their country, he completed
the ruin of the Dutch. The few of thefe republicans
who efcaped the fword and famine evacuated Brazil,
in confequence of a capitulation figned the 28th of January 1654.

What changes are produced in the opinions of men!
Thefe events feem no more to us, and are, in fact, no
more than the confequences of fome political, moral,
or natural caufes; and the orator Vieira appears no
more to us than an elegant enthufiaft. But let us carry
our imaginations back to the times of the Hebrews,
when they had feminaries of infpired men; to thofe
of the Greeks, when people reforted to Delphos from
all parts of the world; to thofe of the Romans, who
never dared to undertake any confiderable enterprife,
without having previoufly confulted the entrails of the
victims, and the facred fowls; and to the times of our
anceftors, at the period of the crufades: let us imagine a prophet, a witch, an augur, or a St. Bernard,
in the room of Vieira, and the revolution in the Brazils will inftantly appear miraculous; it will appear as
if God, moved by the facred boldnefs of an extraordinary perfon, had fent an avenger to the oppreffed
nation.

The peace, concluded three months after between
England and the United Provinces, feemed to put the
latter in a condition to recover a valuable poffeffion,
which they had loft by an ill-judged parfimony, and
by an unfortunate concurrence of circumftances; but
both the republic and the Company fruftrated the general expectation; and the treaty, which put an end
to the divifions between the two powers in 1661, fecured to Portugal the fole poffeffion of all the Brazils,
in confideration of eight millions of livres [333,333l.

B O O K 6s. 8d.], which that crown engaged to pay to the
   IX.   United Provinces either in money or goods.

Thus did the Dutch part with a conqueſt that might
have become the richeſt of all the European colonies,
and would have given the republic a degree of importance it could never acquire from its own territory.
But, in order to keep it, the government ought to
have undertaken the adminiſtration and defence of it;
and, to make it proſper, it ſhould have enjoyed full
liberty. With theſe precautions, Brazil would have
been preſerved, and would have enriched the nation,
inſtead of ruining the Company. Unfortunately, it
was not yet known, that the only way to make lands
uſeful in America was to clear them, and that this
could not be done with ſucceſs, unleſs a free trade
were opened to all the inhabitants under the protection of government.

Situation of   No ſooner were the Portugueſe entirely freed, by a
the Portu-   firm treaty, from an enemy by whom they had been
gueſe in the ſo often conquered, and ſo often humbled, than they
Brazils, af-
ter they had applied themſelves to give ſome ſtability to their poſ-
expelled the ſeſſion, and to increaſe its riches. Unfortunately,
Dutch.   ſome of the ſteps taken in order to promote and en-
ſure proſperity, bore the marks of ignorance and prejudice; but they were ſtill much ſuperior to any thing
that had been practiſed before this memorable era.

While the court of Liſbon was engaged in regulating the interior concerns of the colony, ſome of the
moſt active ſubjects of Portugal were deviſing the
means of extending it. They advanced to the ſouth
towards the river of Plata, and to the north as far as that
of the Amazons. The Spaniards ſeemed to be in poſſeſſion of both theſe rivers. The Portugueſe were determined to drive them away, or to ſhare the navigation with them.

Settlement   The river of the Amazons, ſo famous for the length
of the Por-   of its courſe; that great vaſſal of the ſea, to which it
tugueſe on brings the tribute it hath received from ſo many of its
the river of
the Ama-   own vaſſals; ſeems to be produced by innumerable
zons.

torrents that rufh down from the eaft fide of the An-B O O K
des, and unite in a fpacious plain, to form that immenfe IX.
river. Yet the common opinion is, that it comes from
the lake Lauricocha, as from a refervoir of the Cordeleirias fituated in the diftrict of Guanuco, thirty leagues
diftant from Lima, about the 11th degree of fouth latitude. In its progrefs of a thoufand or eleven hundred leagues, it receives the waters of a prodigious
number of rivers, fome of which come from far, and
are very broad and deep. It is interfperfed with an
infinite number of iflands, that are too often overflow-
ed to admit of culture. It falls into the ocean under
the line, and is there fifty leagues broad.

The mouth of this river was firft difcovered in 1500
by Vincent Pinçon, one of the companions of Columbus; and its fource is thought to have been found out
by Gonzalo Pizarro in 1538. His lieutenant Orellana
embarked on this river, and failed from one end to
the other of it. He was obliged to fight his way along,
and to engage with many nations, who obftructed his
navigation with their canoes, and poured fhowers of
arrows upon him from the fhore. It was certainly at
this time that the fight of favages without beards, as
are all the American nations, ftruck the lively imaginations of the Spaniards, and fuggefted the idea of an
army of female warriors: this muft have induced the
commanding officer to change the name of that river,
which was then called the Maragnon, and to call it
the river of the Amazons; which name it retains to
this day.

It might appear a matter of aftonifhment, that the
difcovery of America had not fuggefted any miraculous ftories to the imagination of the Spaniards, of a
people who, indeed, never poffeffed the delicacy of
tafte, the fenfibility, nor the graces that were allotted
to the Greeks; but whom nature had indemnified for
the want of thefe qualities, by giving them a haughtinefs of character, an elevation of foul, and an imagination as fertile, and more ardent, than fhe had beftowed on any other nation.

The Greeks never travelled, either in or beyond the precincts of their narrow territory, without meeting with something marvellous. On the summit of the Pindus they saw Apollo, surrounded with the nine Muses. They heard the caverns of Lemnos resound with the hammers of the Cyclops. They fastened Prometheus to the top of the Caucasus. They crushed the giants under a weight of mountains. If Ætna roared, and vomited torrents of flame, this was ascribed to the labours of Typhöeus. The plains and forests of the Greeks were peopled with satyrs and fauns, at whose dances there was not one of their poets who had not assisted; while an entirely new system of nature did not excite any new idea in the minds of the Spaniards. They were neither affected with the variety of the plants and animals, nor with the picturesque manners of a race of men till that time unknown. What, then, could engage their attention? Slaughter, carnage, and plunder. The search for gold, which kept them bent towards the foot of the mountains, reduced them to the posture and to the stupidity of brutes.

As early as the times of Hercules and Theseus, the Greeks had imagined the existence of a nation of Amazons. With this fable they embellished the history of all their heroes, not excepting that of Alexander; and the Spaniards, infatuated with this dream of antiquity, transferred it to the New World. We can scarce find a more probable origin of the opinion they established both in Europe and America, of a republic of female warriors actually existing, who did not live in society with men, and only admitted them once a-year, for the purposes of procreation. To give the more credit to this romantic story, it was reported, not without reason, that the women in America were all so unhappy, and were treated with such contempt and inhumanity, that many of them had agreed to shake off the yoke of their tyrants. It was further said, that, being accustomed to follow the men into the forests, and to carry their provisions and baggage when they

went out to fight or to hunt, they muſt neceſſarily B O O K
have been inured to hardſhips, and rendered capable IX.
of forming ſo bold a reſolution.

But it is abſurd to imagine, that women, who had
ſo fixed an averſion for men, would ever conſent to
become mothers; nor is it likely that the men would
go in queſt of their wives, when they had made their
lives inſupportable at home, and always turned them
away as ſoon as they had no more occaſion for them.
Much leſs can it be ſuppoſed, that the ſofter and more
compaſſionate ſex would expoſe or ſtrangle their own
children, becauſe they were boys; and coolly and deliberately agree to commit ſuch enormities as none
would be guilty of, but a few individuals urged by
rage and deſpair. Neither could an ariſtocratical or
democratical republic, which it requires abilities to govern, be ruled by a ſenate of women; though a monarchical or deſpotic ſtate, in which it is only neceſſary to command, hath been, and may ſtill be, ſwayed
by a female.

Let us conſider the weakneſs of organization in women; their almoſt conſtant valetudinarian ſtate; their
natural puſillanimity; the ſeverity of the labours required in a ſocial ſtate, in times of peace or war; their
abhorrence of blood; their fear of dangers; and let
us then endeavour to reconcile all theſe circumſtances
with the poſſibility of a female republic.

If ſome ſtrange prejudices have been able to form
ſocieties of both ſexes amongſt us, who live ſeparate,
notwithſtanding that natural attraction which was intended to unite them, it is not conſiſtent with the nature of things, that chance ſhould have produced a nation of men without women, and ſtill leſs a nation of
women without men. Certain it is, that, ſince this political conſtitution hath been talked of, infinite pains
have been taken to find it out, but no traces of it
could ever be diſcovered. This ſingular prodigy, therefore, will be like many others, which are always ſuppoſed to exiſt, though we know not where.

Whatever may be the caſe with regard to this cir-

cumſtance of the Amazons, the voyage of Orellana
excited more curioſity than it procured information.
An opportunity of ſatisfying it did not occur for ſome
time, on account of the civil wars that diſturbed Peru;
but, when tranquillity was reſtored, Pedro d'Orſua, a
gentleman of Navarre, diſtinguiſhed by his wiſdom
and courage, offered the viceroy, in 1560, to reſume
that navigation. He ſet out from Cuſco with ſeven
hundred men. Theſe ſanguinary people, inveterate
enemies to all worthy perſons, maſſacred their chief,
who was a man of good morals, and attached to order
and regularity. They ſet up at their head, with the
title of king, a native of Biſcay, of a ferocious diſpoſition, whoſe name was Lopez d'Aguirre, and who promiſed them all the treaſures of the New World.

Intoxicated with ſuch flattering hopes, theſe barbarians ſailed down the river Amazon into the ocean,
and, landing at Trinidad, murdered the governor, and
plundered the iſland. The coaſts of Cumana, Caraccas, and St. Martha, were ſtill more ſeverely treated,
becauſe they were richer. They then penetrated into New Granada, and were advancing to Quito, and
into the interior part of Peru, where every thing was
to be deſtroyed by fire and ſword. A body of troops,
haſtily aſſembled, attacked theſe deſperate men, beat
and diſperſed them. D'Aguirre, ſeeing no way to
eſcape, marked his deſpair by an atrocious act. " My
" child," ſaid he, to his only daughter, who attended
him in his expeditions, " I thought to have placed thee
" upon a throne, but the event hath not anſwered my
" expectation. My honour and thine own will not
" permit thee to live, and to be a ſlave to our ene-
" mies; die, therefore, by a father's hand." Saying
this, he inſtantly ſhot her through the body, and then
put an end to her life, by plunging a dagger into her
heart. After this unnatural act, his ſtrength failed,
and he was taken priſoner, drawn and quartered.

After theſe unfortunate events, the river of the
Amazons was entirely neglected, and was totally forgotten for half a century. Some attempts were after-

wards made to resume the discovery of it, but they were ill concerted and no better executed. The honour of conquering these difficulties, and of acquiring a useful knowledge of that great river, was reserved to the Portuguese.

That nation, which still retained some remains of her former vigour, had, some years before, built a town at the entrance of the river, which was called Belem. Pedro Texeira sailed from this place in 1638, and with a great number of canoes, full of Indians and Portuguese, went up the river of the Amazons, as far as the mouth of the Napo, and then up the Napo, which brought him almost to Ouito, where he arrived by land. Notwithstanding the enmity subsisting between the Spaniards and Portuguese, though subjects of the same master, Texeira was received with that regard, esteem, and confidence, which were due to a man who was doing a signal service. He returned in company with d'Acugna and d'Artieda, two learned Jesuits, who were commissioned to verify his observations, and to make others. An accurate account of these two successful voyages was sent to the court of Madrid, where it gave rise to a very extraordinary project.

The communication between the Spanish colonies had long been found very difficult. Some pirates, who were at enmity with them, infested the north and south seas, and intercepted their navigation. Even those of their ships which had got to the Havannah, and joined others, were not perfectly safe. The galleons were frequently attacked and taken by whole squadrons, and always pursued by privateers, who seldom failed to carry off the straggling vessels that were parted from the convoy, either by stormy weather, or by sailing more slowly than the rest. The Amazon river seemed as if it would obviate all these difficulties. It was thought possible, and even an easy matter, to convey thither the treasures of New Granada, Popayan, Quito, Peru, and Chili itself, by navigable rivers, or at a small expence by land. It was thought, that, coming down the river, they would find the galleons

ready in the harbour of Para to receive them. The
fleet from Brazil would then have joined, and confequently ftrengthened the fleet from Spain. They
would then have failed with great fecurity in latitudes
little known and little frequented, and would have arrived in Europe at leaft with a formidable appearance;
or might really have been in a condition to furmount
any obftacles they might have met with. The revolution which placed the duke of Braganza on the throne,
put an end to thefe important projects. Each of the
two nations was then only intent upon fecuring to itfelf that part of the river which beft fuited its own fituation.

The Spanifh Jefuits undertook to fet up a miffion
in the country lying between the banks of the Amazon and of the Napo, as far as to the conflux of both
thefe rivers. Every miffionary, attended only by one
man, took with him hatchets, knives, needles, and all
kinds of iron tools, and penetrated into the thickeft of
the forefts. There they fpent whole months in climbing up the trees, to fee if they could difcover fome hut,
perceive any fmoke, or hear the found of any drum or
fife. When they were affured that fome favages were
in the neighbourhood, they advanced towards them.
Moft of them fled, efpecially if they were at war.
Thofe whom the miffionaries could come within reach
of were eafily bribed by fuch prefents as their ignorance made them fet a value upon. This was all the
eloquence they had in their power, or all they had
any occafion to employ.

When they had affembled a few families, they led
them to the place they had fixed upon to form a village. The favages were not eafily prevailed upon to
take up their abode there. As they were ufed to rove
about, they found it an unfupportable hardfhip to remain always in the fame place. The ftate of independence in which they had lived, they thought preferable to the focial life that was recommended to
them: and their unconquerable averfion for labour,
induced them continually to return to the forefts

where they had paſſed their lives in idleneſs. Even B O O K
thoſe who were reſtrained by the authority or the pa-   IX.
ternal kindneſs of their legiſlator, ſeldom failed to diſperſe in his abſence, though ever ſo ſhort. But his
death at laſt occaſioned a total ſubverſion of the ſettlement.

It is impoſſible that any reader who reflects ſhould
not be deſirous of knowing what ſtrange infatuation
can induce an individual, who enjoys all the conveniences of life in his own country, to undertake the laborious and unfortunate function of a miſſionary; to
quit his fellow-citizens, his friends, and his relations;
to croſs the ſea, in order to bury himſelf in the midſt
of foreſts; to expoſe himſelf to all the horrors of the
moſt extreme miſery; to run the riſk, at every ſtep,
either of being devoured by wild beaſts, or maſſacred
by ſavages; to ſettle in the midſt of them; to conform himſelf to their manners; to ſhare their indigence and their fatigues; to be expoſed to their paſſions, or caprices, for at leaſt as long a time as is required to learn their language, and to make himſelf
underſtood by them.

If this conduct be aſcribed to the enthuſiaſm of religion, what more powerful motive can be imagined?
If to reſpect for the vows of obedience taken to ſuperiors, who have a right to order them to go any where,
and who cannot be aſked the reaſon for thoſe orders,
without committing the crime of perjury and apoſtacy,
what good, or what evil, is it not in the power of hypocritical or ambitious maſters to do, who command ſo
abſolutely, and who are ſo ſervilely obeyed? If it be
the effect of a deep ſenſe of compaſſion for a part of
the human ſpecies, whom it is intended to reſcue from
a ſtate of ignorance, ſtupidity, and miſery, what virtue
can be more heroic? With reſpect to the conſtancy
with which theſe extraordinary men perſevere in ſo
diſguſtful an undertaking; I ſhould have imagined,
that by living ſo long among the ſavages, they would
have become ſavages themſelves: but I ſhould have
been deceived in this conjecture. It is, on the contra-

BOOK IX. ry, one of the moſt laudable of human vanities that ſupports them in their career.

" My friend," ſaid once to me an old miſſionary, who had lived thirty years in the midſt of the foreſts, and who, ſince he had returned into his own country, had fallen into a profound melancholy, and was for ever regretting his beloved ſavages ; " My friend (ſaid " he), you know not what it is to be the king, almoſt " even the God, of a number of men, who owe to you " the ſmall portion of happineſs they enjoy ; and who " are ever aſſiduous in aſſuring you of their gratitude. " After they have been ranging through immenſe fo- " reſts, they return, overcome with fatigue and inani- " tion ; if they have only killed one piece of game, " for whom do you ſuppoſe it to be intended ? It is " for the FATHER ; for it is thus they call us : and in- " deed they are really our children. Their diſſenſions " are ſuſpended at our appearance. A ſovereign does " not reſt in greater ſafety in the midſt of his guards, " than we do ſurrounded by our ſavages. It is among " them that I will go and end my days."

With this perſevering ſpirit, the Jeſuits had conquer- ed, upon the Amazon, obſtacles apparently invincible. Their miſſion, which began in 1637, conſiſted, in 1766, of ten thouſand inhabitants, who were diſtributed in thirty-ſix villages, twelve of which were ſituated along the Napo, and twenty-four on the banks of the Ama- zon. They were from two to ten, fifteen, or ſome- times twenty days journey diſtant from one another. In moſt of the villages lived people belonging to ſeve- ral nations, who were all obſtinately attached to their cuſtoms and to their manners, and could never be brought to conſider themſelves as members of the ſame community. The efforts that were made to extend this ſettlement were not, nor could they be ſucceſsful.

The women of this part of America are not fruitful, and their barrenneſs increaſes when they remove from one place to another. The men are of a feeble habit, and the cuſtom they have of bathing conſtantly, by no means contributes to increaſe their ſtrength. The cli-

mate is not healthy, and contagious diftempers are fre- B O O K
quent.   It hath never been poffible, and probably ne- IX.
ver will be, to· infpire the favages with an inclination
for agriculture.   Their chief delight is in fifhing and
hunting, amufements which are by no means favourable to the increafe of population. In a country which
is almoft all under water, there are few convenient
fituations to form a fettlement upon. Moft of them
are at fo great a diftance from each other, that they
cannot poffibly furnifh any mutual affiftance.   The
nations which one might endeavour to incorporate are
alfo too far feparated ; moft of them are intrenched in
inacceffible places, and are fo inconfiderable, that they
often confift only of five or fix families.

Of all the Indians the Jefuits had collected, and
whom they governed, none were fo lifelefs or fo incapable of being animated as thefe.   Every miffionary
was obliged to put himfelf at their head, in order to
make them pick up the cocoa, vanilla, and farfaparilla,
that nature plentifully offers them, and which are fent
every year to Quito, three hundred leagues off, that
they may be bartered for articles of primary neceffity.
Their whole property confifts of a hut, open on all
fides, made of a few ofiers, and covered on the top
with palm-leaves, a few implements of hufbandry, a
lance, bows and arrows for hunting, fifhing-tackle, a
tent, a hammock, and a canoe.   It hath not been poffible to infpire them with defires beyond thefe.   They
are fo well fatisfied with what they poffefs, that they
wifh for nothing more ; they live unconcerned, and
die without fear.   They may be faid to be happy, if
happinefs confift more in an exemption from the uneafy fenfation that attends want, than in the multiplicity of enjoyments that our wants require.

This infant ftate, the offspring of religion alone, hath
been hitherto of no fervice to Spain, and it can hardly
be expected it ever fhould.   However, the government
of Maynas, with its capital Borja, have been formed
there.   The deftroyers of America have never thought
of eftablifhing any fettlement in a country where there

are no mines, nor any of thofe rich commodities which fo powerfully allured their covetoufnefs; but this country hath fometimes attracted the neighbouring favages.

While fome miffionaries were eftablifhing the authority of the court of Madrid on the banks of the Amazon, others were doing the fame fervice to the court of Lifbon. Six or feven days journey below the fettlements of St. Ignacio de Pevas, the laft under the jurifdiction of Spain, is St. Paul, the firft of the numerous villages formed by the Portuguefe, at a very great diftance from each other, on the banks of the largeft river, and on thofe of the fmall ones that fall into it.

If the Maynas were at liberty to form connections with thefe neighbours, they might acquire by this intercourfe fome conveniencies that they cannot be fupplied with from Quito, being feparated from that place by the Cordeleras, which cut off the communication more effectually than immenfe feas would do. This indulgence of government might perhaps be productive of confiderable advantages; and, poffibly, both Spain and Portugal, though rival powers, might be fenfible that it would be for their mutual intereft to extend it. It is well known that the province of Quito is poor, for want of an opportunity of difpofing of the overplus of thofe very commodities that are not to be had at Para. The two provinces mutually affifting each other by means of the Napo and of the Amazon, would rife to a degree of profperity they could never attain without this intercourfe. The mother-countries would in time reap great advantages from it, and it could never be prejudicial to them, becaufe Quito could never purchafe what is fent from Europe to America, and Para confumes nothing but what Lifbon obtains from foreign countries. But national antipathies, and the jealoufies of crowned heads, are attended with the fame effects as the paffions and prejudices of men in private life. One unfortunate incident is fufficient to divide families and nations for ever, whofe greateft intereft it is to love and affift one another, and to promote the general good. The fpirit of hatred and revenge will

rather induce men to fubmit to fuffer than not be gra- B O O K
tified. Thofe paffions are conftantly kept up by the IX.
mutual injuries and the effufion of blood they occafion.
How different is man in the ftate of nature from man
corrupted by fociety! The latter amply deferves all
the misfortunes he brings upon himfelf.

It is a circumftance we have lefs reafon than ever to
expect, that any kind of confidence can be eftablifhed
in thefe countries, between the two European nations
that are in poffeffion of them. It hath been for a long
time fufpected, that the river Amazon and the Oroonoko communicated with each other by means of the
Black River, where the court of Lifbon hath feveral
fettlements. This circumftance, which had been fo
long a matter of conteft, was demonftrated in 1744, by
fome Portuguefe boats, which having fet out from one
of thefe rivers, failed into the other. This produced a
new fource of jealoufy, to which the two minifters
ought to have put a ftop, when their attention was engaged in fettling the differences which had too often
ftained the river Plata with blood.

The Portuguefe, who had appeared upon this great The Portu-
river foon after the Spaniards, were not long before guefe wifh
to form
they forgot it. They did not come there again till the fettlements
year 1553, when they got as far as Buenos-Ayres, and on the river Plata.
took poffeffion of the northern coaft of the provinces. Their dif-
This act had not been attended with any confequences, Spain. Ac-
when the court of Lifbon ordered, in 1680, that the commoda-
tions be-
colony of St. Sacrament fhould be eftablifhed precifely tween the
at the extremity of the territory which they thought two powers.
belonged to them. This claim appeared to the Spaniards to be ill-founded; and they deftroyed thefe rifing walls without much difficulty.

Violent contefts immediately arofe between the two
powers. Spain proved that the new colony was placed
in the fpace allotted to her, by the boundary marked
by the popes. The Portuguefe did not deny this aftro-
nomical truth, but they maintained, that this agreement was annulled by later arrangements, and in a
more particular manner by the treaty of 1668, which

put a ſtop to hoſtilities, and ſettled the fate of the two nations. It was concluded in 1681, after a multitude of conteſts, that the Portugueſe ſhould again be put in poſſeſſion of the poſt they had occupied; but that the inhabitants of Buenos Ayres, as well as they, ſhould have the enjoyment of all the diſputed domains.

The war between the two crowns, in the beginning of the century, broke off this proviſional agreement, and in the year 1705 the Portugueſe were again driven out of St. Sacrament; but were reinſtated in the poſſeſſion of it by the peace of Utrecht. This treaty granted them even more than they had ever had, ſince it enſured to them excluſively the whole territory of the colony.

At that period a conſiderable ſmuggling trade was begun, between the Portugueſe ſettlement of St. Sacrament, and that of the Spaniards at Buenos-Ayres, in which all parts of the Brazils and of Peru, and even ſome merchants of the mother-countries, were more or leſs concerned.

The court of Madrid ſoon perceived that the treaſures of the New World were conveyed into another channel. In order to bring them back again, they did not think of any more certain method, than that of limiting, as much as poſſible, the ſtaple of theſe fraudulent connections. Their miniſters aſſerted, that the places under the dominion of the Portugueſe ought not to be extended beyond cannon-ſhot; and they cauſed all the northern coaſt of the Plata, from the mouth of that great river, to the ſettlement which occaſioned them ſuch terrible alarms, to be filled up with flocks, ſheep-folds, and with the villages of Maldonado and Montevideo, and contrived other known methods of occupying this intermediate ſpace.

Theſe unforeſeen enterpriſes revived everlaſting animoſities, which had been for a ſhort time ſuſpended by their commercial connections. Theſe neighbouring people carried on a clandeſtine war with one another. The two nations were upon the brink of an open rupture, when, in 1750, a treaty was propoſed, which ap-

peared likely to settle the differences between these
two monarchies. By this treaty, the Portuguese exchanged the colony of St. Sacrament, and its territory,
for the seven missions formerly established on the east-
ern coast of the Uruguay.

It was necessary that this treaty should be executed
in America; and this was not an easy matter. The
Jesuits, who from their earliest origin had opened to
themselves a secret road to dominion, might have ob-
jected to the dismembering of an empire which owed
its existence to their labours. Independent of this great
interest, they might have thought themselves respon-
sible for the felicity of a docile set of people, who, by
throwing themselves in their arms, had intrusted them
with the care of their future welfare. Besides, the
Guaranis had not been conquered; and therefore,
when they submitted to Spain, they did not give that
crown the right of alienating them from their dominion; without having reflected on the incontestable
rights of nations, they might imagine that it belonged
to them alone to determine what was conducive to
their happiness. The horror they were well known to
entertain for the Portuguese yoke, was equally capable
of leading them astray, or of enlightening them. So
critical a situation required the greatest precautions, and
they were attended to.

The forces which the two powers had sent from Europe, and those which could be assembled in the New
World, united themselves in order to surmount the obstacles that were foreseen; but these preparations did
not terrify the people that were the object of them.
Although the seven ceded colonies were not assisted by
the other colonies, at least not openly; although they
were no more headed by the chiefs, who till that time
had led them on to battle, they were not afraid of
taking up arms to defend their liberty. But their military conduct was not such as it ought to have been.
Instead of contenting themselves with harassing their
enemies, and with interrupting the provisions they
were obliged to get from the distance of two hundred

leagues, the Guaranis ventured to wait for them in the open field. They loft a battle which coft them two thoufand men. This confiderable check difconcerted their meafures; their courage feemed to give way, and they abandoned their territory, without making thofe efforts which were expected from their firft refolution, and which were, perhaps, confiftent with their ftrength.

After this event, the Spaniards attempted to take poffeffion of the colony of St. Sacrament. The Portuguefe refufed to give it up, alleging that the inhabitants of the Uruguay were only difperfed; and that, till the court of Madrid fhould fettle them in fome of their own domains, they would always be difpofed to recover that territory which they had quitted with fo much regret. Thefe difficulties, whether real or imaginary, prevented the conclufion of the treaty, which was even entirely put a ftop to by the two courts in 1761, and every thing fell again into confufion.

From that time, thefe deferts have been almoft inceffantly ftained with blood; fometimes by hoftilities that were not publicly avowed, and fometimes by open wars. Portugal, deprived of the affiftance of England, hath at length been obliged to fubmit. The treaties of the firft of October 1777, and of the eleventh of March 1778, have deprived it for ever of the colony of St. Sacrament; but they have reftored it to the territory of the river St. Peter, which had been taken from it, under the pretences fo frequently alleged, of the line of mark.

While thefe reftlefs and enterprifing men were ravaging the Amazon and the Plata, fome laborious and peaceable citizens were employed in multiplying on the coaft of Brazil important productions, which were delivered to the mother-country, which, in return, fupplied them with every thing they were in want of.

Portugal
had fettled
its connec-
tions with
the Brazils
upon a bad
plan; to
The whole trade was carried on by a fleet, which failed every year from Lifbon and Oporto in the month of March. The fhips it confifted of parted when they came to a certain latitude, and proceeded to their refpective deftinations; but they afterwards all met at

B O O K
IX.

which a fyf-
tem of mo-
nopoly, ftill
more de-
ftructive,
was fubfti-
tuted.

Bahia to fail for Portugal, which they reached in September or October the year following, under convoy
of the men of war, which had efcorted them at their
going out.

A regulation fo contrary to maxims generally received was cenfured by many judicious perfons, who
thought it would have been better to have left the
merchants at liberty to fend out their fhips, and order
them home when it fuited them beft. This fyftem
would have reduced the expence of freight, rendered
the voyages more frequent, increafed the maritime
forces, and encouraged every fpecies of agriculture.
The intercourfe between the colonies and the mother-
country, being more conftant, would have given information which would have enabled government to
extend its protection more eafily, and to fecure its authority.

The court of Lifbon feemed frequently inclined to
yield to thefe confiderations, but was deterred by the
fear of feeing the fhips fall into the enemy's hands if
they failed feparately : by cuftom, the fway of which
is ftill more powerful over government than over individuals ; by the infinuations of fome men in power,
whofe intereft would have been affected by the revolution ; and by variety of prejudices, none of which
could have borne the flighteft fcrutiny.

It was upon this principle that the Portuguefe fettlements in the Old and in the New World were
founded, when the difcovery of the gold and diamond
mines, in the beginning of the century, fixed the attention of all nations upon the Brazils. It was generally thought that thofe riches, added to thofe of another kind furnifhed by the colony, would render it
one of the fineft fettlements of the globe. The Europeans were not yet undeceived, when they learned with furprife, that the moft important part of thofe
regions was juft fubjected to the yoke of monopoly.

Portugal hath made immenfe difcoveries in Africa,
and in the Eaft and Weft Indies, without the affiftance
of any Company. This had been done by fome affo-

BOOK ciations, which kings, nobles, and merchants, had oc-
IX. cafionally formed among themfelves, and which fitted
out fleets more or lefs confiderable, for thofe three
parts of the globe.   It was not to be expected that a
nation, which, in the barbarous ages, had purfued
the ineftimable advantages of competition, would, at
laft, in an enlightened age, adopt a pernicious fyftem,
which, by collecting the principles of life and motion
into a fmall part of the body politic, leaves all the reft
in a ftate of inactivity and ruin.

This plan was formed among the ruins of Lifbon,
when the earth had, as it were, caft out her inhabitants, and left them no afylum or place of fafety but
on the fea, or in the New World.   The dreadful
fhocks which had fubverted that fuperb capital were
ftill repeated, and the flames that had reduced it to
afhes were fcarce extinguifhed, when an exclufive Company was eftablifhed, for the purpofe of felling to foreign nations, at the Brazils, and even in retail, within the fpace of three leagues, the wine fo well known
by the name of Port, which is drunk in many of the
colonies, in part of the north, and efpecially in England.   This Company hath a capital of 3,000,000 livres
[125,000l.], divided into two hundred fhares, of 2500
livres [104l. 3s. 4d.] each.   They lend to the proprietors of the vines half the price they are allowed to
charge for the vintage ; a price which they can never
raife, however favourable the year may be.   For the
beft wines, they are paid at the rate of 156 livres five
fols [6l. 10s. 2½d.] per ton ; but they receive no more
than 125 livres [5l. 4s. 2d.] for thofe of an inferior
quality.   How great foever the dearth may be, or however confiderable the vent, the cultivator can never
expect an increafe of more than 31 livres five fols
[1l. 6s. 2½d.] per ton, and the ton confifts of about
220 gallons.

Oporto, which is become the firft city in the kingdom for its population, riches, and commerce, fince
Lifbon had, as it were, difappeared, juftly took the
alarm, thinking that her trade would be ruined by

this fatal alienation of the rights of the whole nation in favour of a Company. The province between the Douro and the Minho, the moſt fruitful in the kingdom, formed no further expectations from its cultures. Deſpair excited a ſpirit of ſedition among the people; and this gave occaſion to the cruelties of the government. Twelve hundred perſons were either executed, condemned to public labour, baniſhed to the forts in Africa, or reduced to poverty by odious confiſcations of their poſſeſſions.

On the 6th of June 1755, an excluſive Company, with a capital of 3,000,000 livres [125,000l.], divided into twelve hundred ſhares, was eſtabliſhed for the great Para, and for the Maragnan. Four years after, the province of Fernambucca was put under a ſimilar yoke, with this difference, that the latter monopoly had a fund of 3,500,000 livres [145 833l. 6s. 8d.], which was divided into three thouſand four hundred ſhares. The two ſocieties were authoriſed to gain fifteen *per cent.* excluſive of all expences, on articles of proviſions, and to ſell their merchandiſe for forty-five *per cent.* more than they would have coſt even at Liſbon. They were allowed to pay as little as they choſe for the proviſions furniſhed by the diſtricts ſubject to their tyranny. Such extraordinary favours were to laſt twenty years, and might be renewed, to the great detriment of the colony.

The Brazils are at preſent divided into nine provinces, which are all governed by a ſeparate commander. Although theſe ſeveral chiefs are expected to conform to the general regulations which the viceroy thinks proper to make, they are independent of his authority, becauſe they receive their orders directly from Liſbon, and becauſe they themſelves give an account to that court of the affairs in their department. They are only appointed for three years, but their commiſſion is uſually extended beyond that period. They are prohibited by the law from marrying in the country under their juriſdiction; from being concerned in any branch of trade; from accepting any

present whatfoever; from receiving any emoluments for
the functions of their office ; and this law hath been
rather ſtrictly obferved for ſome years paſt. Accordingly, fortunes are at prefent very feldom made, or
even begun, in thofe poſts in the New World. The
perfons who voluntarily refign are obliged, as well as
thofe who are recalled, to give an account of their
conduct to the commiſſioners appointed by the mother-country ; and citizens of all ranks are indifcriminately admitted to impeach them. If they happen
to die in their poſt, the biſhop, the higheſt military
officer, and the firſt magiſtrate, jointly aſſume the reins
of government till the arrival of the fucceſſor.

The jurifprudence of the Brazils is entirely the fame
as that of Portugal. There is a judge eſtabliſhed in
each diſtrict, from whofe decifion an appeal may be
made to the fuperior tribunals of Bahia, and of Rio
Janeiro, and even to thofe of Lifbon, if it be upon
matters of confequence. The great Para and Maragnan alone are allowed to appeal immediately to the
mother-country, without being obliged to appear before the two intermediate tribunals. In criminal cafes,
rather a different plan is adopted. The judge of each
diſtrict hath a right to puniſh, without appeal, ſmall
mifdemeanours. The crimes are judged by the governor, aſſiſted by ſome aſſeſſors appointed by the law.

A particular tribunal is eſtabliſhed in every province,
to take care of the legacies which belong to heirs,
whofe refidence is acrofs the feas. They are allowed
to deduct five *per cent.* for their falaries, and the reſt
is fent to Portugal, to be depofited in a place deſtined
to receive it. The inconvenience of this otherwife
judicious inſtitution is, that the Brazilian creditors can
only be paid in Europe.

The finances of each province are adminiſtered by
the commandant and four magiſtrates. Their account
is fent every year to the royal treafury of the mother-
country, and fcrutinized with great feverity.

Every town, and every village, in the leaſt confiderable, hath a court of judicature. Their bufinefs is to

attend to the fmall concerns they are intrufted with, B o o k and to fettle, under the infpection of the commandant, IX. the trifling taxes that are neceffary. Several privileges have been granted to this tribunal, efpecially that of having the right to carry any complaint they may have againft the head of the colony immediately to the fovereign.

The military are upon the fame footing in the Brazils, as in Portugal, and in the reft of Europe. The troops are at the difpofal of every governor, who appoints to all the vacant commiffions under the rank of captain. He hath the fame authority over the militia, which confifts of all the citizens that are not *fidalgos*, that is to fay, of the firft nobility, or who have no public employment. This body of men, who are all obliged to wear a uniform at their own expence, are never affembled in the interior parts of the country, except in cafes of abfolute neceffity; but at Fernambucca, at Bahia, and at Rio Janeiro, they are exercifed during one month every year, and are then paid by the government. The Negroes and Mulattoes have ftandards of their own; and the Indians fight under the fame banners as the white men. The colony, at this prefent time, confifts of fifteen thoufand eight hundred and ninety-nine regulars, and of twenty-one thoufand eight hundred and fifty militia.

Though the King, as Grand Mafter of the Order of Chrift, be folely in poffeffion of the tithes; and though the produce of the Crufade belong entirely to him; yet, in this extenfive part of the New World, fix bifhoprics have been fucceffively founded, which acknowledge for their fuperior the archbifhopric of Bahia, eftablifhed in the year 1552. The fortunate prelates, moft of them Europeans, who fill thefe honourable fees, live in a very commodious manner upon the emoluments attached to the functions of their miniftry, and upon a penfion of twelve hundred, and from that to thirty thoufand livres [from 5ol. to 125ol.] granted to them by the government.

Among the inferior clergy, none but the miffiona-

B O O K ries who are fettled in the Indian villages are paid by
 IX.   government; but the others find fufficient refources
among the fuperftitious people, whom they are to edi-
fy, to inftruct, and to comfort.   Befide an annual tribute, paid by every family to the clergyman, he is entitled to forty fols [1s. 8d.] for every birth, every wed-
ding, and every burial.   The law which reduces this
contribution to one-half for poor people, and to nothing for thofe that are entirely indigent, is feldom obferved.   The avidity of the priefts hath even been carried fo far as to double this fhamelefs falary, in the diftricts of the mines.

Some few afylums for maidens have been fuffered at
Bahia, and at Rio Janeiro; but it hath never been allowed to eftablifh nunneries in the Brazils.   The monks
have been more fuccefsful; and there are at prefent
twenty convents of different orders, the two richeft of
which are occupied by Benedictines, who are as idle as
they are licentious.   None of thefe fatal eftablifhments
are founded in the gold countries.   The Jefuits had
taken advantage of the influence they had over government, to evade the law, which forbade any regular orders to fettle in thofe regions.   No inftitution hath
been powerful enough fince their expulfion, to extort
fo fignal a favour.

Though there be not abfolutely an inquifition in the
Brazils, the people of that country are not protected
from the outrages of that barbarous inftitution.   The
ecclefiaftics of the colony, who are appointed by that
tribunal to be their agents, are all of them imbued with
the fame fanguinary maxims.   Their mercilefs feverity
is moftly provoked by accufations of Judaifm.   This
fort of fury rofe to fuch an enormous height, from 1702
to 1718, that the minds of all men were impreffed with
terror, and moft of the cultures were neglected.

There is no particular ordonnance in the Brazils for
flaves, and they ought to be tried by the common law.
As their mafters are obliged to feed them, and that it
is become a general cuftom to allot them a fmall piece
of ground, which they are allowed to cultivate for their

own emolument, thofe among them who are induftrious and laborious are, fooner or later, enabled to purchafe their liberty. It is feldom refufed them; and
they may even demand it, at the price fettled by the
regulations, when they find themfelves oppreffed. It
is, probably, for this reafon, that, notwithftanding the
great facility they have for eloping, yet there are few
fugitive Negroes throughout this vaft continent. Thofe
few who are found in the country of the mines only
employ themfelves quietly at a diftance, in cultivating
the productions neceffary for their fubfiftence.

Such of the Negroes as have purchafed their liberty
enjoy the rights of citizens as well as the Mulattoes;
but they are both excluded from the priefthood, and
from any civil employment. Even in the fervice they
can have no commiffion, except in their own battalions. The white men feldom marry the Negro women; moft of them go no farther than to form illegal
connections with them. Thefe connections, which
have the fanction of the manners of the country, differ fcarcely from matrimony, in regions where men
difpofe of their fortunes in conformity to their caprices
and paffions.

The ftate of the Indians hath not always been the Former and
fame: at firft they were feized upon, fold in public prefent
markets, and compelled to work like flaves in the plan- ftate of the
tations. Indians
fubject to
Portugal in
In 1570, Sebaftian forbade that any Brazilian fhould the Brazils.
be made a flave, except fuch as had been taken prifoners in a juft war: but this law was not attended to,
becaufe the Portuguefe would have thought themfelves
difgraced in tilling the ground; and at that time few
cultivators had been fent to Africa.

The edict of Philip II: which, in 1595, confirmed
the orders of Sebaftian, and which even reduced to
ten years the term of flavery, to thofe whom that
prince had allowed to be kept in perpetual fervitude,
was equally difregarded.

Two mandates, of 1605 and 1609, again declared
all the Indians, without exception, to be entirely free.

Philip III. being informed that his commands were not obeyed, iffued a third law, by which thofe who infringed it were condemned to fevere penalties. But, at that period, the colony was ftill governed by a court of judicature, moft of the members of which were born in America itfelf; fo that the new arrangements were not much more refpected than the old ones had been.

In the meanwhile, the miffionaries were every day exclaiming, with greater vehemence, againft the tyranny with which their converts were oppreffed. In 1647, the new court of Lifbon gave way to their preffing folicitations, and formally renewed the orders which forbade the detaining of any Brazilian in flavery. The fpirit of independence, which manifefted itfelf throughout the whole colony, convinced that ftill tottering power, that they were not allowed to do every thing that was juft; and, eight years after, their orders were qualified, by permitting that thofe individuals who were born of a Negro mother and of an Indian father might be kept in flavery.

The Dutch had juft then been driven from this part of the New World. The connections with the coaft of Africa, which had been interrupted by the bloody wars the Portuguefe had been obliged to fuftain againft thofe republicans, refumed their former courfe. The population of the Negroes was increafed in the Brazils. Their fervices foon difgufted the Portuguefe of the natives of the country, who were weaker, and not fo laborious. Thofe who perifhed were not replaced; and that fpecies of fervitude was, by degrees, abolifhed every where, except at St. Paul, at Maragnan, and on the Amazon river, at which places there were not yet any rich fettlements, and where the Portuguefe were not capable of purchafing flaves. The decrees iffued in 1680, 1713, and 1741, to extirpate thefe remains of barbarifm, were of no effect; and it was not till 1755 that all the Brazilians became really free.

At this period they were declared citizens by government; they were to enjoy that title in the fame manner as their conquerors. The fame road was laid

open to their talents ; and they were allowed to afpire B o o K
at the fame dignities. An event fo much calculated ___ IX.
to excite the emotions of a feeling heart, was fcarce
attended to. Pleafure, fortune, war, politics, engrofs
every body's attention, while a revolution, fo favourable to humanity, almoft generally efcapes our notice;
and that even in the eighteenth century, in the midft
of that enlightened and philofophical age. The happinefs of nations is much talked of, but is neither perceived nor felt.

All the faulty operations of government are attacked with feverity ; and when they, by chance, happen
to do any good act, a general filence is obferved. Is
this the kind of acknowledgment which the people
owe to thofe who attend to their happinefs? Or, is this
fort of ingratitude calculated to attach them to their
laborious offices? Is it thus they can be induced to
fill them with diftinction? If the people expect that
their murmurs and their difcontents fhould be attended to when they are oppreffed, they fhould exprefs
their joy in the moft lively manner when they have
obtained redrefs. Whenever the burden of the taxes
hath been alleviated, let the houfes be illuminated;
let them affemble in multitudes, and fill the houfes
and the ftreets ; let them light up bonfires, and dance
and fing round them; let them pronounce with tranfport the name of their benefactor. Is there one among
all the directors of the empire who would not be gratified with fuch homage? Is there one who could ever
refolve to quit his place, or who could die without
having received it ? Is there a man who would not be
defirous of increafing thefe triumphs? Is there one
whofe grandchildren would not feel a noble pride in
hearing it faid of him, his anceftor was the man who
occafioned the lighting up of bonfires four or five
times, during the courfe of his adminiftration? Is there
one who would not be ambitious of bequeathing fuch
a mark of diftinction to his defcendants? Is there a
man who would dare to have engraved upon his tomb
the poft he had filled in his lifetime, without mention-

ing the public feftivals that had been celebrated in his honour? Such a filence would transform the infcription into a fatire. The people are equally abject in profperity as in adverfity; they know not how to complain, or how to rejoice.

Some men, more attentive to the interefting fcenes that are difplayed from time to time on the furface of the globe, conceived a good opinion of the new fyftem. They flattered themfelves that the Indians would apply themfelves to cultivation, and multiply the productions; that their labours would enable them to procure for themfelves numberlefs conveniences which they had not yet enjoyed; that the fight of their happinefs would difguft the favages of their forefts, and would determine them to a more quiet way of living; that an entire confidence would gradually be eftablifhed between the Americans and the Europeans; and that they would in time become one people. They flattered themfelves that the court of Lifbon would have the prudence not to difturb fo defirable a harmony by any particular diftinctions; that they would endeavour, by all poffible means, to obliterate the memory of thofe evils which they had brought upon the New Hemifphere.

But how far are we from feeing thefe flattering hopes fulfilled! In the provinces of Fernambucca, of Bahia, of Rio Janeiro, and of Minas-Geraes, the Brazilians continue to be mixed with the Portuguefe and with the Negroes, but without any change in their characters, becaufe no pains have been taken to enlighten them; becaufe no efforts have been made to overcome their natural lazinefs; becaufe no lands have been diftributed to them; and becaufe nothing hath been given them in advance, by which their emulation might probably have been excited.

At Para, at Maragnan, at Matto-Groffo, at Goyas, and at St. Paul, the Indians have been united in a hundred and feventeen villages, over each of which a white man prefides. It is his bufinefs to fettle the occupations, to direct the cultures, to buy and to fell for the community, to punifh and to reward. It is he who delivers to the agents of government the tenth of the territorial productions. It is he who appoints thofe among them who are obliged to fubmit to the labours of vaffalage with which they are oppreffed. Thefe fubaltern agents, difperfed in the feveral colonies, are fuperintended by a chief, who is vefted with great authority.

The opinions of men have been divided refpecting thefe regulations. A writer, who hath never been out of Europe, would be confidered as a very bold man, fhould he venture to decide between two parties, which an experience of three centuries hath not been able to reconcile. But let me at leaft be permitted to obferve, that one of the moft enlightened men that ever lived at the Brazils, hath frequently told me, that the Indians, who are fuffered to be their own mafters in the Portuguefe colony, are very fuperior in underftanding and induftry to thofe who are kept under perpetual tuition.

The government of Para is the moft northern of any of thefe colonies. It comprehends that portion of Guiana which belongs to the Portuguefe; the borders of the Amazon, from the conflux of the Madeira and the Mamore; and to the eaft, all that fpace which extends as far as the river of the Tocantines. This is the moft barren and the moft unwholefome country in thefe regions.

Prefent
ftate of the
govern-
ment of
Para.

No productions can be expected in Guiana, except on the Black River, the elevated banks of which would be very fit for all the productions that enrich the beft colonies of America. But this country is only inhabited by Indians, who are almoft folely employed in the turtle fifhery, and whom it hath not yet been poffible to fix to any thing but the cutting of fome woods for cabinet-work. This river receives that of Cayari, where, in 1749, a filver mine was difcovered, which undoubtedly, for fome political reafons, hath never been worked.

The borders of the Amazon, on the north fide, are

B O O K almoſt under water. The ſmall quantity of dry land
IX. that is found there is perpetually infeſted with all kinds
of infects.

Though the ſouth part of the Amazon be marſhy
in many places, yet its ſoil is commonly more firm,
and leſs infeſted with reptiles. The great and numerous rivers which empty themſelves into it afford ſtill
greater reſources for cultivation, and yet there is no
ſettlement formed upon them.

The Portugueſe navigators did not enter the Amazon before the year 1535. Ayres d'Acunha and his
followers were almoſt all ſhipwrecked there. It was
not till 1615, that Francis Caldeira laid the foundations of a town, which was called Belem, on the banks
of the rivers. In 1663, the territory of Macapa was
given by government to Bento Maciel Parente, and
afterwards the iſland of Joanna to Macedo: but theſe
two grants have been ſince reunited to the crown; the
firſt by the extinction of the family that had obtained
it, and the ſecond by exchanges.

The Portugueſe contented themſelves, for a long
time, with making excurſions of greater or leſs extent,
to carry off ſome Brazilians. They were a ſet of turbulent and daring ſavages, who were endeavouring to
ſubdue other ſavages leſs ſtrong and leſs courageous
than themſelves. Theſe deſtructive fatigues, theſe unavailing cruelties, had laſted for the ſpace of a century,
when ſome miſſionaries undertook to civilize the wandering Indians. They have aſſembled no inconſiderable number of them in ſeventy eight villages, but
without being able entirely to fix them there. After
having ſpent four or five months in a ſedentary and
idle life, theſe men, attracted by their ancient habits,
forſook their habitations and families, in order to gather in the foreſts the productions of uncultivated nature, which, with very little labour, they might have
procured at home, or might have ſubſtituted to them
others of a ſuperior quality. The wild cacao, the vanilla, the tortoiſe, and crab-ſhells, the ſarſaparilla, the
capivi balſam, and the vegetable wool, which are col-

lected in thefe ruinous excurfions, that are renewed B O O K
every year, are carried to Belem, the capital of the IX.
government.

This town, which is built at the diftance of twenty
leagues from the fea, and upon a foil that rifes thirteen
feet above the level of the ocean, was for a long time
nothing more than a ftaple, to which the riches of the
favages were conveyed from the inland country. Some
Negroes, whom it hath at laft procured, have cultivated in its neighbourhood a fmall quantity of cotton,
which is afterwards manufactured in the country itfelf; and fome fugar-canes, the indifferent produce of
which is afterwards made into brandy. ¯ They have alfo cultivated coffee, rice, and cacao, for exportation.
The fale of the flocks, which grazed in the ifland of
Marajo, was for a confiderable time one of their refources. At prefent they have fcarce oxen enough remaining for their own confumption.

Before the year 1755, this eftablifhment received
every year from the mother-country from thirteen to
fourteen fhips. Since it hath been fubjected by a miftaken or corrupted miniftry to a monopoly, it receives
no more than five or fix. The value of its exports feldom exceeds 600,000 livres [25,000l.]. This feeble
produce is not much increafed by the wood for building, which the government buys up, and carries away
upon its fhips.

The population of the colony confifts of four thoufand one hundred and twenty-eight white men, of
nine thoufand nine hundred and nineteen black flaves,
or free Mulattoes, and of thirty four thoufand eight
hundred and forty-four Indians.

This country, which in 1778 hath been relieved
from the oppreffion neceffarily attending an exclufive
privilege, will undoubtedly avail itfelf of its liberty.
The port of Belem, which is called Para, a name which
is likewife fometimes given to the city, doth not oppofe fo many obftacles to the fuccefs of any enterprie
as is commonly imagined. It is, indeed, difficult of
accefs. Currents which run in contrary directions,

B O O K and which are occafioned by a multitude of fmall
IX. iflands, render the navigation of fhips flow and uncertain. But when once they get into the harbour, they
anchor in a muddy bottom, with four, five, or fix fathom of water. The canal which leads up to it grows,
however, more fhallow every day ; and in a fhort time
it will not be practicable, if, as it muft be fuppofed, the
waters continue to depofit as much earth as they have
dragged into it for this laft century.

State of the   The Maragnan is feparated from Para on the north
govern-   by the river of the Tocantines, from Goyaz on the
ment of   fouth by that of the Cordeleirias mountains, which is
Maragnan.   called Guacuragua, and on the weft from Fernambucca by the Ypiapaba mountains.

The Portuguefe arrived for the firft time in this province in 1535; and they were caft upon it by a ftorm ;
but they did not fettle there till 1599. The French
feized upon it in 1612, and were driven from thence
three years after. It remained under the yoke of the
Dutch from 1641 to 1644 ; at which period the firft
ufurpers again took poffeffion of it, and have kept it
ever fince.

The bufinefs of collecting the ambergrife upon the
coafts, which was the amufement of the favages, became the occupation of the firft Europeans. This
trifling refource was foon exhaufted; and no other was
fubftituted to it, as there ought to have been. The
fettlement continued for a long time in a languifhing
ftate ; and it hath been but lately perceived, that the
cotton which grew upon this territory was the beft in
the New World. The culture of this plant increafes
daily ; and, for fome years paft, that of rice hath been
joined to it, though it be of an inferior quality to the
rice of the Levant, and even to that of North America. Several attempts have been made to produce
filk there ; but the climate hath been found totally
unfit for it. The project, however, of enriching the
country by the culture of indigo, feems to promife
much fuccefs. The fineft arnotto of the Brazils is already gathered there.

The part of the colony firft peopled was the ifland
of Saint Louis, which is feven leagues long, and four
broad, and which is feparated from the continent only
by a very fmall river. There is a town of the fame
name in it, where all the trade is tranfacted, although
it hath a bad harbour. Some cultivations are carried
on there; but the moft confiderable are on the continent, upon the rivers of Ytapicorié, of Mony, of Iqua-
ra, of Pindare, and of Meary.

In the fame government, and towards the back of
the province, is the country of Pauchy, where the inhabitants of St. Paul penetrated in 1571. It was not
conquered without much difficulty, and is not yet entirely fubdued on the eaftern fide. Its foil is uneven
and fandy, though exceedingly elevated. It is inhabited by fhepherds. Upon this foil, which is covered
with faltpetre, they rear a confiderable number of
horfes and horned cattle, which are fold to tolerable
advantage in the neighbouring countries; but the
fheep degenerate there, as well as in the reft of the
Brazils, except in the Coritibe. Unfortunately, the
too frequent droughts, and the exceffive heats, very often deftroy whole flocks, when fufficient attention is
not paid to lead them in time to diftant paftures.

The mines of fulphur, alum, copperas, iron, lead,
and antimony, are very common and very fuperficial
in thefe mountains, and yet none of them have been
opened. Permiffion was, indeed, given, in 1572, to
work the filver one which had been difcovered three
or four years before; but very foon after the court re-
tracted this permiffion, for reafons that are not known
to us.

This government confifts of eight thoufand nine
hundred and ninety-three white men, feventeen thoufand eight hundred and forty-four Negroes, or free
Mulattoes, and flaves; and of thirty-eight thoufand
nine hundred and thirty-feven Indians, either fcattered, or affembled in ten villages. The exportations
have not as yet been equal to this degree of population. Their value was little more than 6 or 700,000

livres [from 25,000l. to 29,166l. 13s. 4d.]; but since the monopoly hath been abolished, it must become more considerable.

The province which follows that of Maragnan, and which is called Fernambucca, was formed out of four private estates.

Fernambucca itself was given, in 1527, to Edward Coelho; and was reunited to the crown as a conquest, after the Dutch had been driven from it in 1654.

The historian De Barros obtained the district of Paraiba from John III., but he neglected the peopling of it. Some vagabonds went over in 1560, and in 1591 were subdued by the French, who were soon obliged to evacuate it. Philip III. caused a city to be erected upon this royal domain, which is at present known by the name of Notre Dame de Neves.

The property of Rio-Grande, a district which had till then been entirely neglected, was ceded to Emanuel Jordan in 1654. The shipwreck of this enterprising man, at the entrance of the harbour, restored to the hands of government, lands, which were soon after cultivated by some individuals.

It is not known at what time, nor to whom, Tamaraca had been granted; but it became a national possession again soon after the elevation of the house of Braganza to the throne of Portugal.

This flourishing government is at present surrounded by the river St. Francis, and by several branches of the Cordeleirias. The coasts afford a small quantity of cotton. In no country of these regions sugar is to be found in such great perfection as upon those plains which are well watered. The mountains are covered with horned cattle, which supply a great quantity of leather. This district alone furnishes the Brazil wood.

The tree which it is taken from is not perfectly known by the botanists. It is, however, believed, that it is in some respects analogous to the *bresillet* of the Antilles, and to the tara, or poinciana spinosa, of Peru. Those who have described it affirm, that it is tall, very branchy, and covered with a brown bark full of

thorns. Its leaves are compofed of a common cofta, B o o k
which fupports from four to fix other coftæ, furnifhed IX.
with two rows of fmall green leaves, fhining, and refembling the leaves of box. The flowers, difpofed in
clufters towards the extremity of the branches, are
fmall, and more odoriferous than thofe of the lily :
they have a calix with five divifions, ten ftamina, and
five petals, four of which are yellow, and the fifth is
of a beautiful red colour. Their piftil becomes an oblong flattened pod, ftuck full of points, and filled with
fome red feeds.

The bark of this tree is fo thick, that the wood is
reduced almoft to nothing when ftripped of it. This
wood is very fit for works of turnery, and takes a good
polifh : but its principal ufe is in the red dye, where
it fupplies the place of double the quantity of logwood. The moft arid foils, and the moft craggy rocks,
are the places which it chiefly delights in.

The trade of this wood is monopolized, and it belongs to the queen's houfehold. The firft dealers in
this article agreed to receive annually in the magazines
of government, where it is depofited, thirty thoufand
quintals of it, at 30 livres [1l. 5s.] the quintal. It
was difcovered, after feveral experiments, that this
quantity was not confumed in Europe ; and they were
obliged to take no more than twenty thoufand quintals ; but it was raifed to 40 livres [1l. 13s. 4d.] the
quintal. Such is the prefent contract, which is in the
hands of two Englifhmen fettled in Portugal. They
give 800,000 livres [33,333l. 6s. 8d.] for the wood
with which they are furnifhed, and fell it at Lifbon itfelf for 1,000,000 livres [41,666l. 13s. 4d.]. The expences they are at amount to 128,000 livres [5333l.
6s. 8d.] ; and therefore the profits are 72,000 livres
[3000l.].

The population of Fernambucca confifts of nineteen thoufand fix hundred and fixty-five white men,
thirty-nine thoufand one hundred and thirty-two Negroes or Mulattoes, and thirty-three thoufand feven
hundred and twenty-eight Indians. There are four

B O O K
IX.

harbours fit to receive fmall veffels. That where the fhoal is, which is the port of Olinda, can admit larger fhips; but they are neither conveniently fituated, nor in fafety.

The ifland of Fernando de Noronha is at fixty leagues diftance from thefe coafts of Fernambucca; but it is under its dependence. The Portuguefe, who had at firft fettled there, foon forfook it; but in 1738, the court of Lifbon, fufpecting that the French Eaft India Company meant to take poffeffion of it, built feven forts there, conftructed with great fkill. They are provided with artillery, and defended with a garrifon of regular troops, which is relieved every fix months. There are no other inhabitants but a few exiles, a fmall number of very indigent Meftees, and the Indians who are employed in the public labours. Though this foil be deep and good, no kind of cultivation hath ever fucceeded there, becaufe the rains do not fall for three or four years together. From the month of December till the month of April, turtles are the only food; after that time they difappear, and the inhabitants have no refource but in the provifions fent from the continent. There are two harbours for foreign veffels in the ifland, where fhips of all rates are in fafety, when north and weft winds do not prevail.

State of the govern-ment of Bahia.

The government of Bahia is enclofed by the river St. Francis on the north, by the river Doce on the fouth, and by the river Preto, one of the arms of the Green River, on the eaft. It confifts of the captainfhip of Xegerippe, the revolutions of which are not known to us; of the captainfhip of Itheos, of which George de Figueredo was deprived, after its deftruction by the Aimorés Indians; of the captainfhip of Porto Seguro, which returned to the crown after the extinction of the family of the Tourinhos; and of the country of Bahia, which was never a private property.

San Salvador, the capital of this fettlement, was for a long time that of all the Brazils. The way to it is by the bay of All Saints, which is two leagues and a half broad at the entrance. On each fide ftands a fortrefs, intended rather to prevent landing, than to hinder fhips from paffing by. It is thirteen or fourteen leagues in length, and interfperfed with little iflands, which are full of cotton trees, and form an agreeable profpect. It grows narrow towards the bottom, which is fheltered from every attack, and makes an excellent harbour for the moft numerous fleets. The town commands this harbour, being built on the flope of a fteep hill.

This city contains two thoufand houfes, which are moft of them built with great magnificence. The furniture here is the more rich and elegant, as extravagance in drefs is ftrictly prohibited. By a very old law, which hath often been broken, and which extends to the New World fince the year 1749, the Portuguefe are forbidden to wear any gold or filver ftuffs, or any laced clothes; but their paffion for fhow, which no laws can eradicate, hath induced them to contrive fome fubftitute, and to wear diamond croffes, medals, and chaplets, or beads, the rich enfigns of a poor religion. The gold they cannot wear themfelves, they lavifh to adorn their domeftic flaves.

As the fituation of the town will not admit of coaches, the rich, who will always be diftinguifhed from the vulgar, have contrived to be carried in cotton hammocks. Supinely ftretched upon velvet cufhions, and furrounded with filken curtains, which they open and fhut at pleafure, thofe proud and lazy mortals move about more voluptuoufly, though with lefs expedition, than in the moft eafy and elegant carriages.

The women feldom enjoy this luxury. Thefe people, who are fuperftitious to a degree of fanaticifm, will hardly allow them to go to church, covered with their cloaks, on high feftivals; and no one is fuffered to fee them in their own houfes. This reftraint, which is the effect of an ungovernable jealoufy, doth not prevent them from carrying on intrigues, though they are fure of being ftabbed to death upon the flighteft fufpicion. By a lenity more judicious than ours, a girl who, without her mother's confent, or even under her protection,

yields to the importunities of a lover, is treated with
lefs feverity.   But if the father cannot conceal her infamy, by difpofing of her in marriage, he abandons her
to the fcandalous trade of a courtezan. Thus it is that
riches bring on a train of vices· and corruption, efpecially when they are acquired by bloodfhed and murder, and are not preferved by labour.

The want of fociety, confequent upon the feparation
of the fexes, is not the only impediment to the pleafures and enjoyments of life at Bahia.   The hypocrify
of fome, the fuperftition of others; avarice within, and
pompous parade without; extreme effeminacy, bordering upon extreme cruelty, in a climate where all the
fenfations are quick and impetuous; the diftruft that
attends weaknefs; the indolence that trufts every thing
to flaves, whether it relate to pleafure or bufinefs; all
the vices that are to be found, either feparately or col-
lectively, in the moft corrupt fouthern countries, con-
ftitute the character of the Portuguefe at Bahia. However, the depravity of their manners feems to decreafe,
fince they are become rather more enlightened.   The
acquifition of knowledge, the abufe of which will fometimes corrupt virtuous nations, may refine, if not reform, a degenerate nation; it will at leaft make crimes
lefs frequent, will caft a varnifh of elegance over corruption, and will introduce an hypocritical kind of ur-
banity, and a contempt for the groffer vices.

Though San Salvador be no longer the capital of the
Brazils, yet the province is ftill the moft populous of
the colony.   It confifts of thirty-nine thoufand feven
hundred and eighty-four white men, and fixty eight
thoufand and twenty-four Negroes. It fhares with the
other colonies the culture of fugar, cotton, and of fome
other productions; and hath the advantage over them
of the fifhery, and of tobacco.

The whale-fifhery hath been very anciently eftablifhed in the Brazils.   All the Portuguefe of the Old
and of the New World had enjoyed, from its firft rife,
the natural rights of this fifhery; but it hath been, for
a long time paft, fubjected to an exclufive privilege,

purchased by a Company formed at Lisbon, whose ships are freighted at Bahia. Its annual produce consists, at present, of three thousand five hundred and thirty pipes of oil, which, at the rate of 175 livres [7l. 5s. 10d.] the pipe, amounts to 617,750 livres [25,740l. 1s. 8d.]; and of two thousand and ninety quintals of whalebone, which, at the rate of 150 livres [6l. 5s.] the quintal, amount to 313,500 livres [13,062l. 10s.] These two sums added together, amount to 931,250 livres [38,802l. 1s. 8d.]. The monopolizers give to government 300,000 livres [12,500l.]. Their expences do not exceed 268,750 livres [11,198l. 8s. 4d.]; and their profits amount to 362,500 livres [15,154l. 3s. 4d.].

This branch of industry must be entirely given up, unless it be immediately put upon a different footing. Nothing but an unlimited freedom of trade can possibly sustain the competition of the American traders, whose activity hath already extended itself as far as those distant seas, and still beyond them. The court of Lisbon ought even to encourage, by all possible means, the whale-fishery in the Cape de Verde Islands, and in the other islands near the burning shores of Africa, which are at present so useless to them.

Though most of the countries of Brazil furnish a small quantity of tobacco, it may be said, that this article hath not become an object of consequence any where, except at Bahia. It thrives in a space of ninety leagues, and in the district of Cachoeira still better than in any other place. This production had for a long time been enriching the province, when the taxes with which it was loaded, on its exportation from Portugal, raised its price so high as to prevent the consumption of it. There was so little demand for it in foreign markets, that in 1773, the cargoes of it did not exceed eight-and twenty thousand quintals. The year following, the duties, which amounted to 27 livres 12 sols [1l. 3s.] per hundred weight, were suppressed, and this cultivation immediately recovered its former prosperity. The colonist then received for

B O O K this commodity 22 livres 16 fols [19s.] per quintal,
IX.   inftead of 12 livres 10 fols [10s. 5d.], which he received before.

Ten thoufand quintals of inferior tobacço are fent
annually from the Brazils to the coafts of Africa,
which being purchafed in the colony itfelf, even at
the rate of 18 livres [15s.] per hundred weight, bring
in 180,000 livres [7500l.]. Fifty-eight thoufand five
hundred quintals are fent into Portugal, which, at
their firft entrance into the country, are fold for 40
livres [1l. 13s. 4d.] the hundred weight; the total value of which is 2,340,000 livres [97,500l.], and the
two fums put together, amount to 2,520,000 livres
[105,000l.].

Every fpeculator is allowed to purchafe the tobacco that is conveyed to the mother-country; but it
muft be depofited in a public warehoufe, where it pays
two fols fix deniers [about five farthings] per quintal
to the government for ftore-room. From this warehoufe is taken that quantity of tobacco which the
kingdom is not in want of, and which is to be difpofed of to foreign nations. Genoa purchafes that
of the beft quality. Spain, as well as Portugal, confumes only the fecond fort, and Hamburgh is fatisfied
with the moft inferior kind of tobacco. It is this
which is alfo purchafed by the French, and other navigators who are in want of it for their Negro trade.

The purchafer freely applies to the merchants in
whom he confides; but the court of Madrid, who
never have any tobacco bought but for fmoking, ufually employ only one agent, to whom they pay for it
at the rate of nine fols [4½d.] the pound.

Portugal, Madeira, and the Azores, where the tobacco is equally monopolized by the crown, do not
confume annually, for fmoking, more than feven hundred thoufand weight of it, which, at the rate of five
livres [4s. 2d.] the pound, muft amount to 3,520,000
livres [146,666l. 13s. 4d.]; and in fnuff, only five
hundred and twenty-eight thoufand pounds, which,
at the rate of feven livres ten fols [6s. 3d.] per pound,

muft produce 3,960,000 livres [165,000l.]; fo that B o o k
the whole amount of this article is 7,480,000 livres ___IX.___
[311.666l. 13s. 4d.]. The government, however,
does not receive more than 5,431,250 livres [228,385l.
8s. 4d.]. The remainder of the fum is expended in
the purchafe of materials, the expences of preparing
the tobacco, and the profits of the people who farm it.

The fnuff which is confumed in Africa, and in the
Eaft Indies, is likewife under the yoke of monopoly;
but it is the queen's revenue. She receives 450,000
livres [18,750l.] for one hundred and fifty quintals,
which are annually fent to thofe diftant regions; exclufive of the profits which muft arife from the fale of
the pepper that is fent from Goa in exchange.

The government of Rio Janeiro almoft totally oc- State of the
cupies the long coaft, which commences at the river government of Rio
Doce, and ends at that of Rio Grande of St. Peter; Janeiro.
and in the inland countries, it is bounded only by
the enormous chain of mountains which extends from
Una to Minas-Geraes. It has abforbed the captain-
fhips of St. Efprit, of Cabofrio, and of the South Paraiba, granted by government at different periods, and
which have fallen in again in feveral ways to the domains of the crown.

The cultures remained for a long time in a languid ftate, in this fpacious and beautiful province:
but they daily acquire fome importance. Tobacco, indeed, is neither better, nor in greater plenty,
than it was formerly; but for thefe three years paft
the fugar-canes have multiplied there, and more efpecially in the plains of Guatacazès. Twelve modern
plantations of excellent indigo, announce a more confiderable number, and a tolerable quantity of coffee
hath been brought from thence by the laft fhips.
The fouthern diftricts of the colony, as far as Rio
Grande, furnifh a great many hides, fome flour, and
very good falt provifions. There are fourteen or fifteen different kinds of wood for dyeing, which will
foon be cut down; and feven or eight forts of gums,
which will at laft be gathered. Two plants were dif-

covered at Bahia, about twenty years ago, which are known by the names of Curuata and Tocum, and which might be employed for fails and cordage. A fmall fhrub, infinitely more fit for thefe purpofes, hath been lately difcovered on the territory of Rio Janeiro, and is very common. It is fometimes white, fometimes yellow, and fometimes purple; but the firft of thefe colours is the beft.

There is no deficiency of hands for the carrying on the labours. The province reckons forty-fix thoufand two hundred and feventy-one white men, thirty-two thoufand one hundred and twenty-fix Indians, and fifty-four thoufand and ninety-one Negroes.

The riches that are produced by the labours of thefe men, either free or flaves, are carried to Rio Janeiro, formerly the capital of all the Brazils, and the place of the viceroy's refidence.

It is one of the fineft harbours that is known; though narrow at its beginning, it widens gradually. Ships of all denominations enter it with eafe, from ten or twelve o'clock in the morning, till the evening, and are carried in by a regular and moderate fea breeze. It is fpacious, fafe, and convenient. It hath an excellent bottom of mud, and five or fix fathom of water in every part.

It was firft difcovered in 1525 by Dias de Solis. Some French Proteftants, who were perfecuted in their own country, made a fmall fettlement there under the guidance of Villegagnon. This fettlement confifted only of fifteen or twenty huts, made of boughs and covered over with grafs, after the manner of the favages in thofe parts. Some fmall bulwarks that were erected for planting of cannon, occafioned the name of Fort Coligni to be given to it. It was deftroyed three years after by Emanuel de Sa, who, in a fertile foil, under a beautiful fky, and at the foot of feveral mountains, which are difpofed in form of an amphitheatre, laid the foundation of a city, which is become famous, fince fome confiderable mines have been difcovered in its neighbourhood.

This city is the grand ſtaple of the riches which flow from the Brazils to Portugal, and the harbour where the fineſt fleets deſtined for the ſupply of that part of the New World put in. Beſide the treaſures that this continual circulation muſt produce, 3,000,000 livres [125,000l.] remain there every year for the expences of government, and a much larger ſum, when the miniſtry of Liſbon think it ſuitable to their ſyſtem of politics to have men of war built there.

A town, where buſineſs is ſo conſiderable and ſo conſtant, muſt have been ſucceſſively enlarged and peopled. Moſt of the citizens live in houſes two ſtories high, built with freeſtone, or bricks, covered with tolerably fine ſlate, and ornamented with a balcony, ſurrounded with lattices. It is at theſe balconies that the women, either by themſelves, or attended by their ſlaves, make their appearance ; it is from thence that they caſt flowers on the men whom they chooſe to diſtinguiſh, and upon thoſe whom they wiſh to invite to the moſt intimate connection between the two ſexes. The ſtreets are large and even, terminated by a chapel, where the people ſing hymns every evening before a ſaint, magnificently habited, and fixed up in a gilded nitch, well illuminated, and covered with the cleareſt mirror. There is no public edifice worthy of attention, except a large aqueduct, which conveys the water from the neighbouring heights, and the mint. The churches are all gloomy, low, and overcharged with ornaments, executed without taſte.

The morals are the ſame at Rio Janeiro as at Bahia, and in all the mine countries. Similar thefts, ſimilar treaſons, ſimilar revenges, and ſimilar exceſſes of all kinds prevail, and with equal impunity.

It hath properly been ſaid, that gold was the repreſentative of all kinds of riches ; but it might have been added, that it was likewiſe the repreſentative of happineſs and misfortune, of almoſt all the vices, and of almoſt all the virtues : for what good or bad action cannot be done by means of gold ? It cannot, therefore, be ſurpriſing that nothing ſhould be a check upon us in our attempts to obtain fo important an object! It cannot be furprifing, that, when obtained, it fhould become the fource of the moft fatal abufes, and that thefe abufes fhould be multiplied in proportion to the vicinity and to the abundance of this precious and pernicious metal.

The fituation of the city, in twenty-two degrees twenty minutes of fouthern latitude, placed it at fuch a diftance from the Old World, that it might have been prefumed moderate fortifications only would be required for its defence ; but as the temptation for attacking it might become greater, in proportion to the increafe of its riches, it was thought proper to add to the works. Thefe were already very confiderable, when Du Guay Trouin took it in 1711, with fuch intrepidity and fkill, as redounded much to his honour, and was a great addition to the fame he had already acquired. The new fortifications that have fince been added to thofe the French had maftered, have not made the town more impregnable, as it may be attacked on other fides, where the landing is very practicable. If gold can make its way into brazen towers through iron gates, much more will iron break down the gates that defend gold and diamonds. And, indeed, the court of Lifbon has not thought it fufficient to fortify Rio Janeiro.

In the government of Rio Janeiro, we meet with the ifland of St. Catherine, nine leagues in length, and two in breadth, and feparated from the continent by a narrow channel. Though the land be not low, it is not feen at a diftance, becaufe it is fhaded by the neighbouring mountains on the continent. Navigators find there a perpetual fpring, excellent water, great plenty of wood, a variety of delicious fruits, vegetables, which are fo welcome to failors, and a pure air, except in the harbour, where the hills intercept the circulation of air, and make it conftantly damp and unwholefome.

Towards the year 1654, the court of Lifbon gave Saint Catherine to Francis Dias Velho, in the fame tnanner as the other countries in Brazil had been ced- ed. This captain was killed by an Englifh pirate; and his ifland became the refuge of vagabonds. Thefe adventurers acknowledged, in a vague manner, the authority of Portugal, but did not adopt the exclufive fyftem of that ftate. They admitted indifcriminately the fhips of all nations that were failing to the South Seas, or to India, and gave them their oxen, their fruits, their pulfe, and all their productions, in exchange for arms, brandy, linen, and wearing apparel. Befide their contempt for gold, they fhowed an indifference for all the conveniences that nature did not fupply them with, which would have done honour to a virtuous people.

The fcum and refufe of civilized bodies may fometimes form a well regulated fociety. The iniquity of our laws, the unjuft diftribution of property, the miferies of want, the infolence and impunity of wealth, and the abufe of power, often make rebels and criminals. If we collect together all thofe unfortunate men who are banifhed from fociety by the too great rigour, and often the injuftice, of the laws, and give them an intrepid, generous, humane, and enlightened chief, we fhall make thefe profligate men become honeft, tractable, and rational. If their neceffities urge them to war, they will become conquerors; and to aggrandife themfelves they will violate the rights of nations, though ftrict obfervers of their own reciprocal duties: fuch were the Romans. If, for want of an able leader, they be left to chance and natural events, they will be mifchievous, reftlefs, rapacious, unfettled, for ever at war, either among themfelves or with their neighbours: fuch were the Paulifts. Laftly, if they can more eafily live upon the natural fruits of the earth, or by agriculture and trade, than by plunder, they will contract the virtues proper to their fituation, and the mild inclinations that arife from a rational love of eafe. Civilized by the happinefs and fecurity of an honeft and peaceable life, they will refpect in others thofe rights which they themfelves enjoy, and will barter

BOOK
IX.
the fuperfluities of their produce for the conveniences of other nations : fuch were the people who had taken refuge at St. Catherine's.

They lived with freedom and tranquillity, when, towards the year 1738, it was thought proper to give them an adminiftration, to fend them troops, and to furround their harbour, which was one of the beft in America, with fortifications. Thefe means of defence have drawn upon them, in 1778, the arms of Spain, and have not preferved them from an invafion. Since they are returned under the dominion of their former mafter, in confequence of the reconciliation between the two crowns, they have acquired the cochineal, from which they expect great advantages in future.

The town of St. Paul is thirteen leagues diftant from the ocean, in a delightful climate, and in the midft of a country equally favourable for the productions of the two hemifpheres. It was built about the year 1570, by the malefactors with which Portugal had infefted the coafts of the New World. No fooner did thefe villains perceive that it was intended to fubject them to fome fyftem of police, than they abandoned the fhores upon which they had been caft by chance, and took refuge on fome diftant fpot, where the power of the laws could not reach them. A fituation which a fmall number of men could defend againft a greater number of troops than could be fent againft them, infpired them with the boldnefs of determining to be their own mafters ; and their ambition was crowned with fuccefs. They were recruited and multiplied by other banditti, and by the defcendants proceeding from their connections with the women of the country. It is faid that all travellers were ftrictly forbidden to enter this new republic. To obtain an admittance, it was previoufly neceffary to promife to fettle there ; and candidates were to undergo a fevere trial. Thofe who could not go through that kind of noviciate, or who were fufpected of perfidy, were barbaroufly murdered, as were likewife all who fhowed any inclination to quit the fettlement.

A pure air, a serene ſky, a very temperate climate, B O O K though in the 24th degree of ſouth latitude, and a land IX. abounding with corn, ſugar, and excellent paſture; all theſe circumſtances conſpired to induce the Pauliſts to lead a life of indolence, eaſe, and effeminacy; but that reſtleſſneſs ſo natural to reſolute banditti; that deſire of dominion which is nearly connected with a love of independence; the advances of liberty, which lead men to wiſh for glory of ſome kind or other, and to diſtinguiſh themſelves; perhaps, all theſe motives combined, prompted them to forego an eaſy life, and to engage in hazardous and troubleſome excurſions.

They over-ran all the inland parts of the Brazils, from one extremity to the other. All the Indians who reſiſted them were put to death; fetters were the portion of cowards; and ſeveral of the inhabitants hid themſelves in the mountains, to avoid ſlavery or death. It would be impoſſible to enumerate the devaſtations, cruelties, and enormities, of which theſe atrocious men were guilty. In the midſt of theſe horrors, however, ſome colonies were forming under a municipal government, which may be conſidered as the origin of all the ſettlements Portugal is at preſent in poſſeſſion of in thoſe territories. Theſe ſmall republics, detached, in ſome meaſure, from the great one, gradually yielded to the entreaties that were made uſe of, in order that they ſhould be ſubjected to an authority which they had never entirely diſavowed; and, in proceſs of time, the Pauliſts ſubmitted to the crown in the ſame manner as the other ſubjects.

That diſtrict then became a government; to which were added, the captainſhips of St. Vincent and of St. Amaro, which had been given to the two brothers, Alphonſo and Peter Lopès de Souſa, their two towns having been deſtroyed by pirates. This arrangement, for which it is difficult to aſſign a cauſe, divides the province of Rio Janeiro in two parts.

The country of St. Paul does not at preſent conſiſt of more than eleven thouſand and ninety-three white men, thirty-two thoufand one hundred and twenty-fix Indians, and eighty-feven Negroes, or Mulattoes. It fends nothing to Europe, except a fmall quantity of cotton; and its inland trade is confined to the furnifhing of Rio Janeiro with flour and falt provifions. It hath been found by fome, that flax and hemp would fucceed very well there; and there is no doubt of its being as eafy and important to grow filk in the country. The plentiful mines of iron and tin, which are found between the rivers Thectè and Mogyaffu, in the Cordeleirias of Paranan-Piacaba, at the diftance of four leagues from Sorocoba, might alfo be worked to great advantage.

State of the three inland governments where the mines are fituated. The fix provinces we have juft been fpeaking of are fituated along the coafts: there are three others, extending from the Weft to the Eaft, which occupy, in the centre of the Brazils, the large plain from which all the rivers fpring that empty themfelves into the Paraguai, into the Amazon, and into the Ocean. It is the moft elevated fpot of Portuguefe America, and is filled with mountains, running in various directions. Gold is found almoft throughout the whole of it; for which reafon it is called the mine country.

The moft important of thefe rich governments is known by the name of Minas Geraes. It reckons thirty-five thoufand one hundred and twenty-eight white men, twenty-fix thoufand and feventy-five Indians, and one hundred and eight thoufand four hundred and fix flaves. Its capital is Villa Rica.

Joyas, the capital of which is Villa Boa, contains eight thoufand nine hundred and thirty-one white men, twenty-nine thoufand fix hundred and twenty-two Indians, and thirty-four thoufand one hundred and four Negroes.

Matto Groffo, the only villàge of which is Villa Bella, hath not yet increafed its population beyond two thoufand and thirty-five white men, four thoufand three hundred and thirty-five Indians, and feven thoufand three hundred and fifty-one flaves. It is the

moft weftern part of the Portuguefe dominions. It is
bounded by the Chiquitos, and by the Maxos, who
were fubjected to Spain by the labours of the Jefuits.

The knowledge of the gold mines, in this part of
the New World, is traced to much more diftant periods than is generally thought. As far back as the
year 1577, the Paulifts difcovered fome near the mountains of Jaguara ; but the unfortunate death of King
Sebaftian foon occafioned this fource of wealth, which
at that time had not been of any great advantage either to the ftate or to individuals, to be forgotten.

Hiftory of
the gold
mines
found in
the Brazils.
The man-
ner of
working
them.

In the heights of Jacobino, in the diftrict of Rio das
Velhas, new mines were again difcovered in 1588, and
to as little effect. Philip II. being determined to contain by mifery people who bore the Spanifh yoke with
too much impatience, would not permit them to be
worked. If he apparently confented to this, in 1603,
it was with a refolution to prevent it ; and his bafe
fucceffors adopted his tyrannical policy.

The fortunate revolution which, in 1640, freed the
Portuguefe of their fetters, was followed by long and
obftinate wars. During the courfe of this violent crifis, the attention of the nation was wholly taken up in
the defence of its liberty, and the miniftry were always
engaged in looking out for the refources of which they
were continually in want.

The ftate of the monarchy began to be fearched into, and its improvement to be thought of ; when, in
1699, chance offered to fome enterprifing men great
treafures in the province of Minas Geraes. The gifts
of bounteous nature were no more difregarded ; and,
three years after, the court of Lifbon formed the fettlements that were neceffary to fecure the benefit of
them. Sabara, Rio das Mortes, Cachoeira, Paracatu,
Do Carmo, Rio das Velhas, Rio Doce, and Auro Preto, are the places in that government where gold hath
been fucceffively found, and where it is ftill difcovered
at this day.

The mines of Goyas were not difcovered till 1726 :

they are fituated in the diftricts of San Felix, Meia
Ponta, O Fanado, Mocambo, and Natividade.

In the year 1735, new ones were found in the province of Matto Groffo, at St. Vincent, at Chapada, at
St. Anne, at Cuiaba, and at Araès.

Befide thefe countries, which are called by preference the Mine Regions, the mines of Jacobino and of
Rio das Contas are worked in the government of Bahia, as are alfo thofe of Parnaguay and Tibogy, in the
government of St. Paul; but neither of them are very
abundant.

The extraction of gold is neither very laborious, nor
dangerous, in thofe parts of the New World. It is
fometimes on the furface of the foil, and this is the
pureft kind; and, at other times, it is neceffary to dig
for it to the depth of three or four fathoms, but feldom lower. A layer of fandy earth, known in the
country by the name of *Saibro*, then ufually informs
the miners that it would be ufelefs to fearch any further. Although, in general, the veins that are regular,
and in the fame direction, be the richeft, it hath been
obferved, that thofe fpaces, the furface of which was
moft fpangled with cryftals, were thofe which furnifhed the greateft plenty of gold. It is found in larger
pieces upon the mountains, and barren or ftony rocks,
than in the valleys, or on the borders of rivers. But
whatever place it may have been gathered in, it is of
three-and-twenty carats and a half on coming out of
the mine, unlefs it be mixed with fulphur, filver, iron,
or mercury; a circumftance that is common only at
Goyas and Araès.

Every man who difcovers a mine, muft give notice
of it to government. If the vein be thought of little
conféquence, by perfons of the art appointed to examine it, it is always given up to the public. If it be
declared to be a rich vein, the government referve a
portion of it to themfelves. Another fhare is given to
the commandant; a third to the intendant, and two
fhares are fecured to the difcoverer; the reft is divided

amongft all the miners of the diftrict, in proportion to their circumftances, which are determined by the number of their flaves. The difputes which this fpecies of property may give rife to, are under the cognizance of the intendant: but an appeal lies from his decrees to the fupreme court eftablifhed at Lifbon, under the title of Council *d'Outremer*.

The miners are obliged to deliver to the king the fifth part of the gold, which they extract by operations more or lefs fuccefsful. This fifth was formerly confiderable, as it exceeded 9,000,000 of livres [375,000l.] annually, from the year 1728 to 1734; but it hath fince gradually decreafed. At prefent the annual produce of Minas Geraes amounts only to 18,750,000 livres [781,250l.]; that of Goyas to 4,687,500 livres [195,312l. 10s.]; that of Matto Groffo to 1,312,500 livres [54,687l. 10s.]; and that of Bahia and St. Paul together, only to 1,562,500 livres [65,104l. 3s. 4d.]. This makes, upon the whole, 25,312,500 livres [1,054,687l. 10s.], of which the government receives 5,062,500 livres [210,937l. 10s.]. The duties for the working of the gold into fpecie yield 1,647,500 livres [68,645l. 16s. 8d.]; and, at the rate of 2 per cent. they get 393,000 livres [16,375l.] for the conveyance, which is executed by their fhips, of all the gold that belongs to trade; fo that upon the 25,312,500 [1,054,687l. 10s.] which the mines produce, the miniftry take 7,103,000 livres [295,958l. 6s. 8d.]. They would even receive fomething more, if to the amount of about 600,000 livres [25,000l.] were not annually fmuggled without paying the two laft mentioned taxes.

The amount of all the metals conftantly circulating in the Brazils is not computed at more than 20,000,000 livres [833,333l. 6s. 8d.]

The firft political writers who turned their thoughts towards the difcoveries made in this region of the New World, did not hefitate to foretel, that the difference of value between gold and filver would be diminifhed. The experience of all countries and of all ages had taught them, that though many ounces of filver had

B O O K always been given for an ounce of gold, becaufe mines
of the former had always been more common than of
the latter, yet the value of both metals had varied in
every country, in proportion to the abundance of either.

In Japan, the proportion of gold to filver is as one
to eight ; in China, as one to ten ; in other parts of
India, as one to eleven, twelve, thirteen, or fourteen, as
we advance further weft.

The like variations are to be met with in Europe.
In ancient Greece, gold was to filver as one to thirteen.
When the produce of all the mines in the univerfe was
brought to Rome, the miftrefs of the world, the moft
fettled proportion was one to ten. It rofe as far as one
to thirteen under Tiberius. Numberlefs and infinite
variations are to be met with in the barbarous ages.
In a word, when Columbus penetrated into America,
the proportion was lefs than one to twelve.

The quantity of thefe metals, which was then
brought from Mexico and Peru, not only made them
more common, but ftill increafed the value of gold a-
bove filver, as there was greater plenty of the latter in
thofe parts. Spain, that was of courfe the beft judge
of the proportion, fettled it as one to fixteen in the
coin of the kingdom; and this fyftem, with fome flight
variations, was adopted throughout Europe.

This proportion ftill exifts ; but we have no reafon
on that account to contradict thofe who had foretold
that it would alter. If gold hath fallen but little in
the markets, and not at all in the coin, fince the Brazils furnifh a great quantity of it, this is owing to particular circumftances, which do not affect the principle.
A great deal of gold is now ufed for fetting of jewels,
and for gilding, which has prevented the price of it
from falling fo much as it would have done if our fa-
fhions had not altered. It is this fame fpirit of luxury
that hath always kept up the price of diamonds, though
they are grown more common.

History of   At all times men have affected to make a parade of
the dia-   their riches, either becaufe they were originally the re-
mond mines   ward of ftrength and the mark of power, or becaufe
difcovered

they have every where obtained that regard, which is
due only to abilities and virtue. A defire of attracting
the attention of others, prompts a man to ornament
himfelf with the choiceft and moft brilliant things na-
tufe can fupply. The fame vanity, in this refpect,
prevails among the favages as in civilized nations. Of
all the fubftances that reprefent the fplendour of opulence, none is fo precious as the diamond ; nor hath
any been of fuch value in trade, or fo ornamental
in fociety. Our women are fometimes dazzling with
them. It fhould feem as if they were more anxious to
appear rich than handfome. Are they not then fenfible, that a neck and an arm elegantly turned, are a
thoufand times more attracting when uncovered, than
when they are concealed under jewels? that the
weight of their ear-rings disfigures their ears? that the
luftre of the diamond only diminifhes that of their
eyes? that this expenfive drefs is rather a fatire upon
their hufbands or their lovers, than an encomium upon
their charms? that the Venus de Medicis hath nothing
but a plain bracelet? and that he who only admires in
a fine woman the brilliancy of her jewels, is a man de-
void of tafte?

There are diamonds of all colours, and of every
fhade of the feveral colours. The diamond hath the
red of the ruby, the orange of the hyacinth, the blue
of the fapphire, and the green of the emerald. This
laft is the moft fcarce, and the deareft when it is of a
beautiful tint. The rofe diamonds, blue and yellow,
are the next in value. The yellowifh and the black-
ifh are leaft efteemed. Tranfparency and clearnefs
are the natural and effential properties of the diamond,
to which art hath added the brilliant and fparkling
luftre of the feveral faces.

The diamond is a cryftallized ftone, of the form of
an octohedron, more or lefs well-fhaped. Its furfaces
are in the fhape of a pyramid, either long or flat ; but
its folid angles are never fo clearly nor fo regularly terminated, as they appear in the other cryftallized ftones,
and efpecially in the rock cryftal.

BOOK
IX.

in the Bra-
zils. Re-
marks upon
the nature
of that
ftone.

But this does not prevent its cryſtallization from be-ing regular in the inſide. This ſtone is compoſed of ſmall layers, exceedingly thin, and ſo cloſely joined to-gether as to form a ſmooth and brilliant ſurface, even at the parts where they are broken. Notwithſtanding this very cloſe connection between the elements of cry-ſtallization in the diamond, it can only be poliſhed by finding out the diſpoſition of the layers in their tranſ-verſe direction, at the point where the extreme end of one layer lies over the other. Without this precaution, the lapidaries would not ſucceed, and the diamond would not take the poliſh, as is always the caſe with thoſe which they call *veiny diamonds*, in which theſe extremities are not uniform, and in the ſame direction. The diamond-cutters compare the compoſition of theſe ſtones to the arrangement of the fibres of wood in the knotty parts, where they interſect each other in every direction.

The diamond is ſuperior to any other precious ſtone, in its luſtre, its fire, and its ſolidity. To theſe advan-tages are added thoſe of being more electrical, of re-ceiving a greater quantity of light, when gently warm-ed by the fire, or expoſed to the rays of the ſun, and of retaining this light longer than other bodies, when it is afterwards placed in the dark. Theſe properties, and perhaps likewiſe ſome imaginary qualities, have in-duced natural philoſophers to think, that the diamond was formed of a more pure ſubſtance than any other ſtone. Several perſons have even imagined it contain-ed ſome of that primitive adamitical earth, which hath been for ſo long a time the object of ſo many laborious inquiries and extravagant ſpeculations.

The hardneſs of the diamond ſuggeſted the idea of its being impoſſible to be deſtroyed, even by the moſt intenſe fire ; and this opinion appeared to be very well founded. Notwithſtanding this, the analogy upon this point, deduced from other ſtones, and eſpecially from thoſe that are compoſed of quartz, which do not undergo any alteration by fire, was never more defec-tive than in this inſtance.

There are no accounts of the diamond having been ſubmitted to the action of fire previous to the years 1694 and 1695, when the celebrated Averani expoſed one to the focus of a burning glaſs, for the information of his pupil John Gaſton de Medicis. The celebrated natural philoſophers of thoſe times, who aſſiſted at this experiment, beheld with aſtoniſhment that the diamond was exhaled in vapour, and diſappeared entirely, while the ruby, of a leſs compact texture than the diamond, only grew ſofter; and while other precious ſtones, of a ſtill ſofter texture, did not experience ſuch conſiderable alterations. This ſingular experiment was repeated upon ſeveral diamonds with equal ſucceſs; but the intenſeneſs of the fire employed was a convincing proof that it could not have been done by any other means. Theſe firſt experiments were buried in oblivion, till the reign of the Emperor Francis I. who repeated them at Vienna; expoſing diamonds, and other precious ſtones, to the moſt intenſe fire of a furnace. The reſult was a confirmation of the fact, that diamonds are deſtroyed with the greateſt eaſe by fire, while other precious ſtones, even thoſe of the ſofteſt kind, are at moſt but ſlightly affected.

The facts, though well atteſted, appeared ſo extraordinary, and were ſo contrary to the received prejudices, that they ſunk again into oblivion. Though recorded by the cotemporary writers, they were nevertheleſs either unknown, or denied by thoſe who had not been witneſſes of them.

At length M. Darcet undertook in France, in 1758, to expoſe the diamond to the ſame heat as porcelain. After he had ſatisfied himſelf of the truth of the experiments made in Germany, he communicated them to the Academy of Sciences, and afterwards repeated them in the midſt of Paris, in order that they might be eſtabliſhed with all poſſible authenticity. As this able philoſopher hath ſince varied and combined his experiments, the inconteſtible reſult of them, and of thoſe that have been made after him, is, that the diamond evaporates and burns away readily in the fire

and in the open air ; and that the complete deftruction of it, far from requiring the intenfe heat which
it had been expofed to before his time, fcarce requires the degree of heat neceffary to keep fine filver
in fufion.

M. Darcet hath moreover proved, that the diamond
can be deftroyed, not only in the open air, but likewife in crucibles made of the beft baked porcelain, and
hermetically fealed, provided the crucibles be put in
the fire of large glafshoufes, or in the intenfe fires for
making porcelain, and which have been long kept
up.

The moft active menftruums, fuch as alkaline falts
in fufion, and the moft concentrated minerals, affifted
even by the heat of fire, have no effect upon the diamond. It is not affected by their action ; it does not
mix with any glafs in vitrification ; it does not unite
with any fubftance that is yet known ; and thefe qualities are equally common to the diamonds of India as
to thofe of Brazil ; to the white diamonds, as to thofe
that are black or coloured ; to the perfect diamonds,
and to the veiny diamonds, which cannot be worked.

Such are the particular properties of this fubftance,
which is hitherto unparalleled in nature ; that although
it poffeffes all the external appearances of other ftones,
it hath not the leaft affinity to them in the nature of
its compofition ; that, notwithftanding its exceffive
hardnefs, it is the only one of the fpecies which doth
not refift the action of even a moderate fire, but is entirely diffipated by it. Thus it is that Nature, in her
three kingdoms, difplays an infinite variety of furprifing irregularities. Sometimes fhe feems to confine
herfelf in the chain and fcale of beings, to the order
of almoft imperceptible differences ; and fometimes,
breaking through every kind of feries, fhe takes a fudden flight, leaving an immenfe void behind her, and
fixes two diftant boundaries, the intervals of which it
is impoffible to fill up. Thus it is that certain vegetables already enjoy fome of the advantages of animal
life ! It is the fame thing with gold, with mercury.

and with fulphur, compared to other mineral and me- tallic fubftances. It is the fame, in a word, with man, who leaves all other animals at fo great a diftance behind him.

There are very few diamond mines. Till of late years, we knew of none but in the Eaft Indies. The oldeft is on the river Gouel, that iffues from the mountains, and falls into the Ganges. It is called the mine of Solempour, from the name of a village built near that part of the river where the diamonds are found. Very few diamonds have ever been taken out of it, any more than out of the Succadan, a river in the ifland of Borneo. The chain of mountains that extends from Cape Comorin to Bengal hath yielded much more.

There is a great variety in the foil from whence the diamonds are extracted. Several of thefe mines are fix, eight, and fometimes as far as twelve feet deep, in a fandy and ftony foil; others are found in a fpecies of ferruginous mineral, where they are fifty fathoms deep. But in all parts this fingular ftone is infulated, and doth not feem to adhere to any bafis, or to any rock. It is furrounded on all fides by a thin pellicle, rather opaque, and of the nature of the diamond itfelf. This pellicle is commonly covered over with a cruft not very folid, which is formed by the furrounding earth or fand.

The Europeans, except a few inquifitive travellers, do not frequent the mines of Indoftan. They are worked by the natives, who deliver the diamonds to the rich Banians, who carried them formerly to Madras; but who, fince the roads have been made, begin to convey them to Calcutta. The whole of this branch of commerce is almoft entirely fallen, for a confiderable time paft, into the hands of a few Englifhmen, who trade on their own account. They fort the ftones of different weight and of different qualities, and put them into proper bags, which are fealed up, and fold in London with their invoice. Reckoning the fix laft years as one common year, the

B O O K united value of all these diamonds hath amounted an-
    IX.   nually to 3,420,000 livres [142,500l.] To this esti-
mate, which only comprehends what is registered, must
be added what hath been concealed, in order to avoid
the duty of two and three quarters *per cent.* which
must be paid to the India Company.

Among these diamonds there was one found of an
irregular shape, and which weighed 193 carats when
cut. It was the property of an American, who refused to cede it to the empress of Russia for the sum
of 2,500,000 livres [104,166l. 13s. 4d.], beside a life
annuity of 25 000 livres [1041l. 13s. 4d.]. This merchant met with no purchaser, and thought himself
very fortunate when count Orloff, some time after, renewed the offer of 2,500,000 livres [104,166l. 13s. 4d.],
but without the annuity. In 1722, Catherine conde-
scended to accept, on her festival day, this valuable
present from the hands of her favourite.

It was to be feared, that the revolutions which so
frequently subvert Indostan would occasion a scarcity
of diamonds; but this apprehension was removed by
a discovery which was made in 1728, at Brazil, upon
some branches of the river das Caravelas, and at Serro
de Frio, in the province of Minas-Geraes.

Some slaves, condemned to search for gold, used to
find some little bright pebbles mixt with it, which they
threw away as useless among the sand and gravel. An-
tonio Rodrigues Banha suspected the value of them,
and communicated his idea to Pedro de Almeida, the
governor of the country. Some of these brilliant
pebbles were sent to the court of Lisbon, who, in
1730, commissioned d'Acunha, their minister in Holland, to have them examined. After repeated experiments, the artists pronounced them to be very fine
diamonds.

The Portuguese immediately gathered them with so
much diligence, that the Rio Janeiro fleet brought
home eleven hundred and forty-six ounces. This plenty lessened their price considerably; but the measures
taken by an attentive ministry soon made them rise to

their original value. They conferred the exclusive right of searching for diamonds on a few wealthy associates; and in order even to restrain the avidity of the Company itself, it was stipulated that it should employ no more than six hundred slaves in that business. It hath since been permitted to increase their number at pleasure, paying 100 sols [4s. 2d.] *per* day for every miner.

To ensure the business of the chartered Company, the gold mines, which were worked in the neighbourhood, were in general shut up; and those who had founded their expectations of fortune upon this frequently deceitful basis, were compelled to turn their activity into some other channel. The other citizens were suffered to remain upon their estates; but capital punishments were decreed by the law against any person who should encroach upon the exclusive rights granted to the Company. Since the sovereign hath succeeded to the Company, all the citizens are allowed to search for diamonds, but under the restriction of delivering them to the agents of the crown at the price it hath stipulated, and on paying twenty *per cent.* upon this sum.

The diamonds that are intended to be sent from the New World to the Old, are enclosed in a casket which hath three locks, the keys of which are separately put into the hands of the chief members of administration; and those keys are deposited in another casket, which is to be sealed with the viceroy's seal. While the exclusive privilege subsisted, this precious deposit, on its arrival in Europe, was remitted to government, who retained, according to a settled regulation, the very scarce diamonds which exceeded twenty carats, and delivered every year, for the profit of the Company, to one, or to several contractors united, forty thousand carats, at prices which have successively varied. An engagement was made on one hand to receive that quantity; and on the other, not to distribute any more; and whatever might be the produce

B O O K of the mines, which neceffarily varied, the contract
  IX. was faithfully adhered to.

At prefent, the court throws fixty thoufand carats
of diamonds into trade. Thefe are monopolifed by one
fingle merchant, who gives 3,120,000 livres [130,000l.],
at the rate of 25 livres [1l. 10d.] the carat, for them.
If the fmuggling amounts to a tenth, as well-inform-
ed perfons fuppofe, the fum of 312,000 livres [13,000l.]
muft be added to the fum received by government :
it will be found that the produce of thofe mines, the
riches of which there is fo great a propenfity to ex-
aggerate, doth not amount annually to more than
3,432,000 livres [143,000l.]. Thefe rough diamonds
are purchafed by England and Holland, who furnifh
them to other nations, more or lefs well cut.

The diamonds of Brazil are not found in quarries ;
moft of them are fcattered in the rivers, the courfe of
which is more or lefs frequently altered. It is a queftion not yet decided, whether they be formed there,
or whether they have been carried there by the waters which empty themfelves into thefe rivers. The increafe of their quantity in the rainy feafons, and after
violent ftorms, would induce one to believe that they
have been wafhed away by the torrents which have
detached them from the rocks and mountains.

In the Eaft and Weft Indies, the mines are fituated
at a fmall diftance from the equator ; fome of them in
the firft degrees of northern latitude, and others in the
correfpondent degrees of fouthern latitude. The cruft
which the rough diamonds are furrounded with is
thicker in the diamonds of Brazil than in thofe of Indoftan ; and it is an eafy matter, or at leaft poffible,
to diftinguifh them in that primary ftate. But the
moft fkilful lapidaries are deceived in them, after they
have been once cut ; they are accordingly of equal
value in trade ; but this equality is to be underftood
only of the fmall diamonds. Moft of the American
diamonds, beyond four or five carats, have blemifhes,
which are feldom found in thofe of Afia ; and in that

case the difference in the price is prodigious. Some B O O K artists are likewise of opinion, that the latter are harder IX. and more brilliant than the former; but this opinion is not generally received.

Some very imperfect amethists and topazes are likewise found in the diamond and gold country, as well as some tolerable fine cryfolites. These precious ftones were never under the yoke of monopoly; and those who difcover them are at liberty to difpofe of them in whatever manner they think moft fuitable to their intereft. Their annual exportation, however, does not amount to more than 150,000 livres [6250l.], and the duties which government receives from them, at the rate of one *per cent.* do not exceed 1500 livres [62l. 10s.].

Mines of iron, fulphur, antimony, tin, lead, and quickfilver, are likewife found in thefe rich countries, and in fome other provinces of Brazil; but no care hath been taken to open any of them. Copper only feems to have been refufed by nature to this vaft and fruitful region of the New Hemifphere.

A colony fo interefting hath been ufeful to Portugal Prefent in feveral ways. The increafe of the public revenue, ftate of Brazil. by the Brazils, feems to have been the kind of advantage which hitherto hath moftly engaged the attention of the government. The obligation to pay for the tranfportation of the metals, which is referved for fhips of war; the exclufive trade of diamonds, the fale of a great number of monopolies, the overloading of the cuftoms; fuch are the principal fources of wealth, which, even in Europe, an infatiable treafury hath opened to itfelf.

Thefe vexations have been carried ftill farther in America. A fifth of the profits upon gold and diamonds is required, which amounts to 6 or 7,000,000 livres [from 250,000l. to 291,666l. 13s. 4d.]. A tenth is demanded upon all kinds of productions, which, though collected without feverity, amounts to 2,873,000 livres [119,708l. 6s. 8d.]. The inhabitants are obliged

B O O K to purchafe crufades, which do not exceed 160,000
  IX.   livres [6666l. 13s. 4d.]. A duty is alfo exacted upon
flaves, which amounts to 1,076,650 livres [44,860l.
8s. 4d.]. Another for the rebuilding of Lifbon, and
for public fchools, which amounts to 385,000 livres
[16,041l. 13s. 4d.]; another from all fubaltern officers
of juftice, which amounts to 153,000 livres [6375l.].
Ten *per cent.* is likewife required upon every import
and export, which may yield 4,882,000 livres [203,416l.
13s. 4d.]; and 1,124,000 livres [43,833l. 6s. 8d.] are
demanded for the liberty of conveying to inland countries the liquors and the commodities that are brought
into port. Government hath alfo referved to itfelf the
monopoly of falt, foap, mercury, aqua fortis, and cards,
which it farms out for 710,320 livres [29,596l 13s.
4d.].

Notwithftanding all thefe taxes, which bring in annually 18,073,970 livres [753,082l. 1s. 8d.] to the
crown, it hath ftill contracted engagements in the Brazils. It owes 713,000 livres [29,708l. 6s. 8d.] to Para,
517,600 [21,791l. 13s. 4d.] to St. Paul and to Matto
Groffo, 10,110,000 livres [421,250l.] to Rio Janeiro;
in all 11,344,600 livres [472,525l.]. In the former of
thefe governments, the debt hath been occafioned by
the recent conftruction of fome forts, more or lefs neceffary; and in the latter, by the wars which were obliged to be carried on againft the Guaranis in 1750, and
by thofe which it hath been requifite to fuftain againft
Spain.

On the other hand, in 1774, the Brazils were indebted to the merchants of the mother-country to
the amount of 15,165,980 livres [631,915l. 16s. 8d.].
This was the opinion of a man who hath attended moft
to this great fettlement, and hath acquired the beft information concerning it.

Foreign
connections
of Brazil.

The colony hath formed fome commercial intercourfe with feveral countries of the globe. Formerly the fhips which returned from the Eaft Indies to
Portugal ufed to put in there, and to difpofe of part

of their cargo. This intercourse hath been interrupted in latter times, for reasons with which we are unacquainted, but which cannot be good ones.

The western coast of Africa, from the Cape de Verde
Islands to beyond the country of Angola, is more than
ever frequented by the Brazilian navigators ; and those
of Rio Janeiro have begun, not long ago, to trade on
the northern coast. Vessels are employed in these
voyages which are built in the colony itself, and which
are not of less than sixty tons burden, nor more than
one hundred and forty. The crew is either entirely or
mostly composed of Negroes and Mulattoes. It is for
the working of the mines, and for the cultivation of
the lands, that this great exertion is made. It is evident from some very authentic memorials which are
now before us, that for these eight years past, sixteen
thousand three hundred and three slaves have been
carried off from these unfortunate shores every year.
These slaves, at the rate of 312 livres [13l.], one with
another, must have cost 5,161,536 livres [215,064l.].
They have been paid for with the gold, the tobacco,
the rums, and the cottons, which come from Brazil ;
and with the glass manufactures, the mirrors, the ribands, and several kinds of toys brought from Europe.

The connections of the colony with the Portuguese
islands are maintained for another purpose. It receives
annually from Madeira, by means of eight or nine
small ships, to the amount of 400,000 livres [16,666l.
13s. 4d.] in wine, vinegar, and brandy ; and from the
Azores, by means of four or five more vessels, to the
amount of 610,000 livres [25,416l. 13s. 4d.] in liquors ; to which are added, linens, salt provisions, and
flour. The agents of this trade lade themselves, in return, with those productions of Brazil, the exclusive
property of which the mother-country hath not reserved to itself. These several branches of trade united do not carry away annually more than to the a-
mount of 2,271,000 livres [94,625l.] of the production
of the colony.

Almost all the riches of this vast region of the New

World are carried into Portugal. From the year 1770 to 1775, they amounted annually to the fum of 56,949,290 livres [2,372,887l. 1s. 8d.]. Gold, diamonds, four hundred and forty-three thoufand quintals of fugar, fifty-eight thoufand five hundred quintals of tobacco, four thoufand five hundred quintals of cotton, twenty thoufand quintals of wood for dyeing, one hundred fourteen thoufand and twenty hides, together with fome other objects of lefs importance, made up this great fum.

After the period we have been fpeaking of, a few variations took place. We are not fufficiently acquainted with them to afcertain them with precifion; but we know to a certainty that the mother-country hath received every year from Rio Janeiro a fmall quantity of coffee and of indigo, together with one thoufand quintals of fugar, more than it received formerly. We know to a certainty that it hath received from Para and from Maragnan every year three hundred and twenty-one quintals of rice, and one hundred and ninety-two quintals of cotton, more than were formerly fent; and we alfo know that there hath been an annual diminution of four thoufand hides and of 965,000 livres [40,208l. 6s. 8d.] in the gold, among the feveral remittances that have been made.

The colony is paid with merchandife, which have not coft originally above fifteen or fixteen millions of livres [from 625,000l. to 666,666l. 13s. 4d.]. The duties received by the fovereign himfelf, feveral monopolies, exorbitant taxes, the dearnefs of freighting, and the profits of the trade, abforb the remainder.

Portugal did not formerly fend from its own country to its colonies any thing befide liquors; but, fince the induftry of the province is in fome degree revived, it furnifhes one half of the confumptions made in the part of the New Hemifphere that is under its dominion.

It is with two-thirds of the productions of Brazil, which are fold to foreigners; it is with the go   and the diamonds which come from thefe regions; it is with the wines, the woollen cloths, the falt, and the fruits of the mother-country itfelf, that Portugal is enabled to pay fixty millions [2,500,000l.] for the merchandife which they annually receive from the feveral countries of Europe. The fhare which the feveral nations have taken in this trade hath experienced great variations. At this prefent time, England is in poffeffion of fourteen parts of it, Italy of eight, Holland of feven, Hamburgh of fix, France of five, Sweden of four, Denmark of four, Spain of two, and Ruffia of one only. The fpoils of this nation have not always been thus divided.

The firft conquefts of the Portuguefe in Africa and Afia did not ftifle the feeds of their induftry. Though Lifbon was become the general warehoufe for India goods, her own filk and woollen manufactures were ftill maintained, and were fufficient for the confumption of the mother-country and of Brazil. The national activity extended to every thing, and made fome amends for the deficiency of population, which. was becoming daily more confiderable. Amidft the various calamities that Spanifh tyranny oppreffed the kingdom with, the Portuguefe could not complain of a ceffation of labour at home; nor was the number of manufactures much leffened at the time when they recovered their liberty.

The happy revolution that placed the duke of Braganza upon the throne was the period of this decay. A fpirit of enthufiafm feized upon the people. Some of them croffed the feas, in order to defend diftant poffeffions againft an enemy who was imagined to be more formidable than he really was. The reft took up arms to cover the frontiers. The intereft of the whole nation prevailed over private views, and every patriot was folicitous only for his country. It might naturally be expected, that, when the firft enthufiafm was paft, every one would refume his ufual employment; but, unfortunately, the cruel war which followed that great event, was attended with fuch devaftations in an open country, that the people chofe rather to forego

BOOK their labours than to expofe themfelves to fee the fruits
of them continually deftroyed. The miniftry encouraged this fpirit of indolence by meafures which cannot be too feverely cenfured.

Their fituation put them under a neceffity of forming alliances. Political reafons fecured to them all the
enemies of Spain. The advantages they muft neceffarily reap from the diverfions made in Portugal, could
not fail of attaching them to its intereft. If the new
court had formed fuch extenfive views, as from the
nature of their enterprife it might be prefumed they
had, they would have known that they had no need
to make any facrifices in order to acquire friends. By
an ill-judged precipitation they ruined their affairs.
They gave up their trade to other powers, who were
almoft as much interefted in their prefervation as they
were themfelves. This infatuation made thofe powers
imagine they might venture any thing, and their avidity ftill prompted them to encroach upon the privileges that had been fo improperly lavifhed upon them.
The induftry of the Portuguefe was deftroyed by this
competition, but was again revived, in fome degree,
by an error of the French miniftry.

This crown had, for a confiderable time paft, been
in poffeffion of fome iflands in America. The fhackles
with which they had been reftrained had till then impeded their fertility. The cultures would fpeedily and
infallibly have been improved, by a well-digefted plan
of liberty. The crown chofe rather to fecure to the
monopoly, to which they were fubjeded, the exclufive
right of fupplying the kingdom; and the fugars and
tobaccos of Brazil were ftrictly prohibited there in
1664. The court of Lifbon, irritated, as they had reafon to be, with this inconfiderate prohibition, forbade,
on their parts, the importation of French manufactures, the only ones, at that period, which were efteemed in Portugal. Genoa immediately feized upon the
filk trade, and hath kept it ever fince; and England
appropriated to itfelf the woollen trade, though with
lefs uninterrupted fuccefs. The Portuguefe, inftruded

by workmen from all quarters, began, in 1681, to ma- nufacture the fleeces of their own flocks. The progress of this manufacture was sufficiently rapid, to enable the government to proscribe several kinds of foreign woollen cloths, and, soon after, to forbid those of all kinds.

Great Britain was much chagrined at these arrangements. For a long time, the English strove, with great assiduity, to open the communication afresh, which had been shut against them. Their endeavours were sometimes likely to be attended with success; but they were soon after obliged to give up those hopes, which they had reason to think so well founded. It was impossible to discover in what manner these attempts would end, when a revolution happened in the political system of Europe, which at once overturned all the former ideas.

A grandson of Lewis XIV. was called to the throne of Spain. All nations were alarmed at this accession of power to the house of Bourbon, which they already thought too formidable and too ambitious. Portugal, in particular, which had always considered France as a firm friend, now beheld in her an enemy, who must necessarily desire, and perhaps promote, her ruin. This induced her to apply for the protection of England, which being accustomed to turn every event to her own commercial advantage, could not fail of availing itself, with warmth, of a circumstanc so favourable to its interest. The English ambassador Methuen, a profound and able negotiator, signed a treaty, on the 27th of December 1703, by which the court of Lisbon engaged to permit the importation of all British woollen goods, on the same footing as before the prohibition; upon condition that the Portugal wines should pay a duty one third less than those of France, to the customhouse in England.

The advantages of this stipulation were very certain for one of the parties, but only probable for the other. England obtained an exclusive privilege for her manufactures, as the prohibition remained in full force with

B O O K regard to thofe of other nations ; but granted nothing
   IX. on her part, having already fettled, for her own intereft, what fhe now artfully reprefented to her ally as a
great favour.   Since France had bought no more
cloths of the Englifh, they had obferved that the high
price of French wines was prejudicial to the balance
of trade, and had therefore endeavoured to leffen the
confumption, by laying heavier duties upon them.
They have again increafed them from the fame motive, and ftill made a merit of it to the court of Lifbon, as being a proof of their friendfhip.

The Portuguefe manufactures fell, being unable to
fupport the competition of the Englifh.   Great Britain
clothed her new ally ; and as the wine, oil, falt, and
fruit fhe bought, was a trifle in comparifon to what fhe
fold, it was neceffary that the deficiency fhould be fupplied with the gold of Brazil.   The balance inclined
more and more in favour of the Englifh, and it was
fcarce poffible that it fhould not.

All perfons who are converfant with the theory of
commerce, or have attended to its revolutions, know
that an active, rich, and intelligent nation, which hath
once appropriated to itfelf any confiderable branch of
trade, will foon engrofs all the lefs important branches
of it.   It hath fuch great advantages over its competitors, that it difgufts them, and makes itfelf mafter of
the countries where its induftry is exerted.   Thus it is
that Great Britain hath found means to engrofs all the
productions of Portugal and her colonies.

It furnifhed Portugal with clothing, food, hardware,
materials for building, and all articles of luxury, and
returned her own materials manufactured.   Thefe ufeful labours employed a million of Englifh artificers or
hufbandmen.

It furnifhed her with fhips, and with naval and warlike ftores for her fettlements in America, and carried
on all her navigation in other parts of the world.

It had engroffed the whole money trade of Portugal.
Money was borrowed in London at three or three and
a half *per cent.* and negotiated at Lifbon, where it was

worth ten. In ten years time, the capital was paid by the interest, and still remained due.

It engroffed all the inland trade. There were Englifh houfes fettled at Lifbon, which received all the commodities of their own country, and diftributed them to merchants, who difpofed of them in the provinces, moftly for the benefit of their employers. A fmall profit was the only reward of this induftry, which is difgraceful to a nation that worked at home for the benefit of another.

It carried off even the agency bufinefs. The fleets deftined for the Brazils were the fole property of the Englifh. The riches they brought back belonged to them. They would not even fuffer them to pafs through the hands of the Portuguefe, and only borrowed or purchafed their name, becaufe they could not do without it. Thefe ftrangers difappeared as foon as they had acquired the fortune they intended, and left that nation impoverifhed and exhaufted, at whofe expence they had enriched themfelves. It is demonftrable from the regifters of the fleets, that in the fpace of fixty years, that is, from the difcovery of the mines to the year 1756, 2,400,000,000 livres [100,000,000l.] worth of gold had been brought away from Brazil, and yet, in this latter period, all the fpecie in Portugal amounted to no more than 15 or 20,000,000 [from 625,000l. to 833,333l. 6s. 8d.], and at that time the nation owed one hundred million [4,166,666l. 13s. 4d.], or more.

But what Lifbon was lofing, London gained. England, by her natural advantages, was only intended for a fecondary power. Though the changes that had happened in the religion, government, and induftry of the Englifh, had improved their condition, increafed their ftrength, and unfolded their genius, they could not poffibly act a capital part. They knew by experience that the means which, in ancient governments, could raife a nation to any height, when, without any connection with its neighbours, it emerged, as it were, fingly out of nothing, were infufficient in modern times, when the intercourfe of nations, making the ad-

B O O K vantages of each common to all, left to numbers and
  IX.   ftrength their natural fuperiority. Since foldiers, generals, and nations, had hired themfelves to engage in
war ; fince the power of gold had opened every cabinet, and made every treaty ; England had learned
that the greatnefs of a ftate depended upon its riches,
and that its political power was eftimated in proportion to its millions. This truth, which muft have a-
larmed the ambition of the Englifh, became favourable
to them, as foon as they had prevailed upon Portugal
to depend upon them for neceffaries, and had bound
them by treaties to an impoffibility of procuring them
from any other power. Thus was that kingdom made
dependent on a falfe friend for food and raiment.
Thefe were, to borrow the expreffion of a certain po-
litician, like two anchors which the Britons had faftened upon that empire. They went further ftill : they
made the Portuguefe lofe all confideration, all weight,
all influence in the general fyftem of affairs, by per-
fuading them to have neither forces nor alliances.
Truft to us, faid the Englifh, for your fafety ; we will
negotiate and fight for you. Thus, without bloodfhed
or labour, and without experiencing any of the evils
that attend upon conqueft, they made themfelves more
effectually mafters of Portugal, than the Portuguefe
were of the mines of Brazil.

All things are connected, both in nature and politics. It is fcarce poffible that a nation fhould lofe its
agriculture and its induftry, without a vifible decay of
the liberal arts, letters, fciences, and all the found principles of policy and government. The kingdom of
Portugal furnifhes a melancholy inftance of this truth.
As foon as Great Britain had condemned it to a ftate
of inaction, it is fallen into fuch barbarifm as is fcarce
credible. The light which had fhone all over Europe
did not extend itfelf to the frontiers of Portugal. That
kingdom was even obferved to degenerate, and to attract the contempt of thofe whofe emulation and jealoufy it had before excited. The advantage of having
tolerable laws, while all other ftates were involved in

horrible confusion; this inestimable advantage has BOOK IX.
been of no service to the Portuguese. They have lost
the turn of their genius, by forgetting the principles
of reason, morality, and politics. The efforts they may
make to emerge from this state of degeneracy and infatuation might possibly prove ineffectual; because
good reformers are not easily to be found in that nation which stands most in need of them. Men who
are qualified to cause revolutions in empires are generally prepared to it by previous circumstances, and seldom start up at once. They have generally had their
forerunners, who have awakened the minds of the people, disposed them to receive the light, and prepared
the necessary means for bringing about great revolutions. As there is no appearance of any such prepa-
ratory steps in Portugal, the nation must still continue
for a long time in this humiliating condition, unless it
will adopt the principles followed, with so much success, by the most enlightened states.

The first step towards its recovery, that firm and vi- Means which the court of Lisbon ought to employ to extricate the mother-country, and her colonies, from their languid state.
gorous one without which all the rest would be unstea-
dy, uncertain, useless, and perhaps dangerous, would
be to shake off the yoke of England. Portugal, in
her present situation, cannot subsist without foreign
commodities; therefore, it is her interest to promote
the greatest competition of sellers she possibly can, in
order to reduce the price of what she is obliged to
buy. As it is no less the interest of the Portuguese to
dispose of the overplus of their own produce and that
of the colonies, they ought, for the same reason, to invite as many purchasers as possible to their harbours,
to enhance the price, and increase the quantity of
their exports. These political measures are certainly
liable to no objection.

By the treaty of 1703, the Portuguese are only
obliged to permit the importation of woollen goods
from England, on the terms stipulated before the prohibition. They might grant the same privilege to
other nations, without incurring the reproach of having broken their engagement. A liberty granted to

B O O K one nation was never interpreted as an exclufive and
IX. perpetual privilege, that could deprive the prince who
granted it of his right of extending it to other nations.
He muft neceffarily be the judge of what fuits his own
kingdom. It is not eafy to conceive what rational objection a Britifh miniftry could make to a king of Portugal who fhould tell them, I will encourage merchants
to come to my dominions, who will feed and clothe
my fubjects as cheap and cheaper than you, merchants
who will take the produce of my colonies, from whence
you will receive nothing but gold.

We may judge of the effect this wife conduct would
have, by the events that have taken place, independent of this fpirited refolution. It appears from the
regifters of the cuftoms, that in the fpace of five years,
from 1762 to 1766 inclufively, England, which, till
very lately, engroffed the whole trade of Portugal, hath
only fent there goods to the value of 95,613,547 livres
10 fous [3,983,897l. 16s. 3d.], and hath received commodities to the amount of 37,761,075 livres [1,573,378l.
2s. 6d.]; fo that the balance in money hath been but
57,692,475 livres [2,403,853l. 2s. 6d.].

The circumftance which deceives all Europe, with
regard to the extent of the Englifh trade, is, that all
the gold of Brazil is conveyed by the road of the
Thames. This feems to be a natural and neceffary
confequence of the affairs carried on by that nation.
But the truth is, that metals are not allowed to go out
of Portugal, and, therefore, can only be brought away
by men of war, which are not liable to be fearched;
that Great Britain fends two every week, as regularly
as the fea will permit; and that thefe fhips bring the
riches of all nations into their ifland, from whence the
merchants, difperfed in the feveral countries, receive
them, either in kind, or in bills of exchange, paying
one *per cent.*

The Britifh miniftry, who are not the dupes of thefe
dazzling appearances, and are but too fenfible of the
diminution of this moft valuable branch of their trade,
have, for fome time paft, taken incredible pains to re-

ſtore it to its former ſtate. Their endeavours will ne- B O O K
ver ſucceed, becauſe this is one of thoſe events which ___IX.___
are not within the reach of political wiſdom. If the
evil aroſe from favours granted to rival nations, or if
England had been debarred from her former privileges, ſome well-conducted negotiations might occaſion a new revolution. But the court of Liſbon hath
never varied its conduct neither with Great Britain
nor with other ſtates. Her ſubjects have had no other
inducement to give the preference to the merchandiſe
brought them from all parts of Europe, than becauſe
thoſe of their former friends were ſo loaded with taxes,
that they bore an exorbitant price. The Portugueſe
will procure many articles at a ſtill more reaſonable
rate, whenever their government ſhall eſtabliſh a perfect equality in their ports between all nations.

The court of Liſbon, after removing, in ſome meaſure, the diſadvantages of their trade, which is merely
paſſive, ſhould endeavour to make it active. Their
miniſters, in conformity with the prevailing taſte of
the age, have already eſtabliſhed ſome manufactures
of ſilk, of cotton, and of ſteel. We think that they
ought to have begun by reſuming the cultures that
have been dropped, and by reanimating thoſe that are
languid.

The climate of Portugal is favourable to the production of ſilk, of which there was formerly great
plenty. The baptized Jews made it their buſineſs to
breed worms, and to prepare the ſilk, till they were
perſecuted by the inquiſition, which was ſtill more ſevere and more powerful under the houſe of Braganza,
than it had ever been under the Spaniſh dominion.
Moſt of the manufacturers fled to the kingdom of Valencia; and thoſe who ſold the produce of their labours removed, with their effects, to England and Holland, which improved the activity of both thoſe countries. This diſperſion was the ruin of the ſilk trade in
Portugal ſo that no trace of it remains at preſent;
but it might be reſumed.

The next cultivation that ought to be attended to,

B O O K is that of the olive tree. It is now carried on, and
   IX.   constantly supplies all the oil that is wanted for home
consumption, beside a small quantity every year for
exportation; but this is not sufficient. It would be
an easy matter for Portugal to share, in a more direct
manner, with other nations, the profits they derive
from this production, which is wholly confined to the
southern provinces of Europe.

Their wool is likewise capable of improvement.
Though it be inferior to that of Spain, the French,
the Dutch, and even the English, buy up twelve or
thirteen thousand quintals of it every year, and would
purchase a greater quantity, if it were brought to market. Those who have travelled through Portugal,
with that spirit of observation which enables men to
form a right judgment of things, are of opinion that
double the quantity might be obtained, without injuring the other branches of industry; and that, on the
contrary, it might tend to their improvement.

The trade of salt seems to have been more closely
attended to. The North annually takes off a hundred
and fifty thousand tons, which may cost 1,500,000 livres [62,500l.]. It is corrosive, and takes off from
the weight and flavour of our food; but hath the advantage of preserving fish and meat longer than French
salt. This property will occasion a greater demand for
it, in proportion as the navigation of the country is extended.

The Portuguese found a greater vent for their wines
than might have been expected from their flavour and
quality. Particular circumstances had rendered them
most commonly used in the North of Europe and of
America. It was impossible to foresee, that the court
of Lisbon itself would put a stop to the sale of them.
The order for rooting up the vines in Portugal could
only be dictated by private interest. The pretence
for so extraordinary a law is so absurd, that no one has
given credit to it. It is very well known, that the
ground where the vines have stood can never be fit
for the culture of corn.

But if this were ever fo practicable, it would ftill be an unwarrantable infringement of the facred and un-alienable right of property. In a monaftery, every thing belongs to all: nothing is the property of any individual, but the joint property of the whole com-munity: it is one fingle animal with twenty, thirty, forty, a thoufand, or ten thoufand heads. But it is not the fame in fociety. Here every individual hath the difpofal of himfelf and of his property: he poffeffes a fhare of the general wealth, which he is abfolute mafter of, and may ufe, or even abufe, as he thinks proper. A private man muft be at liberty to let his ground lie fallow, if he choofes it, without the inter-vention of adminiftration. If government fhould af-fume a right to judge of the abufe of property, it would foon take upon itfelf to judge of the ufe of it; and then every true idea of liberty and property will be deftroy-ed. If it can require me to employ my own property according to its fancy; if it fhould inflict punifhments on my difobedience, my negligence, or my folly, and that, under pretence of general and public utility, I am no longer abfolute mafter of my own, I am only an adminiftrator, who is to be directed by the will of another. The man who lives in fociety muft, in this refpect, be left at liberty to be a bad citizen, becaufe he will foon be feverely punifhed by poverty, and by contempt, which is worfe than poverty. He who burns his own corn, or throws his money away, is a fool too rarely to be met with, to make it neceffary to bind him by prohibitive laws, which would be injuri-ous in themfelves, by their infringement of the uni-verfal and facred idea of property. In every well-re-gulated conftitution, the bufinefs of the magiftrate muft be confined to what concerns the public fafety, inward tranquillity, the conduct of the army, and the obferv-ance of the laws. Wherever authority is extended be-yond this, we may affirm that the people are expofed to oppreffion. If we take a furvey of all ages and na-tions, that great and fublime idea of public utility will prefent itfelf to our imagination under the fym-

BOOK IX.

BOOK
IX.

bolical figure of a Hercules, crufhing one part of the people with his club, amidft the fhouts and acclamations of the other part, who are not fenfible that they are foon to fall under the fame ftrokes.

To return to Portugal: that country ftands in need of other meafures than have hitherto been purfued, to reftore the culture of corn; it is in fo languid a ftate, that the Portuguefe annually import three-fourths of the corn they confume. They never, perhaps, will be able to gather their whole fubfiftence from a foil which is not fufficiently well watered; but it behoves them to leffen, as much as they poffibly can, their dependence upon foreign fuccours. The population is fufficient to carry on the labours with fpirit, fince, by allowing four perfons and a half to each fire-fide, it amounts to one million nine hundred and fixty thoufand fouls, exclufive of the monks.

The court of Lifbon would lie under a fatal miftake, if they fhould imagine that time alone will bring about fo great a revolution. It behoves them to pave the way for it, by a complete reformation of the taxes, which have never been well regulated fince the foundation of the monarchy, and the confufion of which increafes every year. When the impediments are removed, every kind of encouragement muft be given. One of the moft fatal prejudices, and moft deftructive of the happinefs of men and the profperity of nations, is that which fuppofes that men only are wanting for the purpofes of agriculture. The experience of all ages hath fhown, that much cannot be required of the earth, till much hath been beftowed upon it. There are, in all Portugal, very few farmers who are able to advance the neceffary fums. Government fhould, therefore, affift them. A revenue of 46,884,531 livres [1,953,523l. 2s. 6d.], properly difpenfed, would facilitate this liberality, which is frequently more economical than the moft fordid avarice.

This firft change will be productive of others. The arts neceffary to agriculture will infallibly rife and grow up with it. Induftry will extend its feveral branches, and Portugal will no longer exhibit an in- stance of a savage people in the midst of civilized nations. The citizen will no longer be forced to devote himself to celibacy, or to leave his country in search of employment. Commodious houses will be erected upon ruins ; and manufactures supply the place of convents. The subjects of this almost ruined state, which now resemble those scattered and solitary shrubs that are found upon the soil of the richest mines, will no longer be reduced to those necessities they now experience, notwithstanding their mountains and rivers of gold. The wealth of the state will be kept in constant circulation, and will no longer be buried in the churches. Superstition will be banished, together with ignorance, despair, and indolence. Those who have no other object in view, but to commit excesses, and expiate them, who are fond of miracles and magic arts, will then be inflamed with public spirit. The nation, freed from its fetters, and restored to its natural activity, will exert itself with a spirit worthy of its former exploits.

Portugal will recollect, that she was indebted to her navy for her opulence, her glory, and her strength, and will attend to the means of restoring it. It will no longer be reduced to seventeen men of war, to twenty-five warlike ships of smaller rates, and about a hundred merchantmen, from six to eight hundred tons burden, which are still in a more ruinous state. Her population, reduced to one million nine hundred and sixty thousand souls, will increase and fill her harbours and roads with active fleets. The revival of her navy will be doubtless difficult for a power, whose flag is not known on any of the European seas, and which, for a century past, has given up her navigation to any power that would attend to it ; but every obstacle will be surmounted by a wise and prudent government. When once it carries on all the navigation that should belong to it, considerable sums will be retained in the kingdom, which are now constantly expended for freight.

BOOK IX.

This change will extend its influence to the islands that are dependent on the crown. Madeira, the annual exports of which amount to 4,658,800 livres [194,116l. 13s. 4d.], will extend its labour, its prosperity, and its riches. The Azores will be still more improved. We know that this Archipelago, consisting of nine islands, of which Tercera is the principal, hath no more than one hundred and forty-two thousand inhabitants; and sells at present, to the mother-country, to Brazil, and to North America, its wines, its linens, its corn, and its cattle, to the amount only of 2,440,000 livres [101,666l. 13s. 4d.]. Even the Cape de Verde islands, notwithstanding the frequent droughts they experience, will be able to multiply their mules, and more especially to cultivate the perella, that species of grass of the colour of moss, which the North of Europe employs with so much advantage in dyeing. The government will not confine themselves to the encouragement in their possessions, of the cultures only that are known there; they will take care to introduce new ones, which the fertility of the soil, and the temperature and variety of the climate, seem incessantly to require.

These new improvements will be principally felt in Brazil, that great colony, which hath never been what it ought.

Before the year 1525, it received only some banished persons, without either morals or fortune.

The grandees, who at this period obtained provinces there, made it a scene of carnage and destruction. For the space of sixty years, there was a continual struggle between the Portuguese, who wished to enslave all; and the Indians, who refused to bear the chains that were intended for them, or who broke them after they had been obliged to submit to them.

Even the labours of a few Brazilians, who were kept under the yoke by a watchful exertion of tyranny, were inconsiderable. Those of the Europeans were nothing, because they would have thought themselves degraded by slavish occupations. The only suc-

cefs that could be expected was from the Negroes; BOOK
but they did not begin to multiply there till towards IX.
the year 15▪0.

Ten years after this, Portugal was enflaved; and we
may readily fuppofe that the Spanifh government,
which fuffered its own ancient poffeffions in the other
hemifphere to fall into confufion, did not exert itfelf
in improving the colonies of a nation, which, though
fubdued, ftill excited its fufpicions.

The long and bloody wars which Brazil had to fuftain againft the Dutch retarded its progrefs in every
particular.

This was alfo again impeded, by the revolution
which freed Portugal from the yoke of Spain, while
it kept the two nations in arms during eighteen years.

While thefe contefts were fubfifting, the European
nations that had formed fettlements in America began
to cultivate there productions, which till that time had
been peculiar to Brazil. This competition lowered
the price of them; and the colony, difcouraged, did
not export more than half of what they previoufly
fold. So great a misfortune warned the miniftry of
the neceffity of freeing thefe commodities from the
taxes with which they were laden at their entrance into the mother-country. The difcovery of the mines
occafioned thefe objects to be neglected, which, from
that time, appeared to be lefs important than they
really were.

Gold and diamonds, which are articles of value
merely by convention, were themfelves prejudicial to
cultures, which they might have encouraged. The
hopes of making a brilliant fortune, by collecting
thefe fugitive and precarious riches, determined a great
number of proprietors to abandon their plantations.

This fatal illufion began to be diffipated, when the
fyftem of monopolies put a ftop to the inclination generally fhown, of refuming a plan which was more
fafe, and even more lucrative, than that which had at
firft fo much inflamed the imaginations of men.

The laft difputes with Spain were, in a word, a new

source of defolation to the colony. The inhabitants
were compelled by violence to quit their labours; loans
were extorted from them without intereſt, for which
they have not yet been reimburſed; they were expoſed to the utmoſt outrages of the moſt barbarous
deſpotiſm.

At preſent, that theſe obſtacles to every kind of
good are moſt of them removed, the riches which Brazil offers in vain, for three centuries paſt, are no longer
to be rejected. The climate is wholeſome in that part
of the New World; the harbours are numerous; and
the coaſts, which are of eaſy acceſs, are generally fertile. The inland part of the country, which is ſtill
more fruitful, and interſected by a great number of
navigable rivers, may be cultivated for the wants or
for the luxuries of Europe. All the productions peculiar to America thrive there, notwithſtanding the
havock made by the ants, and without apprehenſion
of ſeeing them deſtroyed by thoſe terrible hurricanes
and by thoſe devouring droughts which ſo frequently
lay waſte the beſt iſlands of this hemiſphere. It gives
encouragement to labour, from the plenty of proviſions, of cattle, and of ſlaves: nothing is wanting to
make it one of the fineſt eſtabliſhments upon the face
of the globe.

It will become ſo, when it ſhall be freed from that
number of impoſts, and from that multitude of contractors which keep it in a ſtate of humiliation and oppreſſion, when its activity ſhall no longer be reſtrained
by numberleſs monopolies; when the price of the merchandiſe conveyed to it ſhall not be doubled by the
taxes impoſed upon them; when its productions ſhall
pay no more duties, or ſhall only pay ſuch as are not
more conſiderable than thoſe of its competitors; when
its intercourſe with the other national poſſeſſions ſhall
have been diſencumbered from the ſhackles which
confine it; when the Eaſt Indies ſhall be laid open to
it, and when it ſhall be permitted to draw from its own
produce the money required to carry on this new connection.

The colony hath hands fufficient to multiply and to extend thefe labours. At the time of our writing, it reckons one hundred feventy-fix thoufand and twenty-eight white men ; three hundred forty-feven thoufand eight hundred and fifty-eight flaves ; two hundred feventy-eight thoufand three hundred and forty-nine Indians ; which together forms a population of eight hundred and two thoufand two hundred and thirty-five perfons. The number of favages, ftill wandering about in the Brazils, is computed at two hundred thou-fand. Perhaps it might not be impoffible to induce them to acknowledge the authority of the court of Lifbon ; but this would not be attended with much advantage, unlefs directors, more enlightened than their predeceffors, fhould contrive methods that have efcap-ed the reflection of men for three centuries paft.

A more certain method of increafing the mafs of productions, would be to admit into the Brazils all foreigners who would undertake the cultivation of them ; an infinite number of Americans, Englifh, French, or Dutch, whofe plantations are exhaufted ; and many Europeans prompted by the ardent defire, at prefent grown fo common, of making a rapid for-tune, would convey their activity, their induftry, and their capitals into the country. Thefe enterprifing men would introduce a better fpirit into the colony, and would infufe into the degenerate race of the Por-tuguefe Creoles, that kind of animation which they have loft for fo long a time.

This order of things might be eftablifhed without prejudice to any other intereft. Two thirds of the borders of the great rivers are cultivated. Thefe vir-gin lands belong to the crown, whofe fyftem it hath always been to grant gratuitoufly one league of terri-tory, under the exprefs condition of cultivating it in a given time. By diftributing thefe domains to their new fubjects, they would not fpoil their old ones, and they would increafe their cultures, as well as the num-ber of their defenders.

But in order to accelerate the advantages of this

new plan, it would be neceſſary to efface even the
ſlighteſt veſtige of the inquiſition, that horrible tribunal, the very name of which makes all people ſhudder
who have not entirely given up their reaſon. This
would even be a matter of little importance, if at the
ſame time the influence of the clergy were not alſo
diminiſhed in the public deliberations and in the affairs
of individuals.

Some ſtates have been known to favour the corruption of prieſts, in order to weaken the aſcendant that
ſuperſtition gives them over the minds of the people.
That this method is not always infallible, appears from
what has happened in the Brazils, nor is this execrable
policy reconcileable with the principles of morality.
It would be more ſecure and more eligible to open the
doors of the ſanctuary to all the citizens without diſtinction. Philip II. when he became maſter of Portugal, enacted, that they ſhould be ſhut againſt all ſuch
whoſe blood was tainted with any mixture with Jews,
Heretics, or Negroes. This diſtinction hath given a
dangerous ſuperiority to a ſet of men who were already
too powerful. It hath been aboliſhed in the African ſettlements; and why ſhould it be continued in
America? Why, after taking from the clergy the authority they derived from their birth, ſhould they not
be abridged of the power they aſſume on account of
their riches?

Some politicians have aſſerted, that no government
ought ever to appoint a fixed income for the clergy,
but that their ſpiritual ſervices ſhould be paid by thoſe
who have recourſe to them. That this method would
excite their zeal and vigilance. That they would grow
daily more expert in the care of ſouls by experience,
ſtudy, and application. Theſe ſtateſmen have been
oppoſed by philoſophers, who maintained that an economy which would tend to increaſe the activity of the
clergy, would be fatal to public tranquillity; and that
it was better to lull that ambitious body into idleneſs,
than to give it new ſtrength. It is obſerved, ſay they,
that churches and religious houſes, which have no

settled income, are so many repositories of superstition, B O O K
maintained at the expence of the lower class of people, IX.
where saints, miracles, relics, and all the inventions with
which imposture hath loaded religion, are made. So
that it would be a benefit to society, if the clergy had
a stated provision; but so moderate, as to restrain the
ambition of the body and the number of its members.
Poverty makes them fanatical; opulence independent;
and both concur to render them seditious.

Such at least was the opinion of a philosopher, who
said to a great monarch : There is a powerful body in
your dominions, which hath assumed a power of sus-
pending the labour of your subjects, whenever it thinks
proper to call them into its temples. This body is
authorised to speak to them a hundred times a-year,
and to speak in the name of God. It tells them that
the most powerful sovereign is no more in the sight of
the Supreme Being than the meanest slave ; and that,
as it is inspired by the Creator of all things, it is to be
believed in preference to the masters of the world. The
effects of such a system threaten the total subversion of
society, unless the ministers of religion are made dependent on the magistrate ; and they will never be effectually so, unless they derive their subsistence from
him. This is the only way to establish a harmony between the oracles of heaven and the maxims of government. It is the business of a prudent administration to bring, without disturbances or commotions, the
clergy to that state in which they will be able to do
good, without having it in their power to do mischief.

Till the court of Lisbon hath attained this salutary
end, all projects of reformation will be ineffectual. The
defects of ecclesiastical government will still subsist,
notwithstanding all endeavours to reform them. The
clergy must be brought to depend upon the magistrate,
before the Portuguese who live in Brazil can venture
to oppose their tyranny. Perhaps even the prejudices
these inhabitants have imbibed from a faulty and mo-
nastic education, may be too deeply rooted in their
minds, to be ever eradicated. These enlightened views

BOOK IX. feem to be referved for the next generation. This revolution might be haftened, by obliging the chief proprietors to fend their children to Europe for education, and by reforming the plan of public education in
Portugal.

All ideas are eafily impreffed upon tender organs.
The foul, without experience as without reflection,
readily admits truth and falfehood in matters of opinion, and equally adopts what is either conducive or
prejudicial to the public welfare. Young people may
be taught to value or depreciate their own reafon; to
make ufe of it, or to neglect it; to confider it as their
beft guide, or to miftruft its powers. Fathers obftinately defend the abfurdities they were taught in their
infancy; their children will be as fond of the leading
principles in which they have been trained. They will
bring back into Brazil notions of religion, morality,
adminiftration, commerce, and agriculture. The mother-country will confer places of truft on them alone.
They will then exert the talents they have acquired,
and the face of the colony will be totally changed.
Writers who fpeak of it, will no longer lament the
idlenefs, the ignorance, the blunders, the fuperftitions
which have been the ground-work of its adminiftration. The hiftory of this colony will no longer be a
fatire upon it.

Whether the court of Lifbon ought to put a stop to their projects of reformation from the apprehen-fion of a rupture with Eng-land. The fear of incenfing Great Britain muft not protract
thefe happy alterations one fingle moment. The mo-
tives which, perhaps, have prevented them hitherto,
are but prejudices, which will be removed upon the
flighteft examination. There are numberlefs political
errors, which, once adopted, become principles. Such
is the prevailing notion at the court of Lifbon, that the
ftate cannot exift or profper but by means of the Englifh. It is forgotten that the Portuguefe monarchy
was formed without the help of other nations; that
during the whole time of their contefts with the Moors,
they were fupported by no foreign power; that their
greatnefs had been increafing for three centuries fucceffively, when they extended their dominion over

Africa and the Eaſt and Weſt Indies by their own B O O K
ſtrength. All theſe great revolutions were performed IX.
by the Portugueſe alone. Was it neceſſary then that
this nation ſhould diſcover a great treaſure, and be a
proprietor of rich mines, merely to ſuggeſt the idea of
its being unable to ſupport itſelf? Are the Portugueſe
to be compared to thoſe fooliſh individuals, whoſe
heads are turned by the embarraſſment which their
newly-acquired riches occaſion?

No nation ought to ſubmit to be protected. If the
people are wiſe, they will have forces relative to their
ſituation, and will never have more enemies than they
are able to withſtand. Unleſs their ambition be unbounded, they have allies, who, for their own ſakes,
will warmly and faithfully ſupport their intereſt. This
general truth is peculiarly applicable to thoſe ſtates
that are poſſeſſed of mines. It is the intereſt of all
other nations to be in amity with them ; and, if there
be occaſion for it, they will all unite for their preſervation. Let Portugal but hold the balance even between all the powers of Europe, and they will form
an impenetrable barrier around her. England herſelf,
though deprived of the preference ſhe hath too long
enjoyed, will ſtill ſupport a nation whoſe independence
is eſſential to the balance of power in Europe. All
nations would quickly join in one common cauſe, if
Spain ſhould ever be ſo mad for conqueſt, as to attempt any thing againſt Portugal. Never would the
jealous, reſtleſs, and quick-ſighted policy of our age,
ſuffer all the treaſures of the New World to be in the
ſame hands, or that one houſe ſhould be ſo powerful
in America, as to threaten the liberties of Europe.

This ſecurity, however, ſhould not induce the court
of Liſbon to neglect the means of their own preſervation, as they did when they truſted to the Britiſh arms
for their defence, or indolently reſted on the ſupine-
neſs of their neighbours ; when deſtitute of land or
ſea forces, they were accounted as nothing in the political ſyſtem, which is the greateſt diſgrace that can
befal a nation. If the Portugueſe will regain the con-

fequence they have loft, they muft put themfelves in
fuch a ftate, as not to be afraid of war, and even to
declare it themfelves, if their rights or their fafety
fhould require it. It is not always an advantage to a
nation to continue in peace, when all the reft are in
arms. In the political as in the natural world, a great
event will have very extenfive effects. The rife or fall
of one empire will affect all the reft. Even thofe which
are furtheft removed from the feat of war, are fometimes the victims of their moderation or of their weaknefs. Thefe maxims are directly applicable to Portugal, particularly at this juncture, when the example of
her neighbours, the critical fituation of her haughty
allies, the folicitations of the powers who are jealous
of her friendfhip; in fhort, every thing calls upon her
to roufe, and to exert herfelf.

If the Portuguefe will not at length frequent the
feas, where alone they can diftinguifh themfelves, and
from whence they muft derive their profperity; if
they do not appear with a powerful force at the extremity of Europe, where nature hath fo happily placed them; their fate is decided, the monarchy is at an
end. They will fall again into the chains they had
fhaken off for a moment, as a lion that fhould drop
afleep at the door of his den, after he had broken it
open. The little circulation there is ftill within, would
but indicate thofe feeble figns of life, which are the
fymptoms of approaching death. The few trifling regulations they might make from time to time, refpecting the finances, the police, commerce, and the navy,
whether at home or for the colonies, would be but
weak palliatives, which, by concealing their fituation,
would make it only the more dangerous.

Is it reafon-
ably to be
expected
that Portu-
gal will im-
prove its
ftate and
that of its
colonies? It cannot be denied that Portugal hath fuffered the
moft favourable opportunity that could have offered
of refuming her former fplendour to efcape. They are
not politics alone that prepare revolutions. Some deftructive phenomenon may change the face of an empire. The earthquake of the firft of November 1755,
which overthrew the capital of Portugal, ought to have

reſtored the kingdom. The deſtruction of a proud city
is often the preſervation of a whole ſtate, as the opulence of one man may be the ruin of thouſands. State-
ly edifices might be ſubverted; effects, moſtly belonging to foreigners, might be deſtroyed; idle, debauch-
ed, and corrupt men, might be buried under heaps of
ruins, without affecting the public welfare. The earth,
in a tranſient fit of rage, had only taken what ſhe was
able to reſtore; and the gulfs ſhe opened under one
city, were already digged for the foundations of another.

But we cannot flatter ourſelves with the hopes of
future improvements, while we do not ſee a better order of things, a new ſtate, and a new people, a better
management riſing out of the ruins of Liſbon. The
nation that is not improved by a great cataſtrophe is
ruined without reſource, or the period of its reſtoration is reſerved for ſuch diſtant ages, that it is probable
it will ſooner be annihilated than it can be regenerated. May Heaven preſerve Portugal from this fatal
event! May it remove from my mind the preſage
which cannot be impreſſed upon it without plunging
me into the deepeſt affliction! But at this inſtant I
cannot conceal from myſelf, that as much as the great
ſhocks of nature give energy to enlightened minds, ſo
much do they depreſs thoſe that are vitiated by the
habit of ignorance and ſuperſtition. Government,
which every where takes advantage of the credulity
of the people, and which nothing can divert from the
ſettled purpoſe of extending the boundaries of authority, became more encroaching at the very inſtant that
the nation grew more timorous. Men of bold ſpirits
oppreſſed thoſe that were weak; and the epocha of
that great phenomenon turned out to be the epocha
of accumulated ſlavery; a melancholy but common
effect of the cataſtrophes of nature. They uſually
make men a prey to the artifices of thoſe who are ambitious of ruling over them. Then it is that they take
large ſtrides, by repeated acts of arbitrary power; whether it be that thoſe who govern do really believe that

B O O K the people were born to obey, or whether they think,
IX.   that, by extending their own power, they increafe the
ftrength of the public.   Thofe falfe politicians are not
aware, that, with fuch principles, a ftate is like an
over-ftrained fpring, which will break at laft, and re-
coil againft the hand that bends it.   The prefent fituation of the continent of South America but too plainly evinces the juftnefs of this comparifon.   Let us now
proceed to fhow the effects of a different conduct in
the American iflands.

BOOK X.

Settlement of the European nations in the great Archipelago of America.

B O O K HITHERTO we have been only proceeding from
X.   one fcene of horror to another, in following the fteps
Confidera- of the Spaniards and of the Portuguefe.   Let us now
tions upon fee whether the Englifh, French, Hollanders, and
the conduct
of all the Danes, whom we are going to accompany into the
European iflands, have fhown themfelves lefs favage than thofe
nations in
the New who took poffeffion of the continent.   Will the inha-
World. bitants of thefe limited fpaces be expofed to the deplorable deftiny of the Peruvians, of the Mexicans,
and of the Brazilians?   Is it poffible that civilized men,
who have all lived in their country under forms of government, if not wife, at leaft ancient; who have all
been bred up in places where they were inftructed
with the leffons, and fometimes with the example of
virtue; who were all brought up in the midft of polifhed cities, in which a rigid exercife of juftice muft
have accuftomed them to refpect their fellow-creatures; is it poffible that all fuch men, without exception, fhould purfue a line of conduct equally contrary
to the principles of humanity, to their intereft, to their
fafety, and to the firft dawnings of reafon; and that
they fhould continue to become more barbarous than
the favage?   Shall I for ever be reduced to the necef-

fity of prefenting none but horrid images? Good God! For what an office was I deftined? This change of character, in the European who quits his country, is a phenomenon of fo extraordinary a nature, the imagination is fo deeply affected with it, that, while it attends to it with aftonifhment, reflection tortures itfelf in endeavouring to find out the principle of it, whether it exift in human nature in general, or in the peculiar character of the navigators, or in the circumftances preceding or pofterior to the event.

It is a queftion which naturally occurs, Whether a man who is freed, by whatfoever caufe, from the reftraint of the laws, be not more wicked than the man who hath never felt this reftraint? Perfons who are fufficiently diffatisfied with their lot, fufficiently deprived of refources in their own country, fufficiently poor, or fufficiently ambitious to entertain a contempt for life, and to expofe themfelves to infinite dangers and labours, upon the precarious hope of making a rapid fortune, do they not carry about with them the fatal feeds of a fpirit of depredation, which muft unavoidably have manifefted itfelf with inconceivable rapidity and violence when they came into another climate, far from the effects of public refentment, and when they were no longer awed by the prefence of their fellow-citizens, or reftrained by fhame or fear? Doth not the hiftory of all focieties prove to us, that thofe men on whom nature hath beftowed an extraordinary degree of energy, are moft commonly villains? The danger of a long ftay, and the neceffity of a fpeedy return, added to the defire of juftifying the expences incurred in the enterprife, by a difplay of the riches of the lately difcovered countries, muft neceffarily have occafioned and accelerated the violent fteps taken to acquire the poffeffion of them. Did not the chiefs of the enterprife, and their companions, terrified by the dangers they had undergone, by thofe which they were ftill to undergo, and by the miferies they had fuffered, did they not determine to make themfelves amends for their fufferings, like men who were refolv-

B O O K ed not to expose themselves to them a second time?
X. Did the idea of forming a colony in those distant regions, and of increasing the dominions of their sovereign with them, ever present itself distinctly to the
minds of these first adventurers; and did not the New
World rather appear to them as a rich prey that was
to be devoured, than as a conquest which they ought
to protect? Was not the mischief begun by these atrocious motives, perpetuated, sometimes by the indifference of ministers, and sometimes by the divisions between the European nations; and was it not arrived
to the utmost pitch, when times of tranquillity inspired our governments with more rational principles?
Had the first deputies, to whom the authority and inspection of those countries had been intrusted, or could
they have the knowledge and the virtue requisite to
make themselves beloved by the natives, to conciliate
their respect and confidence, and to establish a system
of police and laws among them? Did they not, on the
contrary, carry along with them, to those distant regions, the same thirst of gold which had laid them
waste? Could it be expected, that, at the origin of
these settlements, a plan of administration could be
formed, which the experience of several centuries hath
not been capable of establishing? Is it possible, even
in our days, to rule nations which are separated by
immense seas from the mother-country, in the same
manner as subjects who are situated immediately under the eye of the sovereign? Since distant posts are
never solicited and filled, unless by indigent, rapacious
men, without talents or morals, strangers to all senti-
ment of honour, and to every idea of equity, the refuse of the higher ranks of the state, must we not consider the splendour of the colonies, in after-times, as a
chimerical notion; and will not the future happiness
of these regions be a phenomenon still more surprising
than their first devastation was?

Accursed, therefore, be the moment of their discovery! And you, European sovereigns, what motive
can excite your jealous ambition for possessions, the

mifery of which you can only perpetuate? And why B O O K
X.
do ye not reftore them to themfelves, if ye defpair of
making them happy? I have, more than once, ventured, in the courfe of this work, to point out to you
the means of accomplifhing this: but I am much
afraid that my voice hath only exclaimed, and will
only exclaim in the defert.

America contains, between the eighth and the thir-
ty-fecond degree of northern latitude, the moft numerous, extenfive, and rich Archipelago, the ocean hath
yet difplayed to the curiofity, the induftry, and avidity of the Europeans. The iflands that compofe it are
known, fince the difcovery of the New World, by the
name of the Caribbees. Thofe that lie neareft the
eaft have been called the Windward Iflands, the others
the Leeward, on account of the wind's blowing generally from the eaftern point in thofe quarters. They
form a continued chain, one end of which feems to be
attached to the continent near the Gulf of Maracaybo,
the other to clofe the entrance of the Gulf of Mexico.
They may, perhaps, with fome degree of reafon, be
confidered as the tops of very high mountains formerly belonging to the continent, and which have been
changed into iflands, by fome revolution that hath laid
all the flat country under water.

All the iflands of the world feem to have been detached from the continent by fubterraneous fires or
earthquakes.

The celebrated Atlantica, the very name of which Is it proba-
ble that the
American
hath been buried in oblivion fome thoufand years ago,
was a large tract of land fituated between Africa and iflandshave
been de-
America. Several circumftances render it probable tachedfrom
that England was formerly a part of France; and Si- the neigh-
cily hath evidently been detached from Italy. The bouring
continent?
Cape de Verde iflands, the Azores, Madeira, and the
Canaries, muft have been part of the neighbouring
continents, or of others that have been deftroyed.
The late obfervations of Englifh navigators leave us
fcarce any room to doubt that all the iflands of the
South Sea formerly compofed one entire continent.

BOOK New Zealand, the largest of them, is full of mountains
  X.   on which may be perceived the marks of extinguished
volcanos. Its inhabitants are neither beardless nor
copper-coloured, as those of America; and, though
they be separated six hundred and eighty leagues from
each other, they speak the same language as the natives of the island of Otaheite, discovered a few years
ago.

Indisputable monuments evince that such changes
have happened, of which the attentive naturalist every
where perceives some traces still remaining. Shells of
every kind, corals, beds of oysters, sea-fish, entire or
broken, regularly heaped up in every quarter of the
globe, in places the most distant from the sea, in the
bowels and on the surfaces of mountains; the vari-
ableness of the continent, subject to all the changes
of the ocean, by which it is constantly beaten, worn
away, or subverted: while at a distance, perhaps, on
one side it loses immense tracts of land; on the other
discovers to us new countries, and long banks of sand
heaped up before those cities that formerly were celebrated sea-ports: the horizontal and parallel position
of the strata of the earth, and of marine productions
collected and heaped up alternately in the same order,
composed of the same materials, that are regularly ce-
mented by the constant and successive exertion of the
same cause: the correspondent similarity observable
between such coasts as are separated by an arm of the
sea; on one side of which may be perceived salient
angles opposite to re-entering angles on the other; on
the right hand, beds of the same kind of sand, or similar petrifactions, disposed on a level with similar strata
extending to the left: the direction of mountains and
rivers towards the sea as to their common origin: the
formation of hills and valleys, on which this immense
body of fluid hath, as it were, stamped indelible marks
of its undulations: all these several circumstances at-
test, that the ocean hath broken its natural limits, or,
perhaps, that its limits have never been insurmount-
able; and that varying the surface of the globe, ac-

cording to the irregularity of its own motions, it hath B o o κ
alternately taken the earth from its inhabitants, and   x.
reſtored it to them again. Hence thoſe ſucceſſive,
though never univerſal, deluges that have covered the
face of the earth, but not rendered it totally inviſible
to us at once ; for the waters, acting at the ſame time
in the cavities and on the ſurface of the globe, cannot
poſſibly increaſe the depth of their beds, without di-
miniſhing their breadth ; or overflow on one ſide,
without leaving dry land on the other ; nor can we
conceive any alteration in the whole ſyſtem that can
poſſibly have made all the mountains diſappear at
once, and occaſioned the ſea to riſe above their ſummits. What a ſudden transformation muſt have forced all the rocks and every ſolid particle of matter to
the centre of the earth, to draw out of its inmoſt re-
ceſſes and channels all thoſe fluids which animate it ;
and thus blending its ſeveral elements together, produce a maſs of waters and uſeleſs germina floating in
the air ? Is it not enough that each hemiſphere alternately becomes a prey to the devaſtations of the ocean?
Such conſtant ſhocks as theſe have doubtleſs ſo long
concealed from us the New World, and, perhaps, ſwallowed up that continent, which, as it is imagined, had
been only ſeparated from our own.

Whatever may be the ſecret cauſes of theſe particular revolutions, the general cauſe of which reſults from
the known and univerſal laws of motion, their effects,
however, will be always ſenſible to every man, who
hath the reſolution and ſagacity to perceive them.
They will be more particularly evident in regard to
the Caribbee Iſlands, if it can ever be proved that they
undergo violent ſhocks whenever the volcanos of the
Cordeleras throw out their contents, or when all Peru
is ſhaken. This Archipelago, as well as that of the
Eaſt Indies, ſituated nearly in the ſame degree of latitude, ſeems to be produced by the ſame cauſe ; namely, the motion of the ſea from eaſt to weſt: a motion
impreſſed by that which cauſes the earth's revolution
from weſt to eaſt ; more rapid at the equator, where

the globe of the earth, being more elevated, revolves
in a larger circle, and in a more agitated zone ; where
the ocean feems, as it were, willing to break through
all the boundaries nature oppofes to it, and, opening
to itfelf a free and uninterrupted courfe, forms the equinoctial line.

The direction of the Caribbee Iflands, beginning
from Tobago, is nearly North and N. N. W. This
direction is continued from one ifland to another, forming a line fomewhat curved towards the north-weft,
and ending at Antigua. In this place the line becomes
at once curved, and, extending itfelf in a ftraight direction to the W. and N. W. meets, in its courfe, with
Porto-Rico, St. Domingo, and Cuba, known by the
name of the Leeward Iflands, which are feparated from
each other by channels of various breadths. Some of
thefe are fix, others fifteen or twenty leagues broad ;
but the foundings, in all of them, are from a hundred
to a hundred and twenty or a hundred and fifty fathom. Between Grenada and St. Vincent's, there is
alfo a fmall Archipelago of thirty leagues, in which
fometimes the foundings are not ten fathom.

The mountains in the Caribbee Iflands run in the
fame direction as the iflands themfelves. This direction is fo regular, that if we were to confider the tops
of thefe mountains only, independent of their bafis,
they might be looked upon as a chain of hills belonging to the continent, of which Martinico would be the
moft north-wefterly promontory.

The fprings of water which flow from the mountains in the Windward Iflands run all in the weftern
part of thefe iflands. The whole eaftern coaft, that
which, according to our conjectures, hath always been
covered by the fea, is without any running water. No
fprings come down there from the mountains ; they
would, indeed, have been ufelefs, for, after having run
over a very fhort tract of land, and with great rapidity, they would have fallen into the fea.

In Porto-Rico, St. Domingo, and Cuba, there are
a few rivers which difcharge themfelves into the fea on

the northern fide, and the fources of which rife in the B O O K
mountains, running from eaft to weft, that is, through X.
the whole length of thefe iflands. Thefe rivers water
a confiderable extent of low country, which hath certainly never been covered by the fea. From the other
fide of the mountains facing the fouth, where the fea,
flowing with great impetuofity, leaves behind it marks
of its inundations, feveral rivers flow into thefe three
iflands, fome of which are confiderable enough to receive the largeft fhips.

Thefe obfervations, which feem to prove that the
fea hath feparated the Caribbee Iflands from the continent, are further confirmed by others of a different
kind, though equally conclufive in fupport of this conjecture. Tobago, Margaretta, and Trinidad, iflands
that are the neareft to the continent, produce, as well
as the Caribbees, trees, the wood of which is foft, and
wild cocoa. This particular fpecies is not to be found,
at leaft in any quantity, in the northern iflands. In
thefe the only wood we meet with is hard. Cuba, fituated at the other extremity of the Caribbees, abounds,
like Florida, from which, perhaps, it hath been feparated, with cedars and cyprefles, both equally ufeful
for the building of fhips.

The foil of the Caribbees confifts moftly of a layer
of clay or gravel, of different thicknefs; under which
is a bed of ftone or rock. The nature of fome of
thefe foils is better adapted to vegetation than others.
In thofe places where the clay is drier and more fri-
able, and mixes with the leaves and remains of plants,
a layer of earth is formed, of greater depth than where
the clay is moifter. The fand or gravel has different
properties, according to its peculiar nature; wherever
it is lefs hard, lefs compact, and lefs porous, fmall
pieces feparate themfelves from it; which, though
dry, preferve a certain degree of coolnefs ufeful to vegetation. This foil is called in America, a pumice-
ftone foil. Wherever the clay and gravel do not go
through fuch modifications, the foil becomes barren,
as foon as the layer, formed by the decompofition of

Nature of the foil of the Carib-bee iflands. Vegetables found there before the invafion.

the original plants, is deftroyed, from the neceffity
there is of weeding it, which too frequently expofes
its falts to the heat of the fun.   Hence, in thofe cultures which require lefs weeding, and where the plant
covers with its leaves the vegetable falts, there the fertility of the ground has been preferved.

When the Europeans landed at the Caribbee Iflands,
they found them covered with large trees, connected,
as it were, to one another by a fpecies of creeping
plant ; which, rifing up in the fame manner as the
ivy, wove itfelf around all the branches, and concealed them from the fight.   There was fo great a plenty
of this plant, and it grew fo thick, that it was impoffible to penetrate into the woods before it was cut
down.   From its great degree of flexibility it was called Liane.   In thefe forefts, as old as the world itfelf,
there were varieties of trees, which, from a fingular
partiality of nature, were very lofty, exceeding ftraight,
and without any excrefcences or defects.   The annual
fall and breaking down of the leaves, and the decay
of the trunks rotted away by time, formed a moift
fediment upon the ground ; which being cleared, occafioned a furprifing degree of vegetation in thofe
plants that were fubftituted to the trees that were rooted up.

In whatever foil thefe trees grew, their roots were
fcarcely two feet deep, and generally much lefs : though
they extended themfelves on the furface, in proportion
to the weight they had to fupport.   The exceffive
drynefs of the ground, where the moft plentiful rains
never penetrate very deep, as they are foon attracted by the fun-beams, and the conftant dews that
moiften the furface, made the roots of thefe plants extend themfelves horizontally, inftead of defcending per-
pendicularly, as they generally do in other climates.

The trees that grew on the tops of mountains and
in fteep places were very hard.   The fharpeft cutting
inftrument could fcarcely make any impreffion upon
them.   Such were the agouti, the palm-tree, the ba-
rata wood, which have fince been ufefully employed

in building. Such were the courbari, the acajou, B O O K the manchineel, and the iron-wood, which have been X. found fit for joiner's work. Such is the acoma, which being either put into the ground, or expofed to the air, is preferved for a long time without being attacked by the worms, or rotted by the damp. Such the maple, the trunk of which, being four or five feet in diameter, and the ftem from forty to fifty feet high, ferved to make a canoe of one fingle piece.

The valleys, which are rendered fertile by the mountains, are covered with foft wood. At the foot of thefe trees grow promifcuoufly thofe plants that the liberality of the foil produced for the fubfiftence of the natives of the country. Thofe in moft general ufe were the yam, the Caribbee cabbage, and the battata, the roots of which being tuberofe, like thofe of the potato, might equally afford a wholefome nourifhment. Nature, which appears to have eftablifhed a certain analogy between the characters of people and the provifions intended for their fupport, had provided the Caribbee Iflands with fuch vegetables as could not bear the heat of the fun, flourifhed beft in moift places, required no cultivation, and were renewed two or three times in the year. The iflanders did not thwart the free and fpontaneous operations of nature, by deftroying one of her productions, to give the greater vigour to another. The preparation of the vegetating falts was entirely left to the mere effect of the foil; nor did the natives pretend to fix the place and time of her fertility. They gathered, as chance threw in their way, or the feafon pointed out, fuch fruits as fpontaneoufly offered themfelves for their fupport. They had obferved, that the putrefaction of the weeds was neceffary to the reproduction of thofe plants that were moft ufeful to them.

The roots of thefe plants were never unwholefome; but they were infipid when raw, and had very little flavour even when boiled, unlefs they were feafoned with pimento. When mixed with ginger, and the acid juice of a plant fomewhat refembling our forrel, they

BOOK produced a ftrong liquor, which was the only com-
X. pound drink of the favages. The only art they made
ufe of in preparing it, was fuffering it to ferment fome
days in common water, expofed to the heat of the
fun.

Exclufive of this nourifhment, the iflands alfo fupplied the inhabitants with a great variety of fruits, but
very different from ours. The moft ufeful among
thefe was the banana. The root of the banana tree
is tuberofe and hairy. Its ftem, which is flender and
foft, grows to feven feet at its utmoft height, and is
eight inches in diameter: it is compofed of feveral
coats, or concentric fheaths, tolerably thick, and each
of them terminated by a firm petiole, hollowed in
form of a gutter, and which fupports a leaf of fix feet
long, and two feet wide. Thefe leaves, collected in
a fmall number at the bottom of the ftem, bend by
their own weight, and dry up one after the other.
They are thin, very fmooth, green on the upper furface, of a paler colour on the under, and furnifhed
with parallel fibres, which are very clofe to each other,
are joined at the cofta, and give the leaf a fatiny appearance. At the end of nine months, the banana
tree pufhes out from the midft of its leaves, when they
are all unfolded, a fprig of three or four feet long, and
two feet in diameter, furnifhed at intervals with femi-
circular bands, which each of them fupports, a clufter
of a dozen or more flowers, covered with a fpatha, or
membranous enclofure. Each piftil is charged with a
ftile of fix ftamina and one calix, with two leaves, one
external, lengthened out, and terminated by five in-
dentations; the other internal, fhorter, and concave.
This piftil, and one of the ftamina, are abortive in the
flowers at the extremity, the clufters of which are fmall,
clofe, and concealed under coloured and permanent
enclofures. In the other flowers, five of the ftamina
are found abortive; but the piftil becomes a flefhy
fruit, elongated, flightly arched, covered with a yellow
and thick pellicle, and filled with a pulpy, yellowifh
fubftance, of a fweetifh tafte, and very nourifhing. The

assemblage of these fruits, to the number of fifty and upwards, upon the same stem, is called a *regime* of bananas; which is as much as a man can carry. While it is upon the stem, its weight makes it bend towards the ground. As soon as it is gathered, this stem dries up, and is succeeded by fresh sprigs, which come out of the root, and flower nine months after, or later, when they are transplanted. There is no other way of multiplying the banana tree, which never yields any seed.

This plant exhibits a number of varieties, which consist only in the form, the size, and the goodness of the fruit. It is agreeable to the taste, and is eaten raw, or prepared in several ways.

One singular circumstance worthy of remark is, that while the voracious plant, which we have termed Liane, climbed round all the barren trees, it avoided the fertile ones, though promiscuously blended with the former. Nature seemed, as it were, to have prescribed to it, to respect what she had destined for the sustenance of man.

The islanders were not so plentifully supplied with pot-herbs, as with roots and fruits. Purslain and cresses were the only herbs of this kind they had.

Their other food was confined within a very narrow compass: they had no tame fowl; and the only quadrupeds that were fit for food did not amount to more than five sorts, the largest of which did not exceed in size our common rabbits. The birds, more pleasing to the eye, though less varied than in our climates, were valuable almost only on account of their feathers: few of them warbled forth those melting notes that are so captivating to the ear; most of them were extremely thin, and very insipid to the taste. Fish was nearly as plentiful as in other seas, but generally less wholesome and less delicate.

The virtues of the plants that nature had placed in these islands, to cure the very few disorders the inhabitants were subject to, can scarce be exaggerated. Whether they were applied externally, or taken in-

BOOK ternally, or the juice of them given in infufion, their
X. effects were as fpeedy as falutary. The invaders of
thofe formerly peaceable regions have employed thefe
fimples, which are always green and in full vigour,
and preferred them to all the medicines that Afia can
furnifh to the reft of the world.

Is the climate of thefe iflands agreeable and wholefome? The generality of the inhabitants of thefe iflands
confider but two feafons among them, that of drought
and that of rain. Nature, whofe operations are conftant, and concealed under a perpetual verdure, appears to them to act always uniformly. But thofe who
attentively obferve her progrefs, difcern, that in the
temperature of the climate, in all the revolutions and
the changes of vegetation, fhe obferves the fame laws
as in Europe, though in a lefs fenfible manner.

Thefe almoft imperceptible changes are no prefervative againft the dangers and inconveniences of fuch a
fcorching climate as muft be naturally expected under
the torrid zone. As thefe iflands are all under the tropics, their inhabitants are expofed, allowing for the varieties refulting from difference of fituation and of foil,
to a perpetual heat, which generally increafes from the
rifing of the fun till an hour after noon, and then decreafes in proportion as the fun declines. A covered
fky, that might ferve to alleviate this heat, is feldom
feen. Sometimes, indeed, clouds appear for an hour
or two; but the fun is never hid for four days during
the whole year.

The variations in the temperature of the air depend
rather upon the wind, than the changes of the feafons.
In thofe places where the wind doth not blow, the air
is exceffively hot, and none but the eafterly winds contribute to temperate and refrefh it; thofe that blow
from the fouth and weft afford little relief, but they
are much lefs frequent and lefs regular than that which
comes from the eaft. The branches of the trees expofed to its influence are forced round towards the
weft, in that direction which they feemed to be thrown
into by the conftant and uniform courfe of the wind.
But their roots are ftronger, and more extended under

ground towards the eaſt, in order to afford them, as it **BOOK** were, a fixed point, the reſiſtance of which may coun- **X.** teract the power of the ruling wind. Accordingly, it hath been obſerved, that, whenever the weſterly wind blows with any violence, the trees are eaſily thrown down: in order, therefore, to judge of the violence of a hurricane, the number of trees, as well as the direction in which they fall, is equally to be conſidered.

The eaſterly wind depends upon two invariable cauſes, the probability of which is very ſtriking. The firſt ariſes from the diurnal motion of the earth from weſt to eaſt, and which muſt neceſſarily be more rapid under the equinoctial than under the parallels of latitude, becauſe a greater ſpace muſt be paſſed over in the ſame time. The ſecond is owing to the heat of the ſun, which, as ſoon as it riſes above the horizon, rarefies the air, and cauſes it to blow towards the weſt, in proportion as the earth revolves towards the eaſt.

The eaſterly wind, therefore, which at the Caribbee Iſlands is ſcarcely felt before nine or ten o'clock in the morning, increaſes in proportion as the ſun riſes above the horizon, and decreaſes as it declines. Towards the evening it ceaſes entirely to blow on the coaſts, but not on the open ſea. The reaſons of this difference are very evident. After the ſetting of the ſun, the air from the land, that continues for a conſiderable time rarefied, on account of the vapours which are conſtantly riſing from the heated globe, neceſſarily flows back upon the air of the ſea: this is what is generally called a Land Breeze. It is moſt ſenſibly felt in the night, and continues till the air of the ſea, rarefied by the heat of the ſun, flows back again towards the land, where the air hath been condenſed by the coolneſs of the night. It hath alſo been obſerved, that the eaſterly wind blows more regularly, and with greater force, in the dog-days, than at any other times of the year; becauſe the ſun then acts more powerfully on the air. Thus nature cauſes the exceſſive heat of the ſun to contribute to the refreſhment of thoſe climates that are parched up by its rays. It is thus, that in fire-en-

B O O K gines art makes the fire inftrumental in fupplying con-
  X.   ftantly with frefh water the copper veffels from which
          it is exhaufted by evaporation.

The rain contributes alfo to the temperature of the
American iflands, though not equally in them all. In
thofe places where the eafterly wind meets with nothing to oppofe its progrefs, it difpels the clouds as
they begin to rife, and compels them to break, either
n the woods, or upon the mountains. But whenever
the ftorms are too violent, or the blowing of the eafterly wind is interrupted by the changeable and temporary effect of the fouthern and wefterly ones, it then
begins to rain. In the other Caribbee Iflands, where
this wind doth not generally blow, the rains are fo frequent and plentiful, efpecially in the winter feafon,
which lafts from the middle of July to the middle of
October, that, according to the moft accurate obfervations, as much water falls in one week, during this
time, as in our climates in the fpace of a year. Inftead
of thofe mild and refrefhing fhowers which we fometimes enjoy in Europe, the rains in thefe climates are
torrents, the found of which might be miftaken for
that of hail, if this were not almoft unknown under fo
burning a fky.

Thefe fhowers, it muft be allowed, refrefh the air;
but they occafion a dampnefs, the effects of which are
no lefs difagreeable than fatal. The dead muft be interred within a few hours after they have expired.
Meat will not keep fweet above four-and-twenty hours.
The fruits decay, whether they are gathered ripe, or
before their maturity. The bread muft be made up
into bifcuits, to prevent its growing mouldy. Common wines foon turn four; and iron grows rufty in a
day's time. The feeds can only be preferved by conftant attention and care, till the proper feafon returns
for fowing them. When the Caribbee Iflands were
firft difcovered, the corn that was conveyed there for
the fupport of thofe who could not accuftom themfelves to the food of the natives of the country, was
fo foon damaged, that it became neceffary to fend it

in the ears. This neceſſary precaution enhanced the B O O K
price of it ſo much, that few people were able to buy X.
it. Flour was then ſubſtituted in lieu of corn, which
lowered, indeed, the expences of tranſport, but was
attended with this inconvenience, that it was ſooner
damaged. It was imagined by a merchant, that if
the flour were entirely ſeparated from the bran, which
contributes to its fermentation, it would have the
double advantage of cheapneſs and of keeping longer.
He cauſed it therefore to be ſifted, and put the fineſt
flour into ſtrong caſks, and beat it cloſe together with
iron hammers, till it became ſo hard a body, that the
air could ſcarce penetrate it. Experience juſtified ſo
ſenſible a contrivance: the practice of it hath become
general, and been conſiderably improved ever ſince.

It was thought that nothing more remained to be
done, when M. du Hamel propoſed another precaution, that of drying the flour in ſtoves, before it was
embarked. This idea attracted the attention of the
French miniſtry. Flour prepared in the new way, and
ſome according to the former mode, was ſent to the
other hemiſphere. Upon their return, the firſt had
loſt nothing, and the laſt was half rotten, and deprived of its glutinous property. The ſame reſult hath attended all the experiments. It is pleaſing to hope, that
a diſcovery ſo uſeful will not be loſt, for the nations
that have formed ſettlements to the ſouth of America.
If it doth not ſecure to the proviſions the ſame degree
of duration that they have in our dry and temperate
climates, they will not at leaſt be corrupted ſo ſoon,
and will be preſerved for a longer time.

However troubleſome theſe natural effects of the Ordinary
rain may be, it is attended with ſome ſtill more for- phenomenon in the
midable; ſuch as frequent and ſometimes dreadful iſlands.
earthquakes in the iſlands. As they generally happen
during the time, or towards the end of the rainy ſeaſon, and when the tides are higheſt, ſome ingenious
naturaliſts have therefore ſuppoſed that they might be
owing to theſe two cauſes.

The waters of the ſky and of the ſea undermine,

B O O K dig up, and ravage the earth in feveral ways. The
   X.   ocean, in particular, exerts its fury upon this globe
with a violence that can neither be forefeen nor prevented. Among the various fhocks to which it is conftantly expofed, from this reftlefs and boifterous element, there is one, which, at the Caribbee Iflands, is
diftinguifhed by the name of *raz de marée*, or whirl-
pool. It conftantly happens once, twice, or three
times, from July to October, and always on the weftern coafts; becaufe it takes place after the time of the
wefterly and foutherly winds, or while they blow.
The waves, which at a diftance feem to advance gently within four or five hundred yards, fuddenly fwell
againft the fhore, as if acted upon in an oblique direction by fome fuperior force, and break with the greateft impetuofity. The fhips which are then upon the
coaft, or in the roads beyond it, unable either to put
to fea or keep their anchors, are dafhed to pieces
againft the land, leaving the unhappy failors entirely
without hopes of efcaping that certain death, the ap-
proaches of which they have been expecting for feveral hours.

So extraordinary a motion of the fea hath been hitherto confidered as the confequence of a ftorm. But
a ftorm follows the direction of the wind, from one
point of the compafs to another; and whirlpools are
felt in one part of an ifland that is fheltered by another
ifland, where the fhock is not at all perceived. This
obfervation hath induced Mr. Dutafta, who has travelled through Africa and America, as a natural philofopher, a merchant, and a ftatefman, to feek for a more
probable caufe of this fingular phenomenon. He hath
not only difcovered this, but alfo feveral other truths
that may be ufeful to many of the fciences, if he
fhould ever make them public. We fhall then, probably, acquire more certain information concerning
hurricanes.

The hurricane is a violent wind, generally accompanied with rain, lightning, and thunder, fometimes
with earthquakes; and always attended with the moft

melancholy and fatal confequences that the wind can produce. The day, which in the torrid zone is ufually bright and clear, is fuddenly changed into a dark and univerfal night; the appearance of a perpetual fpring into the drearinefs and horror of the moft gloomy winter. Trees, as ancient as the world itfelf, are torn up by the roots, and inftantly difappear. The ftrongeft and the moft folid buildings are in a moment buried in ruins. Where the eye delighted itfelf with the profpect of rich and verdant hills, nothing is to be feen but plantations entirely deftroyed, and frightful caverns. The unhappy fufferers, deprived of their whole fupport, weep over the carcafes of the dead, or fearch among the ruins for their friends and relations. The noife of the waters, of the woods, of the thunder, and of the winds, that break againft the fhattered rocks; the cries and howlings of men and animals, promifcuoufly involved in a whirlwind of fand, ftones, and ruins of buildings: all together feem to portend the laft ftruggles of expiring nature.

Thefe hurricanes, however, contribute to produce more plentiful crops, and to ripen the fruits of the earth. Whether thefe violent concuffions tear up the ground, in order to render it more fertile, or whether the hurricane brings along with it certain fubftances fit to promote the vegetation of plants, is not eafily determined: but it hath been obferved, that this feeming and temporary confufion was not only a confequence of the uniformity of nature, which makes even diffolution itfelf inftrumental to regeneration, but alfo the means of preferving the general fyftem, the life and vigour of which is maintained by an internal fermentation, the fource of partial evil and of general good.

The firft inhabitants of the Caribbee Iflands imagined that they had difcovered infallible prognoftics of this alarming phenomenon. They obferved, that, when it was near at hand, the air was mifty, the fun red, and yet the weather calm, and the tops of the mountains clear. Under the earth, and in the refer-

BOOK
X.

voirs of water, a dull found was heard, like that arifing from pent-up winds. The ftars were clouded by a
vapour, that made them appear larger. The fky, in
the north-weft, was overfpread with dark and black
clouds, that feemed very alarming. The fea fent forth
a ftrong and difagreeable fmell, and, in the midft of a
calm, was fuddenly agitated. The wind changed in a
moment from eaft to weft, and blew very violently at
different intervals, each of which continued for two
hours together.

Though the truth of all thefe obfervations cannot be
afcertained, yet to pay no attention to the ideas, and
even prejudices, of favage nations on times and feafons,
would be a feeming indication of imprudence, or of a
mind too little addicted to philofophical inquiries. The
want of employment of thefe people, and their being
habituated to live in open air, afford them an opportunity, and put them under a neceffity, of obferving
the fmalleft alterations in the air, and of acquiring fuch
informations on this point, as have efcaped the more
enlightened nations, which are more employed, and
more devoted to works of a fedentary nature. Poffibly
we muft be indebted to the man who dwells in the forefts for the difcovery of effects, and to the learned
man for the inveftigation of caufes. Let us trace, if
poffible, the caufe of hurricanes, a phenomenon fo frequent in America, that this alone would have been
fufficient to make it be deferted, or render it uninhabitable many ages ago.

No hurricanes come from the eaft, that is, from the
greateft extent of the fea at the Caribbee Iflands. As
this is an acknowledged fact, it would induce us to believe, that they are formed on the continent of America. The weft wind which blows conftantly, and fometimes very violently in the fouthern parts, from July to
January, and the north wind blowing at the fame time
in the northern parts, muft, when they meet, oppofe
each other with a force proportionate to their natural
velocity. If this fhock happens in the long and narrow paffes of the mountains, it muft occafion a ftrong

current of air, that will extend itself in a compound ratio of the moving power, and the diameter of the narrow pass of the mountain. Every solid body that meets this current of air, will be impressed with a degree of force proportioned to the extent of surface it opposes to the current; so that if the position of that surface should be perpendicular to the direction of the hurricane, it is impossible to determine what effect might be produced upon the whole mass. Fortunately, the different bearings of the coast of these islands, and their angular or spherical figure, occasion these dreadful hurricanes to fall upon surfaces more or less oblique, which divert the current of air, break its force, and gradually destroy its effects. Experience also proves, that their action is by degrees so much weakened, that even in the direction where the hurricane falls with most force, it is scarce felt at ten leagues distance. The most accurate observers have remarked, that all the hurricanes which have successively subverted the islands, came from the north-west, and consequently from the narrow passes formed by the mountains of St. Martha. The distance of some islands from this direction, is not a sufficient reason for rejecting this opinion; as several causes may contribute to divert a current of air to the south or east. We cannot help thinking, therefore, that those persons have been in an error, who have asserted, that the violence of a hurricane was felt under whatever point of the compass the wind came from. Such are the destructive phenomena Nature hath opposed to the acquisition of the riches of the New World: but what barrier could restrain the daring spirit of the navigator who discovered it?

Christopher Columbus having first formed a settlement at St. Domingo, one of the Greater Antilles, discovered the Less. The islanders he had to encounter there, were not so weak and cowardly as those he had at first subdued. The Caribs, who thought they originally came from Guiana, were of moderate stature, thick set and strong, and such as seemed adapted to form men of superior strength, if their manner of life

BOOK and exercifes had feconded thefe natural appearances.
X. Their legs, thick and mufcular, were generally well
made ; their eyes black, large, and fomewhat promi-
nent. Their whole figure would have been pleafing,
had they not fpoiled their natural beauty by fancied
and artificial ornaments, which could only be agreeable
among themfelves. The eye-brows and the head were
the only parts of the body on which they fuffered any
hair to grow. They wore no garment, nor had this
any influence on their chaftity. In order to guard a-
gainft the bite of infects. they painted all their bodies
over with the juice of the rocou, or arnotto, which
gave them the appearance of a boiled lobfter.

Their religion confifted only in fome confufed belief
of a good and bad principle ; an opinion fo natural to
man, that we find it diffufed among the moft favage
nations, and preferved even among many civilized
people. They were little concerned about the tute-
lary divinity, but had the greateft dread of the evil
principle. Their other fuperftitions were more abfurd
than dangerous, and they were but little attached to
them. This indifference did not contribute to render
them more ready to embrace Chriftianity when it was
propofed to them. Without entering into difpute
with thofe who expounded the doctrines, they contented themfelves with rejecting the belief of them,
for fear, as they faid, *that their neighbours fhould laugh
at them*.

Though the Caribs had no regular form of government among them, yet they lived quietly and peaceably
with one another. The tranquillity they enjoyed,
was entirely owing to that innate principle of compaffion which precedes all reflection, and is the fource
of all focial virtues. This humane fpirit of benevolence
arifes from the very frame and nature of man, whofe
felf-love alone is fufficient to make him abhor the fufferings of his fellow-creatures. To infufe, therefore, a
fpirit of humanity into the minds of tyrants, it would
only be neceffary to make them the executioners of
thofe victims they facrifice to their pride, and of thofe

cruelties they order to be practifed upon others. The B O O K
hands of thofe voluptuaries fhould be obliged to muti- X
late the eunuchs of their feraglios; they fhould be
forced to attend the field of battle; they fhould there
behold the bleeding wounds, hear the imprecations,
and be witneffes of the agonies and convulfions of their
dying foldiers; they fhould next attend the hofpitals,
and at leifure contemplate the wounds, the fractures,
the difeafes occafioned by famine, by labours equally
dangerous and unwholefome, by cruel fervices and
taxes, and by the other calamities which arife from the
vices and profligacy of their manners. How greatly
would fcenes like thefe, occafionally introduced in the
education of princes, contribute to leffen the crimes
and fufferings of the human race! What benefits
would not the people derive from the compaffionate
emotions of their fovereigns?

Among the Caribs, whofe hearts were not depraved
by the pernicious inftitutions that corrupt us, neither
adultery, treafon, nor maffacres, fo common among civilized nations, were known. Religion, the laws, and
penal punifhments, thofe barriers raifed to protect old
cuftoms from the encroachments of new ones, were
ufelefs to men who followed nature alone. Theft was
never heard of among thefe favages, before the Europeans came among them. When they difcovered any
thing miffing, they obferved, *that the Chriftians had
been with them.*

Thefe iflanders were little acquainted with the ftrongeft paffions of the foul, not even with that of love.
This paffion was with them merely a fenfual appetite.
They never fhowed the leaft marks of attention or
tendernefs for that fex, fo much courted in other countries. They confidered their wives rather in the light
of flaves than of companions; they did not even fuffer them to eat with them, and had ufurped the right
of divorcing them, without granting them the indulgence of marrying again. The women felt themfelves
born to obey, and fubmitted patiently to their fate.

In other refpects, a tafte for power had little influ-

ence on the minds of the Caribs; as they had no distinction of ranks among them, they were all on a footing of equality, and were extremely surprised to find
degrees of subordination established among the Europeans. This system was so repugnant to their ideas,
that they considered those as slaves, who had the
weakness to receive the commands of a superior, and
obey them. The subjection of the women among
them, was a natural consequence of the weakness of
the sex. But in what manner, and for what reason,
the stronger men submitted themselves to the weaker;
and how one man commanded the whole body, was a
problem, that neither war, treachery, nor superstition,
had been able to resolve.

The manners of a people, neither influenced by interest, vanity, or ambition, must be very simple. Every
family formed within itself a republic, distinct in some
degree from the rest of the nation. They composed a
hamlet, called *carbet*, of greater or less consequence,
in proportion to the space of ground it occupied. The
chief or patriarch of the family lived in the centre,
with his wives and younger children. Around him
were placed the huts of such of his descendants as were
married. The columns that supported these huts were
stakes; the roofs were thatched; and the whole furniture consisted of some weapons, cotton beds made
very plain and simple, some baskets, and utensils made
of calabashes.

In these huts the Caribs spent the greatest part of
their life, either in sleeping or smoking. When they
went out, they retired into some corner, and sat upon
the ground, seemingly absorbed in the most profound
contemplation. Whenever they spoke, which was not
very often, they were heard without interruption or
contradiction, and without any answer, but the sign of
a tacit approbation.

They were not much troubled in providing for their
sustenance. Savages, who spent their life in the con-
densed air of the forest, who had the custom of covering themselves with a layer of rocou, which closed up

the pores of the ſkin ; who ſpent their days in idleneſs and indolence ; ſuch ſavages muſt neceſſarily perſpire very little, and be very moderate in their eating. Without being compelled to the labours of cultivation, they found conſtantly, at the foot of the trees, a wholeſome food, fitted to their conſtitution; and which required no great preparation. If they ſometimes added to theſe gifts of liberal and uncultivated nature, what they had taken in hunting and fiſhing, it was moſtly upon occaſion of ſome public feaſt.

Theſe extraordinary feſtivals were not holden at any ſtated times. The gueſts themſelves ſhowed no alteration in their uſual characters. In theſe meetings they were not more gay or ſprightly than at other times. A ſpirit of indolence and liſtleſſneſs appeared in their countenances. Their dances were ſo grave and ſolemn, that the motions of their bodies were expreſſive of the dullneſs of their minds. But theſe gloomy feſtivals, like thoſe clouded ſkies that are the forerunners of a ſtorm, were ſeldom concluded without bloodſhed. Theſe ſavages, who were ſo temperate when alone, grew drunk when aſſembled in companies, and their intoxication excited and revived thoſe family diſſenſions, that were either only ſtifled, or not entirely extinguiſhed : and thus theſe feſtivals terminated in maſſacres. Hatred and revenge, the only paſſions that could deeply agitate the minds of theſe ſavages, were thus perpetuated by convivial pleaſures. In the height of theſe entertainments, parents and relations embraced one another, and ſwore that they would wage war upon the continent, and, ſometimes, in the great iſlands.

The Caribs uſed to embark upon boats, made of a ſingle tree, that had been felled by burning its roots. Whole years had been employed in hollowing theſe canoes, by hatchets made of ſtone, or by means of fire, ſkilfully applied within the trunk of the tree, in order to bring it to the moſt proper form. Theſe free and voluntary warriors being arrived on the coaſts, to which they were led, ſometimes by a blind caprice, and ſome-

BOOK
X.
times by violent hatred, went in queſt of nations to exterminate. They made their attack with a kind of club, nearly as long as the arm, and with poiſoned arrows. At their return from this military expedition, which was the more ſpeedily brought to a concluſion, as mutual enmity rendered it more cruel and ſpirited, the ſavages fell again into their former ſtate of indolence and inactivity.

The Spaniards, notwithſtanding the advantage of fire-arms, did not continue long at war with this people, nor were they always ſucceſsful. At firſt they fought only for gold, and afterwards for ſlaves ; but not meeting with any mines, and the Caribs being ſo proud and ſullen that they died when reduced to ſlavery, the Spaniards gave up all thoughts of making conqueſts which they thought of little conſequence, and which they could neither acquire nor preſerve without conſtant and bloody wars.

The Engliſh and French ſettled in the Windward Iſlands on the ruin of the Caribs.

The Engliſh and French, being appriſed of theſe tranſactions, ventured to equip a ſmall fleet, in order to intercept the Spaniſh veſſels which frequented theſe latitudes. The advantages gained increaſed the number of pirates. Peace, which frequently took place in Europe, did not prevent theſe expeditions. The cuſtom that prevailed among the Spaniards, of ſtopping all ſhips that ſailed beyond the tropic, juſtified ſuch piracies.

The two nations had long been acquainted with the Windward Iſlands, without ever thinking of making any ſettlement there, or having been able to fix upon the mode of doing it. They were, perhaps, apprehenſive of irritating the Caribs, by whom they had been favourably received ; or, perhaps, they conſidered that a ſoil which afforded none of thoſe productions that were of uſe in the Old World was unworthy of their attention. At length, however, ſome Engliſh and French, the former headed by Warner, and the latter by Denambuc, landed at St. Chriſtopher's on the ſame day, at two oppoſite parts of the iſland. The frequent loſſes they ſuſtained, ſerved to convince them both, that they certainly would never triumph over, and enrich themselves with the spoils of the common enemy, unless they had some fixed residence, ports, and a place of general rendezvous. As they had no notion of commerce, agriculture, or conquest, they amicably divided the coasts of the island where they accidentally met together. The natives of the country retired from the spot they were fixed upon, telling them at the same time, that *land must either be very bad or very scarce with them, since they were come from so great a distance, and had exposed themselves to so many dangers, to seek for it among them.*

The court of Madrid were not so peaceably inclined. Frederick of Toledo, who was sent to Brazil in the year 1630, with a powerful fleet, to attack the Dutch, was ordered, in his passage, to destroy the pirates, who, according to the prejudices of that nation, had invaded one of their territories. The vicinity of two active and industrious nations occasioned the greatest anxiety to the Spaniards. They were sensible that their colonies would be exposed to attacks, if any other people should come to settle in that part of America.

The French and English in vain united their weak powers against the common enemy: they were beaten; and those who were not either killed in the action, or not taken prisoners, fled for shelter, with the utmost precipitation, into the neighbouring islands. When the danger was over, they most of them returned to their former settlements. Spain, whose attention was engrossed by objects she considered as of greater importance, disturbed them no more; taking it for granted, perhaps, that their mutual jealousies would occasion their destruction.

Unfortunately for the Caribs, the two nations, thus conquered, suspended their rivalship. The Caribs, already suspected of forming a conspiracy in St. Christopher's, were either banished or destroyed. Their wives, their provisions, and even the lands they occupied, were seized upon. A spirit of anxiety, the con-

sequence of ufurpation, inclined the Europeans to believe that the other favage nations had entered into
the confpiracy; and they were therefore attacked in
their iflands. In vain did thofe plain and inoffenfive
men, who had no inclination to contend for the poffeffion of a land which they confidered not as their property, remove the boundaries of their habitations, in
proportion as the Europeans advanced with their encroachments; they were ftill purfued with the fame
eagernefs and obftinacy. As foon as they perceived
that their lives or liberties were in danger, they at
length took up arms; and the fpirit of revenge, which
always goes beyond the injury, muft have fometimes
contributed to render them cruel, though not unjuft.

In earlier times, the Englifh and the French confidered the Caribs as their common enemy; but this
kind of cafual affociation was frequently interrupted.
It implied not a lafting engagement, much lefs the becoming guarantee for their mutual poffeffions. The
favages artfully contrived to be at peace, fometimes
with one nation, and fometimes with the other; and
thus they gained the advantage of having only one
enemy at a time. This management would have been
but of little fervice to thefe iflanders, had not Europe,
fcarce paying any attention to a few adventurers,
whofe excurfions had as yet been of no ufe to her,
and not fufficiently enlightened to penetrate into fu-
turity, neglected both the care of governing them, as
well as that of putting them into a condition to extend
or recover the advantages they had already acquired.
The indifference fhown by the two mother-countries,
determined their fubjects of the New World, in the
month of January 1660, to enter into an alliance, fecuring to each people thofe poffeffions the various
events of war had procured them, and which till then
had been totally unfettled. This alliance was accompanied with an offenfive and defenfive league, to compel the natives of the country to join in this plan; to
which their fears induced them to accede the very
fame year.

By this treaty, which eftablifhed tranquillity in this
part of America, France obtained Guadalupe, Martinico, Granada, and fome lefs confiderable acquifitions.
England was confirmed in the poffeffion of Barbadoes,
Nevis, Antigua, Montferrat, and feveral other iflands
of little value : St. Chriftopher's belonged to both nations. The Caribs were confined to Dominica and St.
Vincent's, where all the fcattered body of this people
united, and did not at that time exceed in number
6000 men.

At this period, the Englifh fettlements had acquired under a government, which, though not free from
defects, was yet tolerable, fome kind of form, and were
in a flourifhing ftate. On the contrary, the French colonies were abandoned by a great number of their inhabitants, reduced to defpair, from the neceffity they
were under of fubmitting to the tyranny of exclufive
privileges. Thefe men, paffionately attached to liberty, fled to the northern coaft of St. Domingo, a place
of refuge for feveral adventurers of their own country,
fince they had been driven out of St. Chriftopher's
about thirty years before.

They were called Buccaneers, becaufe they imitated
the cuftom of the favages, in drying the food they lived upon by fmoke, in places called Buccans. As they
had no wives nor children, they ufually affociated two
in a company, to affift one another in family duties.
In thefe focieties property was common, and the laft
furvivor inherited all that remained. Theft was unknown among them, though no precautions were taken againft it ; and what was wanting at home was
freely borrowed from fome of the neighbours, without
any other reftriction than that of a previous intima-
tion, if they were at home ; if not, of making them
acquainted with it at their return. Cæfar found in
Gaul the fame cuftom, which bears the double character, both of a primitive ftate, in which every thing was
in common, and of times pofterior to that in which the
idea of private property was known and refpected.
Differences feldom arofe, and, when they did, were

B O O K
X.

The French
take poffef-
fion of part
of St. Do-
mingo.
Character
of thefe ad-
venturers.

BOOK easily adjusted. If the parties, however, were obsti-
X. nate, they decided the matter by fire-arms. If the
ball entered at the back or the sides, it was considered
as a mark of treachery, ·and the assassin was immediately put to death. The former laws of their country
were disregarded, and by the usual sea baptism they
had received in passing the tropic, they considered
themselves exempted from all obligation to obey them.
These adventurers had even quitted their family name
to assume others, borrowed from terms of war, most of
which have been transmitted to their posterity.

The dress of these barbarians consisted of a shirt
dipped in the blood of the animals they killed in
hunting ; a pair of drawers dirtier than the shirt, and
made in the shape of a brewer's apron ; a girdle made
of leather, on which a very short sabre was hung, and
some knives ; a hat without any rim, except a flap before, in order to take hold of it ; and shoes without
stockings. Their ambition was satisfied, if they can
but provide themselves with a gun that carried balls
of an ounce weight, and with a pack of about five-
and-twenty or thirty dogs.

The buccaneers spent their life in hunting the wild
bulls, of which there were great numbers in the island,
since the Spaniards had brought them. The best parts
of these animals, when seasoned with pimento and
orange juice, were the most common food of their de-
stroyers, who had forgotten the use of bread, and who
had nothing but water to drink. The hides of these
animals were conveyed to several ports, and bought by
the navigators. They were carried thither by men
who were called *engagés*, or bondsmen, a set of persons who were used to sell themselves in Europe to
serve as slaves in the colonies during the term of three
years. One of these miserable men presuming to represent to his master, who always fixed upon a Sunday
for this voyage, that God had forbidden such a practice, when he had declared, *Six days shalt thou labour,
and on the seventh day shalt thou rest ;* And I, replied the
brutal Buccaneer, say to thee, *Six days thou shalt kill*

bulls, and strip them of their skins, and on the seventh
day thou shalt carry their hides to the sea-shore. This
command was followed by blows, which sometimes
enforce obedience, sometimes disobedience to the laws
of God.

Men of such a cast, habituated to constant exercises, and feeding every day on fresh meat, were little
exposed to diseases. Their excursions were only suspended by a flight fever, which lasted one day, and
was not felt the next. They must, however, have been
weakened by length of time, under a climate of too
intense a heat, to enable them to support so hard and
laborious a manner of life.

The climate, indeed, was the only enemy the Buccaneers had reason to fear. The Spanish colony, at
first so considerable, was reduced to nothing. Neglected and forgotten by the mother-country, it had even
lost the remembrance of its former greatness. The
few inhabitants that survived lived in a state of indolence : their slaves had no other employment but to
swing them in their hammocks. Confined to those
wants only that are satisfied by nature, frugality prolonged their lives to an old age, rarely to be met with
in more temperate climates.

It is probable they would not have been roused from
their indolence, had not the enterprising and active
spirit of their enemies pursued them in proportion as
they retreated. Exasperated at length, from having
their tranquillity and ease continually disturbed, they
invited from the continent, and from the neighbouring islands, some troops, who fell upon the dispers-
ed Buccaneers. They unexpectedly attacked these
barbarians in small parties in their excursions, or in
the night-time, when retired into their huts, and many
of them were massacred. These adventurers would
most probably have been all destroyed, had they not
formed themselves into a body for their mutual defence.
They were under an absolute necessity of separating
in the day-time, but met together in the evening. If
any one of them was missing, it was supposed that he

was either taken prisoner or killed, and the chase was delayed, till he was either found, or his death revenged. We may easily conceive how much blood must have been shed by such ruffians, belonging to no country, and subject to no laws; hunters and warriors from the calls of nature and instinct; and excited to murder and massacres from being habituated to attack, and from the necessity of defending themselves. In the height of their fury, they devoted every thing to destruction, without any distinction of sex or age. The Spaniards, at length despairing of being able to get the better of such savage and obstinate enemies, took the resolution of destroying all the bulls of the islands, by a general chase. The execution of this design having deprived the Buccaneers of their usual resources, put them under the necessity of making settlements, and cultivating the lands.

France, which till that time had disclaimed for her subjects these ruffians, whose successes were only temporary, acknowledged them, however, as soon as they formed themselves into settlements. In 1665, she sent them over a man of probity and understanding to govern them. Several women attended him, who, like most of those who have at different periods been sent into the New World, were noted for their vices and licentiousness. The Buccaneers were not offended at the profligacy of their manners; each of them said to the woman who fell to his lot :

" I take thee without knowing, or caring to know,
" whom thou art. If any body from whence thou
" comest would have had thee, thou wouldst not have
" come in quest of me; but no matter. I do not de-
" sire thee to give me an account of thy past conduct,
" because I have no right to be offended at it, at the
" time when thou wast at liberty to behave either
" well or ill, according to thy own pleasure; and be-
" cause I shall have no reason to be ashamed of any
" thing thou wast guilty of when thou didst not be-
" long to me. Give me only thy word for the fu-
" ture. I acquit thee of what is past." Then striking

his hand on the barrel of his gun, he added, " This B o o k
" will revenge me of thy breach of faith; if thou   x.
" fhouldſt prove falſe, this will certainly be true to my
" aim."

The Engliſh had not waited till their rivals had ob- The En-
tained a firm ſettlement in the Great Antilles to pro- gliſh con-
cure themſelves an eſtabliſhment there. The declining quer Ja-
ſtate of the kingdom of Spain, weakened by its in- maica.
ternal diviſions, by the revolt of Catalonia and Portugal, by the commotions of Naples, by the deſtruction of its formidable infantry in the plains of Rocroy,
by its continual loſſes in the Netherlands, by the in-
capacity of its miniſters, and even by the extinction
of that national pride, which, after having been kept
up and maintained by fixing itſelf on great objects,
had degenerated into an indolent haughtineſs: all theſe
circumſtances, tending to the ruin of the Spaniſh monarchy, left no room to doubt that war might be ſuc-
ceſsfully waged againſt her.   France ſkilfully took the
advantage of theſe confuſions ſhe had partly occaſioned; and Cromwell, in the year 1655, joined her, in
order to ſhare in the ſpoils of a kingdom haſtening to
deſtruction in every part.

This conduct of the Protector cauſed a revolt among
the beſt Engliſh officers, who, conſidering it as an inſtance of great injuſtice, determined to quit the ſervice.   They thought that the will of their ſuperiors
could not give ſanction to an enterpriſe which violated all the principles of equity; and that by concur-
ring in the execution of it, they would be guilty of
the greateſt crime.   The reſt of the Europeans looked upon theſe principles of virtue and honour as the
effect of that republican and fanatical ſpirit which then
prevailed in England; but they attacked the Protector with other motives.

Spain had long threatened to enſlave all other nations.   Perhaps the multitude, who are little able to
eſtimate the ſtrength of nations, and to weigh the variations in the balance of power, were not yet recovered from their ancient prejudices.   An univerſal pa-

nic had feized the minds of thofe able men who attentively ftudied the general progrefs of affairs. They
were fenfible, that, if the rapid and extraordinary fucceffes of France were not checked by fome foreign
power, fhe would deprive the Spaniards of their poffeffions, impofe on them what laws fhe thought proper, compel them to the marriage of the Infanta with
Lewis the XIV., fecure to herfelf the inheritance of
Charles the V., and opprefs the liberty of Europe that
fhe had formerly protected. Cromwell, who had lately fubverted the government of his country, feemed a
fit perfon to give a check to the power of kings : but
he was looked upon as the weakeft of politicians, when
he was obferved to form connections, which his own
private interefts, thofe of his country, as well as thofe
of Europe in general, ought abfolutely to have prevented him from entering into.

These obfervations could not poffibly efcape the
deep and penetrating genius of the ufurper. But, perhaps, he was defirous of preferving the idea the nation
already entertained of his abilities, by fome important
conqueft. If he had declared himfelf on the fide of
Spain, the execution of this project muft have been
chimerical; as the utmoft he could poffibly expect
was to reftore the balance of power between the two
contending parties. He imagined it more favourable
to his defigns, to begin to form a connection with
France, and afterwards to attack her, when he had
made himfelf mafter of thofe poffeffions that were the
object of his ambition. Whatever truth there may be
in thefe conjectures, which, however, may be fupported from the evidence of hiftory, and are, at leaft, confiftent with the character of the extraordinary politi-
cian who is fuppofed to have adopted this mode of
reafoning, the Englifh went into the New World to
attack an enemy they had juft brought upon themfelves.

Their firft attempts were directed againft the town
of St. Domingo, the inhabitants of which retired into
the woods as foon as they faw a large fleet command-

ed by Penn, and nine thousand land forces headed by
Venables, appear before the city. But the errors committed by their enemies inspiring these fugitives with
fresh courage, they returned, and compelled the enemy to reimbark with disgrace. This misfortune was
the consequence of the ill-concerted plan of this expedition.

The two commanders of this enterprise were men
of very moderate abilities. They entertained a mutual
hatred against each other, and were not attached to
the Protector. Inspectors had been appointed to watch
over them, who, under the name of commissaries,
checked their operations. The soldiers who were sent
from Europe were the refuse of the army; and the militia, taken from Barbadoes and St. Christopher's, were
under no kind of discipline. The hope of plunder,
that stimulus so necessary for the success of distant and
difficult enterprises, was prohibited. Matters were arranged in such a manner, as to render it impossible for
any kind of harmony to subsist between the several
persons who were to concur in their success. Proper
arms, provisions fit for the climate, and the information
necessary to conduct the enterprise, were all wanting.

The execution of the attack was answerable to the
plan. The landing of the troops, which might have
been effected without danger, even in the port itself,
was accomplished without a guide, at forty miles distance. The troops wandered about for four days without water or provisions. Exhausted by the excessive
heat of the climate, and discouraged by the cowardice
and misunderstanding of their officers, they did not
even contend with the Spaniards for victory. They
scarce thought themselves in safety when they had got
back to their ships.

But ill success contributed to reconcile the irritated
parties. The English, who had not yet contracted the
habit of bearing disgrace, reclaimed by the very faults
they had committed, and restored to the love of their
country, to a sense of their duty, and to a thirst of glo-

B O O K ry, failed for Jamaica, with a determined refolution,
   X.   either to perifh, or to make the conqueft of it.

The inhabitants of this ifland, fubject to Spain fince
the year 1509, were ignorant of what had happened
at St. Domingo, and did not imagine they had any
enemy failing in the neighbouring feas. The Englifh,
therefore, landed without oppofition. They were boldly marching to lay fiege to St. Jago, the only fortified
place in the colony, when the governor gave a check
to their ardour, by offering them terms of capitulation.
The difcuffion of the articles, artfully prolonged, gave
the colonifts time to remove their moft valuable effects
into fecret places. They themfelves fled for fhelter to
inacceffible mountains, leaving only to the conquerors
a city without inhabitants, moveables, treafures, or provifions.

This artifice exafperated the befiegers. They fent
out detachments on every fide, with exprefs orders to
deftroy every thing they met with. The difappointment they felt on finding thefe parties return without
having difcovered any thing; the want of every convenience, more fenfibly felt by this nation than any
other; the mortality which increafed among them
every day; the dread they were under of being attacked by all the forces of the New World: all thefe
circumftances confpired to make them clamorous for
a fpeedy return into England The cowardly defer-
tion of fo rich a prize as Jamaica, which they had almoft refolved upon, would foon have expofed them to
the mortifying reproaches of their country, had they
not difcovered at laft fome pafture land, where the fugitives had conveyed their numerous flocks. This unexpected good fortune occafioned a change in the fentiments of the Englifh, and made them refolve to complete their conqueft.

The fpirit of activity, which this laft refolution had
excited, convinced the befieged, that they could not.
remain with fafety in the forefts and precipices where
they had concealed themfelves. They unanimoufly,

therefore, agreed to fet fail for Cuba. Here they were received with fuch marks of difgrace as the weaknefs of their defence deferved, and they were fent back again; but with fuch fuccours as were unequal to the forces they had to contend with. From that principle of honour, which in moft men arifes rather from a fear of fhame than a love of glory, they made a more obftinate refiftance than could have been expected from the few refources they had. They did not evacuate this confiderable ifland, till they were reduced to the greateft extremities; and from that period it hath remained one of the moft valuable poffeffions of Great Britain in the New World.

BOOK
X.

Before the Englifh had made any fettlement at Jamaica, and the French at St. Domingo, fome pirates of both nations, who have fince been fo much diftinguifhed by the name of Freebooters, had driven the Spaniards out of the fmall ifland of Tortuga, fituated at the diftance of two leagues from St. Domingo; and fortifying themfelves there, had made excurfions with amazing intrepidity againft the common enemy. They formed themfelves into fmall companies, confifting of fifty, a hundred, or a hundred and fifty men each. A boat, of a greater or fmaller fize, was all their naval force. Thefe boats were fcarce big enough for a perfon to lie down in; and they had nothing to fhelter them from the ardent heats of a burning climate, nor from the rains, which fall in torrents in thofe regions. They were often in want of the moft neceffary fupports of life. But all thefe calamities were forgotten at the fight of a fhip. They never deliberated on the attack, but proceeded immediately to board the fhip, of whatever fize it might be. As foon as they threw out the grappling, the veffel was certainly taken.

The freebooters ravage the American feas. Origin, manners, expeditions, and decline of thefe pirates.

In cafes of extreme neceffity, thefe banditti attacked the people of every nation, but fell upon the Spaniards at all times. They thought that the cruelties they had exercifed on the Americans, juftified the implacable averfion they had fworn againft them. But this extraordinary kind of humanity was heightened

by perſonal reſentment, from the mortification they
felt, in ſeeing themſelves debarred from the privilege
of hunting and fiſhing, which they juſtly conſidered
as natural rights. ·Such was their infatuation, that
whenever they embarked on any expedition, they uſed
to pray to Heaven for the ſucceſs of it ; and they never came back from the plunder, but they conſtantly
returned thanks to God for their victory.

The ſhips that arrived from Europe ſeldom tempted
their avidity. Theſe barbarians would have found nothing but merchandiſe in them, the ſale of which
would not have been very profitable, and would have
required too conſtant an attention. They always waited for them on their return, when they were laden
with the gold, ſilver, and jewels of the other hemiſphere. If they met with a ſingle ſhip, they never
failed to attack her. They followed the fleets themſelves ; and any ſhip that ſtraggled, or remained behind, was inevitably loſt. The Spaniards, who trem-
bled at the ſight of theſe implacable enemies, immediately ſurrendered. Life was granted to them, if the
cargo proved a rich one ; but if the conquerors were
diſappointed in their expectations, all the crew were
frequently thrown into the ſea.

Peter Legrand, a native of Dieppe, had no more
than four pieces of cannon and twenty-eight men in
his boat : yet, with this trifling force, he ventured to
attack the vice-admiral of the galleons. He boarded
him, having firſt given orders to ſink his own veſſel ;
and the Spaniards were ſo much ſurpriſed at this bold-
neſs, that not one of them attempted to oppoſe him.
When he came to the captain's cabin, who was engaged at play, he preſented a piſtol to him, and compelled him to ſurrender. This commander, with the
greater part of the crew, they landed at the neareſt
cape, as a uſeleſs burden to the ſhip they had ſo ill defended, and reſerved only a ſufficient number of ſailors to work her.

Fifty-five freebooters, who had ſailed into the ſouth-
ern ſea, proceeded as far as California. To return in-

to the northern fea, they were obliged to fail two B O O K
thoufand leagues againft the wind in a canoe. When X.
they were at the Straits of Magellan, they were feized
with rage at having made no plunder in fo rich an
ocean, and fteered again towards Peru. They were
informed, that there was in the port of Yauca a fhip,
the cargo of which was valued at feveral millions:
they immediately attacked, took her, and embarked
upon her.

Michael de Bafco, Jonqué, and Lawrence le Graff,
were cruifing before Carthagena with three fmall and
bad veffels, when two men of war failed out of the
harbour to attack thefe freebooters, and to bring them
alive or dead. The Spaniards were fo much deceived
in their expectations, that they were themfelves taken
prifoners. The victors kept the fhips; but they fent
back the crews with a degree of fcorn, which greatly
enhanced the fhame of a defeat in itfelf fo humiliating.

Michael and Brouage having received intelligence
that a very valuable cargo had been fhipped from Carthagena in veffels carrying a foreign flag, in order to
fecure it from their rapine, attacked the two fhips that
were loaded with this treafure, and plundered them.
The Dutch captains, exafperated at their being beaten
by fhips fo inferior to theirs, ventured to tell one of
thefe adventurers openly, that, if he had been alone,
he would not dare to attack them. *Let us begin the
fight again*, replied the Buccaneer with haughtinefs,
*and my companion fhall remain a quiet fpectator of the en-
gagement. If I fhould be conqueror again, both your fhips
fhall alfo be mine.* The prudent republicans, far from
accepting the challenge, quickly made off, apprehend-
ing, if they fhould ftop, that they might not have the
liberty of declining it.

Lawrence, who was on board a very fmall veffel,
was overtaken by two Spanifh fhips, carrying each fixty guns. *You have*, faid he, addreffing himfelf to his
companions, *too much experience not to be fenfible of your
danger, and too much courage to fear it. On this occa-*

BOOK *fion we muſt avail ourſelves of every circumſtance, hazard*
X.   *every thing, attack and defend ourſelves at the ſame time.*
Valour, artifice, raſhneſs, and even deſpair itſelf, muſt now
be employed.   Let us dread the ignominy of a defeat ; let
us dread the cruelty of our enemies ; and let us fight, that
we may eſcape them.

After this ſpeech, which was received with general
applauſe, the captain called to the braveſt of the freebooters, and publicly ordered him to ſet fire to the
gunpowder, on the firſt ſignal he ſhould give him ;
ſhowing, by this reſolution, that they muſt either expect death, or defend themſelves.   Then extending his
hand toward the enemy, *We muſt*, ſays he, *paſs between*
their ſhips, and fire upon them from every ſide, according
to your uſual cuſtom.   This plan of operation was executed with equal courage and diſpatch.   The ſhips indeed were not taken ; but the crews were ſo reduced
in number, that they either were not able, or had not
courage enough, to continue the combat againſt a
handful of reſolute men, who, even in their retreat,
carried away the honour of the victory.   The Spaniſh
commander atoned, by his death, for the diſgrace his
ignorance and cowardice had ſtamped upon his country.   In every engagement the freebooters ſhowed the
ſame ſpirit of intrepidity.

When they had got a conſiderable booty, at firſt
they held their rendezvous at the iſland of Tortuga, in
order to divide the ſpoil ; but afterwards the French
went to St. Domingo, and the Engliſh to Jamaica.
They all took an oath, that they had ſecreted none of
the ſpoil.   If any one among them was convicted of
perjury, which ſeldom happened, he was left, as ſoon as
an opportunity offered, upon ſome deſert iſland, as an
infamous perſon.   The firſt ſhares of the booty were
always given to thoſe who had been maimed in any of
their engagements.   If they had loſt a hand, an arm,
or a leg, they received two hundred crowns [25l.].
An eye, or a finger, loſt in fight, was valued only at
half the above ſum.   The wounded were allowed three
livres [2s. 6d.] a-day for two months, to enable them

to have their wounds taken care of. If they had not
money enough to fulfil thefe facred obligations, the
whole company were bound to engage in fome frefh
expedition, and to continue it, even till they had acquired a fufficient ftock to enable them to fatisfy fuch
honourable contracts.

After this act of juftice and humanity, the remainder
of the booty was divided. The commander, in ftrictnefs, could only lay claim to a fingle fhare as the reft ;
but they complimented him with two or three, in proportion as they were fatisfied with his fkill, valour, and
conduct. When the veffel was not the property of the
company, the perfon who had fitted it out, and furnifhed it with neceffary arms and provifions, was entitled
to a third of the prizes. Favour never had any influence in the divifion of the booty ; for every fhare was
rigidly determined by lot. This probity was extended
even to the dead. Their fhare was given to their fur-
viving companion. If the perfon who had been killed
had none, his part was fent to his family. If there were
no friends or relations, it was diftributed in charity to
the poor and to churches, which were to pray for the
perfon in whofe name thefe benefactions were given,
the fruits of inhuman but neceffary piratical plunder.

They afterwards indulged themfelves in profufions
of all kinds. Unbounded licentioufnefs in gaming,
wine, women, every kind of debauchery was carried to
the utmoft pitch of excefs, and was ftopt only by the
want which fuch profufions brought on. Thofe men
who were enriched with feveral millions, were in an
inftant totally ruined, and deftitute of clothes and provifions. They returned to fea, and the new fupplies
they acquired were foon lavifhed in the fame manner.
If thefe madmen were afked, what fatisfaction they
could find in diffipating fo rapidly, what they had
gained with fo much difficulty? they made this very
ingenuous reply : " Expofed as we are to fuch a va-
" riety of dangers, our life is totally different from that
" of other men. Why fhould we, who are alive to-
" day, and may be dead to-morrow, think of hoarding

" up? We reckon only the day we live, but never " think upon that which is to come. Our concern is " rather to fquander life away, than to preferve it."

The Spanifh colonies, flattering themfelves with the hopes of feeing an end to their miferies, and reduced almoft to defpair in finding themfelves a perpetual prey to thefe ruffians, grew weary of navigation. They gave up all the power, conveniences, and fortune their connections procured them, and formed themfelves almoft into fo many diftinct and feparate ftates. They were fenfible of the inconveniences arifing from fuch a conduct, and avowed them; but the dread of falling into the hands of rapacious and favage men had greater influence over them than the dictates of honour, intereft, and policy. This was the rife of that fpirit of inactivity which continues to this time.

This defpondency ferved only to increafe the boldnefs of the freebooters. As yet they had only appeared in the Spanifh fettlements, in order to carry off fome provifions; and even this they had done very feldom. They no fooner found their captures begin to diminifh, than they determined to recover by land what they had loft at fea. The richeft and moft populous countries of the continent were plundered and laid wafte. The culture of lands was equally neglected with navigation; and the Spaniards dared no more appear in their public roads, than fail in the latitudes which belonged to them.

Among the freebooters who fignalized themfelves in this new fpecies of excurfions, Montbar, a gentleman of Languedoc, particularly diftinguifhed himfelf. Having, by chance, in his infancy, met with a circumftantial account of the cruelties practifed in the New World, he conceived an averfion, which he carried to a degree of frenzy, againft that nation that had committed fuch enormities. Upon this point a ftory is told of him, that when he was at college, and acting in a play the part of a Frenchman, who quarrelled with a Spaniard, he fell upon the perfon who perfonated the Spaniard with fuch fury, that he would have ſtrangled him, had he not been reſcued out of his hands. His heated imagination continually repre-ſented to him innumerable multitudes of people maſ-ſacred by ſavage monſters who came out of Spain. He was animated with an irreſiſtible ardour to avenge ſo much innocent blood. The enthuſiaſm this ſpirit of hu-manity worked him up to, was turned into a rage more cruel than the thirſt of gold, or the fanaticiſm of reli-gion, to which ſo many victims had been ſacrificed. The manes of theſe unhappy ſufferers ſeemed to rouſe him, and call upon him for vengeance. He had heard ſome account of the *brethren of the coaſt*, as of the moſt inveterate enemies to the Spaniſh name : he therefore embarked on board a ſhip in order to join them.

In the paſſage they met with a Spaniſh veſſel, attack-ed it, and, as it was uſual in thoſe times, immediately boarded it. Montbar, with a ſabre in his hand fell upon the enemy, broke through them, and, hurrying twice from one end of the ſhip to the other, levelled every thing that oppoſed him. When he had com-pelled the enemy to ſurrender, leaving to his compa-nions the happineſs of dividing ſo rich a booty, he contented himſelf with the ſavage pleaſure of contem-plating the dead bodies of the Spaniards lying in heaps together, againſt whom he had ſworn a conſtant and deadly hatred.

Freſh opportunites ſoon occurred, that enabled him to exert this ſpirit of revenge, without extinguiſhing it. The ſhip he was upon arrived at the coaſt of St. Domingo. The French who were ſettled in the iſland brought him only a ſmall quantity of refreſhment, and alleged, in excuſe, that the Spaniards had laid waſte their ſettlements. " Why," replied Montbar, " do " you ſuffer ſuch inſults ?" " Neither do we," anſwer-ed they in the ſame tone ; " the Spaniards have expe-" rienced what kind of men we are, and have there-" fore taken advantage of the time when we were en-" gaged in hunting. But we are going to join ſome " of our companions, who have been ſtill more ill-

" treated than we, and then we fhall have warm work."
" If you approve it," anfwered Montbar, " I will
" head you, not as your commander, but as the fore-
" moft to expofe myfelf to danger." The Buccaneers
perceiving, from his appearance, that he was fuch a
man as they wanted, cheerfully accepted his offer.
The fame day they overtook the enemy, and Montbar
attacked them with an impetuofity that aftonifhed the
braveft. Nothing efcaped the effects of his fury. The
remaining part of his life was equally diftinguifhed as
this day. The Spaniards fuffered fo much from him,
both by land and fea, that he acquired the name of
the *Exterminator.*

His favage difpofition, as well as that of the other
Buccaneers who attended him, having obliged the
Spaniards to confine themfelves within their fettlements, thefe freebooters refolved to attack them
there. This new method of carrying on the war required fuperior forces ; and their affociations, in confequence, became more numerous. The firft that was
confiderable was formed by Lolonois, who derived his
name from the fands of Olone, the place of his birth.
From the abject ftate of a bondfman, he had gradually raifed himfelf to the command of two canoes, with
twenty-two men. With thefe he was fo fuccefsful,
as to take a Spanifh frigate on the coaft of Cuba. A
flave having obferved that all the men who were
wounded were put to death, and fearing left he fhould
fhare the fame fate, wanted to fave himfelf by a perfidious declaration, but very confiftent with the part he
had been deftined to take. He affured them, that the
governor of the Havannah had put him on board, in
order to ferve as executioner to all the Buccaneers he
had fentenced to be hanged, not doubting in the leaft
but they would be all taken prifoners. The favage
Lolonois, fired with rage at this declaration, ordered
all the Spaniards to be brought before him, and cut
off their heads one after another, fucking, at each
ftroke, the drops of blood that trickled down his fabre.
He then repaired to the Port-au-Prince, in which were

four fhips, fitted out purpofely to fail in purfuit of him. B O O K
He took them, and threw all the crews into the fea,   X.
except one man, whom he faved, in order to fend him
with a letter to the governor of the Havannah, ac-
quainting him with what he had done, and affuring
him, that he would treat in the fame manner all the
Spaniards that fhould fall into his hands, not excepting the governor himfelf, if he fhould be fo fortunate
as to take him. After this expedition, he ran his canoes and prize-fhips aground, and failed with his frigate only to the ifland of Tortuga.

Here he met with Michael de Bafco, who had fo
much diftinguifhed himfelf in having taken, even under the cannon of Porto-Bello, a Spanifh fhip, eftimated at five or fix millions of livres [from 208,333l.
6s. 8d. to 250,000l.], and by other actions equally
brave and daring. Thefe two adventurers gave out,
that they were going together upon fome important
project, and they were joined by four hundred and
forty men. This corps, the moft numerous the Buccaneers had yet been able to mufter, failed to the Bay
of Venezuela, which runs up into the country for the
fpace of fifty leagues. The fort that was built at the
entrance of it for its defence was taken ; the cannon
fpiked, and the whole garrifon, confifting of two hundred and fifty men, put to the fword. They then re-
imbarked, and came to Maracaybo, built on the weftern coaft of the lake of the fame name, at the diftance
of ten leagues from its mouth. This city, which had
become flourifhing and rich by its trade in fkins, tobacco, and cocoa, was deferted. The inhabitants had
retired with their effects to the other fide of the bay.
If the Buccaneers had not loft a fortnight in riot and
debauch, they would have found at Gibraltar, near the
extremity of the lake, every thing that the inhabitants
had fecreted, to fecure it from being plundered. On
the contrary, they met with fortifications lately erected, which they had the ufelefs fatisfaction of making
themfelves mafters of, at the expence of a great deal
of blood ; for the inhabitants had already removed at

BOOK a diftance the moft valuable part of their property.
X. Exafperated at this difappointment, they fet fire to
Gibraltar. Maracaybo would have fhared the fame
fate, had it not been ranfomed. Befide the fum they
received for its ranfom, they alfo carried off with them
all the croffes, pictures, and bells of the churches, intending, as they faid, to build a chapel in the ifland
of Tortuga, and to confecrate this part of their fpoils
to facred purpofes. Such was the religion of thefe
barbarous people, who could make no other offering
to Heaven, than that which arofe from their robberies
and plunder.

While they were idly diffipating the fpoils they had
made on the coaft of Venezuela, Morgan, the moft re-
nowned of the Englifh freebooters, failed from Jamaica
to attack Porto-Bello. His plan of operations was fo
well contrived, that he furprifed the city, and took it
without oppofition. In order to fecure the fort with
the fame facility, he compelled the women and the
priefts to fix the fcaling-ladders to the walls, from a
full conviction that the gallantry and fuperftition of the
Spaniards would never fuffer them to fire at the perfons they confidered as the objects of their love and
reverence. But the garrifon was not to be deceived
by this artifice, and was only to be fubdued by force
of arms; the treafures that were carried away from
this famous port were acquired at the expence of much
bloodfhed.

The conqueft of Panama was an object of much
greater importance. To fecure this, Morgan thought
it neceffary to fail in the latitudes of Cofta-Ricca, to
procure fome guides in the ifland of St. Catherine, to
which the Spaniards tranfported their malefactors.
This place was fo ftrongly fortified, that it ought to
have ftopped the progrefs of the moft intrepid commander for ten years. Notwithftanding this, the governor, on the firft appearance of the pirates, fent pri-
vately to concert meafures how he might furrender
himfelf without incurring the imputation of cowardice.
The refult of this confultation was, that Morgan, in

the night-time, fhould attack a fort at fome diftance, B O O K and that the governor fhould fally out of the citadel X. to defend this important poft; that the befiegers fhould then attack him in the rear, and take him prifoner, which would confequently occafion a furrender of the place. It was agreed that a brifk firing fhould be kept up on both fides, without doing mifchief to either. This farce was admirably carried on. The Spaniards, without being expofed to any danger, appeared to have done their duty ; and the freebooters, after having totally demolifhed the fortifications, and put on board their veffels a prodigious quantity of warlike ftores, which they found at St. Catherine's, fteered their courfe towards the river Chagre, the only channel that was open to them, to arrive at the place which was the object of their utmoft wifhes.

At the entrance of this confiderable river, a fort was built upon a fteep rock, which the waves of the fea conftantly beat againft. This bulwark, very difficult of accefs, was defended by an officer, whofe extraordinary abilities were equal to his courage, and by a garrifon that deferved fuch a commander. The freebooters, for the firft time, here met with a refiftance that could only be equalled by their perfeverance : it was a doubtful point, whether they would fucceed, or be obliged to raife the fiege, when a lucky accident happened, that proved favourable to their glory and their fortune. The commander was killed, and the fort accidentally took fire : the befiegers then, taking advantage of this double calamity, made themfelves mafters of the place.

Morgan left his veffels at anchor, with a fufficient number of men to guard them, and failed up the river in his boats for thirty-three miles, till he came to Cruces, where it ceafes to be navigable. He then proceeded by land to Panama, which was only five leagues diftant. Upon a large and extenfive plain that was before the city, he met with a confiderable body of troops, whom he put to flight with the greateft eafe, and entered into the city, that was now abandoned.

BOOK
X.

Here were found prodigious treasures concealed in the wells and caves. Some valuable commodities were taken upon the boats that were left aground at low water. In the neighbouring forests were also found several rich deposits. But the party of freebooters who were making excursions into the country, little satisfied with this booty, exercised the most shocking tortures on the Spaniards, Negroes, and Indians they discovered, to oblige them to confess where they had secreted their own as well as their masters riches. A beggar, accidentally going into a castle that had been deserted through fear, found some apparel that he put on. He had scarcely dressed himself in this manner, when he was perceived by these pirates, who demanded of him where his gold was. The unfortunate man showed them the ragged clothes he had just thrown off. He was instantly tortured; but, as he made no discovery, he was given up to some slaves, who put an end to his life. Thus the treasure the Spaniards had acquired in the New World by massacres and tortures, were restored again in the same manner.

In the midst of such scenes of horror, the savage Morgan fell in love. His character was not likely to inspire the object of his attachment with favourable sentiments towards him. He was resolved therefore to subdue by force the beautiful Spaniard that inflamed and tormented him. *Stop*, cried she to this savage, as she sprung with eagerness from his arms, *Stop : thinkest thou then that thou canst ravish my honour from me, as thou hast wrested from me my fortune and my liberty? Be assured that I can die, and be revenged.* Having said this, she drew out a poignard from under her gown, which she would have plunged into his heart, had he not avoided the blow.

But Morgan, still inflamed with a passion which this determined resistance had turned into rage, instead of the tenderness and attention he had made use of to prevail upon his captive, now proceeded to treat her with the greatest inhumanity. The fair Spaniard, immoveably resolute, stimulated, at the same time that she resisted, the frantic desires of Morgan; till at last the pirates, expressing their resentment at being kept so long in a state of inactivity, by a caprice which appeared extravagant to them, he was under the necessity of of listening to their complaints, and giving up his pursuit. Panama was burnt. They then set sail with a great number of prisoners, who were ransomed a few days after, and came to the mouth of the Chagre with a prodigious booty.

Before the break of the day that had been fixed upon for the division of the spoil, Morgan, while the rest of the pirates were in a deep sleep, with the principal freebooters of his own country, sailed for Jamaica, in a vessel which he had laden with the rich spoils of a city, that served as the staple of commerce between the Old and the New World. This instance of treachery, unheard-of before, excited a rage and resentment not to be described. The English pursued the robber, in hopes of wresting from him the booty of which their right and their avidity had been frustrated. The French, though sharers in the same loss, retired to the island of Tortuga, from whence they made several expeditions : but they were all trifling, till, in the year 1683, they attempted one of the greatest importance.

The plan of this expedition was formed by Van Horn, a native of Ostend, though he had served all his life among the French. His intrepidity would never let him suffer the least signs of cowardice among those who were associated with him. In the heat of an engagement he went about his ship, successively observed his men, and immediately killed those who shrank at the sudden report of a pistol, gun, or cannon. This extraordinary discipline had made him become the terror of the coward, and the idol of the brave. In other respects, he readily shared with the men of spirit and bravery the immense riches that were acquired by so truly warlike a disposition. When he went upon these expeditions, he generally sailed in his frigate, which was his own property. But these new designs

requiring greater numbers to carry them into execution, he took to his affiftance Grammont, Godfrey,
and Jonqué, three Frenchmen, diftinguifhed by their
exploits, and Lawrence de Graff, a Dutchman, who
had fignalized himfelf ftill more than they. Twelve
hundred freebooters joined themfelves to thefe famous commanders, and failed in fix veffels for Vera
Cruz.

The darknefs of the night favoured their landing,
which was effected at three leagues from the place,
where they arrived without being difcovered. The
governor, the fort, the barracks, and the pofts of the
greateft confequence ; every thing, in a word, that
could occafion any refiftance, was taken by break of
day. All the citizens, men, women, and children,
were fhut up in the churches, where they had fled for
fhelter. At the door of each church were placed barrels of gunpowder to blow up the building. A free-
booter, with a lighted match, was to fet fire to it upon
the leaft appearance of an infurrection.

While the city was kept in fuch terror, it was eafily
pillaged ; and, after the freebooters had carried off
what was moft valuable, they made a propofal to the
citizens who were kept prifoners in the churches, to
ranfom their lives and liberties, by a contribution of
ten millions of livres [416,666l. 13s. 4d.]. Thefe unfortunate people, who had neither eaten nor drunk for
three days, cheerfully accepted the terms that were
offered them. Half of the money was paid the fame
day : the other part was expected from the inland
parts of the country ; when there appeared, on an
eminence, a confiderable body of troops advancing,
and near the port a fleet of feventeen fhips from Europe. At the fight of this armament, the freebooters,
without any marks of furprife, retreated quietly with
fifteen hundren flaves they had carred off with them,
as a trifling indemnification for the reft of the money
they expected, the fettling of which they referred to
a more favourable opportunity. Thefe ruffians fincere-
ly believed, that whatever they pillaged or exacted by

force of arms, upon the coafts where they made a de-
fcent, was their lawful property, and that God and
their arms gave them an undoubted right not only to
the capital of thefe contributions they compelled the
inhabitants to fign a written engagement to fulfil, but
even to the intereft of that part of the fum that was
not yet paid.

Their retreat was equally glorious and daring. They
boldly failed through the midft of the Spanifh fleet,
which let them pafs without firing a fingle gun ; and
were, in fact, rather afraid of being attacked and beaten.
The Spaniards would not probably have efcaped fo eafily, and with no other inconvenience, but fuch as
arofe from their fears, if the veffels of the pirates had
not been laden with riches, or if the Spanifh fleet had
been freighted with any other effects but fuch merchandife as were little valued by thefe pirates.

A year had fcarce elapfed fince their return from
Mexico, when on a fudden they were all feized with
the rage of going to plunder the country of Peru.
They expected, undoubtedly, to find greater treafures
upon a fea little frequented, than upon one fo long
expofed to plunder. The French and Englifh, and
even the pirate affociations of thefe two nations, pro-
jected this plan at the fame time, without having concerted it together. Four thoufand men directed their
courfe to this part of the New Hemifphere. Some of
them came by the continent, and others by the Straits
of Magellan, to the place that was the object of their
wifhes. If the intrepidity of thefe barbarians had
been directed, by a fkilful and refpectable commander, to one fingle uniform end, this important colony
would have been loft to Spain. But their natural character was an invincible obftacle to fo rare an union ;
for they always formed themfelves into feveral diftinct
bodies, fometimes into fo few in number as ten or
twelve, who acted together, or feparately, as the moft
trifling caprice directed. Grognier, Lécuyer, Picard,
and Le Sage, were the moft diftinguifhed officers among

B O O K the French: Dàvid, Samms, Peter, Wilner, and Town-
    X.   ley, among the Englifh.

Such of thofe adventurers as had got into the South
Sea by the Straits of Darien, feized upon the firft veffels they found upon the coaft. Their affociates,
who had failed in their own veffels, were not much
better provided. Weak, however, as they were, they
beat, funk, or took, all the fhips that were fitted out
againft them. The Spaniards then fufpended their
navigations. The freebooters were continually obliged to make defcents upon the coafts, to get provifions; or to go by land, in order to plunder thofe cities where the booty was fecured. They fucceffively
attacked Seppo, Peubla-Neuvo, Leon, Reulejo, Pue-
blo-Viejo, Chiriquita, Efparfo, Granada, Villia, Ni-
coya, Tecoantepec, Mucmelūna, Chuluteca, New-Se-
govia, and Guayaquil, the moft confiderable of all thefe
places.

As Grognier was returning home from one of thofe
rapid expeditions, he found that a defile through which
he was to pafs was occupied by fome battalions that
were intrenched, who offered not to impede his retreat,
provided he would confent to releafe the prifoners he
had taken. *If,* faid he, *you would have my prifoners,
you muft cut their irons afunder with your fabres; with
refpect to my paffage, my fword fecures that to me.* This
anfwer gained him a victory, and he purfued his march
unmolefted.

Univerfal terror prevailed throughout the empire;
the approach of the freebooters, and even the fear of
their arrival, difperfed the people. The Spaniards,
grown effeminate by the moft extravagant luxury,
enervated by the peaceful exercife of their tyranny,
and reduced to the ftate of their flaves, never waited
for the enemy, unlefs they were at leaft twenty to
one; and even then they were beaten. They retained no impreffion of the pride and nobility of their origin. They were fo much degenerated, that they had
loft all ideas of the art of war, and were even fcarce

acquainted with the ufe of fire-arms. They were but little better than the Americans, whom they trampled upon. . This extraordinary want of courage was increafed, from the idea they had conceived of the ferocious men who attacked them. Their monks had drawn them with the fame hideous features with which they reprefented devils; and they themfelves had overcharged the picture. Such a reprefentation, the offfpring of a wild and terrified imagination, equally imprinted on every mind averfion and terror.

Notwithftanding the excefs of their refentment, the Spaniards only recked their revenge upon their foes when they were no more able to infpire terror. As foon as the Buccaneers had quitted the place they had plundered, and if any of them had been killed in the attack, the body was digged up again, mutilated, or made to pafs through the various kinds of torture that would have been practifed upon the man had he been alive. This abhorrence of the freebooters was extended even to the places on which they had exercifed their cruelties. The cities they had taken were excommunicated; the very walls and foil of the places which had been laid wafte were anathematized, and the inhabitants abandoned them for ever.

This rage, equally impotent and childifh, could only contribute to embolden that of their enemies. As foon as they took a town, it was directly fet on fire, unlefs a fum proportioned to its value was given to fave it. The prifoners taken in battle were maffacred without mercy, if they were not ranfomed by government, or by individuals: gold, pearls, or precious ftones, were the only things accepted of for the payment of their ranfom. Silver being too common, and too weighty in proportion to its value, would have been troublefome to them. In a word, the chances of fortune, that feldom leave guilt unpunifhed, nor adverfity without a compenfation for its fufferings, atoned for the crimes committed in the conqueft of the New World, and the Indians were amply avenged of the Spaniards.

But it happened in this, as it generally does in events

B O O K of this nature, that thofe who committed fuch out-
X.   rages did not long enjoy the fruits of them. Several
of them died in the courfe of thefe piracies, from the
effects of the climate, from diftrefs or debauchery.
Some were fhipwrecked in paffing the Straits of Magellan, and at Cape Horn. Moft of thofe who attempted to get to the Northern Sea by land fell into
the ambufcade that was laid for them, and loft either
their lives or the booty they had acquired. The Englifh and French colonies gained very little by an expedition that lafted four years, and found themfelves
deprived of their braveft inhabitants.

While fuch piracies were committed on the Southern Ocean, the Northern was threatened with the fame
by Grammont. He was a native of Paris, by birth a
gentleman, and had diftinguifhed himfelf in a military
capacity in Europe; but his paffion for wine, gaming,
and women, had induced him to join the pirates. His
virtues, perhaps, were fufficient to have atoned for his
vices. He was affable, polite, generous, and eloquent:
he was endued with a found judgment, and was a perfon of approved valour, which foon made him be confidered as the chief of the French freebooters. As
foon as it was known that he had taken up arms, he
was immediately joined by a number of brave men.
The governor of St. Domingo, who had at length prevailed upon his mafter to approve of the project, equally wife and juft, of fixing the pirates to fome place,
and inducing them to become cultivators, was defirous
of preventing the concerted expedition, and forbade it
in the king's name. Grammont, who had a greater fhare
of fenfe than his affociates, was not on that account
more inclined to comply, and fternly replied, *How can
Lewis difapprove of a defign he is unacquainted with,
and which hath been planned only a few days ago?* This
anfwer highly pleafed all the freebooters, who directly embarked, in 1685, to attack Campeachy.

They landed without oppofition. But, at fome diftance from the coaft, they were attacked by eight
hundred Spaniards, who were beaten, and purfued to

the town, where both parties entered at the fame time. B O O K
The cannon they found there was immediately level- X.
led againſt the citadel. As it had very little effect,
they were contriving ſome ſtratagem to enable them
to become maſters of the place, when intelligence was
brought that it was abandoned. There remained in
it only a gunner, an Engliſhman, and an officer of
ſuch ſignal courage, that he choſe rather to expoſe
himſelf to the greateſt extremities, than baſely to fly
from the place with the reſt. The commander of the
Buccaneers received him with marks of diſtinction, ge-
neroufly releaſed him, gave him up all his effects, and
beſides complimented him with ſome valuable preſents : ſuch influence have courage and fidelity, even
on the minds of thoſe who ſeem to violate all the rights
of ſociety.

The conquerors of Campeachy ſpent two months
in ſearching all the environs of the city, for twelve or
fifteen leagues, carrying off every thing that the inhabitants, in their flight, thought they had preſerved.
When all the treaſure they had collected from every
quarter was depoſited in the ſhips, a propoſal was made
to the governor of the province, who ſtill kept the
field with nine hundred men, to ranſom his capital city. His refuſal determined them to burn it, and de-
moliſh the citadel. The French, on the feſtival of St.
Louis, were celebrating the anniverſary of their king,
and, in the tranſports of their patriotiſm, intoxication,
and national love of their prince, they burnt to the
value of a million [41,666l. 13s. 4d.] of logwood ; a
part, and a very conſiderable one too, of the ſpoil they
had made. After this ſingular and extravagant inſtance of folly, of which Frenchmen only could boaſt,
they returned to St. Domingo.

The little advantage which the Engliſh and French
freebooters had made by their laſt expeditions upon
the continent had infenſibly led them to have recourſe
to their uſual piratical expeditions upon the ſea. Both
were employed in attacking the ſhips they met with ;
when a particular train of circumſtances again enga-

ged the French in that courfe, which every thing had
rendered them diffatisfied with.

A few enterprifing men had fitted out, in 1697, in
the ports of France, and under the fanction of government, feven fhips of the line, and a proportionate number of inferior veffels. This fleet, commanded by Commodore Pointis, conveyed troops for landing ; and its
deftination was againft Carthagena, one of the richeft
and beft fortified towns of the New World. It was
expected that this expedition would be attended with
great difficulties, but it was hoped that they would be
furmounted, if the Buccaneers would affift in it, which
they did engage to do, from motives of complaifance
to Ducaffe, governor of St. Domingo, who was, and
deferved to be, their idol.

Thefe men, whofe boldnefs could not be reftrained,
did ftill more than was expected from them. No
fooner had they perceived a fmall breach in the fortifications of the lower town, than they ftormed the
place, and planted their ftandards upon the walls.
They carried the other works with the fame intrepidity.
The town furrendered, and its fubmiffion was owing to
the Buccaneers.

All kinds of enormities fucceeded this event. The
general, who was an unjuft, covetous, and cruel man,
broke every article of the capitulation. Although the
apprehenfions of an army that was collecting in the inland country, had made him confent that the inhabitants fhould keep half of their moveable effects, yet
every thing was given up to the moft horrible plunder.
The officers were the firft thieves ; and it was not till
they had gorged themfelves with the fpoils, that the
foldiers were fuffered to ranfack the houfes. As for
the Buccaneers, they were kept in employment out of
the town, while the treafure was feized.

Pointis pretended that the fpoils did not exceed feven or eight millions of livres [from 291,666l. 13s.
4d. to 333,333l. 6s. 8d.]. Ducaffe valued them at
30,000,000 [1,250,000l.], and others at 40,000,000
[1,666,666l. 10s. 4d.]. The Buccaneers, according to

agreement, were to receive one quarter of the whole, B O O K whatever it might be. They were however given to underſtand, that their profit would only amount to 40,000 crowns [5000l.].

The ſhips had ſet ſail, when the propoſal was made to theſe intrepid men, who had decided the victory. Exaſperated at this treatment, which ſo evidently affected their rights, and diſappointed their expectations, they reſolved immediately to board the veſſel called *the Sceptre*, where Pointis himſelf was, and which, at that time, was too far diſtant from the reſt of the ſhips, to expect to be aſſiſted by them. This infamous commander was upon the point of being maſſacred, when one of the malcontents cried out : *Brethren, why ſhould we attack this raſcal? He hath carried off nothing that belongs to us. He hath left our ſhare at Carthagena, and there we muſt go to recover it.* This propoſal was received with general applauſe. A ſavage joy at once ſucceeded that gloomy melancholy which had ſeized them ; and, without further deliberation, all their ſhips ſailed towards the city.

As ſoon as they had entered the city, without meeting with any reſiſtance, the Buccaneers ſhut up all the men in the great church, and ſpoke to them in the following words :

" We are not ignorant that you conſider us as men " void of faith and of all religion, as infernal beings " rather than men. The abhorrence you have of us " hath been manifeſted by the opprobrious terms with " which you affect to deſcribe us ; and your miſtruſt " of us, by your refuſing to treat with us of your ca- " pitulation. You ſee us here armed, and capable of " avenging ourſelves. The paleneſs viſible upon your " countenances plainly ſhews that you expect the moſt " ſevere treatment ; and your conſcience tells you, no " doubt, that you deſerve it. Be at length undeceiv- " ed, and acknowledge, in this inſtance, that the in- " jurious appellations with which you ſtigmatize us are " not to be applied to us, but to the infamous gene- " ral under whoſe command we lately fought. The

BOOK
X.

" traitor to whom we have opened the gates of the ci-
" ty, which he would never have entered without our
" affiftance, hath feized upon the fpoils acquired at
" our hazard, and by our courage ; and, by this act
" of injuftice, hath compelled us to return to you.
" Our moderation muft juftify our fincerity. We will
" quit your city immediately, upon your delivering
" 5,000,000 of livres [208,333l. 6s. 8d.] into our
" hands. This is the whole of our claim ; and we
" pledge our honour to you, that we will inftantly re-
" treat. But if you refufe us fo moderate a contribu-
" tion, look at our fabres : we fwear by them that we
" will fpare no perfon ; and when the misfortunes
" which threaten you fhall come upon you, and upon
" your wives and children, accufe none but yourfelves
" and the worthlefs Pointis, whom you are at liberty
" to load with all kinds of execrations."

After this difcourfe, a facred orator mounted the
pulpit, and made ufe of the influence that his character, his authority, and his eloquence gave him, to perfuade his hearers to yield up, without referve, all the
gold, filver, and jewels they had. The collection made
after the fermon not furnifhing the fum required, the
city was ordered to be plundered. From the houfes,
they proceeded to pillage the churches, and even the
tombs, but with no great fuccefs ; and the inftruments
of torture were at length produced.

Two of the citizens of the greateft diftinction were
feized, and after them two more, in order to endeavour to extort from them, where the public money, as
well as that of individuals, was concealed. They all
anfwered, feparately, with fo much candour, as well
as firmnefs, that they were ignorant of it, that avarice
itfelf was difarmed. Some mufkets were, however,
fired off, to induce a belief that thefe unfortunate men
had been fhot. Every one apprehended the fame fate ;
and that very evening one million of livres [41,666l.
13s. 4d.] was brought in to the freebooters. The following days produced alfo fomething more. Defpairing, at length, to add any thing to what they had al-

ready amaſſed, they ſet ſail.   Unfortunately they fell
in with a fleet of Dutch and Engliſh ſhips, both thoſe
nations being then in alliance with Spain, and ſeveral
of their ſmall veſſels were either taken or ſunk ; the
reſt eſcaped to St. Domingo.

Such was the laſt memorable event in the hiſtory of
the freebooters.

The ſeparation of the Engliſh and French, when
the war, on account of the Prince of Orange, divided
the two nations ; the ſucceſsful means they both made
uſe of to promote the cultivation of land in their colonies, by the aſſiſtance of theſe enterpriſing men ; the
prudence that was ſhown, in fixing the moſt diſtinguiſhed among them, and intruſting them with civil
and military employments ; the protection they were
under a neceſſity of affording ſucceſſively to the Spaniſh ſettlements, which, till then, had been a general
object of plunder : all theſe circumſtances, and various
others, beſide the impoſſibility there was of ſupplying
the place of ſo many extraordinary men, who were
continually dropping off, concurred to put an end to
the moſt ſingular ſociety that had ever exiſted.   Without any regular ſyſtem, without laws, without any degree of ſubordination, and even without any fixed revenue, they became the aſtoniſhment of the age in
which they lived, as they will alſo be of poſterity.
They would have ſubdued all America, had they been
animated with the ſpirit of conqueſt, as they were with
that of rapine.

England, France, and Holland, had ſent, at different
times, conſiderable fleets into the New World.   The
intemperance of the climate, the want of ſubſiſtence,
the dejection of the troops, rendered the beſt-concert-
ed ſchemes unſucceſsful.   Neither of theſe nations acquired any national glory, nor made any conſiderable
progreſs, by them.   Upon the very ſcene of their diſgrace, and on the very ſpot where they were ſo ſhame-
fully repulſed, a ſmall number of adventurers, who had
no other reſources to enable them to carry on a war,
but what the war itſelf afforded them, ſucceeded in the

B O O K most difficult enterprifes. They fupplied the want of
  X.   numbers and of power, by their activity, their vigilance, and bravery. An unbounded paffion for liberty
and independence excited and kept up in them that
energy of foul that enables us to undertake and execute every thing; it produced that vigour, that fuperiority in action, which the moft approved military
difcipline, the moft powerful combinations of ftrength,
the beft-regulated governments, the moft honourable
and moft ftriking rewards and marks of diftinction,
will never be able to excite.

The principle which actuated thefe extraordinary
and romantic men is not eafily difcovered. It cannot
be afcribed to want: the earth they trod upon offered
them immenfe treafures, collected ready to their hand
by men of inferior capacities. Can it then be imputed
to avarice? But would they then have fquandered
away in a day the fpoils acquired in a whole campaign? As they properly belonged to no country,
they did not therefore facrifice themfelves for its defence, for the aggrandizing of its territories, or for the
avenging of its quarrels. The love of glory, had they
known it, would have prevented them from committing fuch numberlefs enormities and crimes, which caft
a fhade on all their brighteft actions. Neither could
a fpirit of indolence and eafe ever make men expofe
themfelves to conftant fatigues, and fubmit to the
greateft dangers.

What then were the moral caufes that gave rife to
fo fingular a fociety as that of the freebooters? That
country, where nature feems to have obtained a perpetual and abfolute power over the moft turbulent paffions, where the intemperate riot and intoxication occafioned by public feftivals was neceffary to roufe men
from an habitual ftate of lethargy, where they lived
fatisfied with their tedious and indolent courfe of life;
that country became at once inhabited by an ardent
and impetuous people, who, from the fcorching heat
of their atmofphere, feemed to have carried their fentiments to the greateft excefs, and their paffions to a

degree of frenzy. While the heats of a burning cli- B O O K
mate enervated the old conquerors of the New World; X.
while the Spaniards, who were fo reftlefs and turbulent
in their own country, enjoyed, with the conquered
Americans, a life habituated to eafe and dejection; a
fet of men, who had come out of the moft temperate
climates in Europe, went under the equator to acquire
powers unknown before.

If we fhould be defirous of tracing the origin of this
revolution, we fhall perceive that it arifes from the
freebooters having lived under the fhackles of European governments. The fpirit of liberty being repref-
fed for fo many ages, exerted its power to a degree almoft inconceivable, and occafioned the moft terrible
effects that were ever exhibited in the moral world.
Reftlefs and enthufiaftic men of every nation joined
themfelves to thefe adventurers, as foon as they heard
of the fuccefs they had met with. The charms of novelty; the idea of, and defire excited by, diftant objects; the want of a change in fituation; the hopes of
better fortune; the impulfe which excites the imagination to the undertaking of great actions; admiration, which eafily induces men to imitation; the neceffity of getting the better of thofe impediments that
are the confequences of imprudence; the force of example; and the being equally partakers of the fame
good and bad fortune among thofe who have frequently affociated together: in a word, the temporary ferment which all the elements together, with feveral accidental circumftances, had raifed in the minds of men,
alternately elevated to the greateft profperity, or funk
in the deepeft diftrefs, at one time ftained with blood,
at another revelling in voluptuoufnefs, rendered the
freebooters a people wholly diftinct in hiftory; but a
people whofe duration was fo tranfient, that its glory
lafted, as it were, but a moment.

We are, however, accuftomed to confider thefe ruffians with a kind of abhorrence. This they deferve,
as the inftances of fidelity, integrity, difintereftednefs,
and generofity they fhowed to one another, did not

BOOK
X.

prevent the outrages they perpetually committed a-
gainft mankind. But amidft fuch enormities, it is impoffible not to be furprifed at a variety of brave and
noble actions, that would have reflected honour on the
moft virtuous people.

Some freebooters had agreed, for a certain fum, to
efcort a Spanifh fhip, very richly laden. One of them
ventured to propofe to his companions to enrich themfelves at once, by making themfelves mafters of the
fhip. Montauban, who was the commander of the
troop, had no fooner heard the propofal, than he defired to refign the command, and to be fet on fhore.
What! replied thefe brave men, would you then leave
us? Is there any one among us who approves of the
treachery that you abhor? A council was immediately called; and it was determined that the guilty perfon fhould be thrown upon the firft coaft they came
to. They took an oath, that fo difhoneft a man fhould
never be admitted in any expedition, in which any of
the brave men prefent fhould be concerned, as they
would think themfelves difhonoured by fuch a connection. If this be not confidered as an inftance of heroifm, muft we then expect to meet with heroes in an
age in which every thing great is turned into ridicule,
under the idea of enthufiafm?

Accordingly, the hiftory of paft times doth not offer, nor will that of future times ever produce, an example of fuch an affociation; which is almoft as marvellous as the difcovery of the New World. Nothing
but this event could have given rife to it, by collecting together, in thofe diftant regions, all the men of
the higheft impetuofity and energy of foul that had
ever appeared in our ftates.

Their fword, and their daring fpirit, which they exercifed with fuch terrible effect in America, was the
only fortune which thefe men of fo uncommon a
ftamp poffeffed in Europe. In America, being enemies to all mankind, and dreaded by all; perpetually
expofed to the moft extreme dangers, they muft neceffarily have confidered every day as if the laft of their

life, and they would, confequently, diffipate their
wealth in the fame manner as they had acquired it.
They would give themfelves up to all the exceffes of
debauchery and profufion; and, on their return from
the fight, the intoxication of their victory would accompany them in their feafts; they would embrace
their miftreffes in their bloody arms; they would fall
afleep, for a while, lulled by voluptuous pleafures,
from which they would be roufed only to proceed to
new maffacres. As it was a matter of indifference to
them whether they fhould leave their bodies upon the
furface of the earth, or underneath the waters, they
muft neceffarily look upon life or death with the fame
coolnefs. With a ferocious turn of mind, and a mif-
guided confcience, deftitute of connections, of relations, of friends, of fellow-citizens, of a country, and
of an afylum, and without having any of thofe motives which moderate the ardour of bravery, by the
value which they attach to exiftence, they muft neceffarily have rufhed, like men deprived of fight, upon
the moft defperate attempts. Equally incapable of
fubmitting to indigence or to quiet; too proud to employ themfelves in common labour; they would have
been the fcourge of the Old, had they not been that
of the New World. Had they not gone to ravage
thofe diftant countries, they would have ranfacked our
provinces, and would have left behind them a name
famous in the catalogue of our greateft villains.

America had fcarce recovered from the ravages fhe
had fuftained; fhe had fcarce begun to be fenfible of
the advantages fhe derived from the induftry of the
freebooters, who were now become citizens and hufbandmen; when the Old World exhibited the fcene
of fuch a revolution as alarmed and terrified the New.
Charles the Second, king of Spain, had juft ended a
life of trouble and anxiety. His fubjects, perfuaded
that a defcendant of the houfe of Bourbon alone was
able to preferve the monarchy entire, had urged him,
towards the clofe of his life, to appoint the duke of
Anjou his fucceffor. The idea of having the govern-

Marginal notes:

BOOK X.

Caufes that prevented the Englifh and Dutch from making any conqueft in America during the war for the Spanifh fucceffion.

B O O K ment of two-and twenty kingdoms devolve to a fa-
X. mily that was not only his rival, but his enemy, had
filled him with the moſt gloomy apprehenſions. But
after ſeveral internal ſtruggles, and numberleſs marks
of irreſolution, he at length prevailed upon himſelf to
ſhow an example of juſtice, and greatneſs of ſoul, which
the natural weakneſs of his character gave little reaſon
to expect from him.

Europe, tired out, for half a century, with the haughtineſs, ambition, and tyranny of Lewis XIV. exerted
its combined forces to prevent the increaſe of a power
already become too formidable. The fatal effects of a
bad adminiſtration had entirely enervated the Spaniards ; the ſpirit of ſuperſtition, and conſequently of
weakneſs, that prevailed then in France, had procured
ſuch advantages to the league, as are hardly to be paralleled in the inſtance of the union of ſeveral powers
againſt a ſingle one. This league gained an influence,
that was increaſed by the victories, equally glorious
and beneficial, it obtained every campaign. Both
kingdoms were ſoon left without ſtrength or fame.
To add to their misfortunes, their calamities were a
general object of joy, and none were touched with a
ſenſe of compaſſion at the miſeries they experienced.

England and Holland, after having profuſely laviſh-
ed their blood and treaſures in defence of the emperor, thought it neceſſary to attend to their own intereſts in America. This country invited them to rich
as well as eaſy conqueſts. Spain, ſince the deſtruction
of its galleons at Vigo, had no ſhips; and France, after having experienced that fatal reverſe of fortune
that had reduced her to the loweſt ebb, had neglected
her navy. This inattention was owing to a diſtant
cauſe.

Lewis XIV. who, in his earlier age, was ambitious
of every thing that might add to his glory, thought
that ſomething would be wanting to the ſplendour of
his reign if he did not eſtabliſh a conſiderable naval
force. His numerous fleets were ſoon in a condition
to balance the combined forces of England and of

Holland, and conveyed the terror of his name to the B O O K extremities of the globe. But he foon loft this new X. fpecies of grandeur. In proportion as his inordinate ambition drew upon him frefh enemies, as he found himfelf obliged to maintain a greater number of troops in conftant pay, as the frontiers of the kingdom were extended, and as his forts became more numerous, the number of his fhips decreafed. He made ufe of part of the funds that were deftined to fupport his maritime power, even before his neceffities obliged him to it. The frequent removals of the court, public buildings, that were either ufelefs or too magnificent, objects of oftentation, or of mere pleafure, and various other caufes equally trifling, abforbed that part of the public revenue, which ought to have been employed in his maritime armaments. From that time, this part of the power of France began to grow weak: it infenfibly declined, and was entirely loft in the misfortunes of the war that was raifed for the Spanifh fucceffion.

At this period, the acquifitions the Spaniards and French had made in the Weft Indies were not put in a ftate of defence. They were, therefore, the more likely foon to become the property of Great Britain and the United Provinces; the only modern nations who had eftablifhed their political influence upon the principles of commerce. The vaft difcoveries of the Spaniards and Portuguefe had given them, indeed, an exclufive poffeffion of thofe treafures and productions that feemed to promife them the empire of the world, if riches could obtain it: but thefe nations, intoxicated as they were with the love of gold and the idea of conqueft, had never in the leaft fufpected that their poffeffions in the New World could fupport their power in the Old. The Englifh and Dutch went into the contrary extreme; building their opinions upon the fyftem of the influence they fuppofed America muft neceffarily give to Europe: A fyftem which they not only mifapplied, but carried to excefs.

Thefe two nations, one of which had no natural advantages, and the other very inconfiderable ones, had,

B O O K from the earlieſt period, diſcovered the true principleś
  X. of commerce, and purſued them with greater perſeverance than might have been expected from the different ſituations they had been engaged in. Accidental
circumſtances having at firſt animated the induſtry of
the pooreſt of theſe nations, ſhe found herſelf very
quickly equalled by her rival power, whoſe genius was
more lively, and whoſe reſources were much greater.
The war, occaſioned by a ſpirit of induſtry, and excited by jealouſy, ſoon degenerated into fierce, obſtinate,
and bloody engagements. Theſe were not merely ſuch
hoſtilities as are carried on between two different people ; they reſembled rather the hatred and revenge of
one private man againſt another. The neceſſity they
were under of uniting, in order to check and reſtrain
the power of France, ſuſpended theſe hoſtilities. The
ſucceſs they met with, which was, perhaps, too rapid
and deciſive, revived their former animoſity. From
the apprehenſion they were under, that each ſtate was
labouring for the aggrandizement of the other, they
entirely neglected the invaſion of America. Queen
Anne, at length, availing herſelf of a favourable opportunity for concluding a ſeparate peace, procured
ſuch advantageous terms, as gave the Engliſh a great
ſuperiority over their rivals the Dutch. From that
time, England became of the greateſt importance in
the political ſyſtem of Europe, and Holland was totally diſregarded.

Remark-   The years ſucceeding the peace of Utrecht revived
able activi- the ideas of the golden age to the world, which would
ty that pre-
vailed in be always in a ſufficient ſtate of tranquillity, if the Eu-
the iſlands ropeans did not diſturb its peace, by carrying their
of America
after the arms and their diſſenſions into every quarter of the
peace of globe. The fields were now no more covered with
Utrecht.
dead bodies. The harveſt of the huſbandman was not
laid waſte. The ſailor ventured to ſail in every ſea
without dread of pirates. Mothers no more ſaw their
children forced from them, to laviſh their blood at the
caprice of a weak monarch or an ambitious miniſter.
Nations did no longer unite to gratify the paſſions of

their fovereigns. For fome time, men lived together B O O K
as brethren, as much, at leaft, as the pride of princes,   X.
and the avidity of the people, would allow.

Although this general happinefs was to be attributed
to thofe who held the reins of government, yet the improvement of reafon contributed, in fome degree, to
produce it. Philofophy then began to lay open and
recommend the fentiments of benevolence. The writings of fome philofophers had been made public, or
difperfed among the people, and contributed to polifh
and refine their manners. The fpirit of moderation
had infpired men with the love of the more ufeful and
pleafing arts of life, and abated, at leaft, the defire they
till then had of deftroying one another. The thirft of
blood feemed to be affuaged, and all nations, with the
affiftance of the difcoveries they had made, ardently fet
about the improvement of their population, agriculture, and manufactures.

This fpirit of activity exerted itfelf principally in the
Caribbee Iflands. The ftates upon the continent can
fubfift, and even flourifh, when the rage of war is
kindled in their neighbourhood and on their frontiers;
becaufe the principal object of their attention is the
culture of their lands, their manufactures, their fubfiftence, and internal confumptions. This is not the
cafe with regard to thofe fettlements which different
nations have formed in the great Archipelago of America. In thefe, life and property are equally precarious. None of the neceffaries of life are the natural
produce of the climate. Wearing apparel, and the inftruments of hufbandry, are not even made in the
country. All their commodities are intended for exportation. Nothing but an eafy and fafe communication with Africa, with the northern coafts of the New
World, but principally with Europe, can procure to
thefe iflands that free circulation of the neceffaries of
life they receive, and of thofe fuperfluities they give in
exchange. The more the colonifts had fuffered from
the effects of that long and dreadful commotion that
had thrown every thing into confufion. the greater was

their vigilance in endeavouring to repair the loffes their
fortunes had fuftained. The very hopes entertained
that the general weaknefs would enfure a lafting tranquillity, encouraged the moft cautious merchants to
fupply the colonifts with goods in advance; a circumftance that contributed greatly to quicken the progrefs
they made, which, notwithftanding all their care and
attention, would otherwife have been very flow. Thefe
affiftances enfured as well as increafed the profperity of
the iflands, till a ftorm, that had been a long time ga-
thering, broke out in the year 1739, and difturbed the
peace of the world.

The iflands
of America
are the
caufe of the
war in
1739. E-
vents in
that war,
and the ter-
mination of
it.
The Englifh colonies, but chiefly Jamaica, had carried on a contraband trade with the Spanifh fettlements in the New World, which cuftom had long
made them confider as lawful. The court of Madrid
becoming better acquainted with its interefts, concerted meafures to put a ftop to, or at leaft to check, this
intercourfe. The plan might poffibly be prudent;
but it was neceffary it fhould be carried into execution
with equity. If the fhips that were intended to prevent this fraudulent trade had only feized upon thofe
veffels that were concerned in it, this meafure would
have deferved commendation. But the abufes infeparable from violent meafures, the eagernefs of gain, and
perhaps too, a fpirit of revenge, incited them to ftop,
under the pretence of their carrying on a contraband
trade, many fhips which in reality had a legal deftination.

England, whofe fecurity, power, and glory, is founded upon commerce, could not very patiently fuffer
even her ufurpations to be reftrained ; but was highly
incenfed when fhe found that thefe hoftilities were carried to an excefs inconfiftent with the law of nations.
In London, and in the houfe of parliament, general
complaints were made againft the authors of them, and
invectives againft the minifter who fuffered them.
Walpole, who had long ruled Great Britain, and whofe
character and abilities were better adapted to peace
than war, and the Spanifh council, which fhowed lefs

fpirit as the ftorm increafed, concerted together terms B o o k
of reconciliation. Thofe fixed upon, and figned at   X.
Pardo, were not approved by a people equally inflamed by its interefts, its refentments, and by party fpirit,
and efpecially by the number of political writings that
were conftantly publifhed on the fubjeſt.

The fovereign of any country, who forbids the liberty of difcuffing publicly matters of adminiftration,
and politics, gives an authentic atteftation of his propenfity to tyranny, and of the impropriety of his meafures. It is juft as if he were to fay to the people:
" I know full as well as you do, that what I have de-
" termined upon is contrary to your liberty, your pre-
" rogatives, your intereft, your tranquillity, and your
" happinefs; but I do not choofe that you fhould
" murmur at it. I will never fuffer you to be enlight-
" ened, becaufe it is convenient to me that you fhould
" remain in that ftate of ftupidity, which will prevent
" you from difcerning my caprices, my vanity, my ex-
" travagant diffipations, my oftentation, the depreda-
" tions of my courtiers and of my favourites, my ruin-
" ous amufements, and my ftill more ruinous paffions,
" from the public good, which never was, is not, nor
" ever will be, as far as depends upon me and my fuc-
" ceffors, any thing more than a decent pretence.
" Every thing I do is well done, you may either be-
" lieve or not, as you choofe; but you muft be filent.
" I will prove to you, by all the moft extravagant and
" atrocious meafures, that I reign for myfelf alone,
" and neither by you nor for you. And if any one of
" you fhould be rafh enough to contradiſt me, let him
" perifh in the obfcurity of a dungeon, or let him be
" ftrangled, that he may for ever be deprived of the
" powers of committing a fimilar aſt of indifcretion;
" for fuch is my will and pleafure." In confequence
of fuch declarations, a man of genius muft be either
filent or be put to death; and a nation muft be kept
in a ftate of barbarifm, with refpeſt to their religion,
their laws, their morals, and their government, and in
the ignorance of the moft important things relative to

B O O K
X.

their real interefts, to their power, to their trade, to their fplendour, and to their felicity; while all the nations around are improving themfelves by the daring efforts, and the concurrence of numbers of enlightened men, whofe views are directed to thofe objects alone that are really worthy of their attention. The reafoning of an adminiftration, which prohibits information, is defective in every particular; the progrefs of improvement is not to be ftopt, nor even to be checked, without manifeft difadvantage. Prohibition hath no other effect than to irritate men, and to infpire them with an idea of rebellion, and to give all their writings a libellous tendency. It is doing too much honour to innocent fubjects, to be alarmed at a few pages of writing, when two hundred thoufand affaffins are ready to execute the orders of government.

England teems daily with numberlefs productions of the prefs, in which all the concerns of the nation are treated with freedom. Among thefe writings fome are judicious, written by men of underftanding, or citizens well informed and zealous for the public good. Their advice contributes to difcover to the public their true interefts, and to affift the operations of government. Few ufeful regulations of internal economy are adopted in the ftate, that have not firft been pointed out, modelled, or improved in fome of thefe writings. Unhappy are the people who are deprived of fuch an advantage.

' But it may be faid, that among the few fenfible
' men who ferve to enlighten their country, numbers
' are to be met with, who, either from a difguft to
' thofe in power, or from a defire of falling in with the
' tafte of the people, or from fome perfonal motives,
' delight in fomenting a fpirit of diffenfion and difcon-
' tent. The means generally made ufe of for this
' purpofe, are to heighten the pretenfions of their coun-
' try beyond their juft and legal bounds, and to make
' the people confider the fmalleft precautions taken by
' other powers for the prefervation of their poffeffions,
' as vifible encroachments. Thefe exaggerations, equal-

' ly partial and falfe, eftablifh prejudices, the effects of
' which occafion the nation to be conftantly at war
' with its neighbours. If government, from a defire of
' preferving the balance of juftice between itfelf and
' other powers, fhould refufe to yield to popular pre-
' judices, it finds itfelf, at length, compelled to it.'

The liberty of the prefs is undoubtedly attended
with thefe inconveniencies ; but they are fo trifling,
and fo tranfient, when compared with the advantages
refulting from it, that they do not deferve our notice.
The queftion is reduced to this : *Is it better that a people fhould be in a perpetual ftate of ftupidity, than that
they fhould be fometimes turbulent?* Sovereigns, if ye
mean to be wicked, fuffer your people to write ; you
will find men corrupt enough to ferve you according
to your evil defires, and who will improve you in the
art of a Tiberius. If ye mean to be good, permit them
alfo to write ; you will find fome honeft men who will
improve you in the art of a Trajan. How many things
are ye ftill ignorant of, before ye can become great,
either in good or in evil.

The mob of London, the moft contemptible of any
in the univerfe, as the people of England confidered in
a political view are the firft people in the world, abet-
ted by twenty thoufand young men, the fons of diftinguifhed merchants, befet the parliament houfe with
clamours and threats, and influence its deliberations.
Such tumults are frequently excited by a party in the
parliament itfelf. Thefe defpicable men, once roufed,
revile the moft refpectable citizen, who hath incurred
their difpleafure, and been rendered fufpicious to them:
they fet fire to his houfe, and fcandaloufly infult the
moft facred characters. The tumult can never be appeafed, unlefs they force the miniftry to yield to their
fury. This indirect, though continual influence of
commerce upon the public meafures, was, perhaps
never fo fenfibly felt as at the period we are fpeaking
of.

England began the war with much fuperior advantages. She had a great number of failors on foot. Her

BOOK magazines were filled with warlike stores, and her dock-
X. yards were in the most flourishing condition. Her
fleets were all manned and ready for service, and commanded by experienced officers, who waited only for
orders to set sail, and to spread the terror and glory of
her flag to the extremities of the world. Walpole, by
neglecting such great advantages, must not be censur-
ed as having betrayed his country. In this particular
he is above suspicion, since he was never even accused
of corruption, in a country where such charges have
been often made without being believed. His conduct,
however, was not entirely irreproachable. The apprehension he was under of involving himself in difficulties that might endanger his administration; the
necessity he found of applying those treasures in military operations, that he had amassed to bribe and secure to himself a party, joined to that of imposing new
taxes, which must necessarily raise to the highest degree
the aversion that had been entertained both for his
person and principles: all these, and some other circumstances, occasioned an irresolution in his conduct
that was attended with the most fatal consequences.
He lost time, which is of the utmost importance in
every expedition, but particularly decisive in all naval
operations.

The fleet that Vernon commanded, after having destroyed Porto-Bello, was unsuccessful at Carthagena,
rather from the badness of the climate, and the misunderstanding and inexperience of the officers, than from
the valour of the garrison. Anson's fleet was lost at
the doubling of Cape Horn, which some months sooner might have been performed without danger. If we
were to judge of what he might have done with his
whole squadron, from what he actually performed with
a single ship, it is not improbable but that he would
at least have shaken the empire of the Spaniards in the
South Sea. A settlement that was attempted in the
island of Cuba was not prosperous. Those who intended building a city there all died. General Ogle-
thorpe, after having opened the trenches for thirty-

eight days, was forced to raife the fiege of Fort St. Auftin in Florida, vigoroufly defended by Manuel Montiano, who had been allowed time enough to prepare himfelf againft the attack.

Though the firft efforts of the Englifh againft Spanifh America were not fuccefsful, yet the alarm was not appeafed. The navy, the character, and government of the Englifh, were three great refources they had ftill left, fufficient to make the Spaniards tremble. In vain did France unite her naval powers, to act in conjunction with thofe of Spain. This confederacy neither checked the intrepidity of the common enemy, nor animated the minds of fuch as were overwhelmed with fear. Fortunately for both nations, as well as for America, the death of the Emperor Charles the VI. had kindled in Europe an obftinate war, in which the Britifh troops were detained, to fupport an intereft that was extremely doubtful. The hoftilities, commenced in diftant countries with fuch great preparations, terminated at laft infenfibly in a few piracies that were committed on both fides. The moft remarkable event that happened at that time was the taking of Cape-Breton, which expofed the fifhery, commerce, and colonies of France, to the greateft dangers. This valuable poffeffion was reftored to the French at the peace; but the treaty that gave it up was not lefs the object of cenfure.

The French, ever influenced by a fpirit of chivalry, that hath fo long been the dazzling folly of all Europe, imagine the facrifice of their lives fufficiently compenfated, if it hath contributed to extend the frontiers of their country; that is to fay, when they have compelled their prince to the neceffity of governing them with lefs attention and equity than he did before; but if their territory remains the fame as it was before the war, they then think their honour is loft. This rage for conqueft, excufable indeed in a barbarous age, but which more enlightened ones fhould never be reproached with, threw difgrace on the peace of Aix-la-Chapelle, which reftored to Auftria all the places that

B O O K had been taken from her. The nation, too trifling
   X.   and capricious to attend to political difcuffions, could
          not be convinced, that, by forming any kind of efta-
blifhment for the Infant Don Philip, an alliance with
Spain was effectually fecured : that fhe herfelf was
thereby engaged to adjuft, with the houfe of Auftria,
fome interefts of the greateft importance : that, by becoming guarantees to the king of Pruffia for Silefia,
two rival powers would, in confequence of fuch an arrangement, be formed in Germany; to produce which
happy effect had been the labour and care of two centuries : that, by reftoring Friburg, and thofe towns in
Flanders that had been deftroyed, they would be eafily retaken, if war fhould again be declared, and carried on with vigour : befides, that the number of land
forces might always be very eafily diminifhed of fifty
thoufand men, and the faving which fuch a reduction
would produce, might and ought to have been employed in increafing the navy.

If, therefore, the French nation had not even been
obliged to attend to the management of its affairs at
home, which were then in a very alarming ftate ; if
her credit and commerce had not been entirely ruined; if fome of her moft confiderable provinces had
not been in the greateft diftrefs; if fhe had not loft the
key of Canada ; if her colonies had not been threatened with certain and immediate invafion; if her navy
had not been fo entirely deftroyed, as fcarcely to have
a fhip left to fend into the New World ; and if Spain
had not been upon the point of concluding a feparate
treaty with England : independent of all thefe circumftances, yet the peace that was then made would have
deferved the approbation of the moft fenfible and judicious men.

The eafe with which Marfhal Saxe could penetrate
into the internal provinces of the Netherlands, was an
object that particularly attracted the French. It will
readily be allowed, that nothing feemed impoffible to
the victorious arms of Lewis XV.; but it may be
thought paradoxical to affert, that the Englifh were

extremely defirous of feeing the Dutch fubdued. If BOOK
the republic, which could not poffibly feparate itfelf ___X.___
from its allies, had been conquered, its inhabitants,
filled as they were with ancient, as well as prefent prejudices againft the government, laws, manners, and religion of their conqueror, would hardly have fubmitted
to his dominion. Would they not certainly have conveyed their people, their ftock, and their induftry to
Great Britain? And can there be the leaft doubt,
whether fuch confiderable advantages would not have
been infinitely more valuable to the Englifh, than an
alliance with the Dutch?

To this obfervation let us venture to add another,
which, though not attended to before, will, perhaps,
not feem lefs evident. The court of Vienna hath been
thought either very fortunate, or very fkilful, in having
been able, by the means of negotiations, to wreft out
of the hands of the French thofe places which had
been taken from them during the war. But would
they not have been more fortunate, or more fkilful,
had they fuffered their enemy to keep part of the conquefts they had obtained? The period is now paffed,
when the houfe of Auftria was equal, or, perhaps, fuperior in ftrength to the houfe of Bourbon. Policy,
therefore, fhould have engaged her to intereft other
powers in her fortune, even from the loffes fhe had
fuftained. This might have been effected, by facrificing fomething, apparently at leaft, to France. Europe, alarmed at the increafing power of this monarchy, which is naturally an object of hatred, envy, and
fear, would have renewed that fpirit of animofity that
had been fworn againft Lewis XIV.; and more formidable leagues would neceffarily have been formed
in confequence of fuch fentiments. This general difpofition of the people was more likely to have recovered the greatnefs of the new houfe of Auftria, than the
re-acquifition of a diftant and limited territory, always
open to an attack.

It is probable, however, that the French plenipo-
tentiary who managed the negotiation, as well as the

BOOK
X.
minifter who directed it, would have feen through the artifice. We do not even fcruple to affert, that neither of thefe ftatefmen had any view of extending the French dominions. But would they have found the fame penetration to unravel political defigns in the council, to which they were refponfible for their conduct? This is a point we cannot prefume to determine. All governments are generally inclined to extend their territories ; and that of France is, from its conftitution, equally fo.

But whatever truth there may be in thefe reflections, it muft be allowed, that the expectations of the two French minifters, who fettled the peace, were difappointed. The principal object they had in view was the prefervation of the colonies that had been threatened by the enemy. But as foon as the danger was over, this unbounded fource of opulence was neglected. France kept on foot a large body of troops, retained in her pay a great part of Germany, and acted in the fame manner as if another Charles V. had threatened her frontiers, or another Philip II. could have thrown the internal parts of the kingdom into confufion by his intrigues. She was not fenfible that her fuperiority upon the continent was acknowledged ; that no fingle power could venture to attack her; and that the event of the laft war, and the arrangements fettled by the laft peace, had rendered the union of feveral powers againft her impoffible. A number of apprehenfions, equally weak and trifling, difturbed her tranquillity. Her prejudices prevented her from perceiving that fhe had only one enemy really deferving her attention, and that this enemy could only be reftrained by a confiderable fleet.

The Englifh, more inclined to envy the profperity of others than to enjoy their own, are not only defirous of becoming rich, but of being exclufively fo. Their ambition is gain, as that of the Romans was empire. They do not properly feek to extend their dominion, but their colonies. Commerce is the fole object of all the wars they are engaged in, and the defire of engroffing it all to themfelves hath made them perform many great actions, and commit the moft fla-grant acts of injuftice, and obliges them to perfevere in the fame conduct. Will the nations never be tired of that fpecies of tyranny which fets them at defiance, and degrades them? Will they perpetually continue in that ftate of weaknefs which compels them to fub-mit to a defpotifm they would be very defirous of an-nihilating? If they fhould ever form an alliance among themfelves, how could one fingle power be able to refift them, unlefs deftiny were always in its favour, which it would be very imprudent to depend upon? Who is it that hath enfured eternal profperity to the Englifh? and if it could be enfured to them, would it not be too dearly purchafed by the lofs of a tranquil-lity which they could never enjoy? and would they not be too feverely punifhed for it, by the alarms of a fpirit of jealoufy which ever obliges them to keep an anxious and watchful eye upon the flighteft move-ments of the other powers? Is it very glorious; is it very pleafing; is it very advantageous; and is it very fafe, for one nation to reign in the midft of others, as a fultan in the midft of his flaves? Will a dangerous increafe of outward enmity be fufficiently compen-fated by the baneful increafe of inward opulence? Englifhmen, avidity knows no bounds; but patience hath its end, which is almoft always fatal to thofe who urge it to that extreme. But the paffion for trade exerts fuch influence over you, that even your philo-fophers are governed by it. The celebrated Mr. Boyle ufed to fay, that it would be a commendable action to preach Chriftianity to the favages, becaufe, were they to know only fo much of it as would convince them of their obligation to wear clothes, it would prove of great fervice to the Englifh manufactures.

A fyftem of this nature, which the Englifh have fcarce ever loft fight of, difcovered itfelf more openly in 1755, than it had ever done before. The rapid im-provements made in the French colonies furprifed every attentive mind, and awakened the jealoufy of the En-

BOOK X.

America was the caufe of the war in 1755.

glish. Afhamed, however, to let it appear at firft, they
concealed it for fome time under myfterious difguifes;
and a people who have pride or modefty enough to
term negotiations the *artillery of their enemies*, did not
fcruple to employ all the windings and artifices of the
moft infidious policy.

France, alarmed at the confufed ftate of her finances,
intimidated by the fmall number of her fhips, and the
inexperience of her admirals; feduced by a love of
eafe, pleafure, and tranquillity, favoured the attempts
that were made to deceive her. In vain did fome able
ftatefmen continually urge, that Great Britain was, and
ought to be, defirous of a war; and that fhe was compelled to begin it, before the naval eftablifhment of
her rival had attained to the fame degree of perfection
as her trading navy. Thefe caufes of apprehenfion
feemed abfurd in a country where trade had been hitherto carried on by a fpirit of imitation only; where
it had been fhackled by every fpecies of reftraint, and
always facrificed to finance; where it had never met
with any real encouragement, and where men knew
not, perhaps, that they were in poffeffion of the moft
valuable and richeft commerce in the world. A nation, that was indebted to nature for a moft excellent
foil; to chance for her colonies; to the vivacity and
pliancy of her difpofition, for a tafte in thofe arts which
vary and increafe the enjoyments of life; to her conquefts and her literary merit, and even to the difperfion of the Proteftants fhe had unfortunately loft, for
the defire excited in other countries of imitating her:
this nation, that would be too happy, were fhe permitted to enjoy her happinefs, would not perceive that
fhe might be deprived of fome of thefe advantages,
and infenfibly fell a facrifice to thofe arts employed to
lull her into fecurity. When the Englifh thought
there was no further occafion to diffemble, they commenced hoftilities, without having previoufly paid any
attention to thofe formalities that are in ufe among civilized people.

Did the nation, which is reckoned fo proud, fo humane, and fo prudent, reflect upon what was doing? It reduced the moft facred conventions of nations among themfelves, to the artifices of a perfidious policy ; it freed them from the common tie that connects them, by difcarding the chimerical idea of the right of nations. Did thefe people perceive, that they were fixing a conftant ftate of war ; that they were making peace a time of apprehenfion only ; that they were introducing on the globe nothing but a falfe and deceitful fecurity ; that fovereigns were becoming fo many wolves, ready to devour each other ; that the empire of difcord was becoming unbounded ; that the moft cruel and moft unjuft reprifals were authorifed ; and that arms were no longer to be laid afide? At that time there was a half Themiftocles in the miniftry ; but there was not one Ariftides in all Great Britain ; fince, far from exclaiming, in imitation of the Athenians, who were not themfelves the moft fcrupulous men among the Greeks : *The thing is ufeful, but it is not honeft ; let it be mentioned no more :* the Englifh, on the contrary, congratulated themfelves upon an ignominious act, againft which the voice of all Europe was raifed with indignation. Acts of hoftility, without a declaration of war, when there is even no treaty of peace fubfifting, is the proceeding of barbarians. Hoftilities, againft the faith of treaties, but preceded by a declaration of war, by what pretence foever it may be palliated, would be a difgufting act of injuftice, if the habit of it had not been frequent, and if the fhame of it did not light upon almoft all the powers. Hoftilities, without a declaration of war, againft a neighbouring people, who are quietly repofing themfelves upon the faith of treaties, upon the right of nations, upon a reciprocal intercourfe of good will, upon civilized manners, upon the fame God, upon the fame worfhip, upon the reciprocal refidence and protection granted to the citizens of both nations in their refpective countries : fuch hoftilities are a crime, which, in every fociety, would be treated as murder on the highway ; and if there were any exprefs code againft it, as there

B O O K is a tacit one, formed and fubfcribed to between all
X. nations, we fhould then read the following fentence :
LET US ALL UNITE AGAINST THE TRAITOR, AND LET HIM
BE EXTERMINATED FROM THE FACE OF THE EARTH. The
nation that commits fuch a crime, purfues its intereft
with unbounded and fhamelefs jealoufy ; it fhows that
it is deftitute of equity and honour; that it defpifes
equally the judgment of the prefent time, and the cenfure of pofterity ; and that it hath more regard for its
exiftence among nations, than for the colours it will
be painted in in their hiftory. If it be the ftrongeft,
it is a mean tyrant; it is a lion, which debafes itfelf
to act the abject part of a fox. If it be the weakeft,
and be apprehenfive for itfelf, it may, perhaps, be lefs
odious, but it is equally bafe. How much more noble,
and how much more advantageous, was the cuftom of
the Roman people! Let us open, as they did, the gates
of our temples ; let an ambaffador be fent to the enemy's frontiers, and there let him declare war, by fhak-
ing the fkirts of his garments, at the found of the
trumpet of the herald that attends him. Let us not
maffacre an enemy that fleeps. If we dip our hand
into the blood of him who thinks himfelf our friend,
the ftain of it will never be wiped off. It will always
call to mind the Macbeth of the poet.

Though a declaration of war were only a mere ceremony between nations, which feem to be bound by
no ties as foon as they intend to maffacre one another,
yet it is very evident, that the Britifh miniftry were
more than doubtful of the injuftice of their conduct.
The timidity of their meafures, the perplexity of their
operations, the prevaricating modes of juftification they
adopted, and the influence they in vain exerted to make
parliament approve fo fcandalous a violation ; thefe,
with feveral other circumftances, plainly difcovered
the guilt of their proceeding. If thofe weak minifters
of fo great a power had been as bold in committing
crimes, as they appeared regardlefs of the laws of virtue, they would have formed a project of the moft extenfive nature. When they unjuftly gave orders to

attack all the French ſhips upon the northern coaſt of
America, they would have extended theſe orders to
every ſea. The ruin of the only power that was capable of making any reſiſtance, would have been the
neceſſary conſequence of ſuch a ſtrong confederacy.
Its fall would have intimidated all other nations; and,
wherever the Engliſh flag had appeared, it would have
commanded obedience in every quarter of the world.
A ſucceſs ſo remarkable and deciſive would have made
the multitude overlook the violation of public right,
would have juſtified it to the political world, and the
remonſtrances of the wiſe would have been loſt in the
clamours of the ignorant and ambitious.

A timid, but equally unjuſtifiable conduct, was attended with very contrary effects. The council of
George II. was hated, as well as deſpiſed, over all Europe; and the events correſponded to theſe ſentiments.
France, though unexpectedly attacked, was victorious
in Canada, gained conſiderable advantages by ſea, took
Minorca, and threatened London itſelf. Her rival was
then ſenſible of the truth of what men of underſtand-
ing had long ſince obſerved in England, that the French
united the greateſt contrarieties in their character; that
they blended virtues and vices, marks of weakneſs and
ſtrength that had always been thought inconſiſtent
with each other; that they were brave, though effeminate; equally addicted to pleaſure and glory; ſe-
rious in trifles, and trifling in matters of importance;
ever diſpoſed to war, and ready to attack: in a word,
mere children, ſuffering themſelves, as the Athenians
of old, to be diſquieted and moved to anger for real
or imaginary intereſts; fond of enterpriſe and action,
ready to follow any guide, and comforted in the greateſt misfortunes with the moſt trifling ſucceſs. The Engliſh, who, according to a vulgar though ſtrong expreſ-
ſion of Swift's, are *always in the cellar or in the garret,*
and know no medium, began then to be too much
afraid of a nation that they had unjuſtly deſpiſed. A
ſpirit of deſpondency ſucceeded to that of preſump-
tion.

BOOK X.

The begin-
ning of the
war is un-
favourable
to the En-
gliſh.

BOOK The nation, corrupted by the too great confidence
  X.   it had placed in its opulence ; humbled by the intro-
————— duction of foreign troops, and by the moral character
and inability of its governors ; weakened too by the
collifion of factions, which keep up an exertion of
ftrength among a free people in times of peace, but
which deftroy their power in times of war ; the nation, difgraced, aftonifhed, and uncertain what meafures to purfue ; equally fenfible of the diftreffes it had
already been expofed to, as of thofe it forefaw, was incapable of exerting itfelf to avenge the one or prevent
the other. All zeal for the common caufe was confined to the granting of immenfe fupplies. That the
coward is fooner difpofed to part with his money than
the brave man, in order to ward off danger ; and that
the prefent critical fituation of affairs required them
not to confider who fhould pay, but who fhould ftand
forward to fight ; thefe were truths, which, at that
time, feemed to have been forgotten.

The French, on their part, were dazzled with fome
inftances of fuccefs that were of no confequence. Pre-
fuming that the furprife their enemies had been thrown
into was a proof of their weaknefs, they involved themfelves further than was confiftent with their intereft in
the difturbances which then began to divide the Ger-
man powers.

A fyftem, which, if unfuccefsful, muft have been
attended with the greateft difgrace, and, if fortunate,
muft have been deftructive in the end, ferved to con-
found them. Their levity made them forget, that a
few months before they had applauded the wife and
enlightened ftatefman, who, being defirous to avoid a
land war, which fome minifters were willing to enter
into, from their defpairing of fuccefs at fea, had, with
the vivacity and confidence peculiar to genius, addreffed himfelf to them in the following words : *Gen-*
tlemen, faid he, *let us all, who are here prefent in council,*
go out, with torches in our hands, and fet fire to all our
fhips, if they are ufelefs to our defence, and are only con-
ducive to make our enemies infult us. This political in-

fatuation threw them into the greateſt difficulties. Errors of the cabinet were followed by military faults.
The management of the army was ſubjected to the
intrigues of the court. A ſeries of bad ſucceſs was the
conſequence of a perpetual change of commanders.
This light and ſuperficial nation did not perceive, that,
even ſuppoſing, what indeed was impoſſible, that all
thoſe who were ſucceſſively intruſted with the direction of the military operations had really been men of
abilities, yet they could not contend with advantage
againſt a man of genius, aſſiſted by one of diſtinguiſhed capacity. Misfortunes made no alteration in the
plan that had been formed, and the changes of generals were endleſs.

While the French were thus deceived, the Engliſh,
from a ſpirit of dejection, were inflamed with the utmoſt reſentment : they changed a miniſter who had
juſtly excited general diſſatisfaction, and placed at the
head of affairs a man who was equally an enemy to
timid meaſures, to the royal prerogative, and to France.
Although this choice was the conſequence of that ſpirit of party which cauſes the greateſt revolutions in
England, yet it was ſuch as the circumſtances of the
times required. William Pitt had a ſoul formed for
great deſigns ; was diſtinguiſhed by a ſpecies of eloquence that never-failed to captivate his hearers, and
by a character equally firm and enterpriſing. He was
ambitious to make his country riſe ſuperior to all others,
and at the ſame time to raiſe his own fame. His enthuſiaſm fired a nation which will always be inſpired
by a love of liberty. The admiral who had ſuffered
Minorca to be taken was arreſted, thrown into priſon,
accuſed, tried, and ſentenced to death. Neither his
rank, abilities, family, nor friends, could protect him
from the rigour of the law. His own ſhip was fixed
upon as the ſpot where the ſentence paſſed upon him
was to be put in execution. All Europe, at the news
of this melancholy event, was ſtruck with aſtoniſhment, blended with admiration and horror. It recalled the memory of the ancient republics. The death

B O O K of Byng, whether guilty or not, proclaimed, in the
  X.   moft alarming manner, to thofe who were employed
by the nation, what fate they muft expect, if they betrayed the confidence repofed in them. Every man
faid to himfelf, in the inftant of battle, It is on this
field I muft die, rather than with infamy on a fcaffold.
Thus the blood of one man, accufed of cowardice,
was productive of a fpirit of heroifm.

This fyftem of holding out an example of terror to
fubdue the impreffions of fear, was further ftrengthened by an emulation, that feemed to promife the revival of public fpirit. Diffipation, pleafure, indolence,
and often vice and a corruption of manners, occafion
warm and frequent connections in moft kingdoms of
Europe. The Englifh have lefs intercourfe and connection with each other ; they have, perhaps, lefs tafte
for focial life than other nations ; but the idea of any
project that may be ferviceable to the ftate immediately unites them, and they feem, as it were, animated by one foul. All ranks, parties, and fects, contribute to infure its fuccefs, and with fuch liberality as
cannot be paralleled in thofe places where the notion
of a particular native country does not prevail.

And, in fact, why fhould we be concerned for the
glory of a nation, when we can expect no other return
for the facrifices we make, than an increafe of mifery ;
when victories and defeats are equally fatal ; victories,
by giving rife to taxes to pave the way for them ; and
defeats, by occafioning taxes to repair them ? If there
were not fome little remains of honour fubfifting in
us, in fpite of all the efforts that are made ufe of to
ftifle it, and which proves, that, under vexations of
every kind, the people ftill retain fome feeling for the
difgrace of the nation, they would be equally affected
with its profperity or its misfortunes. Will they experience better treatment, whether the fovereign be
victorious or conquered ; whether he acquire or lofe a
province ; whether trade fhould fall or profper ? The
zeal of the Englifh is more remarkably diftinguifhed,
when the nation hath placed an implicit confidence in

the minifter who hath the direction of public mea- B O O K
X.
fures. As foon as Mr. Pitt was made prime minifter, a marine fociety was eftablifhed, which, perceiving that there appeared a remiffnefs in general to enter into the fea fervice, and difapproving the cuftom of prefling men into it, invited the children of the poor-eft clafs in the three kingdoms to become fhip boys, and their fathers failors. They undertook to pay the expences of their voyage; to take care of them in ficknefs; to feed, clothe, and furnifh them with every thing neceffary to preferve their health during the time they were to be at fea. The king, moved by this inftance of patriotifm, gave them 22,500 livres [937l. 10s.], the prince of Wales 9000 livres [375l.], and the princefs of Wales 4500 [187l. 10s.]. The ac-tors of the different theatres, whofe abilities have not been treated with contempt by this enlightened na-tion, acted their beft plays for the increafe of fo re-fpectable an eftablifhment. The theatres were never fo much crowded as on this occafion. A hundred of thefe fhip boys, and a hundred of the failors, clothed from a zeal that may truly be holden facred, appear-ed upon the ftage; a decoration this, furely, not infe-rior to that arifing from the multitude of lights, the elegance of drefs, and the brilliancy of jewels.

This public zeal, and attachment to the interefts of the nation, animated the minds of all the Englifh, and the effects of it were difplayed in the difference of their conduct. They ravaged the coafts of their enemies; beat them every where by fea; intercepted their navi-gation, and gave a check to all their forces in Weftpha-lia. They drove them out of North America, Africa, and the Eaft Indies. Till Mr. Pitt became minifter, all the expeditions of the nation, made in diftant coun-tries, had been unfuccefsful, and muft neceffarily have been fo, becaufe they had been ill-concerted. He, on the contrary, planned fuch prudent and ufeful defigns; his preparations were conducted with fo much fore-fight and difpatch; his means were fo well adapted to the ends he wanted to obtain; he made fuch a prudent

The Eng-
lifh are
roufed from
their lethar-
gy, and feize
the French
and Spanifh
iflands.
Account of
the author
of thefe
fucceffes.

B O O K choice of the perfons whom he intrufted with his de-
X.   figns; he eftablifhed fuch harmony between the land
and fea forces, and raifed the fpirits of the Englifh to
fuch a height, that his whole adminiftration was a feries
of conquefts. His mind, ftill fuperior to his glory,
made him defpife the idle clamours of thofe who cenfured what they called his profufions. He ufed to fay
with Philip, father of Alexander the Great, *That victory was to be purchafed by money, and that money muft
not be fpared at the expence of victory.*

By fuch a conduct, and fuch principles, Mr. Pitt had
at all times, and in all places, triumphed over the
French. He purfued them to their moft valuable
iflands, even to their fugar colonies. Thefe poffeffions, fo juftly prized for their riches, were not, however, better fecured. The fortifications that were e-
rected there were conftructed without judgment, and
were falling to decay. Thefe ruins were equally deftitute of defenders, of arms, and of ammunition. Ever
fince the beginning of hoftilities, all intercourfe between thefe great fettlements and the mother-country
had been at an end. They could neither receive fubfiftence from it, nor enrich it with their productions.
The buildings neceffary for the carrying on of agriculture, were a heap of ruins. The mafters and the flaves,
equally deftitute of the neceffaries of life, were obliged
to feed upon the cattle deftined for the labours of hufbandry. If any rapacious navigators ever reached
them, it was through fo many dangers, that the colonifts were obliged to pay for what they bought of thefe
traders at a very advanced price, and to give them in
exchange whatever they confented to take from them
at the loweft. Though the colonifts did not call in
the aid of any foreign power to their affiftance, yet it
was not to be expected, that their attachments to their
mother-country would induce them to make a vigorous defence againft an enemy that might put an end
to their diftreffes.

In this fituation of affairs, ten fhips of the line, fome
bomb-ketches and frigates, with five thoufand land-

forces, failed from England, and arrived at Guadalupe. B O O K
They appeared before the town on the 22d of January ___X.___
1759, and the next day bombarded the town of Baffe-
Terre. If the befiegers had known how to take advantage of the terror they had fpread, the ifland would
have made a very fhort refiftance : but the flownefs,
timidity, and irrefolution of their operations afforded
the garrifon and the inhabitants leifure to fortify themfelves in a pafs that was only at the diftance of two
leagues from the place. From this fpot they ftopped
the progrefs of the enemy, who were equally diftreffed
from the heat of the climate and the want of provifions. The Englifh, defpairing of making themfelves
mafters of the colony on this fide, proceeded to attack
it in another quarter, known by the name of Grande-
Terre. It was defended by a fort called Fort Lewis,
which made ftill lefs refiftance than that of Baffe-
Terre, that had furrendered in four-and-twenty hours.
The conquerors were again guilty of the error they
had before fallen into, and fuffered the fame inconveniencies from it. The event of the expedition began
to be doubtful, when Barrington, who fucceeded to the
command at the death of Hopfon, changed the plan
of operations. He gave up the idea of penetrating
into the country, and re-embarked his foldiers, who
fucceffively attacked the houfes and villages upon the
coafts. The ravages they committed obliged the colonifts to fubmit. The whole ifland, after three months
defence, furrendered on the 21ft day of April, upon
very honourable terms of capitulation.

The troops that had obtained this victory did not
engage in this expedition, till they had ineffectually
threatened Martinico. Three years after, Great Britain revived a defign that had been too haftily given
up; but greater preparations and more effectual means
were employed to carry it into execution. On the 16th
of January 1762, eighteen battalions, under the command of general Monckton, and eighteen fhips of the
line commanded by admiral Rodney, the firft fent
from North America, and the latter from Europe, ap-

B O O K peared before the capital of the ifland. The landing
   X.   of the troops the next day was foon effected, without
difficulty and without lofs. To take poffeffion of the
eminences that were fortified and defended by Fort
Royal, feemed to be a matter not fo eafily accomplifhed. Thefe obftacles, however, were, after fome warm
engagements, furmounted, and the place, that would
foon have been reduced to afhes by the bombs, capi-
tulated on the 9th of February; and the whole colony
did the fame on the 13th. It is probable that the profperity of Guadalupe under the Britifh government,
contributed to bring about this general furrender;
which might, and ought to have been delayed longer.
Granada and the other Leeward Iflands, whether fubject to France, or which, though peopled by Frenchmen, were neutral, furrendered themfelves, without
making any refiftance.

Even St. Domingo, the only poffeffion the French
ftill retained in the Archipelago of America, was likely to fall into the' hands of the Englifh; and its lofs
feemed to be not far diftant. If it had not even been
known that this was the firft conqueft Great Britain
would attempt, yet it could not be fuppofed that it
would efcape its avidity. Would this ambitious nation have checked the career of its own fucceffes fo far
as to give up all thoughts of a conqueft that would
have completed its profperity? This was a point that
feemed not to admit of a doubt. The colony was generally known to be entirely without any means of
defence, either within or without, and therefore incapable of making the leaft refiftance. It was fo fenfible
of its weaknefs, that it feemed difpofed to furrender as
foon as it fhould be fummoned to do it.

The court of Verfailles was equally aftonifhed and
alarmed at the loffes it had fuftained, and at thofe it
forefaw. It had expected fuch an obftinate refiftance
as would have been fuperior to every attack. The defcendants of thofe brave adventurers, who had fettled
thefe colonies, feemed a rampart fufficient to repel all
the forces of the Britifh empire. They almoft felt a

fecret fatisfaction that the Englifh were directing their
efforts towards that quarter. The miniftry had infpired the nation with the fame confidence that poffeffed
them, and it was the mark of a bad citizen to fhow the
leaft uneafinefs.

It is an obfervation we may now be permitted to
make, that events, which have once happened, will
happen again. A people whofe whole fortune confifts in fields and paftures, will, if influenced by any
degree of fpirit, refolutely defend their poffeffions. The
harveft of one year is the utmoft they can lofe, and
whatever calamity they may experience, does not diftrefs them to fuch a degree as to leave them without
hopes of recovery. The cafe is very different with regard to the wealthy cultivators of thefe colonies.
Whenever they take up arms, they run the rifk of
having the labours of their whole lives deftroyed, their
flaves carried off, and all the hopes of their pofterity
either loft by fire or plunder: they will therefore always fubmit to the enemy. Though fatisfied with the
government under which they live, they are lefs attached to its glory than to their own riches.

The example of the firft colonifts, whofe perfeverance
could not be fhaken by the moft vigorous attacks, does
not affect the truth of this obfervation. The object of
the war was then the acquifition of territory, and the
expulfion of the inhabitants ; at prefent, a war waged
againft a colony is directed only againft the fovereign
of it.

The plan of attacking Martinico was laid by Mr.
Pitt, though he was not in the miniftry when it was
fubdued. The refignation of this great man drew the
attention of Europe, and deferves to be confidered by
every one, who inveftigates the caufes and effects of
political revolutions. An hiftorian, who ventures to
write the tranfactions of his own age, hath feldom, it
muft be granted, fufficient lights to guide him. The
councils of kings are fo fecret, that time alone can
gradually withdraw the veil that furrounds them. Their
minifters, faithful depofitaries of the fecrets they have

B O O K been intrufted with, or interefted to conceal them, ex-
X. plain themfelves no further than is fufficient to miflead
the curious inquirer, who wifhes to difcover them.
Whatever penetration he may poffefs, in tracing the
fource and connection of events, he is at laft reduced
to conjecture. If his conjectures happen to be juft,
ftill he is ignorant that they are fo, or cannot depend
upon them ; and this uncertainty is fcarcely more fa-
tisfactory than a total ignorance. He muft therefore
wait till prudence and intereft, freed from the reftraint
of filence, fhall unfold the truth ; in a word, till fome
valuable and original records be produced for public
infpection, wherein the latent fprings on which the
deftiny of nations hath depended, fhall be difcovered.

Thefe reflections fhould fufpend the inquiries of the
man who wants only to attend to the progrefs of political intrigues. They are diffolved as foon as they
are formed. We could only collect feparate parts of
them, which could not be brought together unlefs by
conjecture, which might be the further diftant from
the truth, in proportion as more fagacity had been
difplayed in the forming of it. We fhould often be
likely to fill up with fome great view, or with fome
profound fpeculation, a vacancy which prefents itfelf,
from our ignorance of fome witticifm, of fome frivolous
caprice, of fome trifling refentment, or of fome childifh
emotion of jealoufy : for thefe are the wonderful levers
with which the earth hath fo often been moved, and
will ftill be moved hereafter. If it be then prudent to
fay nothing of the obfcure caufes of events, it is at
leaft the time to fpeak of the character of thofe who
have conducted them. We know what they were in
their infancy, in their youth, in a more mature age, in
their family and in fociety, in private life, and in public
affairs. We know what their natural and acquired talents were ; their ruling paffions, their vices, their virtues, their inclinations, and their averfions ; their connections, their animofities, and their friendfhips ; their
perfonal and relative interefts ; the marks of favour or
difgrace they have experienced ; the means they have

employed to obtain their high pofts, and to maintain B O O K
themfelves in them ; the conduct they have obferved X.
with regard to their protectors and their dependents ;
the projects they have conceived, and the manner in
which they have executed them ; the character of the
men they have employed ; the obftacles they have met
with, and the manner in which they have furmounted
them : in a word, we know the fuccefs they have had ;
the reward they have obtained in confequence of it ;
the punifhment they have fuffered when they have
mifcarried ; the praife or blame beftowed upon them
by the nation ; the manner in which they have ended
their career, and the reputation they have left behind
them after death.

We are defirous of penetrating into the foul of one
the greateft men of his age, and perhaps we can never do it at a more proper time. The moft confpi-
cuous actions only of a man's life are tranfmitted
to pofterity, which will, therefore, be deprived of a
variety of fimple and artlefs details, that enlighten
the mind of an obferver, who lived at the time they
happened.

Mr. Pitt, after having refcued England from the
kind of difgrace it had been expofed to in the beginning of the war, arrived to a height of fuccefs that
aftonifhed all the world. Whether he forefaw this or
not, he did not feem to be embarraffed with it, and refolved to carry it as far as he could. The moderation
which fo many ftatefmen had affected before him,
feemed to him to be only a pretence to conceal their
weaknefs or their indolence. He thought that all
ftates fhould exert their power to the utmoft, and that
there was no inftance of one nation being able to become fuperior to another, and not effecting it. The
parallel he drew between England and France confirmed him in his opinion. He perceived, with uneafinefs, that the power of England, founded upon a
trade which fhe might and would lofe, was very inconfiderable, when compared with that of her rival, which
nature, art, and particular circumftances, had raifed

B O O K to fuch a degree of ftrength, under favourable admi-
  X.   niftrations, as had made all Europe tremble. Senfible
of this truth, he therefore determined to deprive France
of her colonies, and to reduce her to that ftate, to
which the freedom of the New World, fooner or later
accomplifhed, will bring all nations that have formed
fettlements there.

The means neceffary to complete this project, which
was fo far advanced, appeared to him abfolutely certain. While the imagination of weak minds took fha-
dows for realities, the greateft difficulties appeared tri-
vial to him. Though the nation, of which he was
the idol, was fometimes alarmed at his vaft and uncommon enterprifes, he was not in the leaft difquieted
about them ; becaufe, in his eyes, the multitude was
like a torrent, the courfe of which he knew how to direct which way he would.

Perfectly indifferent with regard to fortune, he was
ftill more fo with regard to power. His fuccesses had
made his adminiftration abfolute. With the people he
was a republican, with the nobles and the fovereign he
was a defpotic minifter. To think differently from
him, was a mark of being an enemy to the common
caufe.

He availed himfelf of the fuperiority he had gained,
in order to excite the ardour of the people. Little
influenced by that fpecies of philofophy, which, diveft-
ing itfelf of the prejudices of national glory, to extend its views to the welfare of all mankind, tries
every thing by the principles of univerfal reafon ; he
kept up a violent and favage fpirit of enthufiafm,
which he called, and perhaps believed to be, a love
of his country ; but which was, in reality, nothing
more than a ftrong averfion for the nation he wanted
to opprefs.

France was perhaps as much difcouraged by this
fpirit of inveteracy, that conftantly purfued her, as
by the diftreffes fhe had undergone. The diminution,
the exhaufted ftate, or, to fay the truth, the total ruin
of her naval powers, afforded her a difcouraging pro-

fpect for the future. The expectation that a fortunate B O O K
fuccefs by land might occafion a change in the face X.
of affairs, was merely imaginary. If one of their fqua-
drons had deftroyed one or feveral of thofe of her rival, the Englifh would not have renounced any of
their claims. This is one general rule; and another
is, that whenever any power hath acquired a very determined fuperiority at fea, it can never lofe it in the
courfe of the war; more particularly, if that fuperiority can be traced from a diftant caufe, and efpecially
if it proceed partly from the character of the nation.
The fuperiority of one continent above another depends entirely on the abilities of a fingle man, and may
be loft in a moment: on the contrary, fuperiority at
fea, as it refults from the vigilance and intereft of each
individual in the ftate, muft always increafe, particularly when it is encouraged by national conftitution: a
fudden invafion can only put a ftop to it.

Nothing but a general confederacy could have reftored the balance of power; the impoffibility of which
Mr. Pitt plainly faw. He knew the reftraints by which
Holland was confined, the poverty of Sweden and Denmark, the inexperience of the Ruffians, and the little
regard that feveral of thefe powers paid to the interefts of France. He was confcious alfo of the terror
which the Englifh forces had fpread among them all,
the miftruft they entertained of each other, and the
apprehenfion that each of them muft have, that they
fhould be diftreffed before they could receive affiftance.

The affairs of Spain were particularly circumftanced.
The ravages that laid wafte the French colonies, and
which every day increafed, might eafily extend to the
fettlements of the Spaniards. Whether this kingdom
was not, or would not be, fenfible of the danger that
threatened it, its ufual indolence accompanied it with
regard to thefe great objects. At length, upon a change
of miniftry, a new fyftem took place. Don Carlos endeavoured to extinguifh the flame; but it was too late.
His overtures were received with a contemptuous

B O O K haughtinefs.   Mr. Pitt, having deliberately confider-
   X.   ed the extent of his power, anfwered every propofal
that was made, in the following manner :   *I will liften
to them*, faid he, *when you have taken the Tower of London fword in hand*.   This mode of expreffion might
difguft, but it was impofing.

Such was the fituation of affairs when the court of
France thought herfelf obliged to make overtures of
peace to that of Great Britain.   Both courts were
equally apprehenfive, and with good reafon, that Mr.
Pitt would oppofe them.   He confented to enter into
a negotiation ; but the event fhowed, as fenfible politicians had conjectured, that his intention was not to
continue it.   His defign was only to furnifh himfelf
with fufficient proofs of the engagements that the two
branches of the houfe of Bourbon had entered into
againft Great Britain, that he might make them evident to his country.   As foon as he had gained this
intelligence, he broke off the negotiation, and propofed declaring war againft Spain.   The fuperiority of the
naval power of England above that of both thefe
kingdoms, and the affurance he had that it would be
infinitely better directed, infpired him with this confidence.

Mr. Pitt's fyftem appeared, to diftinguifhed politicians, the only important, and, indeed, the only reafonable one.   The Englifh nation had contracted fuch
a load of debt, that it could neither free itfelf from it,
nor fupport it, without opening to itfelf new fources
of wealth.   Europe, tired out with the grievances
Great Britain had made her fubmit to, waited impa-
tiently for an opportunity to difable her oppreffor from
continuing them.   The houfe of Bourbon could not
but preferve a ftrong refentment for the injuries it had
fuffered, and for the loffes it had fuftained ; it could
not but make fecret preparations, and gradually work
up a fpirit of revenge, to which a combination of all
its forces might enfure fuccefs.   Thefe motives obliged
Great Britain, though a commercial power, to aggrandife itfelf for its fupport.   This cruel neceffity was not

fo fenfibly felt by the council of George the Third as B o o k Mr. Pitt defired. Moderation appeared to him a work X. of weaknefs, or of infatuation, perhaps of treachery; and he refigned his poft, becaufe he was not allowed to be the declared enemy of Spain.

May we venture to form a conjecture? The Englifh miniftry plainly faw that there was no poffibility of avoiding a frefh war; but equally tired out and difgraced by the power Mr. Pitt had affumed, they were defirous of reftoring that fpirit of equality which is the fpring of a republican government. Defpairing of being able to raife themfelves to a level with a man fo highly efteemed, or of making him ftoop to them, they united their forces to effect his ruin. As open attacks would only have turned againft themfelves, they had recourfe to more artful methods. They attempted to four his temper; the natural fire of his character laid him open to fuch a fnare; and he fell into it. If Mr. Pitt refigned his poft through peevifhnefs, he deferves to be cenfured for not having fupprefled or maftered it. If he hoped, by this expedient, to humble his enemies, he fhowed he had greater knowledge of affairs than of men. If, as he afferted, he refigned, becaufe he would no longer be refponfible for the meafures he did not guide, we may be allowed to think that he was more ftrongly attached to his own perfonal glory, than to the interefts of his country. But whatever may have been the caufe of his refignation, nothing but the blindeft, moft unjuft, and moft violent partiality, can venture to affert, that his virtues and abilities were merely the effect of chance.

However this may be, the firft ftep the new miniftry took was conformable to the principles of Mr. Pitt; and this was a kind of homage they were compelled to pay him. It was thought neceffary to declare war againft Spain; and the Weft Indies were to be the fcene of thefe new hoftilities. Experience had already difcouraged them from making any attempts on the continent of America, and all their views were turned towards Cuba. Men of fenfe and underftanding per-

ceived that the taking of this ifland would not be attended with any apprehenfion of vengeance from the
other colonies; that the empire of the Gulf of Mexico
would be fecured; that the enemy, whofe riches arofe
principally from the amount of its cuftoms, would be
deprived of all their refources; that the whole commerce of the continent would be feized upon, and the
inhabitants would choofe rather to deliver up their
riches to the conqueror of their country, than to give
up thofe commodities they had been ufed to receive
from Europe; in a word, that the power of Spain
would be fo much reduced by this confiderable lofs,
that it would be obliged to fubmit to any terms.

Agreeable to this idea, a fleet, confifting of nineteen fhips of the line, eighteen frigates, and about a
hundred and fifty tranfports, with 10,000 troops on
board, which were to be joined by 4000 more from
North America, fet fail for the Havannah. To arrive
at this formidable place, it was determined to pafs
through the old ftrait of Bahama, not fo long in extent, though more dangerous than the new one. The
obftacles that were to be expected in this paffage, little
known, and too little attended to, were fuccefsfully
furmounted, in a manner worthy the reputation that
Admiral Pocock had acquired. On the 6th of July
he arrived at the place of his deftination; and the
landing of the troops was effected without any oppofition, at the diftance of fix leagues eaftward of thofe
dreadful fortifications that were to be taken.

The operations by land were not fo well conducted
as thofe by fea. If Albemarle, who had the command
of the army, had been a man of abilities, equal to the
commiffion he was intrufted with, he would have begun his attack by the city. The fingle dry wall that
covered it could not have holden out four-and-twenty
hours. It is probable, that the generals, the council,
and the regency, who muft infallibly have fallen into
his hands by this fuccefs, which might fo eafily have
been obtained, would have refolved to capitulate for
the Moro. At all events, he would thus have pre-

vented the fort from receiving any affiftance or provifions that were fupplied from the city during the fiege,
and have fecured the moft likely means to reduce it in
a very fhort time.

The plan he purfued, of beginning his operations by
the attack of the Moro, expofed him to great diftreffes.
The water that was near him was unwholefome, and
he found himfelf under a neceffity of procuring fome
at three leagues diftance from his camp. As the floops
that were fent for this purpofe might be attacked, it
was thought neceffary to poft a body of fifteen hundred men on the eminence of Arofteguy, at a quarter
of a league's diftance from the town, in order to protect them. This body of troops, entirely detached
from the army, and which could not be withdrawn or
fupported but by fea, was perpetually in danger of being cut off.

Albemarle, who might have judged of the difpofition
of the enemy from their not molefting the troops poft-
ed at Arofteguy, fhould have placed another body of
men upon the public road leading to the city. By this
ftep he would have been able almoft to furround it;
he would, moft undoubtedly, have diftreffed it by famine, prevented all removal of the effects into the
country, and opened a lefs dangerous communication
with Arofteguy, than by the detachments he was conftantly obliged to fend, in order to fupport this advanced body of troops.

The fiege of the Moro was carried on without opening the trenches. The foldiers advanced towards the
ditch, and were covered only with barrels of flints,
which were, at length, exchanged for facks of cotton,
that were taken out of fome merchant-fhips arrived
from Jamaica. This want of forefight occafioned the
lofs of a great number of men, always of great value,
but more efpecially fo in a climate where difeafes and
fatigues caufe fo great a confumption of them.

The Englifh general, having loft the greateft part
of his army, and finding the neceffity, for want of
troops, of reimbarking in a few days, determined to

B O O K attempt ſtorming the caſtle : but a large and deep
 X. ditch, cut in the rock, was firſt to be paſſed ; and no
preparations had been made to fill it up.

If the faults of the Engliſh were very confiderable,
thoſe of the Spaniards were ſtill greater. Though ap-
prized above a month before, that war had commenced
between the two nations, they were not rouſed from
their lethargy. The enemy was already upon their
coaſts, and they had made no proviſions of balls of a
proper ſize for their cannons, nor of cartridges ; neither had they one ſingle gun, or even a firelock fit to
make uſe of.

The great number of officers, of the land and ſea
ſervice, who were at the Havannah, occaſioned, during
ſome days of the ſiege, a great uncertainty in the re-
ſolutions, that could not but be favourable to the beſiegers.

Three ſhips of war were funk, to ſtop up the entrance into the port, which the enemy could not paſs.
The road into the harbour was by this means damaged,
and three great ſhips loſt to no purpoſe.

The moſt common prudence would have ſuggeſted,
that the twelve men of war that were at the Havannah ſhould have been got ready to ſail. They could
not poſſibly be of any ſervice in defending the place,
and it was a matter of ſome conſequence to ſave them.
But this was neglected. Neither did the precaution
occur of ſetting them on fire, although this was the
only way left to prevent them from falling into the
hands of the enemy.

The deſtruction of the body of Engliſh troops poſt-
ed at Aroſleguy, where they could not receive any af-
ſiſtance, might have been eaſily effected. This check
would have put the beſiegers to ſome difficulty in procuring water, would have deprived them of men, intimidated them, retarded their operations, and inſpired
the Spaniſh forces with ſome degree of confidence.
But, far from making ſo eaſy an attempt, they did not
attack, even in the open part of the country, any of
the Engliſh detachments, though compoſed entirely

of infantry, and which might have been oppofed by a BOOK regiment of dragoons, and a great number of militia, X. that were provided with horfes.

The communication of the city with the internal parts of the country was fcarce ever interrupted, and yet none of thofe who had a fhare in the adminiftration ever thought of conveying the royal treafure into the inland parts, to prevent it from falling into the hands of the enemy.

The laft inftance of neglect ferved to complete the whole. In the middle of the ditch had been left a piece of rock, terminating in a point, and ftanding by itfelf. The Englifh placed upon this a few tottering planks, which reached from the breach to the counterfcarp. A ferjeant, with fifteen men, paffed over them at one in the afternoon, and concealed themfelves among fome ftones that had fallen down. They were followed by a company of grenadiers, and fome foldiers. When they had collected about a hundred men, in the fpace of an hour, they got upon the breach, under no apprehenfion of being difcovered, and found no men placed there to defend it. Velafco, indeed, informed of what had happened, haftened to fave the place; but he was killed in coming up; and his death putting the Spanifh troops that followed him into confufion, they furrendered to a handful of men. The neglect of placing a centinel to obferve the motions of the enemy lodged upon the ditch, determined this great event. A few days after, a capitulation was entered into for the city, for all the places of the colony, and for the whole ifland. Independent of the great importance of this victory in itfelf, the conquerors found in the Havannah about forty-five millions [1,875,000l.] of filver, and other valuable effects, which fully indemnified them for the expences of the expedition.

The lofs of Cuba, the centre of the power of Spain in the New World, made peace as neceffary to the court of Madrid, as it could poffibly be to that of Verfailles, whofe diftreffes were now brought to the high-

Advantages procured to Great Britain in the iflands by the peace.

BOOK eſt pitch. The Engliſh miniſtry, at that time, con-
X. ſented to a peace; but it ſeemed a matter of much difficulty to ſettle the conditions. The ſucceſſes of Great
Britain had been aſtoniſhing in North and South America. But, however ambitious ſhe might be, ſhe could
not flatter herſelf with the hopes of retaining all the
conqueſts ſhe had made. It was reaſonable to ſuppoſe
that ſhe would give up the poſſeſſions ſhe had gained
in North America, as the advantages ſhe might expect
from them were diſtant, inconſiderable, and uncertain;
and that ſhe would be content with reſerving to herſelf the ſugar colonies ſhe had lately acquired, which
the ſtate of her finances ſeemed more particularly to
require. The increaſe of her cuſtoms, that was a neceſſary conſequence of ſuch a ſyſtem, would have procured her the beſt ſinking fund that could have been
imagined, and which muſt have been ſo much the
more agreeable to the nation, as it would have been
obtained at the expence of the French. This advantage would have been attended with three others, very
conſiderable. It would, in the firſt place, have deprived a rival power, and formidable, notwithſtanding the
faults it had committed, of its richeſt branch of trade.
Secondly, it would have contributed to weaken it,
from its being under a neceſſity of defending Canada;
a colony, which, from the nature of its ſituation, muſt
be detrimental to a nation that had long neglected its
navy. Laſtly, it would have kept New England in a
cloſer and more abſolute dependence on the mother-
country, a part of America that would always want to
be ſupported againſt a reſtleſs, active, and warlike
neighbour.

But though the council of George III. ſhould have
thought it neceſſary to reſtore to their enemies a bad
country of the continent, and to reſerve the valuable
iſlands, yet they would not, perhaps, have ventured to
adopt ſo judicious a meaſure. In other countries the
faults of the miniſters are imputed only to themſelves,
or to their kings, who puniſh them for their miſcon-
duct. In England, the errors of adminiſtration are

generally the errors of the nation, who infift upon obe- dience to their will, though guided by caprice.

The Englifh, who have complained of the terms of the laft peace, when they have been fhown how far fhort they fell of the advantages they expected from them, had, however, in fome meafure, dictated thofe very terms themfelves, by the tenor of their complaints, either previous to, or during the war. The Canadians had committed fome outrages, and the favages many acts of cruelty, in the Englifh colonies. The peaceable inhabitants, terrified at the diftreffes they fuffered, and more fo at thofe they feared, had caufed their clamours to be heard even in Europe. Their correfpondents, interefted to obtain them a fpeedy and powerful re- drefs, had aggravated their complaints. Thofe writers, who eagerly lay hold of every circumftance that can render the French odious, had loaded them with every fpecies of invective. The people, exafperated by the report of the fhocking fcenes that were perpetually prefented to its imagination, wifhed to fee a ftop put to thefe barbarities.

On the other hand, the inhabitants of the fugar co- lonies, fatisfied with the carrying on of their own com- merce, and gaining a part of that of their enemies, were very quiet. Far from wifhing the conqueft of their neighbours fettlements, they rather dreaded it, confi- dering it as deftructive to themfelves, though advan- tageous to the nation. The lands of the French are fo much fuperior to thofe of the Englifh, that no com- petition could poffibly have taken place. Their allies were of the fame opinion, and followed the example of their moderation.

The confequence of fo contrary a plan of conduct was, that the nation was extremely indifferent about the fugar colonies, but very anxious to acquire what they wanted in North America. Let us reprefent to ourfelves the fituation of an enlightened man, who is convinced of the advantages of a project, which he is compelled to give up, by the miftaken notions of a deceived multitude, in order to adopt, in preference to

B O O K it, fome abfurd fchemes contrary to the general good,
   X.   which will difhonour him, if he fhould purfue them,
‿‿‿‿   or which will expofe him to danger, if he fhould refufe : let us reprefent him to ourfelves, as employed
by a fovereign, who will difmifs him, if his rebellious
fubjects fhould infift upon it ; and who cannot afford
him any protection, if they fhould carry their fury fo
far as to demand his life : let us view him divided, as
he muft be, between the miftaken vanity which attaches him to his poft, and the laudable pride which
makes him careful to preferve his reputation : let us
behold him alone, retired in his clofet, and deliberat-
ing upon the fteps he fhould take, amidft the tumult
and clamours of the populace, collected round his
houfe, and threatening to fet it on fire : for fuch is the
alternative, which hath been experienced, and will always be experienced, by thofe who guide the public
affairs of a free country. There is fcarce one fingle
fituation in the world, in which a propriety of conduct
is not attended with inconveniences on both fides. It
is the property of real courage to adapt itfelf to thofe
feveral circumftances and fituations, whatever may be
the refult; but fuch kind of courage is not often to be
met with.

The miniftry, which, in England, can never fupport
its authority againft the people, or, at leaft, cannot
long maintain itfelf fuccefsfully againft its general
odium, turned all their views towards North America,
and found France and Spain readily difpofed to adopt
fuch a fyftem. The courts of Madrid and France gave
up to the Englifh all their former poffeffions, from the
river St. Lawrence up to the Miffiffippi. Befide this,
France ceded the iflands of Granada and Tobago,
and confented that the Englifh fhould keep the
iflands of St. Vincent and Dominica, that had been
confidered as neutral, provided that, on her part,
fhe might appropriate St. Lucia to herfelf. On
thefe conditions, the conquerors reftored to the allied powers all the conquefts they had made in America.

From this time England loft the opportunity, which, perhaps, may never return, of feizing all the avenues, and making itfelf mafter of the fources of all the wealth of the New World. Mexico was in its power, as the Englifh only were in pofieffion of the gulf that opens the way to it; this valuable continent muft, therefore, foon have become their property. It might have been allured, either by the offers of an eafier government, or by the flattering hopes of liberty : the Spaniards might have been invited to fhake off the yoke of the mother-country, which only took up arms to diftrefs its colonies, and not to protect them ; or the Indians might have been tempted to break the chains that enflaved them to an arbitrary government. The whole face of America might, perhaps, have been entirely changed, and the Englifh, more free and more equit-able than other monarchical powers, could not but be benefited by refcuing the human race from the oppref-fions they fuffered in the New World, and by remov-ing the injuries this oppreffion hath brought on Europe in particular.

B O O K
X.
The Britifh miniftry did not extend their views as far as the fituation of things per-mitted

All thofe fubjects, who are victims of the feverity, exactions, oppreffion, and deceit of arbitrary govern-ments; all thofe families that are ruined by the raif-ing of foldiers, by the ravages of armies, by the loans for carrying on war, and by the infractions of peace ; all men born to think and live as men, inftead of obeying and becoming fubject like brutes, would have gladly taken refuge in thofe countries. Thefe, as well as a multitude of workmen without employment; of hufbandmen without land; of men of fcience without any occupation ; and numbers of diftreffed and un-fortunate perfons, would have flown into thefe regions, which require only juft and civilized inhabitants to render them happy. Above all, the peafants of the north, flaves to the nobility, who trample upon them, would certainly have been invited there : thofe Ruf-fian peafants, who are employed as executioners to torture the human race, inftead of cultivating and fer-tilizing the earth. Numbers of them would certainly

B O O K
X.

have been loft in thefe tranfmigrations through extenfive feas, into new climates; but this would have been
an infinitely lefs evil than that of a tyranny, working
by flow and artful means, and facrificing fo many people to the wills of a fmall number of men. In a word,
the Englifh would have been much more glorioufly
employed in fupporting and favouring fo happy a revolution, than in tormenting themfelves in defence of
a liberty, that excites the envy of all kings, and which
they endeavour, by every method, to undermine and
deftroy.

This is a wifh, which, though founded on juftice and
humanity, is yet, alas! vain in itfelf, as it leaves nothing but regret in the mind of him that formed it.
Muft then the defires of the virtuous man for the profperity of the world be for ever loft, while thofe of the
ambitious and the extravagant are fo often favoured
by cafual events?

Since war hath been the caufe of fo much evil, why
does it not run through every fpecies of calamity, that
it may, at length, tend to procure fome good? But
what hath been the confequence of the laft war, one
of thofe that hath been the moft diftrefsful to the human race? It hath occafioned ravages in the four
quarters of the globe; and hath coft Europe alone a-
bove a million of its inhabitants. Thofe who were not
its victims are now diftreffed by it, and their pofterity
will long be oppreffed under the weight of the enormous taxes it hath given rife to. The nation, whom
victory attended in all parts, was ruined by its triumphs. Its public debt, which, at the beginning of the
war, did not exceed 1,617,087,060 livres [67,378,627l.
10s.], arofe, at the conclufion of the peace, to
3,330,000,000 livres [138,750,000l.], for which it
muft pay an intereft of 111,577,490 livres [4,649,062l.
1s. 8d.]

But it is time to quit the fubject of war. Let us
now proceed to confider by what means the nations,
who have divided the great Archipelago of America,
that hath been the origin of fo many quarrels and ne-

gotiations, and hath given rife to fo many reflections, B o o k
have been able to raife it to a degree of opulence, that   x.
may, without exaggeration, be confidered as the firft
caufe of all the great events that at prefent difturb the
peace of the globe.

END OF THE THIRD VOLUME.